Research Methods in Child Language

A Practical Guide

Edited by Erika Hoff

WILEY-BLACKWELL

A John Wiley & Sons, Ltd., Publication

Blackwell Publishing was acquired by John Wiley & Sons in February 2007. Blackwell's publishing program has been merged with Wiley's global Scientific, Technical, and Medical business to form Wiley-Blackwell.

Registered Office
John Wiley & Sons Ltd, The Atrium, Southern Gate, Chichester, West Sussex, PO19 8SQ, UK

Editorial Offices
350 Main Street, Malden, MA 02148-5020, USA
9600 Garsington Road, Oxford, OX4 2DQ, UK
The Atrium, Southern Gate, Chichester, West Sussex, PO19 8SQ, UK

For details of our global editorial offices, for customer services, and for information about how to apply for permission to reuse the copyright material in this book please see our website at www.wiley.com/wiley-blackwell.

Library of Congress Cataloging-in-Publication Data

Research methods in child language : a practical guide / edited by Erika Hoff.
       p.   cm.
    Includes bibliographical references and index.
    ISBN 978-1-4443-3124-0 (alk. paper) – ISBN 978-1-4443-3125-7 (pbk. : alk. paper)
 1. Children–Language.   2. Language awareness in children.   3. Language acquisition–Age factors.   4. Language acquisition–Research–Methodology.   I. Hoff, Erika, 1951–
    P118.3.R47 2011
    401′.93–dc22

                                                                    2011009298

A catalogue record for this book is available from the British Library.

This book is published in the following electronic formats: ePDFs 9781444344004; Wiley Online Library 9781444344035; ePub 9781444344011; Mobi 9781444344028

Set in 10/13pt Sabon by SPi Publisher Services, Pondicherry, India
Printed in Malaysia by Ho Printing (M) Sdn Bhd

1   2012

Contents

List of Figures

List of Plates

Notes on Contributors

Leonard Abbeduto, PhD (University of Illinois–Chicago) is the Charles J. Anderson Professor of Education in the Department of Educational Psychology at the University of Wisconsin–Madison. He is also Associate Director for Behavioral Sciences and Director of the University Center of Excellence in Developmental Disabilities at the University's Waisman Center. His research is focused on behavioral development in atypical populations, with an emphasis on the language problems associated with fragile X syndrome, Down syndrome, and autism. E-mail: Abbeduto@waisman. wisc.edu

Ben Ambridge, PhD (University of Manchester) is Lecturer in Psychology at the University of Liverpool. His research focuses on children's acquisition of syntax and morphology; in particular, on the retreat from overgeneralization error. Dr Ambridge is also a co-author of *Child Language Acquisition*, a recent textbook summarizing the major theoretical debates in the field. E-mail: Ben.Ambridge@Liverpool.ac.uk

Heike Behrens, PhD (University of Amsterdam) is Professor for Cognitive Linguistics and Language Acquisition at the University of Basel, Switzerland. Her research focuses on morphosyntactic development in West Germanic languages (German, Dutch, English) and on input. She is also member and co-speaker of the Graduate School on Frequency Effects in Language at the University of Freiburg, Germany. E-mail: heiki.behrens@unibas.ch

Erica A. Cartmill, PhD (University of St Andrews) is a postdoctoral scholar in the Department of Psychology at the University of Chicago working with Susan Goldin-Meadow on the role that gesture plays in language acquisition and in grounding speech in the physical world. She also studies gestural communication and social cognition in great apes. Her work is aimed at understanding the link between action and communication/language and the role gesture plays in that relationship on both evolutionary and ontogenetic timescales. E-mail: cartmill@uchicago.edu

Cynthia Core, PhD (University of Florida) CCC SLP is an Assistant Professor in the Department of Speech and Hearing Science at the George Washington University in Washington, DC, and a certified Speech–Language Pathologist. She studies the development of phonology and phonological memory and their relationships to language development in young monolingual and bilingual children in collaboration with Erika Hoff. She is also investigating the relationship between the development of speech production and speech perception in young children with cochlear implants with colleagues at The George Washington University and Gallaudet University. E-mail: core@gwu.edu

Roberta Corrigan, PhD (University of Denver) is a Professor of Linguistics and Educational Psychology at the University of Wisconsin–Milwaukee. She is the author of numerous articles on language and cognitive development and recently co-edited *Formulaic Language* (vols 1 and 2, Benjamins, 2009, with Edith Moravcsik, Hamid Ouali, and Kathleen Wheatley). E-mail: corrigan@uwm.edu

Özlem Ece Demir, PhD (University of Chicago) is a postdoctoral scholar in the Department of Psychology at the University of Chicago working with Susan Goldin-Meadow and Susan Levine. Her research focuses on the role of biological and environmental factors underlying children's language, particularly narrative and reading development. E-mail: ece@uchicago.edu

David K. Dickinson, PhD (Harvard) is a Professor at Vanderbilt University's Peabody School of Education. He has studied language and early literacy development among low-income populations, focusing on the role of oral language in literacy development. He also has authored numerous articles and co-authored books that include two volumes of the *Handbook of Early Literacy Research*, created tools for describing support for literacy and language learning in preschool classrooms, developed and studied the effectiveness of professional development efforts, and co-authored a preschool curriculum. E-mail: david.dickinson@vanderbilt.edu

Christopher T. Fennell, PhD (University of British Columbia) is an Associate Professor and Director of the Language Development Lab at the University of Ottawa. His research focuses on monolingual and bilingual infants' discrimination and use of phonemic information in early word learning. E-mail: fennell@uottawa.ca

Susan Goldin-Meadow, PhD (University of Pennsylvania) is the Bearsdley Ruml Distinguished Service Professor in the Departments of Psychology and Comparative Human Development at the University of Chicago. Her work on gesture in both hearing and deaf children has revealed the importance of gesture in facilitating, supporting, and predicting language and cognitive development. E-mail: sgm@uchicago.edu

Roberta Michnick Golinkoff, PhD (Cornell University) is the H. Rodney Sharp Professor of Education at the University of Delaware where she is also a member of the Departments of Psychology and Linguistics. She conducts research in language acquisition, early geometry, and playful learning. Among her awards are a Guggenheim Fellowship and, with K. Hirsh-Pasek, the Urie Bronfenbrenner Award for Lifetime Contribution to Developmental Psychology in the Service of Science and

Society and the Distinguished Service to Psychological Science Award. She is author of 12 books and numerous journal articles, and is committed to the dissemination of developmental science. Her most recent book (with K. Hirsh-Pasek, L. Berk, and D. Singer) is *A Mandate for Playful Learning in Preschool* (Oxford). E-mail: roberta@udel.edu

Ligia Gómez, MA (Boston College) is a PhD candidate in the Applied Developmental Psychology program at the Lynch School of Education, Boston College. Her research interests include language acquisition in monolingual and bilingual speakers, with a particular focus on the crosslinguistic comparison of children's lexical and syntactic skills. E-mail: gomezfra@bc.edu

Kathryn Hirsh-Pasek is the Stanley and Debra Lefkowitz Professor in the Department of Psychology at Temple University, where she serves as Director of the Infant Language Laboratory and Co-Founder of CiRCLE (The Center for Re-Imagining Children's Learning and Education). She received her bachelor's degree from the University of Pittsburgh and her PhD at University of Pennsylvania. Her research in the areas of early language development, literacy, and infant cognition has been funded by the National Science Foundation and the National Institutes of Health and Human Development, resulting in 11 books and more than 100 publications. With her long-time collaborator Roberta Golinkoff, she is a recipient of the APA Bronfenbrenner Award for lifetime contribution to the science of developmental psychology in the service of science and society and the APA Award for Distinguished Service to Psychological Science. She also received Temple University's Great Teacher Award and Paul Eberman Research Award. She is a Fellow of the American Psychological Association and the American Psychological Society, served as the Associate Editor of *Child Development* and treasurer of the International Association for Infant Studies. Her book, *Einstein Never Used Flashcards: How Children Really Learn and Why They Need to Play More and Memorize Less* (Rodale Books) won the prestigious Books for Better Life Award as the best psychology book in 2003. She is deeply invested in bridging the gap between research and practice. To that end, she was a researcher on the NICHD Study of Early Child Care and Youth Development, co-developed the language and literacy preschool curricula for the State of California, and has consulted with toy companies and media programs like Sesame Workshop. E-mail: khirshpa@temple.edu

Erika Hoff, PhD (University of Michigan) is a Professor of Psychology at Florida Atlantic University. She studies early monolingual and bilingual development and its relation to properties of children's language exposure. She is the author of the textbook *Language Development* (Cengage Learning). She is also co-editor of the *Blackwell Handbook of Language Development* and of *Childhood Bilingualism: Research on Infancy through School Age* (Multilingual Matters). E-mail: ehoff@fau.edu

Vikram K. Jaswal, PhD (Stanford University) is Associate Professor of Psychology at the University of Virginia. His research focuses on early cognitive and language development, and recent work has addressed questions about the nature of trust in young children. E-mail: jaswal@virginia.edu

Ioulia Kovelman, PhD (Dartmouth College) is an Assistant Professor at the Department of Psychology, University of Michigan. She is a developmental cognitive neuroscientist interested in bilingual and monolingual language and literacy acquisition. E-mail: kovelman@umich.edu

Sara T. Kover, MS (University of Wisconsin-Madison) is a doctoral student in the Department of Educational Psychology of the University of Wisconsin–Madison. Her research interests include language development in children with fragile X syndrome and children with autism and the evaluation of methods for assessing language ability in children. E-mail: kover@wisc.edu

Aylin C. Küntay, PhD (University of California–Berkeley) teaches in the Psychology Department at Koç University, Istanbul. Her research interests are early morphosyntactic and pragmatic developments, and the interaction of the two. She has adopted the crosslinguistic approach in many of her studies. E-mail: akuntay@ku.edu.tr

Elena Lieven, PhD (University of Cambridge) is a Senior Research Scientist at the Max Planck Institute for Evolutionary Anthropology in Leipzig, Germany, and Director of the Max Planck Child Study Centre at the University of Manchester, UK. Her research areas are syntactic development and crosslinguistic studies of child-directed speech. She is a member of the Chintang/Puma language documentation project and is studying language development in this Tibeto-Burman language. E-mail: lieven@eva.mpg.de

Andrea McDuffie, PhD (Vanderbilt University) CCC is an Assistant Scientist at the Waisman Center of the University of Wisconsin–Madison. Her research is focused on the development of communication and language in children with autism or fragile X syndrome, including the role of parenting in optimizing children's communicative development. E-mail: mcduffie@waisman.wisc.edu

Karla K. McGregor, PhD (Purdue University) CCC SLP is a Professor in the Department of Communication Sciences and Disorders and a member of the Delta Center at the University of Iowa. She is a past editor for language for the *Journal of Speech, Language, and Hearing Research*. E-mail: karla-mcgregor@uiowa.edu

David A. McKercher, PhD (Stanford University) is a Lecturer in the Department of Linguistics at the University of Victoria, British Columbia, Canada. His research interests are in first language acquisition and lexical semantics and he teaches courses on psycholinguistics, semantics, syntax, and morphology. E-mail: davemck@uvic.ca

Letitia R. Naigles, PhD (University of Pennsylvania) is Professor of Psychology at the University of Connecticut. Her research investigates the processes of language acquisition in children with autism and compares language development across languages and cultures. E-mail: letitia.naigles@uconn.edu

Barbara Alexander Pan, PhD (Boston University) studied the language and literacy development of young monolingual and bilingual children for more than 20 years. Her work focused particularly on factors affecting the development of children from low-income families. She retired from the Harvard Graduate School of Education in 2009. Dr Pan passed away in February 2011.

Janina Piotroski, PhD (Miami University) is a cognitive psychologist with a background in learning and human factors. She has spent the last two years working with Letitia Naigles in investigating language development in children with autism and typically developing children. E-mail: janinapiotroski@att.net

Elaine Reese, PhD (Emory University) is an Associate Professor in the Department of Psychology at the University of Otago in Dunedin, New Zealand. Dr Reese also serves as the Education Domain Leader of the *Growing Up in New Zealand* study at the School of Population Health at the University of Auckland. Her research focuses on language, literacy, and memory development, with a particular emphasis on the role of oral language in early literacy. E-mail: ereese@psy.otago.ac.nz

Meredith L. Rowe, EdD (Harvard University) is an Assistant Professor of Human Development at the University of Maryland, College Park. Her research focuses on the role of parents and family factors in child language development and has been supported by the National Institute for Child Health and Human Development and the Institute for Educational Studies. E-mail: mrowe@umd.edu

Rosario Luz Rumiche, BS (Florida Atlantic University) is the Laboratory Manager for the Language Development Lab at Florida Atlantic University. She is a graduate student in the School of Social Work at Florida Atlantic University, and she is the mother of two bilingual children. E-mail: rrumiche@fau.edu.

Alison Sparks, PhD (Clark University) is a Research Associate in the Department of Psychology at Amherst College. Her research focuses on language and literacy development in culturally and linguistically diverse populations, with a particular emphasis on the role of children's narrative productions in developing communicative competence. Dr Sparks consults with early childhood development programs on issues related to literacy learning and fair assessment of bilingual children. E-mail: asparks@amhearst.edu

Sebastian Suggate, PhD (University of Otago) at the time of writing this chapter was an Alexander von Humboldt Postdoctoral Researcher at the University of Würzburg in Germany. His research focuses on the development of reading and language during childhood. E-mail: sebastian.suggate@paedagogik.uni-regensburg.de

Daniel Swingley, PhD (Stanford University) is Associate Professor of Psychology at the University of Pennsylvania, where he is Director of the Infant Language Center. He studies word recognition, lexical representation, and lexical and phonological categorization in infants and young children. He is a pioneer in the use of the looking-while-listening procedure. E-mail: swingley@psych.upenn.edu

John C. Trueswell, PhD (University of Rochester) is Professor of Psychology and Director of the Institute for Research in Cognitive Science at the University of Pennsylvania. Trueswell's lab focuses on understanding how children develop the ability to process language in real time and how this ability interacts with the acquisition of language. Trueswell is known for pioneering eyetracking methods designed for the study of spoken language processing in young children. In addition to his research, Trueswell is actively involved in undergraduate and graduate training in cognitive science at the University of Pennsylvania. He was the co-creator of the Annual Undergraduate Workshop in Cognitive Science and Cognitive Neuroscience, which he continues to direct. He is also director of the NSF-IGERT graduate program in Language and Communication Sciences. E-mail: trueswel@psych.upenn.edu

Marina Vasilyeva, PhD (University of Chicago) is an Associate Professor of Applied Developmental Psychology at the Lynch School of Education, Boston College. Her research interests encompass cognitive development and language acquisition in children. In the linguistic domain, she uses experimental methodology to investigate the role of environmental input in the development of syntactic skills. E-mail: vasilyev@bc.edu

Heidi Waterfall, PhD (University of Chicago) is a Postdoctoral Associate in Developmental Psychology at Cornell University. Her research investigates the role of the linguistic environment, specifically caregiver–child interaction, in child language development. E-mail: heidi.waterfall@gmail.com

Acknowledgments

This book reflects the ideas and efforts of many people. I would like to thank Li Wei, editor of this series, for inviting me to organize a volume on methods of studying child language development and for his guidance and support throughout the process. I would also like to thank Danielle Descoteaux and Julia Kirk at Wiley-Blackwell whose help was invaluable at many points along the way from the conception to the completion of this book. I owe special thanks to Krystal Lago, PhD student at Florida Atlantic University, who serenely managed the task of assembling this collection of chapters and keeping me relatively organized. I am deeply grateful to all the chapter authors who were a pleasure to work with and from whom I have learned a great deal. I note with sadness that the author of Chapter 7, Barbara Pan, passed away as this book was going to press.

Preface

The aim of researchers who study child language is to describe children's language skills and language knowledge at different developmental points and to explain how children progress from their starting state to the achievement of adult-level skills and understandings. Language skills are hard to capture, and both the underlying knowledge and the mechanisms that enable language acquisition are hidden from view inside the mind of the child. Thus, researchers who study child language depend on an array of tools to reveal the object of our study. This book is about those tools. Its aim is to describe the techniques child language researchers use as we go about the business of studying language development.

Some of the methods reviewed in this book are very new, for example the use of functional near infrared spectroscopy (fNIRS) to study the activity of the brain. Others have a longer history – for example the collection, transcription, and coding of speech samples – but have been transformed in recent years by new hardware and software. Each chapter author is a researcher who uses and, in many cases, has contributed to the development of the methods described. The authors were asked to describe the research aims their methods serve, the details of the implementation of those methods, and the type of data the methods yield. Each chapter provides some discussion of the alternative methods available to researchers and their attendant advantages and disadvantages. In many cases, the chapters are part personal travelogue, describing the researcher's journey from research aim to research method.

The book is organized into four parts. The first focuses on laboratory techniques that do not require language production from the participant. Most of these are techniques used to study language in infants. In Chapter 1, Christopher Fennell describes habituation procedures and their use in studying infants' abilities to discriminate the smallest meaningful units of sound. In Chapter 2, Janina Piotroski and Letitia Naigles describe the preferential looking method as it is used to study early language comprehension. In Chapter 3, Daniel Swingley describes the development and use of the looking-while-listening procedure, which provides a window onto the online processing engaged in by prelinguistic infants as they listen to speech. In Chapter 4, Ioulia Kovelman reviews the brain imaging techniques that have been used to peek into the neural activity of infants and older children as they process language. In Chapter 5, the final chapter of this part, Roberta Golinkoff and Kathryn Hirsh-Pasek provide a historical overview of the development of these and other methods that have been used to study language in infants, moving from the early questions of what infants on average can do to the more recently asked question of what individual differences among infants portend for their future language development.

The second part of the book surveys methods that have been used to assess language knowledge in children who do produce speech. In Chapter 6, Cynthia Core provides a short course on phonological development and a survey of methods used to assess phonological development in young children. In Chapter 7, Barbara Pan does likewise for vocabulary development and its assessment. In Chapter 8, Ben Ambridge discusses methods of assessing children's grammatical knowledge, focusing in particular on a new technique – the graded grammaticality judgment paradigm. In Chapter 9, Elaine Reese, Alison Sparks, and Sebastian Suggate describe the story retelling technique they have used to study children's narratives. Chapters 10, 11, and 12 are introductions to three different techniques that have been used to ask questions about children's underlying linguistic knowledge and online processing in both the lexical and the syntactic domains. In Chapter 10, David McKercher and Vikram Jaswal describe the use of judgment tasks. In Chapter 11, Marina Vasilyeva, Heidi Waterfall, and Ligia Gómez describe priming procedures. In Chapter 12, John Trueswell describes eye movement monitoring techniques.

The focus of the third part of the book is on the use of naturalistic methods to capture the speech children hear and the speech they spontaneously produce. In Chapter 13, Meredith Rowe describes methods that have been and are being used to record, transcribe, and code samples of caregiver–child interaction and illustrates the sort of findings such methods can yield. In Chapter 14, Erica Cartmill, Özlem Demir, and Susan Goldin-Meadow describe the methods used to study the gestures children produce and observe as they communicate and the role of gesture in language development. In Chapter 15, Elena Lieven and Heike Behrens describe the dense sampling procedure they and others have used to capture the nature of children's language input and spontaneous speech. In Chapter 16, Letitia Naigles describes techniques that aim for even more than a dense sample – techniques to capture everything a child hears and/or says. In Chapter 17, David Dickinson describes approaches to capturing teacher–child interactions in preschool classrooms. In Chapter 18, Roberta Corrigan provides an introduction to the data archive and analysis tools that are the Child Language Data Exchange System (CHILDES).

The organizing topic for the fourth part is the question of what we can learn and how we go about learning it when we study populations other than typically developing, monolingual children acquiring English. In Chapter 19, Aylin Küntay discusses crosslinguistic research. In Chapter 20, Rosario Rumiche and I describe the particular challenges of research with bilingually developing children and their families, and we describe the methods we have used in our research. In Chapter 21, Karla McGregor discusses methodological issues that are unique to the study of children with language impairment, and she reviews the standards of scientific quality that pertain to research that will provide an evidence base for clinical practice. In Chapter 22, Leonard Abbeduto, Sara Kover, and Andrea McDuffie describe their work studying language development in children with intellectual disabilities.

One aim of this collection is to provide the reader with more background and procedural detail about each method than can be included in a journal article. (Another is to be a bit more readable than the necessarily dense prose of an APA-style method section.) The hope is that the information presented in these chapters will be of use to advanced students beginning research in the field of child language, to established researchers embarking in new directions, and to readers of the scientific literature who would like more background on the procedures that yielded the data they are reading about.

Part I Studying Infants and Others Using Nonverbal Methods

1 Habituation Procedures

Christopher T. Fennell

Summary

In this chapter, the habituation technique will be described in detail, with a focus on infant visual habituation tasks. This easy-to-implement procedure can be used to measure many domains of early language development; however, it has been primarily used to test questions of language discrimination and word learning. In a typical experiment, an infant sits on a parent's lap, or in an infant seat, listening to a repeated sound or word, which can be paired with a visual display. Once her response (e.g., sucking, heart rate, orienting behavior) decreases to a preset criterion, a test trial is presented where the sound or word changes. An increase in response indicates successful discrimination and potential learning of the sound or word. Key advantages of habituation tasks are their use of autonomic responses, broad age range from fetuses to adults, and applicability to multiple populations, including typically and atypically developing children.

"Your child will get bored, and that's ok." Many of us who use habituation to study language development state this to the parents of our participants. In a world of infant videos, playgroups, and exciting toys, the idea that we can glean rich knowledge from purposefully boring an infant can seem strange. Yet, this statement essentially encapsulates the habituation task, a procedure that has answered fundamental questions about early language acquisition and continues to be of great use to the field of developmental psycholinguistics.

Research Methods in Child Language: A Practical Guide, First Edition.
Edited by Erika Hoff.
© 2012 Blackwell Publishing Ltd. Published 2012 by Blackwell Publishing Ltd.

Research Aim

The concept of habituation has a long history in psychology, with forefathers like Wundt and Thorndike exploring human adaptation to a recurring stimulus. Simply defined, habituation is the progressive reduction of an organism's behavior in response to a repeated stimulus. Importantly, the reduction in behavioral response is thought to demonstrate both memory encoding of the stimulus and potential learning. However, as Cohen (2004) and others have stated, the decrease of a response over time may not involve true habituation. The organism may just be fatiguing in general, which may be especially true of infants and children. Thus, habituation procedures require the introduction of a stimulus change after the habituation phase ends. If the organism demonstrates an increase in target behavior in response to the change, the researcher can now state with greater confidence that participants remembered and learned the habituation stimulus on some level. This particularly allows for tests of discrimination by using a similar, but novel, stimulus at test.

Despite its long history, it was not until Fantz's (1964) seminal article that *infant* habituation was broadly introduced into psychological research (see also Golinkoff and Hirsh-Pasek, Chapter 5 this volume). Over the past three and a half decades, there has been an explosion of infant habituation studies, with such pioneers as Leslie Cohen contributing much to our understanding of using this technique with this population. In language development research, habituation tasks have tested such diverse aspects of infants' language abilities as their ability to tell one language from another, the specificity of their phonological representations (e.g., discriminating a /b/ sound from a /d/), their ability to learn word–object associations (e.g., pairing a novel word with a novel object), and their ability to learn grammatical rules (e.g., learning a word order pattern where nonsense syllables follow an ABA configuration like wo fe wo, and then noticing violations of that arrangement – an ABB pattern like li gi gi).

Why have infant habituation procedures enjoyed such broad use? First, while the response measured could be theoretically any form of behavior, it often involves an autonomic physiological response such as sucking, heart rate, or orienting behavior (e.g., looking). This is critical because overt conscious behaviors are harder, and sometimes impossible, to elicit in the prenatal through infant phases of development, exactly when important language abilities are unfolding. Further, these autonomic responses are valid measures across wide populations of participants, including different species, both typically and atypically developing populations, and – most importantly for developmental studies – a wide range of age groups, from fetuses to adults. Using the same task across ages is optimal, as it is difficult to track development when using a variety of different methodologies, each with its own task demands. Another strength is the breadth of possible stimuli; any repeated stimulus is a potential candidate, including phonemes, stress patterns, words, signs, sentences, etc. Finally, and perhaps most importantly, habituation reflects the cognitive structure of the infant mind. Infants' ability to habituate and react to novel stimuli is so fundamental that it is part of neonatal assessment (Brazleton Scale) and correlates with later cognitive skills (Berg and Sternberg, 1985).

Procedure

In my own research, I have found the habituation task to be invaluable. I examine infants' abilities to detect and use the smallest meaningful units of sound in a language: phonemes. For example, /b/ and /d/ are English phonemes because they denote meaningful differences in words, like "bad" and "dad." I and my colleagues, chief among them Janet Werker, have used visual habituation tasks to investigate whether infants can discriminate two phonemes in speech perception and if they can then use that same phonological information when acquiring words in the lab. It is a testament to the power of the task that we can use the same procedure to answer both phonetic and lexical questions over various points of development.

It is no surprise that habituation tasks are commonly used to investigate phoneme distinction in infants, as they are designed to be tests of discrimination. But, why choose habituation over other available methodologies? The main advantage of habituation over its main competitor, the conditioned head turn procedure (CHT), is its use of autonomic responses. CHT, on the other hand, involves an initial phase where infants, via operant conditioning, are rewarded for turning their heads when hearing a stimulus change. This places extra demands on infants and the experimental setup, as CHT requires two experimenters and more equipment (i.e., a reward stimulus – usually an animated toy that is triggered by the first experimenter). Further, CHT cannot be reliably used under 6 months of age, yet a large portion of language development, especially that concerning phoneme perception, occurs prior to this age. However, one advantage of CHT over habituation is that one can meaningfully interpret a single individual's data, as there are multiple change trials. Thus, one can see if an infant can reliably discriminate two stimuli, which is of great importance for clinical applications. The visual habituation task, however, typically involves only one change trial (the novel trial). It is therefore difficult to interpret an individual's data, as she may have had increased, decreased, or equivalent looking times to the novel stimulus compared to a habituation stimulus for any number of reasons (e.g., fatigue, distraction, etc.). For this reason, we can only interpret group data in habituation studies.

Another alternative test of infant phoneme discrimination is the event related potential (ERP) methodology, which measures electrical neural responses to stimuli via electroencephalography (EEG) (see Kovelman, Chapter 4 this volume). There is a standard ERP produced, called the mismatch negativity response, when we detect a change in auditory stimulus. However, more expensive resources and longer experimenter training are required to use ERP than to use the habituation method. Further, there is an added level of difficulty in setup and a corresponding higher level of attrition.

Having chosen a habituation task to test phonological discrimination, for example, it is important to select the appropriate response behavior. Early infant habituation researchers used heart rate and sucking behaviors as dependent variables, demonstrating that these responses decreased as an auditory, olfactory, or visual stimulus repeated. While these measures are less common in modern research, they are both valid, especially with certain populations. For example, during the fetal period, heart rate is one of the few possible behavioral measures. Kisilevsky *et al.* (2009) demonstrated that fetuses will show a novelty response of increased heart rate to maternal speech after being familiarized to a female stranger's speech. In the neonatal and early infancy period, sucking can be preferable to orienting behaviors, such as head turning and looking, given that the very young infant has limited head control and an underdeveloped visual system. Indeed, the first study to demonstrate that young infants can categorically perceive phonemes used a habituation paradigm with sucking as the dependent measure (Eimas *et al.*, 1971). In another example, Shi, Werker, and Morgan (1999) used this response to establish that newborns can discriminate a spoken list of grammar words (e.g., "in," "on") from a list of nongrammatical, or content, words (e.g., "mommy," "chair"). However the major drawback of using heart rate and sucking measures is that they require monitoring equipment to be in contact with infants' bodies: an electrocardiogram or a pacifier outfitted with a pressure transducer. These can be expensive and subject to equipment problems. Sucking is also limited in terms of the age range: a 20-month-old may not easily accept a pacifier to be placed continuously in her mouth during testing.

A third measurement option for auditory language skills – a visual orientation response to a pattern on a screen – was validated by Horowitz's (1975) demonstration of a positive relationship between attention to an auditory stream and visual fixation. This measure is very advantageous, as it requires nothing to be in physical contact with infants. It can even be done without monitoring equipment (i.e., an experimenter observing infants' looks with her own eyes), although it is recommended that a video record be obtained for coding purposes. It should be noted that another orienting behavior could be used: head turns. Using this measure, Swain, Zelazo, and Clifton (1993) showed that newborns could remember a habituated word form for up to 24 hours. However, this blunt measure is used less often than looking time, which has more informative small variations (e.g., small glances, look aways). Even its limitation in the neonatal period (i.e., poor visual capabilities) can be overcome through the use of closer, more contrastive visual stimuli. The ease of measuring looking behavior and its broad age range has led to its wide application,[1] including in my own studies.

We can now turn to an illustration of how to test infants' perceptual discrimination of phonemes using habituation. Note that this same method can be used for any language distinction. Habituation studies necessarily involve two phases, habituation and test, which comprise discrete trials wherein an audio, visual, or audiovisual stimulus is presented. In a phoneme discrimination task, a recording of a female producing syllables in infant-directed speech, which infants prefer to adult-directed speech, is delivered around 65 dB. The visual stimulus is a pattern, usually a checkerboard. Each trial is preceded by an attention-getting stimulus in order to get infants to orient to the screen (e.g., a flashing light; a morphing, colourful shape; the face of a baby accompanied by giggling). Once infants look to the screen, the relevant trial commences. Trials can be of set length, or can terminate once an infant looks away for a set time. The latter infant-controlled option can be more sensitive, as it takes into account individual differences in attention on a trial-by-trial basis. However, it also introduces potential observer bias, as the experimenter decides when infants are no longer attending. Therefore, care should be taken when using this variant, ensuring that the experimenter is blind to both the stimulus and the experimental phases.

The physical setup of the procedure is quite straightforward – another major task advantage. The infant and one parent sit facing a visual display, with the parent wearing sound-masking headphones. Given that looking time is our measure, one important requirement is that the room is dimly lit so that the visual image stands out. Researchers achieve this by turning off any overhead lighting and placing a shaded lamp (or lamps) to the left and/or right of the infant at a 45 degree forward angle. This allows for a clear image of the infants' eyes. Sometimes researchers will surround the visual display with black cloth that stretches the width and height of the room, which will provide a stronger contrast for the presented images. Usually, the task takes place in a small, quiet (or even soundproof) room to aid in the acoustic presentation. Finally, infants' looking times are recorded using a video camera, with this record being used for reliability coding. This camera should be hidden from infants' view so as to not distract them from the visual stimuli.

The software to run the procedure can be created in the lab, or one can use a common freeware program called Habit (Cohen, Atkinson, and Chaput, 2004), which will order stimuli presentation, compute habituation criteria, and accumulate looking time data. Stimuli are usually played from digitized files on the computer and are sent to the display and speaker in the testing room. The experimenter, who should be blind to the audio stimuli being presented and to whether a trial was a habituation or test trial, remotely monitors the infant's looking times. A designated key is pressed on the computer keyboard during infant looks, which this program records.

The habituation phase is, of course, of prime importance to the procedure and where the researcher has many options available. For example, one could end the habituation phase once an infant accrues a certain amount of looking time (e.g., 2 minutes total). These studies are usually termed familiarization rather than habituation and, while they can provide rich data, they can be prone to problems (see Cohen, 2004), as there is no guarantee that all infants would require the same amount of training. Due to individual differences in attention and cognitive skills, one infant may require 2 minutes to learn the stimuli and another may require 3 minutes. To ensure that all infants are on the same page, a true habituation criterion should be used (e.g., looking time across a block of trials falls to 65% of the highest total looking time summed across the same-sized block).[2] Importantly, habituation criteria change based on infant age, decreasing as they get older (using 65% at 14 months, but 50% at 20 months). Selecting the appropriate criterion is critical because if the criterion is too strict, the attrition rate will increase; infants become too bored with the stimuli. If it is too lax, infants will not yet be habituated and one may obtain null results that are not indicative of their true ability. A maximum number of trials should still be included in the design (e.g., 24 trials) so that the experiment does not continue indefinitely. One should compare the results of infants who achieved the true criterion (habituators) and those who reached the maximum number of trials without habituating (nonhabituators) to investigate if there are any performance differences. For example, Werker *et al.* (1998) found that nonhabituators did not successfully learn their habituation stimuli, whereas habituators did.

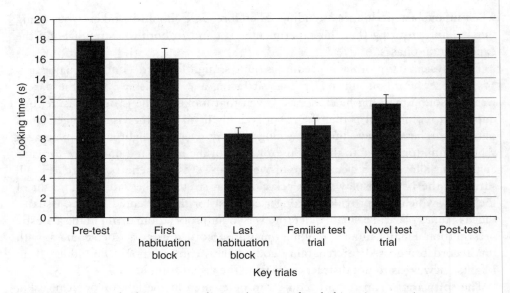

Figure 1.1 Average looking times to key trials in an infant habituation experiment involving a phoneme change at test ($N = 16$). At post-test, infants recovered to pre-test levels and thus were not generally fatigued. Infants habituated, having significantly less looking to the final habituation block than to the first (block = two trials). There is no significant difference between the last habituation block and the familiar test trial, indicating that infants are still bored with the habituation stimulus. Finally, and most importantly, infants noticed the change in stimulus, as the novel test trial is significantly different from both the familiar test trial and the last habituation block.

At test, there are also options available. One possibility is to compare the novel stimulus to the final block of habituation trials to see if they are significantly different. However, this approach has been criticized, as the final block of habituation trials is necessarily low, and may be artificially so (see Cohen, 2004). For example, perhaps an infant was distracted by their loose shoe for one trial and did not attend to the habituation stimuli. The habituation phase ends due to the low response; however, the child was not truly habituated. For this reason, the researcher should include two trials at test – the novel stimuli and another trial of the habituation stimulus – with the order counterbalanced across participants (e.g., Stager and Werker, 1997; Werker *et al.*, 1998). A within-subjects comparison of those two test trials, usually termed novel and familiar, will reveal if participants can detect the difference between the habituated stimuli and something new. Alternatively, one can compare two different groups of infants: one group that received the novel stimulus after habituation, and one that received a familiar stimulus after habituation. Although it removes any possible order effects at test, this last method is less frequently used since it runs into problems of matching the two groups and requires twice the number of participants. The statistical analysis to determine if the novel and familiar trials are significantly different can be a *t*-test, either paired-sample or independent depending on the design. However, an ANOVA that includes the test trials as one variable and gender as the other is recommended, as some work has found female advantages in this type of task (e.g., Fennell, Byers-Heinlein, and Werker, 2007; Werker *et al.*, 1998).

Finally, pre- and post-test trials can be included (see Werker *et al.*, 1998). These two trials consist of the identical stimuli, which are maximally different from the habituation and test trials. The pre-test trial occurs prior to the habituation phase and is presented for two reasons: to allow infants to become accustomed to the presentation, and as a comparison trial for the post-test trial. The post-test trial is presented after the test phase. It is expected that if infants are still engaged in the experiment, looking time would recover to near pre-test level during this final trial. Once again, pre- and post-test looking times can be compared using a *t*-test or an ANOVA that includes gender as a factor.

To determine the reliability of the experimenter's coding, there are three standard procedures. The first requires no extra equipment, but is the least exact. A second trained coder can score the looking times of 25% of the subjects by watching the video records. A Pearson product-moment correlation of original and recoded scores should be greater than 0.95 for the data to be considered reliable. A second method is to have two coders score all the video records using a frame-by-frame analysis to obtain the most exact measures possible. Free software is available to perform this coding (SuperCoder: Hollich, 2005). Finally, but most expensively, a researcher can use an eyetracker (e.g., McMurray and Aslin, 2004). This technology uses the reflection of infrared light to measure the distance between the infant's cornea and pupil, collecting a reading of infant's eye gaze every 20 milliseconds. This provides a very precise recording of an infant's looking behavior (see Piotroski and Naigles, Chapter 2 this volume; Trueswell, Chapter 12 this volume).

Using the recommended setup above, multiple studies have confirmed that after being habituated to audio exemplars from one native-language phoneme category (e.g., /b/), infants look significantly longer to the screen when hearing a new native-language phoneme (e.g., /d/) at test than when hearing the habituated phoneme (e.g., Best *et al.*, 1995; Burns *et al.*, 2007; Polka and Werker, 1994; Stager and Werker, 1997; Sundara, Polka, and Molnar, 2008). The ages tested have ranged from 4 to 20 months and have included both monolingual and bilingual populations.

Visual habituation tasks can therefore be used to test basic language discriminations, including phonemes, quite effectively. When examining infants' use of this phonemic information in early word learning, it would be efficacious to use the same procedure to test both phoneme discrimination and word learning. In this manner, one can directly compare the same response with the same target stimuli. However, it is important to ensure that habituation procedures can truly measure lexical acquisition, which is more complex and occurs developmentally later than phonological acquisition. After all, other valid measures exist. Many word-learning studies have used face-to-face training sessions to teach older infants and toddlers new words and then tested them via picture selection and pointing tasks. However, face-to-face training opens the door for experimenter bias and lacks strict control (i.e., training differences across participants), whereas habituation tasks present the same pre-recorded stimuli to all participants. Further, these testing methods would be too difficult for younger infants, and perhaps even for older infants. For these reasons, my colleagues and I turned to a visual habituation task that involves word–object associations called the "switch" procedure (Werker *et al.*, 1998). The use of this task allowed us to test infants as close to the beginning of the word-learning period as possible, as it does not place undue demands on participants this age, yet it necessitates that infants associate a word and its referent.

In the switch procedure, the exact same physical setup as in phoneme discrimination is used, but infants are now habituated to two word–object pairings[3] and tested on their ability to detect a switch in a pairing. To assess whether infants not only have learned about the words and objects individually, but have linked object A to word A, or object B to word B, they are given two test trials. On the control trial (the "same" trial), a familiar word and object are presented in a familiar combination, e.g., object A with word A. On the test trial (the "switch" trial) a familiar word and object are presented, but in a new combination, e.g., object A paired with word B. If the infants have learned about the words and the objects individually but have not learned the associative link, the "same" and "switch" trials will be equally familiar, and should attract equal looking times. However, if the infants have learned the link between the specific words and objects, the "switch" trial, as a violation, should thus attract greater looking time than the "same" trial. The same statistical analyses as in the phoneme discrimination task are used for test trial comparison. Pre- and post-test trials are included in this design (object C paired with word C, both of which are maximally different from the habituation stimuli).

Werker *et al.* (1998) demonstrated that infants as young as 14 months can learn dissimilar sounding words (e.g., "lif" vs "neem") in the switch task. However, when Stager and Werker (1997) tested the specificity of words by testing phonetically similar labels (e.g., "bih" vs "dih"), they found that 14-month-olds failed to notice the violation at test. This was unexpected as the [b]–[d] contrast is phonemic in English and should therefore be easy for a 14-month-old English-learning infant to discriminate, and therefore use in word learning. Thus, Stager and Werker conducted a series of control studies, all using visual habituation tasks, to further investigate why 14-month-olds failed. Stager and Werker confirmed that infants this age could detect the acoustic difference between "bih" and "dih" by running the phoneme discrimination task discussed earlier. To verify that the problem was specific to word learning, they ran the phoneme discrimination task, but replaced the checkerboard with an object. Infants were thus only habituated to one word–object combination in this task and the "switch" trial entailed a switch from the habituated label (e.g., "bih") to a minimally different label (e.g., "dih"). Even though infants could succeed in discriminating the labels if they ignored the object and only attend to the audio, the 14-month-olds once again failed.

Based on all the above findings, it would seem that infants of 14 months only have difficulty accessing phonetic detail when they are placed in a word-learning situation. The fact that all of these controls could involve the same task points to the versatility and power of the design. Nevertheless, one never knows whether 14-month-olds' continued failure to learn phonetically similar words really reveals something about their word-learning abilities, or instead whether, for any other of an infinite number of reasons, the task simply failed to reveal an underlying capability. Indeed, there have been two prominent criticisms of using habituation tasks to measure word learning: the blunt nature of the test and the ecological validity of the training. First, let us examine the issue of measurement.

In order for infants to succeed in the switch task, they need to demonstrate sufficient surprise at the violation of the link between object and label. In the case where both labels are similar, they may have not learned the words with sufficient confidence to trigger a novelty response. To examine the possibility that our testing method masked infants' detailed phoneme use in word learning, we maintained the same habituation phase as before but altered the testing phase of the switch task by applying the methodology of the "looking-while-listening" procedure (Yoshida *et al.*, 2009; see Swingley, Chapter 3 this volume). After being habituated to object A paired with "bin" and object B paired with "din," infants received target test trials where both habituation objects appeared simultaneously as they heard one of the object labels. We counterbalanced side of object presentation and object label. These trials were interspersed with filler test trials that used familiar objects and labels (e.g., car, shoe) to acquaint infants with the task. This testing method allowed for a subtler analysis of infants' object choice than prior switch studies. We could analyze both proportion looking and latency to the correct object, as well as a timecourse analysis of looking. Test trials were analyzed over 367–2000 ms after the onset of the spoken target word. This window allows for infant reaction time at this age and accounts for the normal duration of their attention. We found that the average proportion of fixation to the target object (53.5%) was significantly greater than chance (50%), an effect generated from the first block of four target test trials (56.8%) rather than the second block (49.4%). Thus, infants of 14 months have encoded enough detail in the word form to distinguish the "bin" object from the "din" object at test. However, as is obvious from the data, it is a very delicate effect, which explains why the traditional switch measure did not reveal it. Future research could use this hybrid procedure, albeit with half the testing trials, to investigate subtle word-learning effects. Nevertheless, this does not necessitate a complete rejection of the traditional testing phase, which has revealed important group differences in the past and may involve a requisite amount of confidence in word knowledge that is more applicable to real-word applications (e.g., correlations between ability in the switch task and phonological processing in later childhood).

To return to the other criticism of the word-learning habituation task, some have argued that the task is too "stripped down" to allow for true word learning; there are no linguistic (i.e., syntax) or pragmatic (e.g., naming routines) cues. Consequently, I and Sandra Waxman took up the challenge to redesign the word-learning version of the visual habituation task to include cues to reference that went beyond the simple temporal contiguity of word and object, while maintaining experimental control (Fennell and Waxman, 2010). We hypothesized that the presence of referential cues would allow infants to learn new words in full phonetic detail. The first issue to address was that, in all previous implementations of the switch habituation task, novel words were presented in isolation, which has adverse consequences for learning object names. In normal conversation, when words appear in isolation, they tend to be proper names ("Daddy!"), commands ("Stop!"), or exclamations ("Wow!"). Importantly, infants are sensitive to this, failing to map isolated words to objects in categorization tasks. We therefore modified the task by presenting the target words in recorded naming phrases that clearly indicated that the to-be-learned word referred to an object (e.g., "Look! It's the bin!"). These naming phrases provide both pragmatic cues (ritualized forms used to present words to infants) and syntactic cues (presence of a determiner) to reference. Another method we employed to invoke referential word learning in the task was to introduce a brief training period wherein infants saw three familiar objects (car, shoe, cat) each paired with its familiar basic-level object name presented in isolation (e.g., "Car!"). This highlighted that words and objects belonged together in the task. We then gave infants a habituation phase (e.g., a novel toy object paired with "bin"), following by the standard testing phase of a novel and familiar pairing of the word–object combination. In both manipulations, infants of 14 months mapped the novel word in all its detail to the accompanying object and were surprised when the word changed (e.g., "bin" changing to "din"). This demonstrates that simple changes to the auditory stimuli or design can invoke a more ecologically valid and powerful word-learning task, while maintaining the strict experimental controls that are so advantageous in habituation procedures.

Remaining Data Issues

Let us now turn to two final points on data analysis. The first concerns the habituation phase, while the second relates to findings in the test phase that do not resemble the standard novelty response.

Habituation phase data can potentially reveal important group differences. If one group receives one stimulus (or set of stimuli) and another group receives a different one, or if both groups receive the same stimuli but are from differing populations (e.g., bilingual versus monolingual, or male versus female), researchers can compare the following measures to explore any differences in adaptation or learning. One can examine the length of habituation via the mean looking time across the entire habituation phase, the mean number of habituation trials, or – better yet – the slope of the habituation curve. Other relevant measures are infants' initial interest in the stimuli (mean looking time in the first block of habituation trials) and infants' final habituation level (mean looking time in the last habituation block). One may see group effects in this last measure, wherein one group has a floor effect of habituation and another group just makes the criterion. Differences between groups in any of these measures could explain eventual group differences at test, and thus all of them should be explored.

A strange effect that can possibly occur at test is discovering, contradictory to the habituation model, a significantly greater response to a familiar stimulus over the novel stimulus. Interestingly, this significant difference indicates that infants can discriminate the familiar and novel stimuli, yet they continue to have active interest in the familiar stimulus from habituation and avoid a novel stimulus. Thus, a significant familiarity preference is still interpretable in terms of discrimination ability; however, the counterintuitive nature of the response requires a clear explanation.

In a key paper, Hunter and Ames (1988) posited that familiarity effects relate to the ease or difficulty with which infants process the habituation stimuli. They hypothesized that infants would prefer stimuli that are at their optimal level of stimulation, and will actively avoid or show a lack of interest in stimuli above or below that level. For a low to moderately complex stimulus, infants would initially have a high response as it is at their optimal level, but as they became familiar with the stimulus, their interest would wane – the standard habituation curve. However, a complex stimulus may actually generate an avoidance response at first, and would only generate interest once the infant has become familiar enough with it to start processing its properties. Thus, if the infants in this latter case were run for the same habituation time as infants exposed to a less complex stimulus, they may show a greater response to a familiar stimulus, as they had not reached the end of the habituation curve and are still trying to process the habituation stimuli. Importantly, younger and older infants may have differing responses to the same stimulus, as its complexity is dependent on the maturity of the cognitive system. Younger infants run for the same length of habituation time with the same stimulus as older infants may demonstrate a familiarity effect, as the stimulus would be more complex to their system. Indeed, data from both of these manipulations (age and stimulus complexity) have borne out the predictions of Hunter and Ames. Cohen (2004) therefore advocates for a strict habituation criterion (e.g., 50% reduction in looking time) to avoid possible familiarity effects.

However, it is important to note that familiarity effects can be interpreted. As mentioned earlier, a significant preference for a familiar over a novel stimulus still demonstrates that infants can discriminate the two stimuli and indicates that the habituation stimulus was overly complex for the developing system of the infants. Hunter and Ames also point out that familiarity effects demonstrate infants' motivation to process information. In an example of the utility of these effects, we recently discovered a strong familiarity preference for a specific novel word in my lab. A subsequent examination of the acoustics of the stimuli revealed that the target phoneme in that word was much more acoustically variable than target phonemes in our other stimuli. That variability increased the complexity of the stimuli and drove the familiarity preference in the study. This familiarity preference therefore led to the finding that infants are acutely sensitive to phonetic variability in stimulus sets.

In conclusion, the habituation task, with its long history and uncomplicated application, is a key tool for developmental psychologists to uncover answers to current and future questions about the very beginnings of language understanding in the mind of the infant, and across the lifespan.

Key Terms

Familiarity preference   An infrequent response in a true habituation task where the participant attends more to the familiar (i.e., habituation) stimulus at test than a novel stimulus. It usually indicates that the wrong habituation criterion was employed and/or that the familiar stimulus was too complex for the participant.

Familiarization study   A study in which all participants experience the target stimuli for the same predetermined amount of time. This is contrasted with a study with a habituation criterion.

Familiar stimulus   The stimulus presented throughout habituation.

Habituation The progressive reduction of an organism's behavior in response to a repeated stimulus.

Habituation criterion The set percentage to which the participant's behavioral response must decrease from its highest point before the test phase begins.

Infant controlled A variation of the habituation task where the length of each test trial is fully determined by infants' attention to the presented stimulus. The trial begins when the infant attends to the stimulus and ends when they stop attending.

Novel stimulus A stimulus presented at test that is distinct from the familiar stimulus. If participants have adapted to or learned the specific stimulus from habituation, they should have an increased response to this stimulus over the familiar stimulus (see *novelty preference*).

Novelty preference The classic test response in a habituation task where the participant attends more to a novel stimulus than a familiar one post-habituation.

Switch procedure An associative word-learning variant of the habituation task where participants receive two word–object associations throughout habituation (object A, word A; object B, word B) and are tested on two test trials, a familiar pairing (object A, word A) and a novel one (object A, word B). If the participants learned the associative link, they will show a novelty response.

Notes

1 Colombo has advocated for combining measures of heart rate and looking time behaviors to obtain a more complete picture of infant habituation (e.g., Colombo *et al.*, 2004).

2 Different block sizes can be used, but are usually two to four trials long. To give a concrete example of a 65% habituation criterion: if an infant looks 100 seconds across the first three trials, the habituation phase would end once her looking time across a set of three trials fell below 65 seconds.

3 When using visual objects paired with audio stimuli, it is important that the object moves across the screen to ensure infant attention. However, one has to ensure that the audio stimulus (i.e., word) does not commence at the same moment that the object changes direction on the screen, as this provides amodal cues to the relationship between word and object (see Werker *et al.*, 1998; 2002).

References

Berg, C., and Sternberg, R. (1985) Response to novelty: continuity versus discontinuity in the developmental course of intelligence. In H. Reese (ed.), *Advances in child development and behavior* (vol. 19, pp. 1–47). New York: Academic.

Best, C.T., McRoberts, G.W., LaFluer, R., and Silver-Isenstadt, J. (1995) Divergent developmental patterns in infants' perception of two non-native consonant contrasts. *Infant Behavior & Development*, 19, 339–350.

Burns, T.C., Yoshida, K.A., Hill, K., and Werker, J.F. (2007) The development of phonetic representation in bilingual and monolingual infants. *Applied Psycholinguistics*, 28, 455–474.

Cohen, L.B. (2004) Uses and misuses of habituation and related preference paradigms. *Infant and Child Development*, 13, 349–352.

Cohen, L.B., Atkinson, D.J., and Chaput, H.H. (2004) A new program for obtaining and organizing data in infant perception and cognition studies (version 1.0). Austin: University of Texas.

Colombo, J., Shaddy, D.J., Richman, W.A., *et al.* (2004) Developmental course of visual habituation and preschool cognitive and language outcome. *Infancy*, 5, 1–38.

Eimas, P.D., Siqueland, E.R., Jusczyk, P., and Vigorito, J. (1971) Speech perception in infancy. *Developmental Issues*, 171, 303–306.

Fantz, R.L. (1964) Visual experiences in infants: decreased attention to familiar patterns relative to novel ones. *Science*, 146, 668–670.

Fennell, C.T., Byers-Heinlein, K., and Werker, J.F. (2007) Using speech sounds to guide word learning: the case of bilingual infants. *Child Development*, 78, 1510–1525.

Fennell, C.T., and Waxman, S.R. (2010) What paradox? Referential cues allow for infant use of phonetic detail in word learning. *Child Development*, 81 (5), 1376–1383.

Hollich, G. (2005) Supercoder: a program for coding preferential looking (version 1.5). Computer software. West Lafayette: Purdue University.

Horowitz, F.D. (1975) Visual attention, auditory stimulation, and language discrimination in young infants. *Monographs of the Society for Research in Child Development*, 39, pp. i–x, 1–140.

Hunter, M.A., and Ames, E.W. (1988) A multifactor model of infant preferences for novel and familiar stimuli. In C. Rovee-Collier and L.P. Lipsitt (eds), *Advances in infancy research* (vol. 5, pp. 69–95). Norwood, NJ: Ablex.

Kisilevsky, B.S., Hains, S.M.J., Brown, C.A., *et al.* (2009) Fetal sensitivity to properties of maternal speech and language. *Infant Behavior and Development*, 32, 59–71.

McMurray, B., and Aslin, R.N. (2004) Anticipatory eye movements reveal infants' auditory and visual categories. *Infancy*, 6 (2), 203–229.

Polka, L., and Werker, J. (1994) Developmental changes in perception of nonnative vowel contrasts. *Journal of Experimental Psychology: Human Perception and Performance*, 20 (2), 421–435.

Shi, R., Werker, J.F., and Morgan, J.L. (1999) Newborn infants' sensitivity to perceptual cues to lexical and grammatical words. *Cognition*, 72 (2), B11–B21.

Stager, C.L., and Werker, J.F. (1997) Infants listen for more phonetic detail in speech perception than in word-learning tasks. *Nature*, 388 (6640), 381–382.

Sundara, M., Polka, L., and Molnar, M. (2008) Development of coronal stop perception: bilingual infants keep pace with their monolingual peers. *Cognition*, 108, 232–242.

Swain, I.U., Zelazo, P.R., and Clifton, R.K. (1993) Newborn infants' memory for speech sounds retained over 24 hours. *Developmental Psychology*, 9 (2), 312–323.

Werker, J.F., Cohen, L.B., Lloyd, V.L., *et al.* (1998) Acquisition of word–object associations by 14-month-old infants. *Developmental Psychology*, 34, 1289–1309.

Werker, J.F., Fennell, C.T., Corcoran, K.M., and Stager, C.L. (2002) Developmental changes in infants' ability to learn similar sounding words. *Infancy*, 3 (1), 1–33.

Yoshida, K., Fennell, C.T., Swingley, D., and Werker, J.F. (2009) Fourteen-month-olds learn similar-sounding words. *Developmental Science*, 12 (3), 412–418.

Further Reading and Resources

Cohen, L.B. (2004) Uses and misuses of habituation and related preference paradigms. *Infant and Child Development*, 13, 349–352.

Hunter, M.A., and Ames, E.W. (1988) A multifactor model of infant preferences for novel and familiar stimuli. In C. Rovee-Collier and L.P. Lipsitt (eds), *Advances in infancy research* (vol. 5, pp. 69–95). Norwood, NJ: Ablex.

Werker, J.F., Shi, R., Desjardins, R., *et al.* (1998) Three methods for testing infant speech perception. In A.M. Slater (ed.), *Perceptual development: visual, auditory, and speech perception in infancy* (pp. 389–420). London: UCL Press.

Habit computer software for running habituation experiments:
http://homepage.psy.utexas.edu/homepage/group/cohenlab/habit.html.
SuperCoder software for coding visual looking:
http://hincapie.psych.purdue.edu/Splitscreen/index.html.

2 Intermodal Preferential Looking

Janina Piotroski and Letitia R. Naigles

Summary

The intermodal preferential looking (IPL) paradigm was developed to investigate the linguistic knowledge of young children through assessing language comprehension. The procedure consists of showing side-by-side dynamic videos depicting different objects, actions, or more complex events, paired with an audio that matches only one of the videos. If children understand the language of the audio, they should look longer at the matching video. The IPL paradigm can be used to study questions concerning the age of acquisition of grammatical constructions and the processes or strategies that children use to learn words. It is suitable for typically developing children between the ages of 12 months and 3.5 years, and for children with speech delays such as those diagnosed with autism spectrum disorder. The IPL method can also be used for crosslinguistic comparisons because the same visual stimuli can be used while varying the audio for the language of interest.

Research Aims

The intermodal preferential looking (IPL) paradigm was developed to investigate the linguistic knowledge of young children, through assessing language comprehension rather than production (Golinkoff *et al.*, 1987; Hirsh-Pasek and Golinkoff, 1996). In addition, this paradigm has begun to be used to study language processing in real time (Candan, Küntay, and Naigles, 2010; Naigles *et al.*, 2010; see also Fernald *et al.*, 2008; and Swingley, Chapter 3 this volume). The IPL paradigm tests comprehension

Research Methods in Child Language: A Practical Guide, First Edition.
Edited by Erika Hoff.
© 2012 Blackwell Publishing Ltd. Published 2012 by Blackwell Publishing Ltd.

by showing children side-by-side dynamic videos depicting different objects, actions, or more complex events. These are paired with an audio that matches only one of the videos. If children understand the language of the audio, they should look longer at the matching video. Thus, this method uses the patterns of children's eye movements as the indicator of comprehension.

The IPL method can be used to study three themes that are crucial to understanding early language acquisition. (1) Which grammatical constructions do children know, and how early do they know them? (2) What processes and strategies do children use to learn words, and when are these in operation? (3) What do children know about the words, especially nouns, that they are already familiar with? (This third theme has also been extensively studied using a similar but not identical paradigm called "looking while listening" [LWL]. For more information, see Swingley, Chapter 3 this volume; also, Houston-Price, Plunkett, and Harris, 2005; Naigles and Gelman, 1995.) Because IPL can be used with children as young as 12–15 months of age, the very beginnings of the mapping of linguistic form and linguistic meaning can be studied.

Theme 1: Acquisition of Grammatical Forms

IPL has been used to demonstrate that children understand very early in life how the word order of their native language illustrates "who does what to whom." For example, children acquiring English look longer at a boy washing a girl than at a girl washing a boy when the audio is "Look, the boy is washing the girl." This preference has also been demonstrated with novel verbs and events (i.e., ones that don't have conventional labels in that language: Gertner, Fisher, and Eisengart, 2006; Dittmar *et al.*, 2008) and in children with autism at the two-word stage of language production (Swensen *et al.*, 2007). Using this method, researchers have also found that 1–2-year-olds understand wh-questions. They are first shown events where an apple hits a flower followed by paired pictures of an apple and a flower. They look longer at the apple for when the audio is "What hit the flower?" and longer at the flower when the audio is "What did the apple hit?" (Seidl, Hollich, and Jusczyk, 2003; Goodwin *et al.*, 2009). Researchers have also found that 2–3-year-olds distinguish specific aspectual markers ("-ing" vs "-ed") when presenting with paired ongoing and completed renditions of the same events. That is, 26–36-month-olds can match past/perfective forms such as "picked" or "drew" onto completed renditions and present/imperfective forms such as "is picking" onto ongoing renditions. Even more impressively, 30-month-olds were able to map novel verbs with "-ing" and "-ed" onto novel ongoing and completed events, respectively (Wagner, Swensen, and Naigles, 2009). This procedure has also been used with children acquiring different languages, revealing that very young children have learned the meaning carried by word order in their language. For example, understanding of subject + verb + object (SVO) order has been found in 17–21-month-old learners of English and Mandarin (Cheung *et al.*, 2009; Hirsh-Pasek and Golinkoff, 1996; Gertner, Fisher, and Eisengart, 2006; Swensen *et al.*, 2007), and understanding of the subject + object + verb (SOV) order that is characteristic of Turkish has been found in 27-month-old learners of Turkish (Candan, Küntay, and Naigles, 2010; see also Dittmar *et al.*, 2008, who tested 2-year-old German learners with both SOV and SVO orders).

Theme 2: Strategies of Word Learning

IPL has also been used to assess children's use of word learning biases such as the shape bias (Tek *et al.*, 2008), the noun bias (Swenson *et al.*, 2007), and syntactic bootstrapping (Naigles, 1990; 1998; Naigles *et al.*, 2010) because it easily enables the teaching of novel words. First, novel words are presented via audio, paired with either two novel objects or a novel object and a novel action. Then, in the testing phase the novel word is presented via audio and the two objects or the object and action are presented on different screens. Whichever screen the infant prefers to look at is taken as evidence of what the infant thinks the novel word means. Using this methodology, typically developing toddlers have been shown to exhibit a noun bias, preferentially mapping novel lexical items onto objects rather than actions, as young as 15 months of age (Swensen *et al.*, 2007; see also Maguire, Hirsh-Pasek, and Golinkoff, 2006). Moreover, children also preferentially map the referent of a novel noun onto the shape of an object as opposed to its color, texture, or size, starting at age 24 months. Interestingly, while 2–3-year-olds with autism have also exhibited a noun bias using IPL, they have not demonstrated a shape bias, even as late as 45 months of age. And a variety of labs have demonstrated that 2–3-year-olds learning English, Spanish, or Japanese can use sentence structure (e.g., the transitive vs intransitive frames) to focus on different types of events as the referents of novel verbs (i.e., syntactic bootstrapping) (Hohenstein, Naigles, and Eisenberg, 2004; Matsuo, Kita, and Naigles, 2009; Naigles, 1990; Yuan and Fisher, 2009). Three-year-olds with autism can also map novel transitive verbs onto novel causative rather than noncausative actions (Naigles *et al.*, 2010).

Data from the IPL procedure also allows asking about the relation between comprehension and production within individual children by comparing children's comprehension of a structure to their production of that structure. In this way, Swensen *et al.* (2007) found that 75% of typically developing children, as well as those diagnosed with autism who understood the meaning carried by word order, nonetheless did not yet consistently produce multiword utterances. Also, the children's preference for the matching video during the IPL test of word order comprehension was not significantly related to their percentage of total utterances in spontaneous production that consisted of multiple words for either group. The same study also found that 80% of the 28-month-old children who understood subject wh-questions and object wh-questions did not yet show evidence of producing these same types of questions. Very recently, we have begun investigating the extent to which variation in maternal input predicts subsequent variation in children's wh-question comprehension, with encouraging preliminary results (Goodwin *et al.*, 2009).

Finally, by increasing the number of behaviors measured IPL has also begun to be used for investigating how language comprehension proceeds in real time. The "standard" measure compares children's amount of looking to the matching screen (percentage of total looking time or duration of longest look) during the test trials with that during baseline control trials, yielding an overall measure of preference. However, one can also assess children's speed and efficiency of processing through a latency to the match (i.e., how quickly, after the start of the trial/test audio, does it take the child to look to the match?). Moreover, one can assess something like children's "certainty" of grasping the form–meaning pairing by analyzing their switches of attention (i.e., how many times do they switch from looking at the match to the nonmatch?). A higher number of switches would indicate a lesser certainty than a lower number of switches. In papers under review, we have found both of these measures to be informative. Turkish 2-year-olds listening to SOV sentences switch attention more than their English-learning peers listening to SVO sentences, possibly indicating more uncertainty interpreting sentences lacking the usual case markers; both groups show highly similar percentages of looking to the matching scene, nonetheless (Candan, Küntay, and Naigles, 2010). Moreover, children with autism who shift quickly to the matching scene when hearing SVO sentences with familiar verbs subsequently (8 months later) show more robust mapping of novel verbs in transitive frames onto causative actions, suggesting that children who are able to process SVO sentences early in development are the ones best able to use sentence frames to learn about verb meanings (Naigles *et al.*, 2010).

Preferential looking is best suited for young children between the ages of 12 months and 3.5 years, and ideal for those younger than 2.5 years, because young children of this age have trouble carrying out explicit tasks and may not talk "enough" to demonstrate the full extent of their current level of linguistic knowledge (Snyder, 2007). That is, toddlers do not always talk or act on demand, so request for enactments or productions of sentences can frequently result in unrelated toy or word play. It has also been found to be a useful technique for assessing the language of children with developmental delays, such as those with autism spectrum disorders (ASDs); these children also have difficulty carrying out explicit requests (e.g., Cauley *et al.*, 1989; Swenson *et al.*, 2007; Tek *et al.*, 2008). Because children are only required to sit relatively still and watch the videos, IPL provides an implicit measure of language understanding. Another useful application involves crosslinguistic comparisons (see Küntay, Chapter 19 this volume), because the same visual stimuli can be used while varying the audio for the language of interest (Cheung *et al.*, 2009; Candan, Küntay, and Naigles, 2010; Hohenstein, Naigles, and Eisenberg, 2004; Maguire *et al.*, 2010).

Procedure

The implementation of the IPL method requires the creation of synchronized videos, and the necessary equipment to present the videos to the children, record their eye movements, and then capture, code, and analyze the data (Tobii offers another way of getting eye movement data: see "Further reading and resources"; see also Gredebäck, Johnson, and von Hofsten, 2010).

Table 2.1 Generic layout of one block of an IPL video[a]

	Left video	Center	Audio	Right video
1	Blank	Flashing light	"Look here!"	Blank
2	**Familiarization video**	**Blank**	**"See this!"**	**Blank**
3	Blank	Flashing light	"Oh, look!"	Blank
4	**Blank**	**Blank**	**"Look now!"**	**Familiarization video**
5	Blank	Flashing light	"Hey, look!"	Blank
6	**Control video 1**	**Blank**	**Nondirecting**	**Control video 2**
7	Blank	Flashing light	Nondirecting	Blank
8	**Test video 1**	**Blank**	**Directing**	**Test video 2**

[a]Bold lines depict actual trials; non-bold lines depict inter-trial intervals.

Video and Audio Stimuli

Creating the videos requires a video camera and either costumed or conventionally dressed people (for enacting the familiar or novel events), or novel or familiar objects. If the videos are to be shown to children of various cultures, it is worthwhile to use people costumed as animals, which would then be matched for ease of labeling, so that the race/clothing of the characters is not a confound. For conventionally costumed characters, both adult and grade-school-aged actors have been used; toddlers find grade-school-aged children especially interesting and fun to watch.

Video layouts are usually created using commercial nonlinear editing software (e.g., Avid, FinalCutPro). These layouts can be arranged in a number of ways, depending on the exact questions under investigation. In general, though, as depicted in Table 2.1, familiarization or teaching trials come first, presented either sequentially on either side or in the middle, so as not to bias the children about which side will carry the match (i.e., sequential trials presented in a left–right (L–R) pattern for one block (i.e., a set of trials) should be presented in an R–L pattern for the next block). Usually, control trials, when the test events are presented without a directing audio, follow (Swensen *et al.*, 2007; Naigles, 1990); however, sometimes control trials are presented first (Naigles, Bavin, and Smith, 2005; Roseberry *et al.*, 2009). These trials provide the critical indication of screen/action/object preference, independent of the linguistic stimulus. Test trials are last in a given block; some use two test trials per item while others use only one, and the jury is out on whether children become confused when asked for the same linguistic match twice in succession (Naigles, 1990; Swensen *et al.*, 2007; Naigles, Bavin, and Smith, 2005; Matsuo, Kita, and Naigles, 2009). The test trials should be counterbalanced for the side of the match both within and across participants; therefore, the side of the match should switch across trials and across children. Because the first trial (i.e., familiarization or teaching) of a block alternates on an XYXY pattern, we usually follow an XYYXXY pattern for the side of the matching screen. That way, the side of the first trial is also the side of the match only half the time. Half of the children would view the match in an LRRLLRR pattern while the other half sees the match in an RLLRRLL pattern.

Some kind of visual centering stimulus needs to be presented during the interstimulus intervals (numbered 1, 3, 5, 7 in Table 2.1) to keep the children on task; some researchers use baby faces (Maguire *et al.*, 2010), but we have found red flashing lights to be attention-getting for both typically developing children and those with ASDs. Audios should be in child-directed speech and should include lots of attention-getting exclamations such as "hey," "wow," "look here" with a tone and a voice that are upbeat and fun. Trials 1–8 are then repeated for each block, or new items to be tested.

These videos are designed for use with children with short attention spans; therefore, videos are usually kept to 3–6 minutes total length (four to eight items in total; trials are 6–8 seconds long, with interstimulus intervals of 2–3 seconds). We have begun to present the same videos multiple times in a longitudinal design (Tek *et al.*, 2008), and have found better comprehension at an earlier age if a video is presented with only two to four blocks at visit N, followed by four to eight blocks at visit $N + 1$ (Naigles, 2009).

One last aspect of stimulus creation involves how to designate where the trials begin and end, so that the appropriate eye movements can be coded. Some paradigms lay a 1 kHz tone on a second (nonprojected) audio channel; this tone is coincident with each trial (bold lines in Table 2.1) and is copied onto the video showing the child's face (via a cable stretching from the laptop to the camera). Coders can then reference the tone signal to see when each trial starts and stops. Alternatively, if the child views the videos in a dimmed room, the added light of every trial will be visible on the film of the child's face and can be used as the indicator of trial onset and offset.

IPL Setups

IPL videos can be shown on a stationary setup or a portable setup. A stationary setup consists of a computer, two video monitors, a centrally placed speaker, a centering light, an audio splitter, and a video camera with tripod. The room is usually darkened to help the children focus on the videos; however, some light is needed so that the child's eyes are visible when filmed. The portable setup includes a portable projector with stand, a large projection screen, a video camera with tripod, a speaker, an audio splitter, and a laptop. Essentially, the video is shunted from the computer to the monitors directly in the stationary setup, or from the laptop to the projector to the screen in the portable version. The portable setup is ideally suited to studying developmentally delayed populations, and/or when longer or more naturalistic sessions are desired, because it can be easily transported to and set up in children's homes. Assessment in children's own homes is desirable for populations who become consistently uncomfortable in unfamiliar settings.

The portable setup involves somewhat different equipment and procedure, because it is used in families' homes. The projection screen must be sturdy, stand on its own and not be easily knocked over by young children, who seem to be fascinated by this novel item and love to hit it. A size of 84 by 63 inches (214 by 160 cm) is good. When the projection screen and camera are being set up in families' homes, the direction of natural light in the room should be assessed as with any filming project. Children should sit as close to the camera as possible (within 2 feet or 60 cm) to increase the size of their eyes on the film and obtain the greatest angle of eye movement, while still allowing for some leeway for head/body movement of the child during video. As when using any electronics equipment, adequate time should be allowed for warm-up, especially when traveling in cold weather!

Children in the stationary setup are usually buckled into booster seats or held on parents' laps; the advantage of the former is that, with parents sitting well behind the children, there is less chance of interference (of course, parents are instructed not to interfere). Children held on parents' laps may sit more calmly, but then parents are usually required not to watch the video (and/or listen to the audio), forestalling any cues from subtle movements parents might make. For some cultures, though, this restriction may be too onerous, in which case the booster-seat setup could be used. Children in the portable setup usually sit on their parents' lap; we typically ask the parent to wear headphones playing distracting music so s/he cannot hear the audio. Children viewing the videos ideally should not be allowed to have toys, food, or drinks in their hands as these often serve as distractions and can at times block the view of their eyes (especially with sippy cups). Interestingly, though, the opposite can hold when some children with autism view the videos: they sit and watch *better* when they are holding something.

Coding

Eye movements are coded offline, frame by frame, at 30 frames per second. This level of detail is needed because toddlers move around a lot while viewing, and because the children's eye movement patterns throughout the trial can be revealing about their level of processing. We use custom programs that tabulate the length and direction of each look for each trial, and then organize these looks according to each dependent measure. A free-use program (SuperCoder) is also available (see "Further reading and resources"). It is important that coders be "deaf" to or unaware of the specific stimuli that the child is experiencing on a given trial, so that they don't know which side is the matching one. If coders are very experienced in coding eye movements and the same coders are used to code all of the children's videos, then an interrater reliability calculation based on the complete data from 10% of participants is sufficient (reliability is usually around 0.98). However, with less experienced coders or if there is high turnover in the coders used across the participants of the study, we would recommend having every video coded by at least two people and requiring that their codes (usually duration to match) be within 0.3 seconds of each other for each trial. If they are not, then a third, fourth, or fifth person should code the video and hopefully they will be reliable with one of the previous coders.

Given that our participants are toddlers and/or children with developmental delays, it is inevitable that they will not look at either screen for some proportion of each trial, and for some trials, never. We have generally applied the following conventions for these lapses of attention:

1 Children need to look to at least one screen for a minimum of 0.3 seconds for that trial to be counted. Otherwise, it is a missing trial.
2 For a given video, children need to provide data for more than half of the test trials in order to be included in the final dataset.
3 Missing trials are replaced with the mean across children in that age group and condition for that item.

Data Analysis

Eye movement coding gives a variety of information about the children's visual fixations during the test trials (see also Trueswell, Chapter 12 this volume; Swingley, Chapter 3 this volume). The most typical measure compares the proportion of time that the child looked to the test video matching the directing audio, i.e., (looking to match)/(looking to match + looking to nonmatch) (so not counting looks to the center or away), compared with the same preference during the control/salience trial video in which there was no directing audio. This measure captures whether the directing audio altered the children's original video/side preference: children should look significantly *longer* at the matching scene during the test trials than they had during the control trials, as calculated by *t*-tests or ANOVAs. Variations of this measure can compare the children's looking during the control trial with their looking during the early or later segments of the test trial, thus revealing additional information about the child's ease of processing. For example, children who find the matching screen early in the trial may be demonstrating mastery of the mapping between the linguistic form and its depicted meaning, whereas those who only find it later may require additional processing to accomplish this mapping. It is not yet clear whether children who find the matching scene early, but then look away from it, understand the form–meaning mapping differently (better or worse) from children who find the matching scene early and then continue looking at it; below we will present some preliminary data suggesting the different patterns of looking do indicate different levels of understanding.

It is also possible to compare the children's latency of looking to the match versus the nonmatch during the test trial, with this latency during the control trial. The assumption is that children who understand the form–meaning mapping better will look to the match more quickly during the test trial (Fernald *et al.*, 2008); however, children's latency of looking at the match during the test trial should be *slower* than that during the control trial because the test trial requires the additional processing of the directing audio which has to be matched to the correct video. A third measure that can provide information about the children's understanding and the certainty of that understanding is the number of times that the child switches where s/he is looking during a given trial. The expectation is that children would switch attention more during the control trials (when there is no directing audio) than during the test trials (when there is a directing audio) if they understood the mapping between form and meaning that the trial is testing. Furthermore, children should display fewer switches of attention as their certainty about which side is the correct match increases.

As mentioned above, researchers have begun to use these latter measures to provide more detailed information about young children's early language comprehension processes. For example, differences have been seen across languages in how quickly children shift to the matching scene during the test trials: English learners tend to find the match early in the trial (Candan, Küntay, and Naigles, 2010; Gertner, Fisher, and Eisengart, 2006) whereas German and Turkish learners tend to find it later in the trial (Candan, Küntay, and Naigles, 2010; Dittmar *et al.*, 2008). Because both German and Turkish are languages that primarily use case markers rather than word order to indicate argument structure, these findings could be interpreted as indicating that even 2-year-old children are aware of the relative strength of the word order cue in their respective languages. The finding that Turkish 1–3-year-olds consistently switched attention during the test trials more than their English-learning peers did may also indicate their relative uncertainty about which scene was the matching one (Candan, Küntay, and Naigles, 2010).

Another new way to assess children's level of language comprehension using IPL involves examining their pattern of looking across the entire trial; i.e., their timecourse. Tek *et al.* (2009) have illustrated how this timecourse changes with age for a novel noun-learning task. In a longitudinal investigation of the shape bias, 16 children were shown five sets of novel target objects followed by two simultaneously presented test objects, one of which had the same shape and one the same color as the target object. During the first block of trials, the five target objects were unlabeled and the test audio simply asked, "Which one looks the same?" (the no-name condition). During the second block of trials in the same video, the five targets were each given a novel label and the test audio asked, "Where is the (novel name)?" (the name condition). With the entire-trial proportion-looking-to-match measure, typically developing toddlers at 20 months of age showed no preference for the shape match during the name condition relative to the no-name condition; however, beginning at 24 months of age, these significant effects were found (Tek *et al.*, 2008). Timecourse analyses of the children's looking patterns illustrate how their development proceeded.

Plate 1 shows the children's average timecourse of looking in each direction, at each age (4 months apart, i.e., at 20, 24, 28, and 32 months). The red and pink lines show the children's looking away and looking to the center, respectively. The blue line shows their looking to the shape match, and the green line shows their looking to the color match. Their proportion of looking in each direction is plotted on the y-axis; thus, at any given time, the four lines should add up to 1.0. The relevant trials of the video are plotted on the x-axis, as follows, starting at the far left. The first set of lines in each panel (to the left of the first green vertical bar) shows the children's looking during the ISI (blank) before the no-name test trial. Here, the red centering light is on, and the children are predominantly looking to the center or away (i.e., red and pink lines are the highest). The next set of lines in each panel (between the vertical green bar and the vertical red bar) shows the children's looking during the no-name test trial itself. Here, the children are asked, "Which one looks the same?" and they look equally at the shape and color matches as well as away; their looks to the center have diminished to zero. The next set of lines in each panel (between the vertical red bar and the next vertical green bar) shows the children's looking during the ISI before the name test trial. Again, the red centering light is on and the children are predominantly looking to the center or away (for the 20-month-olds, mostly away!).

The final set of lines in each panel in Plate 1 shows the children's looking during the name test trial itself, and here is where we can see effects of age. The top left panel shows the children's looking patterns at 20 months of age. During the name test trials, they showed a slight and late preference for the shape match over the color match, but clearly looked away longer than at either scene. The top right panel shows their patterns at 24 months of age. During the name test trials, they show an earlier and more stable preference for the shape match over all other directions; however, they do not look at the shape match for more than half of the time. The bottom left panel shows their patterns at 28 months of age. During the name test trials, their preference for the shape match does reach over 0.5, but only towards the very end of the trial. Finally, the bottom right panel shows their patterns at 32 months, the last time they were tested. During the name test trials, their dominant preference for the shape match is evident much earlier in the trial. What we seem to be seeing, then, is that a shape bias that grows stronger with age – which has already been demonstrated in cross-sectional studies (e.g., Samuelson and Smith, 2000) – is manifested longitudinally by a progressively earlier preference for the shape match during preferential looking.

In sum, IPL is a method that taps children's earliest mappings of linguistic forms (i.e., words and sentences) onto referential (i.e., objects and actions) or propositional (i.e., relations and events) meanings. It can be used to assess the processes by which children of different ages learn new words, as well as the ages at which they understand different types of grammatical forms. By requiring only eye movements as overt indicators of understanding (or not), IPL can be used with toddlers whose behavioral compliance is generally low, as well as with some special populations. Newer ways of analyzing these eye movements are revealing interesting and important effects of learning different types of languages, and of learning words at different ages.

Key Terms

Control trials When the test events are presented on both sides of the screen (a match and a nonmatch) without a directing audio.

Familiarization or teaching trial Video on either the right or the left side in which the child is first introduced to an action or a novel word.

Latency to match How long it takes, after the start of the trial/test audio, for the child to look to the match.

Switches of attention The number of times the child switches from looking at the match to the nonmatch.

Test trials When the test events are presented on both sides of the screen with an audio directing them to only one side of the screen (the match).

Visual fixation Where the child is looking during the trials.

References

Candan, A., Küntay, A., and Naigles, L. (2010) Crosslinguistic variation in sensitivity to word order in sentence comprehension. Poster presented at the conference Let The Children Speak: Learning of Critical Language Skills across 25 Languages, COST (European Cooperation in Science and Technology) Action A33, January, London.

Cauley, K., Golinkoff, R., Hirsh-Pasek, K., and Gordon, L. (1989) Revealing hidden competencies: a new method for studying language in the motorically handicapped. *American Journal of Mental Retardation*, 94 (1), 53–63.

Cheung, H., Küntay, A.C., Wagner, L., *et al.* (2009) Cross-linguistic variation and consistency in 2- and 3-year-olds' sensitivity to word order. Poster presented at the Society for Research in Child Development, April, Denver, CO.

Dittmar, M., Abbot-Smith, K., Lieven, E., and Tomasello, M. (2008) German children's comprehension of word order and case marking in causative sentences. *Child Development*, 79 (4), 1152–1167.

Fernald, A., Zangl, R., Portillo, A., and Marchman, V. (2008) Looking while listening: using eye movements to monitor spoken language comprehension by infants and young children. In I. Sekerina, E. Fernandez, and H. Clahsen (eds), *Developmental psycholinguistics: on-line methods in children's language processing* (pp. 97–135). Amsterdam: Benjamins.

Gertner, Y., Fisher, C., and Eisengart, J. (2006) Learning words and rules: abstract knowledge of word order in early sentence comprehension. *Psychological Science*, 17, 684–691.

Golinkoff, R.M., Hirsh-Pasek, K., Cauley, K.M., and Gordon, L. (1987) The eyes have it: lexical and syntactic comprehension in a new paradigm. *Journal of Child Language*, 14, 23–45.

Goodwin, A., Jaffery, G., Fein, D., and Naigles, L.R. (2009) Wh-questions in toddlerhood: comprehension precedes production and input predicts comprehension. Poster presented at the Society for Research in Child Development, April, Denver, CO.

Gredebäck, G., Johnson, S., and von Hofsten, C. (2010) Eye tracking in infancy research. *Developmental Neuropsychology*, 35 (1), 1–19.

Hirsh-Pasek, K., and Golinkoff, R.M. (eds) (1996) *The origins of grammar: evidence from early language comprehension*. Cambridge, MA: MIT Press.

Hohenstein, J., Naigles, L., and Eisenberg, A. (2004) Keeping verb acquisition in motion: a comparison of English and Spanish. In G. Hall and S. Waxman (eds), *Weaving a lexicon* (pp. 569–602). Cambridge, MA: MIT Press.

Houston-Price, C., Plunkett, K., and Harris, P.L. (2005) Word learning "wizardry" at 1:6. *Journal of Child Language*, 32, 175–189.

Maguire, M.J., Hirsh-Pasek, K., and Golinkoff, R.M. (2006) A unified theory of verb learning: putting verbs in context. In K. Hirsh-Pasek and R.M. Golinkoff (eds), *Action meets word: how children learn verbs* (pp. 364–391). New York: Oxford University Press.

Maguire, M., Hirsh-Pasek, K., Golinkoff, R., *et al.* (2010) A developmental shift from similar to language specific strategies in verb acquisition: a comparison of English, Spanish and Japanese. *Cognition*, 114, 299–319.

Matsuo, A., Kita, S., and Naigles, L. (2009) Morphosyntactic bootstrapping in Japanese verb learning. Paper presented at the conference Generative Approaches to Language Acquisition (GALA), September, Lisbon.

Naigles, L. (1990) Children use syntax to learn verb meanings. *Journal of Child Language*, 17, 357–374.

Naigles, L. (1998) Developmental changes in the use of structure in verb learning. In C. Rovee-Collier, L. Lipsitt, and H. Haynes (eds), *Advances in infancy research* (vol. 12, pp. 298–318). London: Ablex.

Naigles, L.R. (2009) Grammatical understanding in young children with ASD: resilient knowledge and fragmentary deficits. Invited symposium, International Conference on Innovative Research in Autism, April, Tours, France.

Naigles, L., Bavin, E., and Smith, M. (2005) Toddlers recognize verbs in novel situations and sentences. *Developmental Science*, 8, 424–431.

Naigles, L.R., and Gelman, S.A. (1995) Overextensions in comprehension and production revisited: preferential-looking in a study of *dog, cat* and *cow. Journal of Child Language*, 22, 19–46.

Naigles, L., Kelty, E., Jaffery, R., and Fein, D. (2010) Abstractness and continuity in the syntactic development of young children with autism. Unpublished manuscript, University of Connecticut.

Roseberry, S., Hirsh-Pasek, K., Parish-Morris, J., and Golinkoff, R.M. (2009) Live action: can young children learn verbs from video? *Child Development*, 80, 1360–1375.

Samuelson, L.K., and Smith, L.B. (2000) Grounding development in cognitive processes. *Child Development*, 71, 98–106.

Seidl, A., Hollich, G., and Jusczyk, P.W. (2003) Early understanding of subject and object *wh*-questions. *Infancy*, 4, 423–436.

Snyder, W. (2007) *Child language: the parametric approach*. Oxford University Press.

Swensen, L., Kelley, E., Fein, D., and Naigles, L. (2007) Children with autism display typical language learning characteristics: evidence from preferential looking. *Child Development*, 78, 542–557.

Tek, S., Jaffery, G., Fein, D., and Naigles, L.R. (2008) Do children with autism show a shape bias in word learning? *Autism Research*, 1, 202–215.

Tek, S., Jaffrey, G., Piotroski, J., *et al.* (2009) The shape bias: investigations of word learning with children with autism. Poster presented at the International Meeting for Autism Research, May, Chicago.

Wagner, L., Swenson, L.D., and Naigles, L.R. (2009) Children's early productivity with verbal morphology. *Cognitive Development*, 24, 223–239.

Yuan, S., and Fisher, C. (2009) "Really? She blicked the baby?" Two-year-olds learn combinatorial facts about verbs by listening. *Psychological Science*, 20 (5), 619–626.

Further Reading and Resources

Naigles, L. (1990) Children use syntax to learn verb meanings. *Journal of Child Language*, 17, 357–374.

Swensen, L., Kelley, E., Fein, D., and Naigles, L. (2007) Children with autism display typical language learning characteristics: evidence from preferential looking. *Child Development*, 78, 542–557.

Tek, S., Jaffery, G., Fein, D., and Naigles, L.R. (2008) Do children with autism show a shape bias in word learning? *Autism Research*, 1, 202–215.

SuperCoder: http://www1.psych.purdue.edu/~ghollich/Splitscreen/home.html.
Tobii: http://www.diigo.com/list/tobiieyetracking/scientific.

3 The Looking-While-Listening Procedure

Daniel Swingley

Summary

The "looking-while-listening" or "language-guided-looking" procedure is used to closely examine children's interpretation of spoken language. The timecourse of children's eye movements toward pictures or scenes is evaluated while children hear sentences describing one of them. The procedure can be used in virtually any population, and works consistently in children from 14 months onward, with little modification necessary for testing older children or adults. Researchers have examined word recognition and sentence understanding to address a range of questions concerning language representation and performance.

Measuring Performance in Language Acquisition

Linguists and developmental psychologists often focus on the *logical* problems of language acquisition: the discovery of grammar from apparently insufficient evidence, the learning of word meaning despite infinite possible false starts. But for parents observing their children's development, much of the fascination of language acquisition lies in the startling leaps children make from one day to the next as they reveal their thoughts: the words and expressions and sentences that suddenly rush onstage in all their glory. We sense the developing mind struggling to share its thoughts with us, and we ask, "Where on earth did that come from?" And for the most part, we don't know, or we don't know in any detail, because most of what we can determine of any child's linguistic knowledge is revealed by his or her speech – the behavior that surprised us in the first place.

Research Methods in Child Language: A Practical Guide, First Edition.
Edited by Erika Hoff.
© 2012 Blackwell Publishing Ltd. Published 2012 by Blackwell Publishing Ltd.

Comprehension precedes production: young children who can understand multiword sentences may struggle to produce a two-word utterance. Children's corrections of their own attempts are usually improvements rather than random walks, and children can be creative as they strain to give voice to their ideas. For example, children making the transition from one-word utterances to two-word utterances often begin by using one word and one gesture to communicate two separate components of their intended meaning (Iverson and Goldin-Meadow, 2005). These observations show that when young children speak, the semantic target that they are aiming for may be clear in their minds even when the child's utterance is not understandable to others, or when the child fails to produce an utterance at all. It is commonly said that language development is effortless for children, but it's not true: children's difficulties are just different from ours. One stumbling block appears to be the inability to successfully assemble sentences out of components that children seem to *interpret* correctly, according to their language's grammar.

Precisely because comprehension precedes production, mapping out the developmental course of language acquisition requires evaluation of children's receptive knowledge of language. Researchers have risen to the task: we have ways to assess discrimination and categorization of speech sounds and sequences of sounds from birth, using habituation measures like high-amplitude sucking (Fennell, Chapter 1 this volume). We can test infants' recognition of speech sequences using contingent listening tasks like the head turn preference procedure or response training tasks like conditioned head turn. And we can measure correlates of stimulus-driven brain activity using one of a few brain imaging techniques (Kovelman, Chapter 4 this volume). These procedures work with infants, but for the most part they do not depend on (or directly reveal) children's meaningful interpretation of language.

Experimental tests of language comprehension have been available for a long time. There are act-out tasks in which children manipulate toys or other objects under instruction to enact the statements of a researcher (or puppet). There is the truth-value judgment task, which asks children whether a puppet is right or wrong about some statement. These procedures certainly depend on children's interpretation of language. But they are extremely difficult to use in children younger than 2 to 2½ years old.

Eye movement tasks were developed to help fill the gap left by these other procedures. The first "preferential looking" studies examining infant language comprehension showed that children's gaze toward images or films was affected in sensible ways by simultaneously presented spoken language: if the child heard "Look at the doggie!" he or she tended to look at a picture of a dog more than a picture of some other familiar object (e.g., Golinkoff *et al.*, 1987; Reznick, 1990; Thomas *et al.*, 1981). This response allows researchers to draw inferences about children's knowledge: if children increase their looking to a named image or film upon hearing it labeled, they show evidence of understanding the word. Likewise, syntactic interpretation may be probed: if children gaze at a scene that exemplifies a spoken sentence better than another scene (which might exemplify a syntactically different sentence with the same participants, for example), children provide evidence of knowing something about that syntactic structure.

This procedure has been tremendously influential in tracing the earliest development of children's knowledge of words and syntactic structures, as outlined by Piotroski (see Piotroski and Naigles, Chapter 2 this volume) and by Hirsh-Pasek (see Golinkoff and Hirsh-Pasek, Chapter 5 this volume). Over the past decade and a half, preferential looking procedures have been adapted for studying not only children's knowledge of language, but also the details of children's performance in interpreting language online. It is this work that is the focus of the present chapter.

The notion of "performance" is often raised in the literature on language acquisition, traditionally as part of an effort to explain why a child didn't succeed in a task, or botched a grammatical structure, in spite of the researcher's belief that the child had already acquired the relevant grammatical knowledge. The distinction between the child's capabilities and the child's behavior is a necessary one if, like most cognitive scientists, one wishes to maintain a distinction between representation (taken to be relatively static knowledge) and process (taken to be the implementation of this knowledge in cognition under particular circumstances). But in language acquisition, performance has not been the focus of sustained empirical attention to the extent that representation ("competence") has. This state of affairs emerged in part due to a vicious circle: the more "performance" is (often justifiably) derided as an unmotivated "fudge factor," the less it has appeared a compelling research area to work on, and one consequence is performance-based descriptions of behavior without adequate content.

This has begun to change, partly as a result of research using "looking-while-listening," "language-guided-looking," or "eyetracking" methods with infants and young children. In developmental psycholinguistics, these terms all mean the same thing. Where they diverge from the traditional preferential looking methods is the use of characteristic features of eye movement responses to address questions about psychological processes. In particular, looking-while-listening experiments focus on the timing of children's responses. Response times have been an essential component of cognitive psychology from the beginning, starting with Donders and Cattell in the late nineteenth century and carrying on to this day, but they have had a relatively limited impact on developmental psychology simply because of the difficulty of persuading children to make an overt manual response quickly and accurately. However, very young children make rapid eye movements as they seek information, and, it turns out, they do so in response to language.

The Development of Looking While Listening

This part of the story begins around 1990 in Anne Fernald's lab at Stanford. She wanted to know if the infant-directed prosodic register would make words easier for young children to understand. On each of a series of 12 trials, children at 12, 15, and 18 months of age were presented with pairs of pictures, one on each of two screens.

A few seconds later, a pre-recorded speech stimulus was played, in either the infant-directed or the adult-directed register, naming one of the two objects. A film of the child's face was recorded on videotape. The whole apparatus was decidedly low-tech by today's standards: the pictures were beamed onto rear-projection screens by yoked slide projectors, and the speech was presented using a reel-to-reel tape player triggered by a research assistant listening to a recording of a metronome. What distinguished Fernald's implementation, though, was her insistence on frame-by-frame, offline coding of children's eye movements.

At the time, most labs using preferential looking methods recorded looking behavior online, using a button box. This is a speedy way to go – you have the child's results before you say goodbye to the mom – but it inevitably introduces error because of delays and variability in responding to the child. Offline coding removes the response latency component to scoring and allows researchers to draw up precise standards for what counts as a fixation, when a fixation should be considered to begin and end, what to do when the child blinks, and other details that were hashed out in long late-night discussions in the Stanford lab. Originally, the decision to code offline was not based on the anticipation of measuring response latencies; it was simply a matter of getting the best possible record of behavior.

Fernald, McRoberts, and Herrera (in Fernald, McRoberts, and Swingley, 2001) found that young children indeed recognized words more reliably when spoken in the infant-directed register. They also found that target fixation was not uniform over the 6 s test period (starting from the offset of the sentence): among 18-month-olds, performance was better at 0–2 s after sentence offset than at 2–4 s, and worst of all at 4–6 s. As these results were emerging, John Pinto and I joined Anne Fernald's lab. Pinto developed software that could take the lab's detailed records of eye movements and produce a matrix of gaze locations over time, showing for each trial, and at each moment in time, whether the child was fixating the target, the distracter, or neither. We began exploring other possible windows of analysis: 2 s windows, 1 s windows, windows starting mid-word, and so on. At some point in this exploration process I decided to compute every possible 1 s window, starting from the beginning of the trial and going to the end. A plot of the means of each overlapping window revealed a smooth curve starting at 50% and rapidly rising to about 80% before falling off. I was quite proud of this until I showed it to Pinto, who asked why I was taking a moving average rather than simply plotting the raw averages for each time slice. Skipping the 1 s smoothing operation led to the first of our plots of the timecourse of word recognition in children.

Broadly speaking, timecourse analyses of young children's word recognition have yielded two main lines of research, one examining the cognitive processes involved in parsing sentences, and another examining individual differences among children. I will illustrate these research programs using selected results.

Both lines emerged from an early study using language guided looking (Fernald *et al.*, 1998). On each of eight trials, children heard sentences like "Where's the ball?" while viewing a ball on one computer screen and a shoe on the other. Children's eye movements were coded from videotape. Results were reported in three ways, in keeping with much subsequent work. First, children's proportion of fixation to the target during a 2 s window, from target-word onset, was computed. On each trial, the total number of 100 ms intervals (from 0 ms to 2000 ms) on which children were coded as fixating the target was divided by the count of target- and distracter-fixated intervals. Among 15-, 18-, and 24-month-olds, the mean proportions were consistently greater than the 50% that would be expected if children did not respond to the words (each picture served as target and distracter equally often in yoked pairs, so picture preferences could not lead to overall performance above 50%). Mean target fixation increased substantially with age.

Second, children's *response latencies* were computed, defined as the amount of time, from the onset of the target word, it took for children to initiate a refixation away from the distracter picture to the target, for all trials on which children had been fixating the distracter picture when the target word began. Mean response latencies declined substantially as children grew older – from a mean of 995 ms at 15 months to 679 ms at 24 months.

Third, children's proportion of target fixation over time was displayed graphically in *onset-contingent timecourse plots* (e.g., Plate 2). In such graphs, time is given on the *x*-axis. Trials are grouped according to whether the child happened to be fixating the target, or the distracter, when the target word began. This is useful because children are in different states in each case. A child looking at the target is hearing it named as the sentence unfolds; the sentence confirms that the child's focus of attention matches the utterance. Recognition is inferred when children continue fixating the target. A child looking at the distracter hears the spoken target word, and the meaning that the word evokes is inconsistent with the child's focus of attention, which is expected to provoke a refixation (Swingley and Fernald, 2002). Rather than plotting target fixation on the *y*-axis, we plot, for each unit of time, the proportion of trials on which children are, at that moment, fixating a different picture than the one they were looking at when the target word began. Thus, good performance is shown by "target-initial" trials remaining flat near 0, and "distracter-initial" trials rapidly departing from 0 toward 1. The advantage of plotting this way, rather than showing percentage-to-target for each type of trial, is that one can see clearly when the child begins to show evidence of understanding, namely when the lines diverge. The divergence in the lines happens when defections from the target are outnumbered by rejections of the distracter picture.

For example, Plate 2 plots data from Experiment 2 in Swingley (2009), in which 14–22-month-olds responded to correctly pronounced words (black lines on the plot) and mispronounced words (red lines). When hearing correct pronunciations, such as *book*, children's refixations from the distracter (shown with a solid line) began to exceed refixations from the target (dashed line) at around 750 ms. The separation between the distracter-initial and target-initial lines is smaller than, and begins later than, what we would expect from older children or adults, but it is clear that children's responses are, on the whole, responsive to the match between the word and the fixated picture. When children heard mispronunciations, such as *dook*, they shifted away from the target and distracter pictures equally often until about 1450 ms, and the relatively small separation between target-initial and distracter-initial means reveals children's difficulty in understanding the mispronounced word.

The Fernald *et al.* (1998) paper led directly to a series of studies examining detailed aspects of the timecourse of word recognition. In several cases, these studies compared children and adults directly, and found qualitatively (and often quantitatively) similar patterns. For example, Swingley, Pinto, and Fernald (1999) compared how 24-month-olds and adults responded when, for example, hearing *doggie* and looking at a doll versus hearing *doggie* and looking at a tree. At both ages, participants rejected the distracter faster when its initial sounds did not match the spoken word (e.g., the /tr/ of "tree") than when they did (e.g., the /dɔ/ of "doll"). The temporal delay in rejecting the onset-overlapping "doggie" and "doll" distracters was, at both ages, comparable to the amount of time the two spoken words overlapped, as assessed using adults' explicit judgments of fragments of the words. These results showed that children, like adults, interpret speech incrementally, updating their understanding as the words unfolded. Support for the same idea in younger children was shown by Fernald, Swingley, and Pinto (2001) and by Swingley (2009). In the latter study, children from 14 to 22 months of age responded to stimuli that were "mispronounced" at onset (e.g., *cup* as "gup") or offset (e.g., *cup* as "cub"). Relative to the onset of the target words, children's target fixation was disrupted immediately when onsets were altered, and disrupted a few hundred milliseconds later when offsets were altered, in keeping with the acoustic timing of the deviations themselves.

The principle of incremental interpretation holds for other areas of sentence parsing as well, although it is clear that children's proficiency in using linguistic information depends on mastery of the words and constructions they are hearing. By about 36 months, native Spanish learners use grammatical gender encoded in articles to help identify the following noun (Lew-Williams and Fernald, 2007); French learners have been shown to do the same at 25 months (van Heugten and Shi, 2009). On the other hand, at 30 months, English learners do not consistently use prenominal adjectives to constrain reference (Fernald, Thorpe, and Marchman, 2010). For example, confronted with a blue car and a red house, 30-month-olds had only mixed success in using the adjective in sentences like "Which one's the blue car?" to guide their attention away from the red distracter picture. Given that all the children tested were capable of using *blue* and *red* appropriately in their own speech, this result points to the fact that expert language understanding is a skill in itself, over and above knowledge of word meanings and acquisition of grammatical rules.

This notion of language processing as a skill fits well with another major line of research using the looking-while-listening procedure, where quantitative details of children's responses are used to establish individual differences in speech processing. The Fernald *et al.* (1998) paper mentioned earlier explored differences in mean response latency among children of different ages; more recent work has tested whether measurements of speed and accuracy in word recognition are correlated with other cognitive assessments both contemporaneously and predictively. For example, Marchman and Fernald (2008) measured 25-month-olds' response latency to the nouns in sentences like "Where's the doggie?" or "Where's the nice cow?" Response latency made significant unique contributions to prediction of working memory scores on a standarized test given at 8 years; response latency and vocabulary size together predicted high scores on expressive language. More recent studies by the same authors reveal connections between maternal child-directed speech and children's speed of word recognition using the looking-while-listening task (Hurtado, Marchman, and Fernald, 2008). In a low-SES sample of Spanish-speaking families in

California, children of more talkative mothers (assessed at 18 months) recognized words more quickly at 24 months than children whose mothers talked to them less; further, response latency at 24 months was significantly correlated with growth in vocabulary over the prior 6 months.

Both the individual difference studies and the incremental-processing studies take advantage of unique properties of the language-guided-looking procedure by evaluating not only children's overall performance in linking words to referents, but also the details of the timing with which these connections are made. The procedure is also used frequently in answering questions about static representational knowledge, and in these cases the temporal dynamics of children's responses provide an additional dependent measure but are not the focus of the research. For example, following Swingley and Aslin (2000), several studies have evaluated children's looking patterns upon hearing canonical pronunciations of words and phonologically deviant pronunciations. Children typically look to target pictures more rapidly when the words are correctly pronounced than mispronounced, just as adults do; whereas phonetic changes that are not phonologically distinctive in the language do not hinder recognition (e.g., Quam and Swingley, 2010). In these studies, the response latency measures are usually redundant with other measures of target looking (such as proportion of target fixation over a short analysis window).

Implementation

Apparatus

The procedure is not technically demanding to implement. Considering the apparatus, the most common setup is built around a "booth," a three-sided enclosure about 1.5 m on a side. In essence, the booth is a display surrounded by visually featureless space: there is nothing to see but what's on the screen. The display itself is usually a very large video monitor – 42 inch (107 cm) diagonal is common – or a projection system fed by a computer. Projectors allow for larger pictures and a greater amount of space between pictures. Using large, widely spaced pictures was initially motivated by the desire to maximize coding accuracy on grainy, dimly lit videotape, and also by the reasonable supposition that larger images would capture infants' attention better. However, it is not certain that this is necessary. We have been successful in testing children ranging from <12 months to 30 months using a single 20 inch (51 cm) computer monitor. If the child is only 50–60 cm from the screen, the visual angle separating pictures placed near the screen's left and right edges is adequate for judging left and right fixations, particularly using modern cameras that do a good job recording in dim light. Whether giant screens impress infants enough to lower attrition rates is an open question.

Stimulus presentation can be controlled by software designed for experiments (such as Psyscope: http://psy.ck.sissa.it/psy cmu edu/index.html), animations (such as Director: http://www.adobe.com/products/director), or movies (such as

QuickTime: http://www.apple.com/quicktime). Software programs vary in their temporal accuracy. One cannot assume that if the program is told to play sound x at 2000 ms after displaying picture y, this actually happens consistently. In any case, even with a consistently presented stimulus, one still needs a way to line up the experimental events (like the onset of the spoken target word on each trial) and infant events (like an eye movement shift). Different labs have handled this in different ways. One option is to use picture-in-picture video technology to place a recording of the visual display in the corner of the recording of the child's face, so that coders can link the eye movement time stream with the trial onset times. (In this case coders are not blind to the target picture's side of presentation, however.) Another option, which we use, is to play one audio channel of the stereo stimulus signal to the child, and embed target-word-aligned tones in the other channel. A custom-built device detects these tones, and embeds a distinctive visual signal in the video recording of the infant. Other tones (and other visual signals) indicate other trial events. Coders can then note the timing of all infant and stimulus events in the same way, by looking at the recorded video signal.

We audio record each session in two ways at once: one channel records the sequence of timing beeps, and another channel records input from a microphone that captures sound in the booth. The latter permits analysis of children's vocalizations (and parents' too, if they speak), and allows confirmation that the auditory stimuli were presented as intended.

Visual and Auditory Stimuli

Naturally, testing language understanding using eye movements to referents of sentences requires that the sentences have picturable referents. The two main concerns are the *recognizability* of the images, and their relative *salience*. We generally use photographs rather than drawings. Some objects are quite difficult to use as referents because their forms vary across instances in children's experience. For example, we have never used "phone" (toy phone? cell phone?) or "hat" (baseball? cowboy? wool with pom-pom?). Another vexing issue is children's tendency to find certain objects much more attractive to look at than others, particularly in children under 24 months of age. Animate objects are more captivating than inanimates, so even if one searches out the most drab, mangy dog, many children will gaze longingly at it. We often try to pair animates together to offset such effects. For both of these issues, pilot testing is the only way to be sure.

Auditory stimuli should be recorded and selected with care, particularly for studies in which phonetic properties are central. Not all talkers are up to the task, and practice is usually necessary even for a speaker with excellent vocal control. When recording stimuli for an experiment 1, it can be useful to have the speaker read materials for potential experiments 2 and 3 as well, because acoustic characteristics of different recording sessions vary (and our speakers have a tendency to graduate and move away). If similar stimuli are to be compared directly (e.g., a word and a deviant pronunciation of that word), these stimuli should be listed next to one another in the recording script, to mitigate the effects of drift on the part of the speaker. Multiple tokens should be recorded and the best and best-matching instances selected. This process is tedious and time consuming, but a study can only be as good as its materials.

Procedure

Once parent and child and any assorted siblings arrive in the lab, it is up to the researcher to determine when it is time to stop playing and start moving into the room with the booth. As a rule, siblings should not be in the testing room with the toddler during the procedure. Toddlers clinging to lab toys should be separated from them if possible, because toys may distract the child, and because children have an uncanny knack for using toys to obscure their eyes from the camera's view. In most cases the child can sit on the parent's lap, though if toddlers insist on sitting in the chair alone, with the mother crouching nearby, this works too, or at least works better than a tantrum.

Parents need to be prevented from biasing their children's looking. We tell parents to look downward (we can see the parent's face clearly on camera and, if necessary, pause the study between trials if we detect any peeking). A visor or opaque sunglasses may also be used. We ask parents not to speak or point to the screen, but allow that if the child becomes restless, it is okay to say, between stimulus sentences, neutral reassurances like "I'm right here" or "Look up at the pictures." If children begin struggling or crying, we pause the procedure; sometimes a session can be rescued with a brief hiatus, or a short play period. The experimental session itself only takes about 5 minutes.

Stimulus Orders

The two main concerns in setting up trial orders are maximizing the amount of looking data each child is likely to provide, and preventing nuisance effects from interfering with interpretation of the results. Speaking very generally, most 14–20-month-olds can participate through 30 or so trials, and older children can stay on task for 40 or perhaps even more. Increasing variety in the sentences and the pictures increases the number of trials children make it through and reduces attrition. Many researchers include filler trials to provide this variety when the experimental questions require repetitive test trials; another option is to have occasional filler clips that are not trials *per se*, showing interesting pictures or animations.

Once the numbers of trials and stimulus items have been sorted out, the positioning of the pictures (left, right) and the sequential orders need to be determined. Rather than randomizing trial orders, most researchers carefully construct four or eight orders and assign children to them randomly. If pictures are repeated at all (as in most studies) they are usually yoked: for example, a dog and baby might be paired, and on two trials the dog is the named picture and on two trials the baby is. This way a simple preference, e.g., for the dog over the baby, cannot lead to above-chance performance on dog/baby trials taken together. Other properties that are usually maintained if possible include balancing target side (left, right); restricting sequences of target side to a maximum of two or three; placing each item equally often in the first and second half of the experiment; and avoiding adjacent-trial repetition of pictures or words, among others. Putting together the first order of a study is like solving a Sudoku puzzle. But other orders can be constructed from the first order, e.g., by inverting whichever factor is most theoretically important, and by rotating through the items (replacing dog/baby with duck/car, duck/car with shoe/ball, and so on).

Coding

Most of the time, it is easy to tell when a child is looking to the left or to the right. What makes coding difficult is the need to establish precisely when a left or right fixation begins and ends. Research assistants thrown into the coding task without adequate apprenticeship will produce results that correlate fairly well but that do not agree on the details. A lab using the procedure must develop consistent, verbalizable, and complete standards for what counts as fixating a picture and what does not in a given video frame. In general, these standards do not depend on perfecting the ability to determine the horizontal angle of a child's fixation; rather, they depend on learning the dynamics of eye movements over time. Children looking at an object picture typically keep their eyes in a single position for several video frames. A shift to the other picture usually begins as two to three frames in which the eyes move with increasing angular change (acceleration) away from this single position. On the first frame of a shift, the eyes are usually still oriented to the picture, in terms of what light is hitting the fovea, but the dynamics of the movement reveal that a shift is under way. Two well-trained coders can agree on the frame at which a look begins and ends to within zero or one video frame for most looks.

Data Analysis

As described above, the first study using looking while listening with toddlers reported results in terms of proportions of target fixation, response latencies (reaction time, RT), and timecourse plots. Since that time, refinements of the proportional and RT analyses have emerged, as well as other measures.

In most studies the real statistical workhorse is the proportion-to-target analysis. Timecourse is implicated in these analyses in the selection of the window of analysis over which the proportion is computed. In our initial studies a 2 s window, starting from the onset of the target word, was used. Most studies now exclude a few hundred milliseconds from the beginning of this window on the grounds that there are neurophysiological and cognitive limits on how quickly an eye movement could possibly be generated in response to the speech signal; even among children who perform very well, the first one-third of a second or so shows little contingency between stimulus and response. It is important to recognize, though, that the commonplace 367–2000 ms window is *not* an "optimal" window for revealing target recognition. It extends too early. Children initially fixating the distracter take, on average, several hundred milliseconds to decide to shift. For children between 14 and 24 months, an optimal window would extend from approximately 1200–2200 ms, depending on the materials. Why use the earlier window, then? Because it is in the early decision making that much of the *variability* in eye movement responses can be detected. Choosing an "optimal" window for the average 18-month-old, say, could obscure the difference between toddlers who respond quickly and accurately and those who are accurate in their asymptotic interpretation but need more time. Likewise, children tend to respond faster to correct pronunciations of words than mispronunciations, but performance later in the trial can be similar between conditions.

When responses to particular items are of interest, and not just overall performance on a yoked pair of items, counterbalancing alone is not sufficient protection against biases due to picture preference. For example, a child might be presented with a car and a ball and hear "car" and "ball" on separate trials. Now 75% car-looking upon hearing "car," and 50% ball-looking upon hearing "ball," might not mean that the child understands only the word "car." The child could simply prefer to look at cars. In principle, 50% ball-looking might reveal understanding of "ball," if hearing the word pulled the child away from his favorite picture.

This problem is usually managed by comparing looking after hearing the word against looking before hearing the word. If children enjoy looking at cars, this may be revealed to some degree by the initial portion of the trial. Subtracting target-looking proportions before the test window from proportions during the test window is a way to adjust for these picture preferences. This can be done either trial by trial, or pair by pair (i.e., by computing a "preference score" for each picture based on all of the trials in which that picture appears with its yoked partner). This procedure is not without hazard, however. Imagine an adult who likes looking at cars but otherwise fixates where he is instructed. Given 100% car fixation before word onset and 100% fixation afterward (and thus a difference score of zero), one might conclude that he shows no evidence of "car" recognition. The problem is that in good performers whose test-window looking is not affected by picture preferences, subtracting pre-test looking amounts to adding a random number. These considerations suggest that the value of doing this sort of correction depends upon the degree to which looking before and after the word are correlated.

Response latency is a standard measure of cognitive performance, as mentioned above. In the looking-while-listening task, reaction times (RTs) are typically computed only for trials on which children are fixating the distracter when the target word begins (e.g., Fernald, Swingley, and Pinto, 2001). And of course, a child only produces a reaction time when she reacts. A necessary consequence is that analyses of RT are based on fewer trials than analyses of fixation proportion. This problem can be mitigated to some degree by maximizing the number of trials in the session, but it is not unexpected when subtle effects are found in analyses of fixation proportion but not RT.

Other response measures have been developed, sometimes to evaluate specific details of performance. Swingley (2009) computed the likelihood of shifts in fixation from target to distracter and distracter to target, not only for first shifts, but for all refixations throughout the test window. This analysis is one way to distinguish cases in which children shift a great deal, but just as often to the distracter as to the target, from cases in which children shift very little – a distinction that cannot be made from the usual proportional analyses. Plunkett (e.g., Mani and Plunkett, 2007) has examined "longest look duration," which, given a relatively long window of analysis, abstracts away from the response latency component of the fixation task. A child's longest fixation might occur early or late in the analysis window, and will count the same either way. In principle, this might provide a way to equalize differences among younger and older children who tend to respond more quickly.

Future Directions

The literature on word recognition and sentence processing in adults is largely composed of chronometric studies evaluating listeners' interpretation of language over time (e.g., Dahan, 2010; Tanenhaus, 2007). Many of these studies in the past 15 years have been done using eyetracking techniques that are, in all important respects, the same as the looking-while-listening procedure. Although most studies of adults, and increasingly also studies of children, make use of automatic eyetracking systems, the logic of the experiments and the nature of the listener's response are the same whether a machine or a human is coding gaze patterns. The fact that the language-guided-looking task can be used effectively from the second year into adulthood reflects the naturalness and automaticity of the response, and points to the method's potential in measuring and explaining language comprehension performance over the full span of development.

Acknowledgments

Thanks are due to Anne Fernald, Gerry McRoberts, and John Pinto, the team I joined at Stanford in the early 1990s when looking methods were already in development. The present chapter was supported by NIH grant R01-HD049681.

Key Terms

Eyetracking, language guided looking, looking while listening   These terms all refer to procedures in which children are shown scenes or images, and hear language referring to one of the scenes or images. The details of children's fixations to the images, and in particular the timing of children's responses, are evaluated as measures of language understanding. "Eyetracking" is sometimes used to refer specifically to the use of such measures with an automated eyetracking computer.

Onset-contingent timecourse plot   A graph with time on the x-axis, usually starting from the onset of the linguistic stimulus of interest, and a summary measure of children's fixations on the y-axis. Test trials are divided into those on which children initially gazed at the target image or the distracter image. For distracter-initial trials the y-axis reflects moment-by-moment target fixation. For target-initial trials the y-axis reflects moment-by-moment distracter fixation. Thus the vertical separation of these lines, where the distracter-initial line rises above the target-initial line, shows the moment when children begin showing evidence of word recognition.

References

Dahan, D. (2010) The time course of interpretation in speech comprehension. *Current Directions in Psychological Science*, 19, 121–126.

Fernald, A., McRoberts, G.W., and Swingley, D. (2001) Infants' developing competence in recognizing and understanding words in fluent speech. In J. Weissenborn and B. Hoehle (eds), *Approaches to bootstrapping: phonological, lexical, syntactic, and neurophysiological aspects of early language acquisition* (vol. I, pp. 97–123). Amsterdam: Benjamins.

Fernald, A., Pinto, J.P., Swingley, D., *et al.* (1998) Rapid gains in speed of verbal processing by infants in the second year. *Psychological Science*, 9, 228–231.

Fernald, A., Swingley, D., and Pinto, J.P. (2001) When half a word is enough: infants can recognize spoken words using partial acoustic-phonetic information. *Child Development*, 72, 1003–1015.

Fernald, A., Thorpe, K., and Marchman, V.A. (2010) Blue car, red car: developing efficiency in online interpretation of adjective-noun phrases. *Cognitive Psychology*, 60, 190–217.

Golinkoff, R.M., Hirsh-Pasek, K., Cauley, K.M., and Gordon, L. (1987) The eyes have it: lexical and syntactic comprehension in a new paradigm. *Journal of Child Language*, 14, 23–45.

Hurtado, N., Marchman, V.A., and Fernald, A. (2008) Does input influence uptake? Links between maternal talk, processing speed and vocabulary size in Spanish-learning children. *Developmental Science*, 11, F31–F39.

Iverson, J.M., and Goldin-Meadow, S. (2005) Gesture paves the way for language development. *Psychological Science*, 16, 367–371.

Lew-Williams, C., and Fernald, A. (2007) Young children learning Spanish make rapid use of grammatical gender information in spoken word recognition. *Psychological Science*, 18, 193–198.

Mani, N., and Plunkett, K. (2007) Phonological specificity of consonants and vowels in early lexical representations. *Journal of Memory and Language*, 57, 252–272.

Marchman, V.A., and Fernald, A. (2008) Speed of word recognition and vocabulary knowledge in infancy predict cognitive and language outcomes in later childhood. *Developmental Science*, 11, F9–F16.

Quam, C., and Swingley, D. (2010) Phonological knowledge guides two-year-olds' and adults' interpretation of salient pitch contours in word learning. *Journal of Memory and Language*, 52, 135–150.

Reznick, J.S. (1990) Visual preference as a test of infant word comprehension. *Applied Psycholinguistics*, 11, 145–166.

Swingley, D. (2009) Onsets and codas in 1.5-year-olds' word recognition. *Journal of Memory and Language*, 60, 252–269.

Swingley, D., and Aslin, R.N. (2000) Spoken word recognition and lexical representation in very young children. *Cognition*, 76, 147–166.

Swingley, D., and Fernald, A. (2002) Recognition of words referring to present and absent objects by 24-month-olds. *Journal of Memory and Language*, 46, 39–56.

Swingley, D., Pinto, J.P., and Fernald, A. (1999) Continuous processing in word recognition at 24 months. *Cognition*, 71, 73–108.

Tanenhaus, M.K. (2007) Spoken language comprehension: insights from eye movements. In G. Gaskell (ed.), *Oxford handbook of psycholinguistics* (pp. 309–326). Oxford: Oxford University Press.

Thomas, D.G., Campos, J.J., Shucard, D.W., *et al.* (1981) Semantic comprehension in infancy: a signal detection analysis. *Child Development*, 52, 798–803.

Van Heugten, M., and Shi, R. (2009) French-learning toddlers use gender information on determiners during word recognition. *Developmental Science*, 12, 419–425.

Further Reading and Resources

The best detailed introduction to the "nuts and bolts" of the looking-while-listening procedure is Fernald *et al.* (2008). Discussion of the mental processes that are revealed in the task, and defense of the argument that listeners' interpretations are not artificially constrained by the response set, are provided in Dahan and Tanenhaus (2005) and Swingley and Fernald (2002). Overviews of research using the task include Swingley (2008) on infant development and phonology, and Trueswell (2008) on syntactic development.

Dahan, D., and Tanenhaus, M.K. (2005) Looking at the rope when looking for the snake: conceptually mediated eye movements during spoken-word recognition. *Psychonomic Bulletin & Review*, 12, 453–459.

Fernald, A., Zangl, R., Portillo, A., and Marchman, V. (2008) Looking while listening: using eye movements to monitor spoken language comprehension by infants and young children. In I.A. Sekerina, E.M. Fernández, and H. Clahsen (eds), *Developmental psycholinguistics: on-line methods in children's language processing* (pp. 97–135). Amsterdam: Benjamins.

Swingley, D. (2008) The roots of the early vocabulary in infants' learning from speech. *Current Directions in Psychological Science*, 17, 308–312.

Swingley, D., and Fernald, A. (2002) Recognition of words referring to present and absent objects by 24-month-olds. *Journal of Memory and Language*, 46, 39–56.

Trueswell, J.C. (2008) Using eye movements as a developmental measure within psycholinguistics. In I. Sekerina, E.M. Fernández, and H. Clahsen (eds), *Developmental psycholinguistics: on-line methods in children's language processing* (pp. 73–96). Amsterdam: Benjamins.

Information about software mentioned in the chapter can be found online:

Psyscope: http://psy.ck.sissa.it/psy_cmu_edu/index.html.

Adobe Director: http://www.adobe.com/products/director.

QuickTime: http://www.apple.com/quicktime.

4 Neuroimaging Methods

Ioulia Kovelman

Summary

One of the most pervasive questions in the field of language acquisition is, "How does the human brain acquire language?" Noninvasive neuroimaging technologies and the emerging field of developmental cognitive neuroscience now offer both the technology and the growing expertise to examine the neural correlates of language acquisition. In this chapter we review the basic principles of electric (ERP, MEG) and hemodynamic (fMRI, fNIRS) neuroimaging technologies and how they can be used to study children. We also discuss how these neuroimaging methods have now been successfully applied to the study of language acquisition in typically developing children as well as in children with language learning impairments and dyslexia.

Research Aim

Evolutionary processes have endowed humans with the neural tissue and the learning abilities to allow children to develop language. Children require only exposure to their parents' spoken or sign languages in order to acquire them. How does the brain of a child accomplish such a feat? Children can also learn to understand written language. Although reading acquisition frequently depends on explicit instruction, learning, and years of practice, it also depends on structures in the brain and the learning functions that those brain structures support. Modern noninvasive neuroimaging methods have allowed us to address the question of how the brain does what it does when children learn to talk (or sign) and when they learn to read.

Research Methods in Child Language: A Practical Guide, First Edition.
Edited by Erika Hoff.
© 2012 Blackwell Publishing Ltd. Published 2012 by Blackwell Publishing Ltd.

This exploration of the neurological bases of language and reading is part of a larger enterprise. The beginning of the twenty-first century has seen a dramatic shift in the way researchers attempt to unravel the mysteries of human development. Until only very recently, the study of the human brain was distinct from the study of child development; but merging aspects of behavioral child development with aspects of neuroscience has led to the science of the developing human mind, brain, and behavior, or developmental cognitive neuroscience (Johnson, 2005). This field is one of the newest and most rapidly growing fields of science. This new approach to human development creates an inclusive picture of how babies develop into mature adults. This revolutionary shift was facilitated by rapid improvements in noninvasive and child-friendly brain imaging technologies, which now allow systematic investigations of infants and children during the critical ages of early language and literacy acquisition.

The past decade in particular has witnessed a sharp rise in neuroimaging studies in language and reading acquisition and new insight into the relationship between the brain and behavior in those domains. For example, recent infant studies have shown that newborns already have a hemispheric preference for language and that some characteristics of brain activation in infants and preliterate children may indicate future risk of language and reading difficulties. In addition, early learning experiences (e.g., bilingualism) may have a profound effect on how language is organized in the brain (cf. Petitto, 2005). Thus, neuroimaging studies of language both advance the science of language acquisition and also inform clinical and educational practices.

Functional Noninvasive Brain Imaging: Methods, Technology and Application

Functional neuroimaging methods allow researchers to investigate changes in brain activity that occur as the child or adult engages in specific language tasks. There are two major functional neuroimaging methods: methods that measure changes in the brain's electrical activity, and methods that measure changes in the brain's blood flow or *hemodynamic* response. As neuronal electrical activity is rapid and transient, methods that measure the electrical activity of neurons, such as event-related potential (ERP) and magnetoencephalography (MEG), are fast responding, resulting in excellent temporal resolution (on the order of milliseconds); however, these methods provide relatively poor anatomical localization (Luck, 2005). Active neurons expressing electrical activity deplete their energy stores, thereby inducing local changes in blood flow (a hemodynamic change). The hemodynamic response is thus a derivative of neural activity and can be measured with functional magnetic resonance imaging (fMRI), positron emission tomography (PET), or functional near infrared spectroscopy (fNIRS) (Friston, 2009). Change in blood flow is slow and sustained, thus allowing for good spatial yet poor temporal resolution (2–5 seconds) with hemodynamic techniques (Friston, 2009).

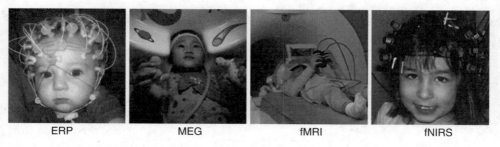

ERP   MEG   fMRI   fNIRS

Figure 4.1 Neuroimaging methods in child language acquisition.

Event-Related Potential (ERP)

Electroencephalogram (EEG) measures the electrical activity occurring in the brain using a set of electrodes positioned on a person's head, which record the brain's spontaneous electrical activity below the scalp. Electrical activity in response to a particular event (internal or external) is referred to as an event-related potential (Luck, 2005) (see also a web-based video publication by Slotnick, 2010). There are several critical advantages of using ERP to study language acquisition. Because ERP has excellent temporal resolution (milliseconds), it is well suited for the study of rapidly changing and temporally ordered verbal information. Another critical advantage of ERP is that it is quiet, is relatively motion tolerant, and can be used with awake infants and children.

New infant-friendly systems may take less than 5 minutes to set up and can yield meaningful data even if the participants are not actively attending to the stimuli and/or are too young to give a behavioral response (Figure 4.1; see Johnson *et al.*, 2001 for a detailed description of infant-friendly ERP setup and data analyses). ERP data yield *components*, or waveforms with a particular *polarity* (whether it is a positive- or a negative-going wave), *latency* (the time following the stimulus onset), and *scalp distribution* (the location of each of these peaks). For instance, Figure 4.2 shows an N400 ERP response to semantically anomalous sentences (e.g., "I like my coffee with cream and *sock*"): N400 is a negative-going wave, peaking at 400 ms after stimulus onset (Holcomb, Coffey, and Neville, 1992). These ERP components are thought to be associated with various aspects of mental processes (language, memory, attention), and they are thought to change over time as a result of cognitive as well as physiological brain maturation. Each event (e.g., seeing a printed word) may incur several components; early components (before 200 ms) are likely associated with sensory processes (e.g., visual detection), while later components are likely to reflect higher cognition (e.g., sentence comprehension). Many of these ERP components and the language processes associated with them have now been extensively explored in both child and adult populations (cf. Friederici, 2005; Kuhl and Rivera-Gaxiola, 2008).

Several ERP components appear associated with key aspects of language competence, as follows.

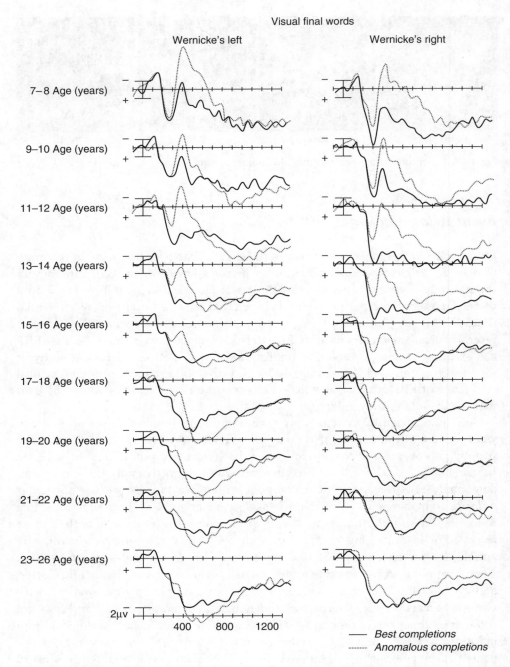

Figure 4.2 N400 ERP response to best (congruous) completion and anomalous (incongruous) final words of visual sentences (best completion, "I like my coffee with cream and *sugar*"; anomalous completion, "I like my coffee with cream and *sock*"), averaged across subjects in each age group (ages 7–26), from left and right parietal (Wernicke) sites. *Source*: Reprinted from Holcomb, Coffey, and Neville (1992).

Phonology

Studies of phonological processing discovered that a mismatch negativity response (MMN; negativity at approximately 200 ms) is typically detected when participants can identify a difference between categorically distinct phonological units (e.g., a difference between /ba/ and /da/ phonemes; see review in Kuhl and Rivera-Gaxiola, 2008). The MMN response appears to emerge and mature quite early in human development, as researchers have reported adult-like amplitude but delayed latency of the response in 3-month-old infants (Cheour *et al.*, 1998).

Semantics

Studies of semantic processing discovered that an N400 response (centro-parietal negativity at approximately 400 ms, Figure 4.2) is typically observed when participants hear a word that does not fit well semantically within the context of a phrase such as, "We bake cookies at the zoo" (Holcomb, Coffey, and Neville, 1992). Children as young as 7 years start showing an adult-like N400 response (Figure 4.2), with both latency and amplitude decreasing with age, which the authors believe reflects both cognitive and physiological changes in the brain (Holcomb, Coffey, and Neville, 1992). Researchers have now studied N400 in children as young as 1 year of age, and have shown that 1-year-olds show an N400 effect when they hear words that do not match the pictures they see (cf. Friederici, 2005).

Syntax

Studies of grammatical processing discovered that adults typically show E/LAN and P600 responses when presented with ungrammatical sentences (e.g., "My uncle watched *about* a movie my family"; Friederici, 2005). E/LAN (early/left anterior negativity at approximately 150–350 ms) response is typically associated with automatic and online grammar processing, whereas P600 (centro-parietal positivity at approximately 600 ms) response is typically associated with structure revision and reanalyses (Friederici, 2005). Researchers report that children as young as 2 years show a P600 response when presented with ungrammatical sentences (cf. Friederici, 2005; Kuhl and Rivera-Gaxiola, 2008). Similarly to N400, children's P600 frequently also has greater amplitude, delayed latency, and broader scalp distribution. Behavioral research suggests that infants and children show rapidly emerging competence in their ability to process language sounds, meaning, and structure. Neuroimaging ERP research suggests that some of the brain mechanisms for language processing, typically observed in adults, may emerge early in development, and that ERP can be useful in helping us understand early language acquisition (Kuhl and Rivera-Gaxiola, 2008; Friederici, 2005).

Magnetoencephalography (MEG)

Magnetoencephalography detects the magnetic field associated with the brain's electric neural activity. To detect and amplify the brain's magnetic signal, superconducting quantum interference devices (SQUIDs) are built into the MEG helmet that surrounds the participant's head. MEG shares many of the advantages of ERP for studying child language development – namely its excellent temporal resolution, safety, low noise level, and suitability for use with infants and children of all ages. The critical advantage of MEG over ERP is better spatial localization. Both ERP and MEG detect dipoles, or active neurons that have differences in polarity between the cell body and the dendrites (Luck, 2005). The neuron's polarity (dipole) generates an electric as well as a magnetic field. ERP detects the electric field, and MEG detects the magnetic field. The skull is an impediment to the dipole's electric signal, forcing it to disperse and shift locations before reaching the surface of the head where ERP sensors can detect the signal (Luck, 2005). The skull is a lesser impediment for the magnetic signal, thus allowing for better localization of the source of the signal with MEG. MEG's SQUID sensors detect the magnetic field as it enters and leaves the head, and therefore small child-sized MEGs with sensors close to the child's head are highly recommended for developmental research (see video publication by Tesan *et al.*, 2010 for details on child-sized MEG technology and its use in language experiments with children). Greater spatial localization for the individual participants can be achieved with magnetic source imaging (MSI), in which a person's functional MEG data are overlaid onto their MRI anatomical image (otherwise, the MEG data can be overlaid onto a generic anatomical template). However, there are drawbacks to MEG. MEG requires a rather large device, and since the magnetic field generated by the brain is relatively small (approximately 10 million times smaller than the Earth's magnetic field) the brain's signals cannot be detected against the background magnetic field unless the equipment is used in a magnetically shielded room. This makes MEG not portable, and it is also more expensive to purchase and use than ERP.

Similar to ERP, MEG data allow measures of response amplitude and latency. However, unlike both ERP and fMRI, MEG data analyses rely on complex source modeling methods which allow for a dynamic localization of brain activity as it transitions from earliest sensory responses (approximately first 200 ms) to later, higher-order cognitive responses (e.g., Halgren *et al.*, 2002). In language, MEG has now been used to investigate various aspects of language processes, including those that have been extensively studied in ERP. Similarly to ERP, MEG systems detect an N400m effect that occurs approximately 400 ms past stimulus onset and is greater in amplitude with incongruous relative to congruous sentence completion (Plate 3; Halgren *et al.*, 2002). Different source modeling methods in MEG may yield different localization results: the use of the equivalent current dipole (ECD) model localizes N400m to the left superior temporal sulcus (Plate 3A; Halgren *et al.*, 2002), while the use of the distributed source model technique suggests that differential activation to incongruous words begins in the left temporal lobe (including Wernicke's area) at 250 ms after word onset and that by 370 ms this activation spreads to other areas, including the frontal lobe (including Broca's area, Plate 3B; see Halgren *et al.*, 2002 for greater detail on MEG computational models). Thus, the critical advantage of MEG is the ability to make full use of both temporal and spatial information. Technological and analytical complexities notwithstanding, the use of MEG systems is rapidly growing in studies of early language and literacy development, in typically developing children as well as in children with language impairments, dyslexia, and autism (Salmelin, 2007).

Functional Magnetic Resonance Imaging (fMRI)

Functional magnetic resonance systems detect changes in blood oxygenation (Friston, 2009). During the measurement the child is placed into the narrow tube of the MRI machine with the child's head confined within a head-coil (Figure 4.1). The system is loud, so well-fitting headphones are necessary for auditory experiments. As a brain region becomes more active during a particular task, neurons in this region expend energy, requiring an increase in the supply of nutrients. As a result, slight increases in blood flow occur, bringing vital glucose and oxygen to the activated region. This change in blood flow, directly correlated with neuronal activity, is known as the *hemodynamic response*. The bloodstream delivers oxygen to neurons via hemoglobin molecules: oxy-hemoglobin carries oxygen whereas deoxy-hemoglobin does not. As brain regions become active, the ratio of oxy- to deoxy-hemoglobin concentration changes. By combining two magnetic fields, one static and one transient, fMRI detects changes in the oxy- to deoxy-hemoglobin concentration ratio by relying predominantly on the magnetic properties of deoxy-hemoglobin, as measured in blood-oxygen-level dependence (BOLD) units (cf. Huettel, Song, and McCarthy, 2008). For instance, when children and adults engage in a rhyming task (i.e., decide if a pair of words, "cat–hat," rhymes), they typically show activation in left inferior frontal, superior temporal, and parietal regions. fMRI measures this hemodynamic change as a BOLD response (Plate 4A), and fNIRS measures this hemodynamic change as an increase in oxy- and a decrease in deoxy-hemoglobin (Plate 4D, E).

The hemodynamic response lags behind the onset of the neural events by about 5 seconds; yet it offers excellent spatial resolution (in millimeters). This great spatial resolution is the critical advantage of fMRI, which allows researchers to test hypotheses about the development and function of specific brain regions. The drawbacks of fMRI are that it requires confinement to a narrow tube within a large machine, it is rather noisy (problem for auditory language experiments), and it requires soundproof facilities and costly maintenance. Nevertheless, significant advances in fMRI application and technology are being made, which are rapidly advancing its use in the study of language acquisition (cf. Freund, 2008; Kuhl and Rivera-Gaxiola, 2008).

In order to take full advantage of the excellent spatial resolution afforded by the fMRI, researchers must take into account that children's brain sizes and structures may change throughout development, which complicates data analyses and interpretation. To compensate for this, technical and analytical methods have been put forth to improve anatomical localization of pediatric data. Child-appropriate data acquisition methods now include the use of child-sized head-coils that improve spatial resolution and minimize head movement. Superior data analysis methods include the use of child-specific and age-appropriate anatomical templates (for details see Freund, 2008) as well as advanced anatomical coregistration methods (for details see Ghosh *et al.*, 2010).

As with any other imaging system, ensuring the cooperation of young participants in fMRI experiments is an art. fMRI studies of children younger than 3 years of age typically include sedated or naturally sleeping participants (for methodological details see Freund, 2008). Fun and engaging experimental paradigms as well as practice with mock scanners are frequently used with older children (for details see video publication by Raschle *et al.*, 2009). Mock scanners are typically made to look and sound like real scanners, allowing children to become comfortable with the fMRI environment and to practice staying still (see video demo in Raschle *et al.*, 2009). Motion artifacts are frequent and can be somewhat corrected during acquisition as well as during analyses (we recommend using Artifact Detection Toolbox developed by Susan Witfield-Gabrieli). Finally, auditory language experiments can take advantage of "silent" fMRI designs, during which the scanner noise is either suspended during the presentation of auditory stimuli, or is reduced overall with the use of "quieter" fMRI sequences (cf. Freund, 2008). Thus, even though at first glance fMRI technology may appear daunting for child research, and its noise level may appear prohibitive for language studies, there are rapidly growing advances in fMRI technology and analyses that allow successful application of the method for the study of language acquisition.

Functional Near Infrared Spectroscopy (fNIRS)

Similar to fMRI, functional near infrared spectroscopy noninvasively measures changes in blood oxygenation, a correlate of brain activity. And similar to ERP, fNIRS systems are small and portable, with a simple headset that is placed on the participant to stabilize the location of optodes (Plate 4B). fNIRS optodes are small emitters and detectors that emit and detect near infrared light at the scalp, and the signal is detected within the region between the emitter and the detector ("banana"; Plate 4C). This "banana" shaped region between the emitter and the detector is created by the intersection of light emitted by the emitter and light detected by the detector; the depth of this "banana" penetration is typically up to 3 cm (Plate 4C). Proper positioning of the optodes on participants' heads is crucial, and there are a variety of methods that have been employed to achieve that positioning (see video publication by Shalinsky *et al.*, 2009 for details on the use of fNIRS technology). During fNIRS imaging, infants can be comfortably seated on their mother's lap, while younger children and adults can be seated separately. In order to minimize physiological noise (e.g., Mayer waves), a footrest and a reclining position are highly recommended (Shalinsky *et al.*, 2009).

The optodes emit two different wavelengths, which allow the system to yield separate measurements of oxy- and deoxy-hemoglobin (e.g., the Hitachi ETG-4000 fNIRS system uses 690 nm and 830 nm wavelengths). Near infrared light noninvasively penetrates the surface of the skull and in most commonly used systems can penetrate up to 2–3 cm into the cortex (Plate 4C). fNIRS is therefore perfectly suited for the study of perception and higher cognition in the human cortex, with temporal resolution of 10 samples per second or higher (compared to fMRI of approximately 1 sample per 2 s) and spatial resolution of 2–3 cm (not as high as fMRI but with greater precision than ERP). See Plate 4D, E for sample fNIRS data, collected as children were deciding if two words rhyme or not. During the task there is an increase in oxy-hemoglobin concentration and a decrease in deoxy-hemoglogin concentration in comparison with resting baseline (looking at a fixation cross). The use of light as opposed to magnetism makes fNIRS completely silent, as well as much smaller than fMRI. Small size and portability mean that fNIRS systems can be taken out of the lab into participants' homes, hospitals' neonatal units, and school systems. Due to the combination of these factors, the system has a critical advantage for the study of early language acquisition as it allows for the use of naturalistic auditory language paradigms with awake infants, children, and adults (Huppert *et al.*, 2009; Petitto *et al.*, in press; Shalinsky *et al.*, 2009). For example, in our own language acquisition research we comfortably use an fNIRS system with awake infants listening to phonemes (Petitto, 2005; Petitto *et al.*, in press; Shalinsky *et al.*, 2009), children reading aloud at school, talking adults, and adult signers who are freely using both hands within the natural signing space (Kovelman *et al.*, 2009).

Akin to fMRI, and when used properly, fNIRS can provide accurate information about the anatomical locus of brain activation. We recommend the use of 10–20 ERP sensor-placement conventions and the use of 3D tracking devices, as well as fMRI coregistration with vitamin E capsules to ensure proper probe placement (for more detail see Kovelman *et al.*, 2009; and Shalinsky *et al.*, 2009). Prior to data acquisition, participants should be trained to keep their head as still as possible during the tasks, and data imaging should be screened for motion artifacts (Huppert *et al.*, 2009; Kovelman *et al.*, 2009). Simultaneous acquisition of imaging data and video data can help better identify body motion artifacts, as well as participants' behavioral performances during imaging tasks (see Shalinsky *et al.*, 2009).

Multimodal and Anatomical Imaging

This chapter has focused on individual methods of functional brain imaging, but nevertheless readers should be made aware of multimodal imaging or "fusion" techniques. Multimodal imaging refers to the concept of acquiring complementary brain data that can answer both "where" and "when" (cf. Friston, 2009). These methods, although more technically difficult to set up than unimodal methods, are becoming increasingly attractive in cognitive neuroscience. One example is the simultaneous use of fMRI and EEG recordings (Friston, 2009). There is also anatomical brain imaging: MRI systems can be used to provide information about the volume and thickness of brain structures, as well as information about the organization of white matter, as afforded by diffusion tensor imaging (DTI). Each of these methods and technologies is being actively used to address the field's questions about the complex nature of language and reading acquisition (cf. Kovelman, Christodoulou, and Gabrieli, in press; Kuhl and Rivera-Gaxiola, 2008).

The two arguably most child-friendly and language-friendly technologies (fNIRS and ERP) can be effectively combined within a single imaging session. This allows researchers to investigate the full range of language acquisition phenomena by examining both timing and location of the underlying brain activity (Friston, 2009). One of the challenges in using combined fNIRS and ERP systems is being able to analyze the data such that they are meaningful with respect to both types of imaging systems. This task is complicated by the fact that while the field has many options for standardized and validated methods of ERP and fMRI data analyses, the best analytical options for fNIRS remain under active investigation (cf. Huppert *et al.*, 2009). The good news is that there have been rapid advancements in fNIRS imaging method and analyses, and publicly available fNIRS analyses software now include HomER (Huppert *et al.*, 2009) and Statistical Parametric Mapping (SPM: Ye *et al.*, 2009). We hope that the near future will bring further improvements in both technology and analytical approaches, allowing us to take full advantage of the simultaneous use of multiple brain imaging methods and modalities.

Neuroimaging Studies of Early Language Acquisition

Words are made up of individual sounds, or phonetic units, which represent the building blocks of language competence (e.g., knowing sounds /b/ and /d/ in English). Among the most fascinating and hotly debated questions in the field is how infants discover this finite set of phonetic units of their native language. It is widely accepted that both environmental and biological factors play a role in children's ability to discover the sounds of their language. Systematic in-person language experience is essential: children exposed to spoken languages discover the phonetic units of their native spoken language (e.g., Werker and Tees, 1992), sign-exposed infants discover phonetic units in their native sign languages (e.g., Petitto, 2005), and children who hear a particular language only from TV may never learn the sounds of this language (cf. Kuhl and Rivera-Gaxiola, 2008). It is also assumed that the ability to discover the sounds of language is closely tied to infant brain development, as there is a maturational change in a child's ability to perceive these phonetic units from different languages. Children before the age of 8 months appear to be "universal" learners, able to perceive phonetic boundaries across all word languages (sign and spoken; Petitto, 2005), and this "universal" categorical perception ability diminishes after the age of 8 months (Werker and Tees, 1992). What are these neural mechanisms that allow a child to discover language, and how do they interact with variation in the language-learning environment?

In our quest to understand the brain mechanisms that drive infants' discovery of language, fNIRS technology has been used to investigate phoneme perception in monolingual and bilingual infants (Petitto *et al.*, in press). Using an oddball paradigm that can be effectively employed with any of the aforementioned imaging methods, a "standard" stimulus appears approximately 80% of the time, and a deviant or "oddball" stimulus appears approximately 20% of time (e.g., /ba/ is heard 80% of the time and /da/ is heard 20% of the time). The difference in the electric or hemodynamic brain response to "oddball" versus standard stimulus is then analyzed. Both "young" (3–4-month-old) and "old" (10–12-month-old) infants, bilingual and monolingual, showed equally robust bilateral activation in the superior temporal region in response to native and nonnative phonetic contrasts. The only region to show a change in activation in response to the sounds of native language as a function of maturation was the posterior aspect of the left inferior frontal region. Both "young" and "old" infants showed greater left IFG activation when hearing a sound that crossed the phonetic boundary (the "oddball"); however the strength of this activation increased in older monolingual infants and decreased in older bilingual infants.

Equally robust was the left STG activation, across ages (3–4 and 10–12 months) and language learning environments (bilingual and monolingual). These findings suggest this brain tissue, known to be important for processing phonological information in adults (Blumstein, 2009), supports early sensitivity to the relevant linguistic information in infants. It has been further hypothesized that the STG is the biologically endowed brain tissue, which is preferentially sensitive to rhythmic modulations of about 1.5 Hz (Petitto, 2005). Research leading to this hypothesis has been extensively exploring the first milestone in infant language production, babbling, which is when babies start producing meaningless, rhythmically alternating syllabi units (e.g., "ba-ba-ba"). Researchers have discovered that hearing babies exposed to speech babble vocally, while hearing and deaf babies exposed to sign language babble with their hands – producing meaningless alternating phonetic units with their hands at a frequency of about 1.5 Hz – leading to the hypothesis that the infant brain is endowed with brain tissue, likely the left STG, which is preferentially sensitive to the slow-rhythmic linguistic stream, be it visual or auditory (cf. Petitto, 2005).

At the age of about 12 months infants transition from "universal" to "native" learners, and begin to lose their ability to discriminate nonnative categories (Werker and Tees, 1992). All infants showed a maturational change in posterior left IFG activation, brain tissue known to be critical for phonologically driven semantic analyses in adults (e.g., in adults, hearing the word "fruit" facilitates hearing ambiguous "bear/pear" as "pear": cf. Blumstein, 2009). This change in left IFG activation at the age of 12 months is thus critical, as at this age first words emerge and stable sound-to-meaning associations become critical. As a monolingual infant's brain becomes dedicated to one language, it shows an increase in activation to changes in native phonological contrasts, while bilingual infants show an opposite pattern and a decrease in left IFG activation (Petitto *et al.*, in press). Researchers have suggested that bilingual children build at least some of their phonetic boundaries differently and on a different timetable compared to their monolingual peers (Ramon-Casas *et al.*, 2009). The decrease in left IFG activation in response to native contrasts may reflect the brain's attempt to "suppress" the closure of the heightened sensitivity period. How long does the bilingual phonological perceptual system remain open, and is this extended phonological sensitivity a "disadvantage"? Bilinguals are frequently observed to have lifelong advantages in language-related learning abilities (e.g., during reading acquisition: Kovelman, Baker, and Petitto, 2008). It is thought this advantage may be afforded by an extended period of heightened sensitivity to language patterns.

Neuroimaging methods thus allow us to investigate the neural tissue that underlies early language acquisition. Behavioral research has shown that children's ability to discriminate nonnative sounds declines and their ability to perceive native sounds improves at around 12 months of age, about the same time as a child starts producing his or her first words. Neuroimaging research now shows that infants' developmental change in the sensitivity to phonetic categories can be linked to maturation changes in the left inferior frontal gyrus (Broca's area), a brain region critical for adjudicating the associations between word sound and word meaning.

Neuroimaging Studies of Reading Acquisition

Just as a critical step towards successful language acquisition is being able to discern the sounds of language, so the ability to manipulate these language sounds, or phonological awareness, is a crucial step toward successful reading acquisition (Wolf, 2007). An example of phonological awareness is knowing that the words "cat" and "hat" rhyme, or that the word "ti-cket" can be broken into syllables "ti" and "cket." Children's phonological awareness precedes and predicts successful transition from language to literacy and is one of the strongest predictors of reading acquisition in early grades and across languages (Wolf, 2007). It is typically thought that children's sensitivity to the sounds of their language ultimately helps them to learn the associations between words sounds and individual letters. A deficit in phonological awareness is thought to be the most common etiology of dyslexia, a lifelong difficulty in learning to read (cf. Kovelman, Christodoulou, and Gabrieli, in press; Wolf, 2007). What might be the mechanism that supports the brain's transition from spoken to printed language, the brain bases of phonological awareness and the ultimate attainment of literacy skills?

It has been hypothesized that children's phonological awareness competence relies on their sensitivity to the slow rhythmic modulations in the speech stream which allow us to perceive syllabic and rime boundaries ("ti-cket," "c-at": Thomson and Goswami, 2008). Researchers have now shown that children with dyslexia are impaired in their ability to discern low-frequency amplitude modulations as well as rhythmic beats of about 1.5–2 Hz (Thomson and Goswami, 2008). This reading acquisition hypothesis and the findings are consistent with language acquisition literature and the babbling milestone, suggesting that infants start language acquisition with a peaked sensitivity to rhythmically alternating language units of about 1.5 Hz (Petitto, 2005). The language acquisition hypothesis is supported by the findings from the very first universal language production milestone: babbling. At approximately 5 months of age all infants start producing rhythmically alternating syllabic units. Hearing infants exposed to speech babble vocally, and sign-exposed infants babble with their hands at a slow rhythmic pace of about 1.5 Hz (cf. Petitto, 2005). Pilot results (Kovelman *et al.*, 2010) now show that typically developing children show greater activation in the left STG region when listening to the "language" frequency of 1.5 Hz, as opposed to slower (0.5 Hz) or faster (3 Hz) "nonlanguage" frequencies, converging on the idea that left STG tissue supports early language acquisition (Kuhl and Rivera-Gaxiola, 2008; Petitto *et al.*, in press) as well as typical reading development (children with dyslexia frequently show under-recruitment of left STG region; cf. Kovelman, Christodoulou, and Gabrieli, in press). Thus, both behavioral and neuroimaging approaches to language and literacy acquisition provide converging evidence that infants are born with neural tissue, the left STG, which is sensitive to slow rhythmic modulations and is present across sign and spoken languages (Kovelman *et al.*, 2010; Petitto, 2005). This sensitivity likely allows the child to identify the language stream itself (sign and spoken), parse it into smaller units, and extract the necessary syllabic, phonetic, and other types of critical linguistic information (Petitto, 2005). In typical development, left STG functioning and slow rhythmic sensitivity can facilitate language acquisition as well as the transition from intuitive to active awareness of the language units. In dyslexia, atypical STG functioning and impaired slow rhythmic sensitivity may impair the child's phonological learning and reading acquisition.

Conclusion

Until almost the beginning of the 1990s, research on the neural bases of language was heavily dominated by clinical and aphasiology research, in which theories of how language is represented in the brain were formed and tested against populations with neurological disorders. The emergence of safe, noninvasive and child-friendly hemodynamic brain imaging methods that do not involve brain surgery or radiation has opened the doors to the anatomical and the functional study of the brain in neurologically intact infants, children, and adults. These neuroimaging methods, including ERP, MEG, fMRI, and fNIRS, are now being actively used to investigate brain regions that support various aspects of early language acquisition across typically developing populations and children with language learning difficulties (cf. Friederici, 2005; Kovelman, Christodoulou, and Gabrieli, in press; Kuhl and Rivera-Gaxiola, 2008).

Neuroimaging tools and the emerging field of developmental cognitive neuroscience can contribute new information, allowing for testing of different hypotheses about the nature of human language acquisition. Neuroimaging tools are rapidly improving with respect to their "child friendliness" and "interpretability" of data – allowing us to test ever younger populations across a wide variety of language paradigms. The field is becoming increasingly "multimethod" and "multimodal," combining behavioral data, functional hemodynamic and electric brain data, and genetic information. This rich study approach allows us to explore the interaction between our biological endowment for language ability (and disability), maturing brain tissue, and maturing learning skills, as well as the learning environments (e.g., bilingualism). In addition to advancing the science of language acquisition, such a systematic and multimethod research approach may also offer new insights into the methods of early identification and targeted treatment for children with language and reading impairments.

Acknowledgments

We thank Dr Mark Shalinsky for technical editorial help and Alyssa Mastic and Kira Mascho for their help with manuscript preparation. A special thank you goes to Patricia O'Loughlin, Dr Stephen Crain, Dr Phillip Holcomb, Dr Eric Halgren, and Melanie Reid for contributing images and figures. We sincerely thank the editor, Dr Erika Hoff, for all her amazing editorial contribution. Finally, we thank the University of Michigan for support.

Key Terms

Blood-oxygen-level dependence (BOLD)   Signal that is dependent on the oxygen concentration in the blood. Changes in BOLD are well correlated with changes in blood flow; however, the relationship with neuronal signals is still being investigated.

Deoxyhemoglobin   When no oxygen is bound to hemoglobin.

Diffusion tensor imaging (DTI)   A related use of MRI to measure anatomical connectivity between areas.

Electroencephalogram (EEG)   Noninvasive brain imaging technology that measures the brain's electrical activity.

Event-related potential (ERP)   Electrical brain events as measured by EEG.

Functional magnetic resonance imaging (fMRI)   An MRI contrast of the BOLD signal.

Functional near infrared spectroscopy (fNIRS)   Measure of oxy- and deoxy-hemoglobin changes through absorption of near infrared light.

Hemodynamic response   Blood flow or circulation.

Hemoglobin   The iron-containing oxygen-transport metalloprotein in the red blood cells.

Magnetic resonance imaging (MRI)   A noninvasive imaging technology that uses a powerful magnetic field to align the nuclear magnetization of (usually) hydrogen atoms in water in the body.

Magnetoencephalography (MEG)   Noninvasive brain imaging technology that measures the brain's magnetic field.

Motion artifacts   Noise in recording due to voluntary or involuntary physical movement.

Multimodal imaging   Simultaneous use of two or more noninvasive imaging modalities in neurovascular coupling.

Oxy-hemoglobin   Oxygen bound to hemoglobin.

Superconducting quantum interference device (SQUID)   Used in MEG brain imaging to enhance the brain's magnetic field.

References

Blumstein, S.E. (2009) Auditory word recognition: evidence from aphasia and functional neuroimaging. *Language and Linguistic Compass*, 3 (4), 824–838.

Cheour, M., Ceponiene, R., Lehtokoski, A., *et al.* (1998) Development of language-specific phoneme representations in the infant brain. *Nature Neuroscience*, 1 (5), 351–353.

Freund, L. (2008) Neuroimaging tools for language study. In M. Rice (ed.), *Infant pathways to language: methods, models, and research directions* (pp. 287–297). New York: Psychology Press.

Friederici, A.D. (2005) Neurophysiological markers of early language acquisition: from syllables to sentences. *Trends in Cognitive Sciences*, 9 (10), 481–488.

Friston, K.J. (2009) Modalities, modes, and models in functional neuroimaging. *Science*, 326 (5951), 399–403.

Ghosh, S.S., Kakunoori, S., Augustinack, J., *et al.* (2010) Evaluating the validity of volume-based and surface-based brain image registration for developmental cognitive neuroscience studies in children 4 to 11 years of age. *NeuroImage*, 53 (1), 85–93.

Halgren, E., Dhond, R.P., Christensen, N., *et al.* (2002) N400-like magnetoencephalography responses modulated by semantic context, word frequency, and lexical class in sentences. *NeuroImage*, 17 (3), 1101–1116.

Holcomb, P., Coffey, S., and Neville, H. (1992) Visual and auditory sentence processing: a developmental analysis using event-related potentials. *Developmental Neuropsychology*, 8 (2–3), 203–241.

Huettel, S.A., Song, A.W., and McCarthy, G. (2008) *Functional magnetic resonance imaging* (2nd edn). Sunderland, MA: Sinauer.

Huppert, T.J., Diamond, S.G., Franceschini, M.A., and Boas, D.A. (2009) HomER: a review of time-series analysis methods for near-infrared spectroscopy of the brain. *Applied Optics*, 48 (10), D280–298.

Johnson, M.H. (2005) *Developmental cognitive neuroscience*. Malden, MA: Blackwell.

Johnson, M.H., de Haan, M., Oliver, A., *et al.* (2001) Recording and analyzing high-density event-related potentials with infants: using the Geodesic sensor net. *Developmental Neuropsychology*, 19 (3), 295–323.

Kovelman, I., Baker, S.A., and Petitto, L.A. (2008) Age of first bilingual language exposure as a new window into bilingual reading development. *Bilingualism (Cambridge, UK)*, 11 (2), 203–223.

Kovelman, I., Christodoulou, C.A., and Gabrieli, J.D.E. (in press) Dyslexia: the brain bases of reading impairments. In M. Faust (ed.), *Handbook of the neurophysiology of language*. Wiley-Blackwell.

Kovelman, I., Mascho, K., Mastic, A., *et al.* (2010) Neural bases of language frequency perception in children and adults. Accepted peer-reviewed conference presentation, 41st Annual Meeting of the Society for Neuroscience, San Diego, CA.

Kovelman, I., Shalinsky, M.H., White, K.S., *et al.* (2009) Dual language use in sign–speech bimodal bilinguals: fNIRS brain-imaging evidence. *Brain and Language*, 109 (2–3), 112–123.

Kuhl, P., and Rivera-Gaxiola, M. (2008) Neural substrates of language acquisition. *Annual Review of Neuroscience*, 31, 511–534.

Luck, S.J. (2005) An introduction to event-related potentials and their neural origins. In *An introduction to the event-related potential technique*. Cambridge, MA: MIT Press.

Pettito, L.A. (2005) How the brain begets language: on the neural tissue underlying human language acquisition. In J. McGilvray (ed.), *The Cambridge companion to Chomsky* (pp. 84–101). Cambridge: Cambridge University Press.

Petitto, L.A., Berens, M.S., Kovelman, I., *et al.* (in press) The "perceptual wedge" hypothesis as the basis for bilingual babies' phonetic processing advantage: new insights from fNIRS brain imaging. *Brain and Language*.

Ramon-Casas, M., Swingley, D., Sebastian-Galles, N., and Bosch, L. (2009) Vowel categorization during word recognition in bilingual toddlers. *Cognitive Psychology*, 59 (1), 96–121.

Raschle, N.M., Lee, M., Buechler, R., *et al.* (2009) Making MR imaging child's play: pediatric neuroimaging protocol, guidelines and procedure. *Journal of Visualized Experiments* 29.

Salmelin, R. (2007) Clinical neurophysiology of language: the MEG approach. *Clinical Neurophysiology*, 118 (2), 237–254.

Shalinsky, M.H., Kovelman, I., Berens, M.S., and Petitto, L.A. (2009) Exploring cognitive functions in babies, children and adults with near infrared spectroscopy. *Journal of Visualized Experiments* 29.

Slotnick, S.D. (2010) High density event-related potential data acquisition in cognitive neuroscience. *Journal of Visualized Experiments* 38.

Tesan, G., Johnson, B.W., Reid, M., *et al.* (2010) Measurement of neuromagnetic brain function in pre-school children with custom sized MEG. *Journal of Visualized Experiments* 36.

Thomson, J.M., and Goswami, U. (2008) Rhythmic processing in children with developmental dyslexia: auditory and motor rhythms link to reading and spelling. *Journal of Physiology, Paris*, 102 (1–3), 120–129.

Werker, J.F., and Tees, R.C. (1992) The organization and reorganization of human speech perception. *Annual Review of Neuroscience*, 15, 377–402.

Wolf, M. (2007) *Proust and the squid: the story and science of the reading brain*. New York: Harper Collins.

Ye, J.C., Tak, S., Jang, K.E., *et al.* (2009) NIRS-SPM: statistical parametric mapping for near-infrared spectroscopy. *NeuroImage*, 44 (2), 428–447.

Recommended Technical Reading

ERP

Print: Luck, S.J. (2005) An introduction to event-related potentials and their neural origins. In *An introduction to the event-related potential technique*. Cambridge, MA: MIT Press.

Video: Slotnick, S.D. (2010) High density event-related potential data acquisition in cognitive neuroscience. *Journal of Visualized Experiments* 38.

MEG

Print: Salmelin, R. (2007) Clinical neurophysiology of language: the MEG approach. *Clinical Neurophysiology*, 118 (2), 237–254.

Video: Tesan, G., Johnson, B.W., Reid, M., *et al.* (2010) Measurement of neuromagnetic brain function in pre-school children with custom sized MEG. *Journal of Visualized Experiments* 36.

fMRI

Print: Huettel, S.A., Song, A.W., and McCarthy, G. (2008) *Functional magnetic resonance imaging* (2nd edn). Sunderland, MA: Sinauer.

Video: Raschle, N.M., Lee, M., Buechler, R., *et al.* (2009) Making MR imaging child's play: pediatric neuroimaging protocol, guidelines and procedure. *Journal of Visualized Experiments* 29.

fNIRS

Print: Gervain, J., Mehler, J., Werker, J.F., *et al.* (2010) Near-infrared spectroscopy: a report from the McDonnell infant methodology consortium. *Developmental Cognitive Neuroscience*, 1 (1), 22–46.

Video: Shalinsky, M.H., Kovelman, I., Berens, M.S., and Petitto, L.A. (2009) Exploring cognitive functions in babies, children and adults with near infrared spectroscopy. *Journal of Visualized Experiments* 29.

5 Methods for Studying Language in Infants: Back to the Future

*Roberta Michnick Golinkoff
and Kathryn Hirsh-Pasek*

Summary

Here we discuss the origins and history of methods of infant research which have allowed researchers to begin to probe questions in language acquisition even before babies can say a single word. Methods involving the use of visual fixation, sucking, auditory preference, and heart rate are treated from a historical standpoint, calling attention to how they have expanded our knowledge base. These methods can be used with a wide range of ages – some starting with neonates – and extending across the first two years of life, in the domains of phonology, semantics, and syntax. Issues arising in data interpretation using these traditional methods are emerging with the use of newer neurophysiological measures as well. Longitudinal assessments of language acquisition are now beginning to inform the field about the meaning and significance of infants' earlier responses in laboratory tasks tapping language origins.

These one-word speakers appear to be five- or six- word listeners ... by 17 months of age ... infants in the beginning stages of language learning can attend to syntactic cues [word order] and use these cues to distinguish between two relatively similar scenes in their environment.

(Hirsh-Pasek and Golinkoff, 1996, p. 122)

[T]his study indicates that long before infants are producing wh-questions, they understand them in ways that few would have suspected ... Infants responded appropriately to subject questions by 15 months of age and to both subject- and object-questions by 20 months.

(Seidl, Hollich, and Jusczyk, 2003, pp. 423, 434)

Research Methods in Child Language: A Practical Guide, First Edition.
Edited by Erika Hoff.
© 2012 Blackwell Publishing Ltd. Published 2012 by Blackwell Publishing Ltd.

This prospective longitudinal study … shows that individual differences in the efficiency of spoken language comprehension at the age of two years predict children's success in cognitive and language tasks in later childhood.

(Fernald *et al.*, 2008, p. 131)

Researchers who study language acquisition wish to understand the very origins of the process, beginning from the earliest stages. To achieve this goal, organisms that cannot speak or even follow commands must be "tricked" into revealing what they know. This is the challenge our field has faced and, to some extent, conquered. Before the advent of methodologies to probe young children's linguistic capabilities, the aforementioned findings would have been inconceivable.

In this chapter, we reflect on the recent history of methodological innovation and ponder how these methods and newer ones might shape the future of our field. The last 40 years took us well beyond counting and cataloguing children's language productions as researchers began to probe children's knowledge of the elements and structures of language, and how this knowledge is used to bootstrap language competence – even before a single word is produced. We can only be selective in our brief review of the field's methodological innovations, highlighting some of the key paradigms and their significance.

In the Beginning

An intervention conducted in ancient Egypt may be the first study of language acquisition. Two infants were reared in silence to see which language would emerge first. While this methodology would now fail to pass human subjects scrutiny, reports of children raised without language input have contributed to our understanding of language development (e.g., Curtiss, 1977; Goldin-Meadow and Mylander, 1984). Baby biographies (e.g., Stern and Stern, 1907) gave way to more sophisticated diary studies (e.g., Naigles, Hoff, and Vear, 2009) enabling us to paint a rich portrait of the growing language system. Studies by Bloom (1973) and Nelson (1973) among others on children's first words and word combinations were landmarks for the field and the CHILDES data exchange system (MacWhinney, 1991), available on the web, continues to illustrate the value of detailed production data.

Methods Moving beyond Production

Two developments enabled researchers to move beyond observations of what children could produce. One was work by Fantz on infants' visual acuity; the other was work on the "orienting response" by Russian psychologists (Sokolov, 1963) which led to the creation of the habituation method.

Fantz's Work

At a time when pediatricians believed that infants were incapable of much vision, Fantz (1961) proved them wrong. Fantz showed that when presented with two cards, one containing broad and one narrow stripes, infants preferred to look at the cards with more narrow stripes. As Fantz and Nevis wrote, "it is now proven that even in the early weeks the young infant can resolve and discriminate patterns" (1967, p. 78). These data suggested that infants' acuity exceeded what was commonly believed and that infants were *selective*. Indeed, Fantz and Nevis argued that this selectivity "is particularly revealing of early perceptual-cognitive development" (p. 78). Fantz and Nevis saw the potential of the *paired comparisons method* for predicting infants' later capabilities, ending their article with "a bit of crystal-ball gazing" when they wrote, "Could it be that the infant's future prospects, as well as his past experiences and present interests, are reflected in his eyes?"

The Orienting Response

Russian psychologists studied what Pavlov referred to as the "what-is-it-reflex," having noticed that his lab dogs turned in the direction of a new stimulus. In what was also called the "orienting reflex" (Sokolov, 1963), both humans and dogs would literally and figuratively "sit up and take notice" at the first presentation of a novel stimulus. The orienting reflex, consisting of a variety of physiological and behavioral responses such as heart rate change, turning toward the new stimulus, eye movements, etc. (Cohen, 1976), is the basis of habituation and familiarization methods. Sokolov grounded habituation in neurological functioning by claiming that it reflected not just moment-to-moment processing but comparison with existing memory traces and the build-up of new ones.

Methods Multiply

Once researchers realized that they could capitalize on infants' attentional responses, additional methods appeared. There is no question that we would not be able to ask the sophisticated questions we do today were it not for the advent of these methods. Just as in chemistry and other sciences, new discoveries follow on the heels of the emergence of new methods. Space does not permit us to treat each and every method and its variations in this chapter. Instead, the chapter favors the most frequently used methods.

The Sucking Response

The orienting response figured in work by Eimas *et al.* (1971). Eimas *et al.* shocked the field by showing that infants but a few weeks of age could discriminate between phonemes and demonstrate categorical perception for speech sounds. After infants' sucking habituated to hearing the same sound in isolation repeatedly, a new sound (either in the same phonemic category or from a new category) was played. Infants then showed an orienting response to the out-of-category sound, recovering their sucking response, and revealing that they could discriminate between phonemes (see Fennell, Chapter 1 this volume). This important research told the field that infants begin language learning with some categories in place. However, as sucking wanes in its utility after about 4 months of age, other methods were needed by researchers to continue to explore infant language discrimination and categorization.

Heart Rate Deceleration

Kagan and Lewis (1965) published the first longitudinal study that used a variety of responses (visual fixation, vocalizations, arm movements, and heart rate) to assess infants' processing of both visual and auditory stimuli. Cardiac deceleration was touted as a way to distinguish between "the empty stare" and "active assimilation" (1965, p. 96) and a way to assess attention to auditory stimuli.

In one fascinating early experiment, Kagan and Lewis (1965) crossed meaningfulness with "inflection" to present 13-month-olds with four kinds of paragraphs: *high meaning, high inflection* (three complete sentences containing highly frequent words such as *baby, mommy, daddy*; read with normal intonation); *high meaning, low inflection* (one word per second; flat intonation); *low meaning, high inflection* (nonsense words; normal intonation): and *low meaning, low inflection* (nonsense words; read one word at a time). Girls showed the greatest deceleration to high meaning, high inflection and to low meaning, high inflection paragraphs, suggesting that girls were motivated to find the meaning and were perhaps attracted to infant-directed speech. Boys, on the other hand, showed the greatest deceleration to the high meaning, low inflection paragraph, as if needing to hear the word-by-word presentation to find meaning. More provocative are the longitudinal links between attention to auditory stimuli (music and tones) at 6 months and attention to the paragraphs at 13 months. Boys showed low attention stability. For girls, high cardiac deceleration at 6 months predicted greater attention to the novel paragraphs (both intonation types) with low meaning. These data suggest that sensitivity to nonlinguistic auditory stimuli at 6 months relates to infant language processing at 13 months.

Visual Fixation

In 1974, Horowitz edited a monograph that asked whether visual fixation might be used as a window into language development. Visual fixation was so new as a dependent variable for this purpose that an appendix was devoted to procedures for establishing an infant laboratory. Papers in that volume reported the discovery that for 10–12-week-olds, introducing auditory stimuli after habituation increased visual fixation time and afforded assessment of infants' discrimination between auditory stimuli. Horowitz suggested that "visual response decrement and recovery may be a very useful procedure for studying infant receptive language abilities" (1974, p. 111).

Infant language capabilities are about more than the auditory signal itself. Learning language entails forming the concepts that languages encode in their semantic structures, such as who does what to whom. Many theorists believed semantic roles were the first way that infants understood sentences (e.g., Golinkoff, 1981; Pinker, 1984). Golinkoff (1975) presented infants with silent, filmed, dynamic events using familiarization and recovery of the visual fixation response or a combination of visual fixation and heart rate deceleration (Golinkoff and Kerr, 1978). Since these studies preceded videotape, human actors were filmed in super 8 mm film. Both studies pitted a change in the *roles* of agent and patient against a change in the event's *direction* across the screen. Fourteen-month-olds watched action role changes more than direction changes, indicating that they could tell agents from patients (Schöppner, Sodian, and Pauen, 2006).

The link between dynamic events and auditory stimuli appeared in Spelke (1976). She showed infants two simultaneous visual displays (a donkey jumping up and down versus a person clapping her hands) accompanied by a single auditory stimulus matching only one of the displays in the paired comparisons method (Fantz, 1961). When 4-month-olds watched the target – the matching event – more than the nontarget, it became clear that this method had great promise for testing language comprehension. Golinkoff *et al.* (1987) capitalized on that promise by developing the "intermodal preferential looking paradigm" (IPLP) for studying language comprehension (see Hirsh-Pasek and Golinkoff, 1996; Piotroski and Naigles, Chapter 2 this volume). That first paper validated the IPLP by testing 17-month-olds on the comprehension of nouns and verbs and 28-month-olds – already using multiword utterances – on the use of word order in sentence comprehension (e.g., "Big Bird is tickling Cookie Monster").

Hirsh-Pasek and Golinkoff (1996) then showed that infants as young as 13 months of age recognized that words come in "packages," specifying unique events in the world. When shown a video of a woman kissing a set of keys and holding a ball in the foreground versus the same woman kissing the ball and dangling the keys in the foreground, babies looked more at the matching event when they heard, "She's kissing the keys!" This result could only have emerged if infants were doing more than processing individual words, as both videos contained a "she," the action of "kissing," and the target item (keys). By 17 months, infants with as few as two words in their productive vocabularies could use word order as a guide to watch specific events that matched the linguistic stimuli (Hirsh-Pasek and Golinkoff, 1996) – if they knew the names of the *Sesame Street* characters. Thus, infants not yet speaking were capable of comprehending not only action role relations in language but probably the grammatical categories of subject and object of the sentence.

Hollich, Hirsh-Pasek, and Golinkoff (2000) introduced a three-dimensional version of the IPLP – the interactive intermodal preferential looking paradigm. It presented real objects to infants (10 to 24 months) and allowed for the manipulation of social cues in an online word learning task. Pruden *et al.* (2006) and Hollich, Hirsh-Pasek, and Golinkoff (2000) reported that the cues infants used for word learning changed over time, moving from perceptual salience, or the attractiveness of the object, to the use of social cues such as eye gaze. Nurmsoo and Bloom (2008), using another paradigm, showed that, by preschool, children do not blindly follow eye gaze but switch to using linguistic cues when these are put into conflict, as the emergent coalition model (Hollich *et al.*, 2000) predicts.

Yet another use of the IPLP is a *nonlinguistic version* (Pruden *et al.*, 2006) that presents single and paired dynamic events to see which ones infants prefer to look at after a familiarization and/or training period. It is designed to assess which *relations* infants can discern that they will later express linguistically (Göksun, Hirsh-Pasek, and Golinkoff, 2010; Golinkoff and Hirsh-Pasek, 2008). Infants appear to form a range of nonlinguistic categories that sometimes change as they learn the particular perceptual distinctions their language encodes. Concepts such as containment and support, path and manner, figure and ground, source and goal have been explored with the nonlinguistic IPLP or single stimulus habituation studies (e.g., Pulverman *et al.*, 2008; Lakusta *et al.*, 2007; Hespos and Spelke, 2004; Casasola, Cohen, and Chiarello, 2003). Thus, methods relying on visual fixation are probing infants' perception of the event components that languages encode and, in some cases, showing language heightening or dampening these distinctions (e.g., Göksun, Hirsh-Pasek, and Golinkoff, 2010).

Conditioned Head Turn and the Head Turn Preference Procedure

Colombo and Bundy (1981) offered a procedure to assess infant auditory selectivity, which was a forerunner of the head turn preference procedure (Fernald, 1985; Hirsh-Pasek *et al.*, 1987; Kemler Nelson *et al.*, 1995). Two- and 4.5-month-olds, in an auditory analogue to Fantz's (1961) paired comparisons method, were offered the opportunity to look at one of two red light rings composed of light diodes placed approximately 1.3 feet (40 cm) apart. A look at one of the rings played a female voice; a look at the other ring yielded silence or white noise. Thus, this was an "infant-controlled" method, as children could make the stimulus begin. Two-month-olds did not look selectively, but 4.5-month-olds preferred the voice over either silence or white noise. Columbo and Bundy wrote, "The finding that, by 4 months, infants show preference for the female voice over both silence and white noise is not an intuitively surprising one, but the demonstration of a valid auditory selectivity paradigm is of more interest" (1981, p. 222).

Werker, Polka, and Pegg (1997) suggested that the conditioned head turn procedure was inspired by research that tested auditory perception in preschoolers. Researchers adapted the procedure to test infants' perception of sounds by conditioning infants to turn their heads to see a reinforcer (e.g., a bear playing cymbals) when they detected a change in the auditory stimulus. For example, babies were able to override changes in voices, gender of the speaker, and age of the speaker to turn to the reinforcer only when a vowel sound changed from /i/ to /a/ (Kuhl, 1983).

Fernald (1985) used a head turn procedure with loudspeakers placed to the left and right behind infants, training them to activate an auditory stimulus by turning their heads. Four-month-old infants turned their heads more to hear passages spoken in infant-directed versus adult-directed speech. Prior to this time, studies had examined infants' sensitivity to phonological aspects of language, taking a bottom-up approach. Fernald's (1985) study suggested that infants might be sensitive to larger stretches of text than just individual phonemes or syllables.

The head turn preference procedure further increased in utility and sensitivity in a study designed to evaluate whether 7–10-month-old infants might be sensitive to the temporal and intonational properties of passages (Hirsh-Pasek *et al.*, 1987). Hirsh-Pasek *et al.* used a passage of infant-directed speech in which 1 second pauses were inserted either at random points or at clausal boundaries where they are usually found. Their methodological innovation was to code not only the side to which infants turned to hear a language sample, but also *how long* infants attended to a side after turning to it. They found that even when the number of head turns to a side did not differ significantly, the *duration* of infants' looks revealed a clear preference for the natural passage. Using this method, a developmental sequence emerged: infants preferred to hear appropriately segmented clauses before they preferred to hear appropriately segmented phrases (Jusczyk *et al.*, 1992) and before they noticed the difference between compound and noncompound words (e.g., "night rate" vs "nitrate": Myers *et al.*, 1996). The head turn preference procedure offered a way to test whether infants conduct top-down analyses as well as bottom-up segmental analyses.

The head turn preference procedure has been used in studies addressing a wide range of questions. For example, Mandel, Jusczyk, and Pisoni (1995) discovered that babies recognize the sound patterns of their own name at 4.5 months. Bortfeld *et al.* (2005) found that if a word in a passage occurred after the baby's own name versus someone else's name, 6-month-old babies recognized the word when played in isolation. The procedure has also been used to test for grammatical sensitivity. Santelman and Jusczyk (1998) found that 18-month-olds preferred to hear an auxiliary and a verb that pattern together (… *is baking*) over an auxiliary and a verb that are ungrammatical (… *can baking*).

The Switch Design

For studying rapid associations between syllables and objects, Werker *et al.* (1998) invented the "switch design." Here, infants are first given the opportunity through repeated pairings to form an association between two novel objects on video and their respective syllables (e.g., object A was accompanied by *lif* and object B by *neem*)(see Fennell, Chapter 1 this volume). Then the pairings were switched. The dependent variable was whether infants recovered their visual fixation time, suggesting that they must have formed the syllable–object associations. This method illustrated how 14-month-olds give preference to forming object + syllable associations over action + syllable association – an interesting point for research on verb learning – as the researchers tested whether the syllable was paired with the object or the movement in which it engaged. They also showed that only 14-month-olds, and not 8- or 12-month-olds, could form rapid associations between syllables and objects.

Stager and Werker (1997) used this method to uncover infants' sensitivity to phonemic distinctions during word learning. They found that 14-month-olds could not perform the task when the syllables used were minimal pairs (i.e., *buh* vs *duh*); they only succeeded when they were phonologically very different (i.e., *lif* and *neem*), as in Werker *et al.* (1998). Werker *et al.* (2002) pursued this finding in an attempt to uncover the reason for the laxity in phonological discrimination during a syllable–object association task. Their research suggested that by 20 months infants were able to map minimal pairs to objects. At 17 months, when Werker *et al.* found a correlation between infants' vocabulary level and their ability to map similar sounding syllables to objects, they concluded that attending to fine phonetic distinctions may contribute to amassing a larger vocabulary more rapidly. Fennell, Byers-Heinlein, and Werker (2007) compared bilingually reared babies' performance on this task. When they found that bilingual infants could not succeed until 20 months, they argued that this pattern reflected an advantage for bilingual babies who must stay "open" longer to the phonological differences that matter for meaning in the languages they are acquiring.

In sum, a variety of methods exists using visual fixation, conditioned head turn, and head turn preference as the dependent variables. These methods have offered researchers a window into infants' language processing.

While progress was surely made, researchers rarely brought infants back to the lab or even tested them concurrently to examine the relationship between performance on the laboratory task and other measures of language knowledge. We attribute this to two factors. First, measures of young children's language knowledge are often difficult to administer and taxing for infants if given concurrent with other assessments. Second, there were few measures for young children. However, a significant methodological tool appeared with the introduction of the MacArthur–Bates Communicative Development Inventory (MCDI), a maternal report questionnaire (Fenson *et al.*, 1994; see Pan, Chapter 7 this volume). Researchers finally had a language instrument that could be given when the child was still less than 3 years of age, and might correlate with contemporaneous performance in the laboratory. The MCDI represented a huge boon to the study of language development: an individual who presumably was the best observer of her own "subject" – the mother – could offer a quick and easy language assessment.

Language achievement, however, as assessed on the MCDI did not always correlate with how children performed in laboratory tasks (e.g., Hirsh-Pasek and Golinkoff, 1996), probably because maternal report and experimental tasks may be measuring different things. The MCDI measures the *product* of what children have already learned about words and grammar, while tests in the laboratory often measure the *processes* by which they learn. This is not to suggest, however, that parent reports or the MCDI are not useful. They have been validated (e.g., Dale, 1991) on numerous populations (e.g., children with cochlear implants: Thal, DesJardins, and Eisenberg, 2007). Mills, Coffey-Corina, and Neville (1993) conducted a study that was not designed to validate parental report *per se* but did do so. Using ERPs with 20-month-olds, Mills, Coffey-Corina, and Neville assessed how learning words changed the words' instantiation in the brain. They found that parental reports of what words their children knew receptively and could say predicted differential brain responses in comparison to unknown and to backward words.

Why Look for Continuity in Precursors of Language Functioning?

Early on, the field of infant language development focused almost exclusively on average sensitivity to aspects of language like sounds, words, and grammatical constructs. Despite calls from researchers, individual differences were largely ignored (but see Tamis-LeMonda, Bornstein, and Baumwell, 2001). So too were questions about whether any of the infant sensitivities that were filling the journal pages predicted *future* language performance.

Bates, Bretherton, and Snyder (1988) were among the first to draw attention to the issue of individual differences in language development. Using data from the MacArthur–Bates Communicative Development Inventory (Fenson *et al.*, 1994), Bates, Dale, and Thal (1995), for example, reported enormous but stable variation over time and a dissociation between comprehension and production in some typical as well as atypical populations. They concluded hauntingly:

> The Average Child is a fiction, a descriptive convenience ... Theories of language development can no longer rely on this mythical being. Any theory worth the name will have to account for the variations that are reliably observed in early language learning. (1995, p. 42)

In the field of developmental psychology writ large, it was Kagan (1970) who challenged us to go beyond the mythical average child and to look at behaviors with a wide-angle lens. His reasons, which are paraphrased below, are still valid today. First, looking at individual variation over time enables us to investigate whether and how early behaviors predict later development. And uncovering these connections can provide signposts for developmental problems. Second, a long range view helps us validate our theories by asking how earlier behaviors unfold and even morph across time. Kagan pointed out that behaviors that look the same may or may not be governed by the same mechanisms at later ages. Despite compelling reasons to look beyond the average child, language development only recently embraced longitudinal research with an eye towards individual variation.

With respect to the predictive value of early behavior, several studies have now emerged. For example, Molfese and colleagues (e.g., Molfese, Molfese, and Espy, 1999) used cortical evoked potential responses to speech and nonspeech auditory stimuli with infants to predict language levels at 5 and reading at 8 years. Benasich *et al.* (2002) argued that difficulties with rapid auditory processing of the cues associated with different speech sounds link to language at 36 months. Studies like these formed the basis for early screening techniques.

Newman *et al.* (2006) also examined the predictive power of early speech processing when they conducted a retrospective analysis of data collected on speech segmentation tasks when infants were between 7.5 and 12 months of age. These data predicted vocabulary at age 2 and to both semantic and syntactic development at 4 and 6 years of age. Importantly, the outcome measures were independent of IQ, suggesting the specificity of Newman *et al.*'s findings to the language domain. Had this study included children who would subsequently have language issues, or who had a familial pattern of language impairment, the relationship between early segmentation skills and later language development might have been even more striking, as Benasich and Tallal (2002) suggest.

Work by Kuhl and her colleagues also suggests that longitudinal research clarifies the significance of early language responses. Kuhl (2009) conducted a prospective study of infants' ability to discriminate between native and nonnative phonemes and later language development. The logic is that if infants discover their native language phonemic distinctions and dampen their sensitivity to nonnative language phonemes, they have achieved a degree of "neural commitment" that represents a more mature brain response. Remaining "open" to nonnative distinctions was predicted to correlate negatively with language skill. Using ERPs, Kuhl reported that children who zeroed in on their native phonemes had more words than children who were slower to do so. The converse was also borne out: children who remained "open" to nonnative phonemic distinctions had lower vocabularies than children who homed in on native phonemes sooner. Input may well influence when infants "go native." Thus early laboratory-assessed speech perception is not just an interesting demonstration of infant capabilities.

Finally, work by Fernald, Perfors, and Marchman (2006), Marchman and Fernald (2008), and Hurtado, Marchman, and Fernald (2008), using a version of the IPLP called the "looking while listening paradigm" (see Swingley, Chapter 3 this volume), is providing important data about the continuity between early processing speed and later language level. The looking while listening procedure also presents paired visual stimuli and a single auditory stimulus. Where it differs is in the calculation of the dependent variable. Using milliseconds, researchers track *how long* it takes for children to land on the visual match. Fernald *et al.* (2008) and Hurtado, Marchman, and Fernald (2008), testing both English- and Spanish-reared children, found strong relationships between speed of processing and vocabulary at 18 and 25 months. Although the direction of causation is unclear, concurrent relationships between real-time language skills and speed of processing are an important new finding. Marchman and Fernald (2008) carried this research further by asking if the processing speed to linguistic stimuli had *predictive* validity. They reported strong correlations between speed of processing at 25 months and measures of expressive language, IQ, and working memory at 8 years of age! These are exciting findings – especially as they also correlate with the amount of input children receive. Thus, these new findings demonstrate that the individual variation in the average ages of early perceptual processing is not merely statistical noise. Rather, this variability might be rich with predictive power as early perception skills lead to later language, offering tremendous potential for early diagnosis and intervention.

As Kagan (1970) predicted, looking at continuities over time also helps us better understand theory. For example, if, as Goldin-Meadow and her colleagues have long argued, gesture plays a key role in early language acquisition, the frequency of parental gesture and children's language learning over time should be correlated (see Cartmill, Demir, and Goldin-Meadow, Chapter 14 this volume). Rowe and Goldin-Meadow (2009) reported a strong link between the number of gestures (such as pointing) children produced at 14 months and the number of vocabulary items they had at 54 months. The number of gestures parents produced mediated this relationship, even controlling for amount of parental and child language – suggesting that parents who use gestures have children who, in turn, produce more gestures. Child gestures apparently become *a tool* for further language learning, suggesting that they play a facilitative role.

Continuity studies, in Kagan's parlance, might "facilitate the understanding of the meaning of responses at particular ages" (1970, p. 105). Two examples of this phenomenon in the language arena are the work of Stager and Werker (1997) and Song *et al.* (under review). In the former, infants at 8 months were able to form syllable–object associations with minimal pairs but 14-month-olds were not. As the older group, but not the younger group, apparently invoked their word learning processes, the two groups of infants were actually engaged in different tasks with the exact same stimuli. In the Song *et al.* work, 10–12-month-olds could form nonlinguistic categories of dynamic action (jumping versus marching) from videotaped events while 19–21-month-olds could not. Again, the older group, already learning verbs, appeared to need the assistance of a verb label to form the category. Both sets of studies suggest that the same laboratory task given to children of different ages might be driven by very different mechanisms.

In 2008, Kagan renewed his call for the study of individual difference in cognitive development. Now commonplace in the area of social development, however, the first *edited* volume dedicated to the study of individual differences and longitudinal prediction in language acquisition was not published until that same year (Columbo, McCardle, and Freund, 2009). As Rice wrote in its foreword, "researchers ... have become increasingly concerned with individual differences, identification of individuals at risk, and prediction of mature function" (2009, p. ix). This emphasis on individual differences and prediction comes at the same time that federal funding agencies are emphasizing "translational science." We predict that such studies will continue to emerge.

Back to the Future

The invention of methods that allow us to probe what happens behind infants' eyes – and ears – has literally transformed our understanding of language development. The next generation of methods slowly coming onto the scene will probe the neurological correlates of language functioning (see Kovelman, Chapter 4 this volume). These neurological methods will prove critical to our understanding when viewed alongside more traditional methods. They offer, however, no panacea. As Columbo, McCardle, and Freund argued:

> Both the extant measures and current paradigms do not easily allow for the study of developmental change over time, and mapping such trajectories is essential to our understanding of brain–behavior relationship as it evolves over time ... Infants, children,

and adults may show the same behavioral outcome but through different underlying mechanisms [or] … may rely on a constant underlying mechanism yet show different behavioral outcomes. (2009, p. 3)

Kagan's (2008) recommendation is thus to use multiple, converging methods such as heart rate deceleration, skin conductance, and emotional responses such as smiling and vocalizing. A trend in this direction is emerging with online brain measures using ERP, MEG, fNIRS, and fMRI (Kuhl and Rivera-Gaxiola, 2008; Kovelman, Chapter 4 this volume). In 2009, Columbo, McCardle, and Freund echoed Kagan's assertions when they wrote, "it will be essential to create paradigms that rely on convergence from multiple assessments of multiple task components using multiple methods … to truly understand developing brain-behavior relations over time" (p. 3).

Using history as our guide, and data generated from multiple methods, the field is now ripe for theories that incorporate individual differences as they play out over the course of development and that look for interrelationships between various aspects of language through the lens of multiple methods. This perspective will no doubt increase the complexity of our designs. As Urie Bronfenbrenner taught us in the area of social systems theory and social development, the understanding of complex behaviors will require additional methodological complexity.

Acknowledgments

We thank Cora-Lee Picone and Sujeet Ranganathan for assistance with the bibliography of this chapter, and Kelly Fisher and Erika Hoff for their helpful comments. This research was funded by joint grants to the authors: from NSF, SBR9615391 and from NIH, RO1HD050199.

Key Terms

Conditioned head turn   Infants can be trained to turn their heads to look at a rewarding stimulus (such as a bear clapping cymbals together) when they hear a new stimulus. The measure is often used to study infants' discriminations between sounds.

Habituation   Used to tell if infants can tell the difference between new and old stimuli. Researchers show (or play) something repeatedly until infants meet a predetermined criterion for boredom. Then the stimulus is changed in systematic ways to see if the orienting response "recovers" or if "dishabituation" occurs. It will recover if infants can tell the difference between the new and old stimuli.

Head turn preference procedure   This is used to gauge what infants think about auditory stimuli. Seated in a three-sided booth, infants see a light blink ahead of them and then a light blinks on one of the two sides of the enclosure at 90 degrees. Researchers measure how long infants look to each side after they turn to it as each side plays a different auditory stimulus.

Intermodal preferential looking paradigm   Infants are shown two side-by-side visual displays (e.g., a boat and a shoe) while they hear a linguistic stimulus (such as a word) that matches only one of the displays (e.g., "boat"). The dependent variable is whether the infant looks more to the side that matches what they hear than to the side that does not match what they hear. This method is used to study language comprehension.

Orienting response What infants do in the presence of a new stimulus. The threshold of their sensory receptors lowers, they turn in the direction of the new stimulus, and they look or listen to it until they get bored. Visual fixation time (how long infants look at a stimulus) is often used as an index of infants' attention and interest in the stimulus.

References

Bates, E., Bretherton, I., and Snyder, L. (1988) *From first words to grammar: individual differences and dissociable mechanisms.* New York: Cambridge University Press.

Bates, E., Dale, P., and Thal, D. (1995) Individual differences and their implications for theories of language development. In P. Fletcher and B. MacWhinney (eds), *Handbook of child language* (pp. 95–151). Oxford: Blackwell.

Benasich, A., and Tallal, P. (2002) Infant discrimination of rapid auditory cues predicts later language impairment. *Behavioral Brain Research*, 136, 31–49.

Benasich, A., Thomas, J., Choudhury, N., and Leppänen, P. (2002) The importance of rapid auditory processing abilities to early language development: evidence from converging methodologies. *Developmental Psychobiology*, 40, 278–292.

Bloom, L. (1973) *One word at a time: the use of single-word utterances before syntax.* The Hague: Mouton.

Bortfeld, H., Morgan, J., Golinkoff, R., and Rathbun, K. (2005) Mommy and me: familiar names help launch babies into speech stream segmentation. *Psychological Science*, 16, 298–304.

Casasola, M., Cohen, L.B., and Chiarello, E. (2003) Six-month-old infants' categorization of containment spatial relations. *Child Development*, 74, 679–693.

Cohen, L.B. (1976) Habituation of infant visual attention. In T.J. Tighe and R.N. Leaton (eds), *Habituation: perspectives from child development, animal behavior, and neuropsychology.* Hillsdale, NJ: Erlbaum.

Colombo, J., and Bundy, R.S. (1981) A method for the measurement of infant auditory selectivity. *Infant Behavior and Development*, 4, 219–223.

Colombo, J., McCardle, P., and Freund, L. (eds) (2009) *Infant pathways to language: methods, models, and research directions.* New York: Psychology Press.

Curtiss, S. (1977) *Genie: a psycholinguistic study of a modern-day wild child.* New York: Academic Press.

Dale, P. (1991) The validity of a parent report measure of vocabulary and syntax at 24 months. *Journal of Speech, Language, and Hearing Research*, 34, 565–571.

Eimas, P.D., Siqueland, E.R., Jusczyk, P.W., and Vigorrito, J. (1971) Speech perception in infants. *Science*, 171, 303–306.

Fantz, R. (1961) The origin of form perception. *Scientific American*, 204, 66–72.

Fantz, R., and Nevis, S. (1967) Pattern preferences and perceptual-cognitive development in early infancy. *Merrill-Palmer Quarterly*, 13, 77–108.

Fennell, C.T., Byers-Heinlein, K., and Werker, J.F. (2007) Using speech sounds to guide word learning: the case of bilingual infants. *Child Development*, 78, 1510–1525.

Fenson, L., Dale, P.S., Reznick, J.S., *et al.* (1994) Variability in early communicative development. *Monographs of the Society for Research in Child Development*, 59 (serial no. 242).

Fernald, A. (1985) Four-month-old infants prefer to listen to motherese. *Infant Behavior and Development*, 8, 181–195.

Fernald, A., Perfors, A., and Marchman, V.A. (2006) Picking up speed in understanding: speech processing efficiency and vocabulary growth across the second year. *Developmental Psychology*, 42, 98–116.

Fernald, A., Zangl, R., Portillo, A.L., and Marchman, V.A. (2008) Looking while listening: using eye movements to monitor spoken language comprehension by infants and young children. In I.A. Sekerina, E.M. Fernandez, and H. Clahsen (eds), *Developmental psycholinguistics: on-line methods in children's language processing* (pp. 97–135). Philadelphia: Benjamins.

Göksun, T., Hirsh-Pasek, K., and Golinkoff, R.M. (2010) Trading spaces: carving up events for learning language. *Perspectives on Psychological Science*, 5, 33–42.

Goldin-Meadow, S., and Mylander, C. (1984) Gestural communication in deaf children: the effects and noneffects of parental input on early language development. *Monographs of the Society for Research in Child Development*, 49 (3–4, serial no. 207).

Golinkoff, R.M. (1975) Semantic development in infants: the concepts of agent and recipient. *Merrill-Palmer Quarterly*, 21, 181–193.

Golinkoff, R.M. (1981) The case for semantic relations: evidence from the verbal and nonverbal domains. *Journal of Child Language*, 78, 413–438.

Golinkoff, R.M., Hirsh-Pasek, K., Cauley, K.M., and Gordon, L. (1987) The eyes have it: lexical and syntactic comprehension in a new paradigm. *Journal of Child Language*, 14, 23–45.

Golinkoff, R.M., and Hirsh-Pasek, K. (2008) How toddlers begin to learn verbs. *Trends in Cognitive Science*, 12, 397–403.

Golinkoff, R., and Kerr, J. (1978) Infants' perception of semantically defined action role changes in filmed events. *Merrill-Palmer Quarterly*, 24, 53–62.

Hespos, S.J., and Spelke, E.S. (2004) Conceptual precursors to language. *Nature*, 430, 453–456.

Hirsh-Pasek, K., and Golinkoff, R.M. (1996) *The origins of grammar: evidence from early language comprehension*. Cambridge, MA: MIT Press.

Hirsh-Pasek, K., Kemler Nelson, D.G., Jusczyk, P.W., *et al.* (1987) Clauses or perceptual units for young infants. *Cognition*, 26, 269–286.

Hollich, G.J., Hirsh-Pasek, K., Golinkoff, R.M., *et al.* (2000) Breaking the language barrier: an emergentist coalition model for the origins of word learning. *Monographs of the Society for Research in Child Development*, 65 (3, serial no. 262).

Horowitz, F.D. (1974) Infant attention and discrimination: methodological and substantive issues. *Monographs of the Society for Research in Child Development*, 39 (5/6, serial no. 158).

Hurtado, N., Marchman, V.A., and Fernald, A. (2008) Does input influence uptake? Links between maternal talk, processing speed and vocabulary size in Spanish-learning children. *Developmental Science*, 11, F31–F39.

Jusczyk, P., Hirsh-Pasek, K., Kemler Nelson, D., *et al.* (1992) Perception of acoustic correlates of major phrasal boundaries by young infants. *Cognitive Psychology*, 24, 252–293.

Kagan, J. (1970) The determinants of attention in the infant. *American Scientist*, 58, 298–306.

Kagan, J. (2008) In defense of qualitative changes in development. *Child Development*, 79, 1606–1624.

Kagan, J., and Lewis, M. (1965) Studies of attention in the human infant. *Merrill-Palmer Quarterly*, 11, 95–127.

Kemler Nelson, D.G., Jusczyk, P.W., Mandel, D.R., *et al.* (1995) The headturn preference procedure for testing auditory perception. *Infant Behavior and Development*, 18, 111–116.

Kuhl, P.K. (1983) Perception of auditory equivalence classes for speech by infants. *Infant Behavior and Development*, 6, 263–285.

Kuhl, P.K. (2009) Linking infant speech perception to language acquisition: phonetic learning predicts language growth. In J. Colombo, P. McCardle, and L. Freund (eds), *Infant pathways to language: methods, models, and research directions* (pp. 213–243). New York: Erlbaum.

Kuhl, P.K., and Rivera-Gaxiola, M. (2008) Neural substrates of early language acquisition. *Annual Review of Neuroscience*, 31, 511–534.

Lakusta, L., Wagner, L., O'Hearn, K., and Landau, B. (2007) Conceptual foundations of spatial language: evidence for a goal bias in infants. *Language Learning and Development*, 3, 179–197.

MacWhinney, B. (1991) *The CHILDES database*. Dublin, OH: Discovery Systems.

Mandel, D.R., Jusczyk, P.W., and Pisoni, D.B. (1995) Infants' recognition of the sound patterns of their own names. *Psychological Science*, 6, 314–317.

Marchman, V.A., and Fernald, A. (2008) Speed of word recognition and vocabulary knowledge in infancy predict cognitive and language outcomes in later childhood. *Developmental Science*, 11, F9–F16.

Mills, D.L., Coffey-Corina, S.A., and Neville, H.J. (1993) Language acquisition and cerebral specialization in 20-month-old infants. *Journal of Cognitive Neuroscience*, 5, 317–334.

Molfese, D.L., Molfese, V.J., and Espy, K.A. (1999) The predictive use of event-related potentials in language development and the treatment of language disorders. *Developmental Neuropsychology*, 16, 373–377.

Myers, J., Jusczyk, P., Kemler Nelson, D., *et al.* (1996) Infants' sensitivity to word boundaries in fluent speech. *Journal of Child Language*, 43, 1–30.

Naigles, L., Hoff, E., and Vear, D. (2009) Flexibility in early verb use: evidence from a multiple-*n* diary study. *Monographs of the Society for Research in Child Development*, 74 (2, serial no. 293).

Nelson, K. (1973) Structure and strategy in learning to talk. *Monographs of the Society for Research in Child Development*, 38 (1–2, serial no. 149).

Newman, R.S., Bernstein Ratner, N., Jusczyk, A., *et al.* (2006) Infants' early ability to segment the conversational speech signal predicts later language development: a retrospective analysis. *Developmental Psychology*, 42, 643–655.

Nurmsoo, E., and Bloom, P. (2008) Preschoolers' perspective-taking in word learning: do they blindly follow eye gaze? *Psychological Science*, 19, 211–215.

Pinker, S. (1984) *Language learnability and language development*. Cambridge, MA: Harvard University Press.

Pruden, S.M., Hirsh-Pasek, K., Golinkoff, R., and Hennon, E.A. (2006) The birth of words: ten-month-olds learn words through perceptual salience. *Child Development*, 77, 266–280.

Pulverman, R., Golinkoff, R.M., Hirsh-Pasek, K., and Sootsman Buresh, J. (2008) Manners matter: infants' attention to manner and path in non-linguistic dynamic events. *Cognition*, 108, 825–830.

Rice, M.L. (2009) Foreword. In J. Colombo, P. McCardle, and L. Freund (eds), *Infant pathways to language* (p. ix). New York: Psychology Press.

Rowe, M.L., and Goldin-Meadow, S. (2009) Differences in early gesture explain SES disparities in child vocabulary size at school entry. *Science*, 323, 951–953.

Santelmann, L., and Jusczyk, P. (1998) Sensitivity to discontinuous dependencies in language learners: evidence for processing limitations. *Cognition*, 69, 105–134.

Schöppner, B., Sodian, B., and Pauen, S. (2006) Encoding action roles in meaningful social interaction in the first year of life. *Infancy*, 9, 289–311.

Seidl, A., Hollich, G., and Jusczyk, P. (2003) Early understanding of subject and object wh-questions. *Infancy*, 4, 423–436.

Sokolov, E. (1963) Higher nervous functions: the orienting reflex. *Annual Review of Physiology*, 25, 545–580.

Song, L., Golinkoff, R.M., Stahl, A., *et al.* (under review). Labeling facilitates 19–21-month-olds' categorization of intransitive human actions.

Spelke, E.S. (1976) Infants' intermodal perception of events. *Cognitive Psychology*, 8, 553–560.

Stager, C.L., and Werker, J.F. (1997) Infants listen for more phonetic detail in speech perception than in word-learning tasks. *Nature*, 388, 381–382.

Stern, C., and Stern, W. (1907) *Die kindersprache*. Leipzig: Barth.

Tamis-LeMonda, C., Bornstein, M., and Baumwell, L. (2001) Maternal responsiveness and children's achievement of language milestones. *Child Development*, 72, 748–767.

Thal, D., DesJardins, J.L., and Eisenberg, L.S. (2007) Validity of the MacArthur–Bates Communicative Development Inventories for measuring language abilities in children with cochlear implants. *American Journal of Speech–Language Pathology*, 16, 54–64.

Werker, J.F., Cohen, L.B., Lloyd, V., *et al.* (1998) Acquisition of word–object associations by 14-month-old infants. *Developmental Psychology*, 34, 1289–1309.

Werker, J.F., Fennell, C.T., Corcoran, K., and Stager, C.L. (2002) Infants' ability to learn phonetically similar words: effects of age and vocabulary size. *Infancy*, 3, 1–30.

Werker, J.F., Polka, L., and Pegg, J.E. (1997) The conditioned head turn procedure as a method for testing infant speech perception. *Early Development and Parenting*, 6, 171–178.

Further Reading and Resources

Clark, E. (2009) *First language acquisition* (2nd edn). New York: Cambridge University Press.

Golinkoff, R.M., and Hirsh-Pasek, K. (2000) *How babies talk: the magic and mystery of language in the first three years*. New York: Dutton/Penguin.

Hirsh-Pasek, K., and Golinkoff, R.M. (eds) (2006) *Action meets word: how children learn verbs*. New York: Oxford University Press.

Hoff, E. (2009) *Language development* (4th edn). CA: Wadsworth.

Jusczyk, P. (2000) *The discovery of spoken language*. Cambridge: MIT Press.

Part II   Assessing Language Knowledge and Processes in Children Who Talk

6 Assessing Phonological Knowledge

Cynthia Core

Summary

This chapter reviews phonology and methods for conducting phonological research in language development and describes several techniques used to assess phonological properties of children's speech productions, focusing on the age range from 18 months to 5 years. The chapter provides a brief overview of the ways that phonological information is relevant to language research and the importance of considering phonological properties of words and phrases in language research. Phonological development and terminology related to phonology are defined. Methodological considerations for data collection for both naturalistic and elicited speech productions and analysis are discussed. Definitions of related constructs are provided.

Why Study Phonology?

Researchers in a variety of disciplines are interested in the phonological development of young children. Phonological development is of interest in the study of typical language development and the study of speech and language disorders, and phonological development is related to the development of reading, spelling, and related skills, such as phonological sensitivity and phoneme awareness. Analysis of phonological development has been used as a way to test linguistic theories of language development and phonology, such as prosodic phonology (e.g., Spencer, 1986; Fikkert, 1994; Goad and Rose, 2004) and optimality theory (e.g., Pater, 1997; Gnanadesikan, 2004), and in investigations of statistical learning in language development (Pierrehumbert, 2003; Saffran, Aslin, and Newport, 1996).

Research Methods in Child Language: A Practical Guide, First Edition.
Edited by Erika Hoff.
© 2012 Blackwell Publishing Ltd. Published 2012 by Blackwell Publishing Ltd.

Children's earliest sound productions are linked to their earliest word productions, forming a natural relationship between the investigations of word learning and sound learning (Stoel-Gammon, 2010a). Before a child begins to produce the words or grammar of his language, he begins with sound production in vocal play and babbling. Children's first words tend to match the phonological properties of their babbling productions (Vihman *et al.*, 1985; Elbers and Ton, 1985). Sound learning and word learning are inextricably related and progress together. In order for children to learn words, they must master both content and form, and the form consists of the phonological properties of the words. Phonological properties of words, such as lexical stress patterns and word shape, can influence the ways in which children produce early words, and the phonological makeup of words may even influence which words children attempt to say (Schwartz and Leonard, 1982).

Basic Concepts and Terminology

Phonology refers to a child's system of speech sound production and the child's mental representations of the sounds of his language. Individual sounds are referred to as segments or phones, and the sounds of a language are called *phonemes*. Phonemes are described in terms of combinations of phonological features that uniquely define each sound. Features include information on voicing, place, and manner of articulation. A child's phonological knowledge consists of the perception and production of the phonemes of his language and knowledge of the organization of the sounds within a language, or the *phonotactics* of the language, such as which sounds are possible as word-initial sequences. Phonology also consists of the *prosodic* or suprasegmental aspects of a language, such as speech rhythm, intonation, word- and phrase-level stress patterns, and phrase boundary cues, such as pitch fall and final lengthening.

Articulation refers to the way (or accuracy with which) a child produces individual speech sounds, e.g., how a child produces the sounds of his or her language, such as whether an /s/ is produced with distortion. *Phonology* goes beyond the surface or phonetic details of speech production to the way a child uses the sounds to change meaning in words, and is often used as an umbrella term to refer to all of the factors of child speech production and phonological knowledge.

The phonological units typically measured and reported on in studies of phonological development include individual speech sounds or phonemes. Researchers typically focus on consonant production rather than vowel production because there is little research available on vowel development, and also because there is more variability in production of vowels across dialects of English. Other phonological units of interest include the syllable and its parts, and words. A *syllable* is the primary unit of phonology that may be composed of a vowel alone, or a vowel in combination with one or more consonants preceding or following the vowel. The

Table 6.1 International Phonetic Alphabet symbols for American English phonemes

Symbol	Key word	Symbol	Key word
Vowels		*Consonants*	
/i/	b<u>e</u>	/p/	<u>p</u>ig
/ɪ/	p<u>i</u>n	/b/	<u>b</u>oy
/e/	<u>a</u>te	/t/	<u>t</u>ea
/ɛ/	r<u>e</u>nt	/d/	<u>d</u>oll
/æ/	h<u>a</u>t	/k/	<u>k</u>ey
/u/	sp<u>oo</u>n	/g/	<u>g</u>irl
/ʊ/	w<u>ou</u>ld	/m/	<u>m</u>ap
/o/	ph<u>o</u>ne	/n/	<u>n</u>ose
/ɔ/	j<u>aw</u>	/v/	<u>v</u>an
/ɑ/	f<u>a</u>ther	/ŋ/	thi<u>ng</u>
/ə/	<u>a</u>head	/f/	<u>f</u>all
/ʌ/	<u>o</u>ven	/θ/	<u>th</u>ink
/ɚ/	finge<u>r</u>	/ð/	<u>th</u>is
/ɜ/	b<u>ir</u>d	/s/	<u>s</u>oup
		/z/	<u>z</u>ipper
Diphthongs		/ʃ/	<u>sh</u>oe
/aʊ/	c<u>ow</u>	/ʒ/	trea<u>s</u>ure
/aɪ/	fl<u>y</u>	/h/	<u>h</u>ouse
/ɔɪ/	t<u>oy</u>	/tʃ/	<u>ch</u>in
/eɪ/	tr<u>ay</u>	/dʒ/	<u>j</u>udge
/oʊ/	t<u>oe</u>s	/w/	<u>w</u>in
		/j/	<u>y</u>ellow
		/r/	<u>r</u>amp
		/l/	<u>l</u>ift

syllable is made up of an *onset* and a *rhyme*, and the *rhyme* is made up of the *nucleus* and the *coda*. The consonants preceding a vowel in the same syllable are referred to as the *onset*, and consonants following a vowel in the same syllable are referred to as the *coda*. The general pattern or frame of a word in terms of the types and sequences of sounds that make up the word is called the *word shape* (or phonotactic pattern) and is expressed in terms of the CV (consonant + vowel) structure of the *phonemes* of the word.

Speech sounds are represented in written form using the International Phonetic Alphabet (IPA), which is a set of symbols designed to represent the sounds of the world's languages with a one-to-one correspondence. The process of transcribing speech using the IPA symbols is called *phonetic transcription*. Table 6.1 contains a list of IPA symbols commonly used to transcribe standard English speech.

Overview of Phonological Development

At the onset of meaningful speech, children tend to use a limited set of early-acquired consonants (nasals, stops, and glides) and simple syllable structures, relying heavily on CV (consonant + vowel) and CVCV productions. The period from 1 year to 2 years is a period of growth from using primarily single words that represent early phonological forms to using word combinations. At the point of word combinations, children expand their phonological system quite quickly, acquiring more consonants, gaining greater accuracy of consonants used, and producing a broader range of word shapes. From around the ages of 2 to 5, children acquire a large vocabulary and their sound system matures to nearly adult-like productions. By the age of 5 years, most children have acquired most consonants in all word positions. Table 6.2 shows proposed ages of acquisition for English organized by early, middle, and late sounds.

Some of the factors that influence how accurately a child produces sounds have to do with the auditory, motoric, and memory abilities of the child, while other factors have to do with the phonological properties of the words and phrases the child attempts to produce (Sosa and Stoel-Gammon, 2007). Frequency of occurrence of a sound in a language, or of a word in the input, seem to facilitate production (e.g., Pye, Ingram, and List, 1987; Zamuner, Gerken, and Hammond, 2004). There are also positional effects such that sounds are produced more accurately in syllable positions that are more acoustically salient, e.g., word-initial position, stressed syllables. These positional effects interact with properties of phrasal stress to affect a child's accuracy of an individual sound in complex ways, typically facilitating production of the sound due to the prosodically strong environment, though this is not always the case (e.g., Inkelas and Rose, 2008; Kent, 1982; Kirk and Demuth, 2006).

Two lexical properties that can affect phonological accuracy are neighborhood density and phonotactic probability. Neighborhood density refers to how phonologically similar two words are by counting the number of phonological neighbors a word has. Phonological neighbors are words that differ from one another by only one phoneme (Luce and Pisoni, 1998), e.g., *sit* has phonological neighbors that include *hit*, *sat*, and *sip*. Phonotactic probability is the likelihood that a sound will occur in a given word position, or that a sound sequence may occur in a word (Jusczyk, Luce, and Charles-Luce, 1994). Sound sequences with high phonotactic probability are produced more accurately than sound sequences with low phonotactic probability in both real words and nonwords (Edwards, Beckman, and Munson, 2004; Zamuner, Gerken, and Hammond, 2004).

What To Study

Phonological investigations may be either qualitative or quantitative in nature. Researchers may be more interested in describing the nature or patterns of a child's productions, or in examining the accuracy of a child's productions. Researchers may

Table 6.2 Proposed ages of acquisition for English organized by early, middle, and late sounds

Phoneme	Age of acquisition (years:months)[b]	GFTA-2 standardized sample ages[c]
Early developing sounds[a]		
/p/	3:0	2:0–3:0
/b/	3:0	2:0–3:0
/d/	3:0–3:6	2:0–3:0
/m/	3:0	2:0
/n/	3:0–3:6	2:0–3:0
/j/	4:0–5:0	5:0
/w/	3:0	3:0
/h/	3:0	2:0
Middle developing sounds[a]		
/t/	3:6–4:0	3:0
/k/	3:6	3:0
/g/	3:6–4:0	3:0
/f/	3:6–5:6	3:0–4:0
/v/	5:6	5:0–6:0
/tʃ/	6:0–7:0	5:0
/dʒ/	6:0–7:0	5:0
/ŋ/	2:0–6:0[d]	3:0–5:0
Late developing sounds[a]		
/θ/	6:0–8:0	7:0–8:0
/ð/	4:6–7:0	7:0
/s/	7:0–9:0	5:0
/z/	7:0–9:0	5:0–7:0
/ʃ/	6:0–7:0	5:0
/ʒ/	6:0–8:0[d]	n/a
/l/	5:0–7:0	5:0
/r/	8:0	5:0–6:0

[a]Order of acquisition: Shriberg (1993).
[b]Age of acquisition: Smit *et al.* (1990).
[c]Age at which 85% of Goldman–Fristoe Test of Articulation–2 standardization sample correctly produced the consonant and consonant cluster sounds (Goldman and Fristoe, 2000).
[d]Sander (1972).

want to know about a child's ability to produce individual sounds, or about the nature of errors in children's productions, or they may want to know about the breadth of the child's phonological system, including such things as the sounds and sound classes and the syllable and word patterns produced by the child (Stoel-Gammon, 2010b).

Quantitative analyses typically rely on a single outcome measure to quantify children's productions. These kinds of measures have been used to report the number of different consonants or syllable shapes used by children, regardless of the accuracy of the child's productions (Paul and Jennings, 1992; Rescorla and Ratner, 1996; Carson *et al.*, 2003). Some researchers have suggested that both elicited tasks and spontaneous speech tasks are needed to assess the phonological abilities of a child (Miccio, 2002; Tyler *et al.*, 2002). Elicited tasks ensure that all the phonemes of interest are sampled, and spontaneous speech tasks provide information on prosody and the relationships between speech production and language.

Spontaneous Speech

Methods of phonological assessment can be divided into those that are applied to children's spontaneous speech and those that elicit speech. Spontaneous speech samples are the most ecologically valid in that they provide the examiner with a picture of the child's typical performance, and they show how a child uses sounds in connected speech, which is often different from the way that words are produced in isolation. They represent the child's typical abilities rather than the optimal or maximal abilities.

One difficulty with using spontaneous speech samples as the basis for phonological assessment is that in naturalistic conditions there is considerably more variability than in elicited tasks. Children may say one word several times, and productions of the same word may vary within a session and across sessions. As a result, there are decisions to be made about how to score the multiple productions of the same target word. Children may avoid saying words that contain sounds they cannot produce, or may select words which they are able to produce most accurately. Some children may not speak much or at all, and some young children limit their speech to simply labeling their toys, or repeating a phrase, such as "Look, a ball … Look, a dog." This limits the variety of linguistic contexts in which a word is produced. Spontaneous sampling may also be problematic for analyzing the speech of young children with limited vocabularies or unintelligible speech.

One way to provide some structure in elicited tasks is to have a standard set of toys for children to play with (e.g., Williams and Elbert, 2003). The toys should contain items that contain a variety of different sounds and provide opportunities for mono- and multisyllabic productions. Spontaneous samples can be collected during any child–caregiver interaction, but toy play and book reading are particularly conducive to eliciting language in young children (see Rowe, Chapter 13 this volume).

One of the biggest threats to recorded child speech data is the interference of background noise, so it is critical to anticipate this problem and plan to prevent it to the degree possible during data collection. Unwanted noise can come from toys, people in the data collection session, or environmental noise, such the child's microphone rubbing against his or her clothing. To help decrease the noise created by toys, we use a soft surface for children to play on, such as a foam mat or a blanket. Many young children are difficult to understand, particularly from a video or audio recording. If the examiner feels that the child's productions are unclear or ambiguous, one strategy to aid in later analysis is to repeat the child's utterance. So, if a child points to a boat and says "da bo" for "That's a boat," the examiner would repeat after the child, "That's a boat."

Other concerns involve the validity of comparing child productions across separate samples. Morris (2009) found that the number of different words produced by ten 18–22-month-old children across two 20 minute sampling sessions was not correlated. The number of different words produced in a single session ranged from 44 to 219 for subjects in this study. Based on her results, Morris determined that a 20 minute conversational session was not necessarily sufficient to get enough different words to provide stable measures of word shape or number of consonants in a child's phonetic inventory. This points to the lack of information we have on measurement in phonology. Researchers have recommended sample sizes for spontaneous speech based on the number of utterances produced during a session (Robb and Bleile, 1994) and the length of session (Carson *et al.*, 2003; Rescorla and Ratner, 1996; Stoel-Gammon, 1987). To date, there are no studies that establish how long a single sampling session should be to obtain reliable data for individual children, nor is there clear guidance on how to handle data from multiple sampling sessions when the number and quality of children's productions vary from session to session. Since children's abilities can change quickly over time during the early stages of development, sessions should be scheduled at frequent intervals, such as weekly or monthly. Dense sampling may help reveal the developmental patterns in more detail (see Lieven and Behrens, Chapter 15 this volume).

Elicited Productions

When speech is elicited, it is often done so to provide a basis for standardized, norm-referenced assessments of articulation and phonology or to provide a basis for researchers to investigate a set of phonological or lexical constructs of interest.

Standardized Tests

Standardized tests of articulation generally measure production of individual speech sounds and provide norm-referenced data to determine how a child's sound production abilities relate to those of his peers in the form of a standard score. For a review of standardized tests of articulation and phonology, see Eisenberg and Hitchcock (2010). The elicitation method for real words is usually a picture-naming task that is designed to sample a variety of consonant sounds. The examiner shows the child a picture of a familiar object and asks the child to name it. If the child does not spontaneously produce the target, then the examiner may ask the child to repeat or imitate the examiner saying the target word. Standardized tests generally yield standard scores that are based on the number of target sounds a child produces in error. Thus, standardized tests do not generally yield information on which sounds a child produces correctly or incorrectly, but are designed to determine whether a child produces the same number of sounds accurately as other children his or her age. In order to tell whether an individual sound is acquired at the expected age, one could consult published normative data (e.g., Smit *et al.*, 1990; Sander, 1972), or consult the norms published in the manual of an articulation test. As a caveat, there is little consensus among the published norms on when sounds are acquired. Differences among studies exist due to the investigator's definition of "acquired" and the methodologies for eliciting productions across studies. Edwards and colleagues (Edwards and Beckman, 2008a) have found that accurate production of sounds develops gradually, so there may be a period in which a child is producing a sound, though less accurately than the adult form, and this period may continue for quite a long time. Age norms for production do not address this phenomenon.

Researcher-Generated Elicitation Tasks

In researcher-developed elicitation tasks, children may name objects or pictures of real words, or they may repeat words or nonword stimuli presented by the researcher. At times, researchers want to control the properties that influence sound production accuracy, such as neighborhood density, frequency of a sound or sound sequence (phonotactic probability), or phonetic complexity of a word. In other cases, researchers may be interested in production of a particular sound or a sound class. In these cases, researchers will want to create their own elicitation tasks. (For examples of researcher-generated tasks, see Munson, Edwards, and Beckman, 2005a; McLeod *et al.*, 1994; Preston and Edwards, 2007; Wolk, Edwards, and Conture, 1993; Yavas and Core, 2006). Real-word repetition has been used in studies of crosslinguistic consonant acquisition (Edwards and Beckman, 2008a), and as a predictor of grammatical development (Dispaldro *et al.*, 2009).

Nonword Repetition

Nonword repetition has become a widely used technique to study phonological short-term memory or phonological working memory (Gathercole and Baddeley, 1989; 1990) and to examine the lexical effects on phonological development (see Stoel-Gammon, 2010a). Phonological working memory skills are associated with word learning in young children (Gathercole and Baddeley, 1989) and adolescents (Gathercole *et al.*, 1997; 1999). Nonword repetition is a measure that seems to differentiate children with and without language impairment (Bishop, North, and Donlan, 1996; Dollaghan and Campbell, 1998; Gathercole and Baddeley, 1990). Nonword repetition measures have been used recently with children as young as 20 months (Hoff, Core, and Bridges, 2008), and also with bilingual children (Ebert *et al.*, 2008; Gutiérrez-Clellen and Simon-Cereijido, 2010; Girbau and Schwartz, 2008; Parra, Hoff, and Core, 2011). In nonword repetition tasks, the examiner produces (or plays a pre-recorded presentation of) a nonword and the child repeats the nonword. For older children, stimuli are recorded to ensure consistency of presentation (e.g., Girbau and Schwartz, 2008; Gathercole and Baddeley, 1989). For very young children (18 to 22 months old) we found that we needed to modify the way we presented stimuli, so we used a toy-naming game in which children were asked to repeat the name of a toy presented by the examiner. Additionally, in order to parse the general articulation abilities of the children from their ability to repeat nonword sound sequences, we administered a real-word repetition task and a phonologically matched nonword repetition task. We found that even controlling for accuracy of real-word repetition, children's nonword repetition abilities predicted their vocabulary size (Hoff, Core, and Bridges, 2008).

Equipment

The current state of digital media recording and storage has brought about a revolution in speech data collection. The state of the art for recording child speech is high quality digital video with high quality digital audio. The video allows the examiner to view the child's face and observe the greater context of the utterance. This enhances the ability to determine which of phonetically similar sounds a child says by watching the child's mouth. High quality digital audio allows the examiner to visually examine the sound wave or spectrogram of an utterance while listening to it, and this also helps improve accuracy of phonetic transcription.

There are three parts of the equipment system to consider in collection of speech data. The first is the microphone that picks up the speech signal from the child; the second is the device that takes the signal from the microphone and records it to a digital file (recorder); and the third is the set of equipment that allows a listener to assess the speech – typically headphones. Investigators should check the specifications for the equipment to make sure that all three parts of the system have the appropriate qualities to capture the physical properties of speech in a way that makes possible both perceptual judgments of speech accuracy and acoustic analysis of speech using speech analysis software. Equipment should be sufficient to transmit or receive an auditory signal ranging from about 50 Hz to 15,000 Hz in order to pick up all of the sound frequencies of speech.

A variety of microphones types are available. As long as a digital video camera has an external microphone jack, the examiner can use a separate microphone to ensure the quality of the audio recording. Boundary microphones, which rest on a flat surface and pick up sound signals from multiple directions, are useful when a child is stationary and the examiner wants to hear the adult and child speech. Wireless microphones worn by the child allow the child freedom of movement, while maintaining a constant distance between the child's mouth and the microphone, improving the quality of the speech signal in the recording.

Data collection procedures should always begin with a check of the sound system. This can be done with an audio output connected to the video recorder. Using headphones or an earbud, the examiner is able to listen to the sound as it is being recorded. This prevents mishaps from battery failure or poor connections. Some researchers choose to collect a separate audio back-up using a digital audio recorder with a good quality external microphone to ensure audio quality.

Data Analysis: Transcription

Once the speech samples have been recorded, they must be phonetically transcribed. The transcriber writes a gloss for the target word, which is the target word as produced by an adult speaker in regular orthography, and typically also in IPA. Then the child's production is transcribed using either broad or narrow transcription. Broad transcription is phonemic and does not include information about fine phonetic details such as aspiration or degree of voicing. Use of additional diacritics can increase the level of detail in the transcription, but more detailed transcriptions usually make it more difficult to achieve good intertranscriber agreement. Broad transcription is generally used to represent a child's phonemic ability, while narrow transcription includes phonetic detail and represents the phonetic accuracy of a child's sound production.

There are several limitations to consider with phonetic transcription, the first being that it is extraordinarily time consuming and requires trained listeners who are knowledgeable about speech science (the properties of individual sounds) and the phonological and phonetic characteristics of the sounds of the language they are transcribing. Phonetic transcriptions are influenced by a transcriber's experience with child speech, experience with phonetic transcription, and knowledge of phonetics and the sounds of the language they are transcribing, and by the transcriber's native language (Edwards and Beckman, 2008b). In studies making crosslinguistic comparisons or studies of bilingual children, it is important to have a native speaker of each language provide the transcriptions in order to prevent the perceptual biases of a nonnative listener (Munson *et al.*, 2010).

Because phonetic transcription relies on the subjective judgments of individual transcribers, researchers usually report on transcription agreement or reliability. Reliability is expressed as a percentage of agreement between the transcriptions produced by two transcribers. This method of validating the transcriptions used in analysis is problematic because interrater agreement can be related to many factors, including the type of speech being transcribed and the training of the transcribers. The degree of transcriber agreement contributes to the power of a study. In a study in which there is low agreement between transcribers, the validity of all analyses based on the transcription is called into question. Transcribers may agree on a majority of sounds a child produces and use the same IPA symbol to transcribe the sounds. But for intermediate productions and distorted sounds, the transcribers are more likely to disagree. It is precisely these points of disagreement that may provide the most information about a child's abilities; so without transcriber agreement on these less accurate productions, a considerable amount of information about the child's abilities is lost (Pye, Wilcox, and Siren, 1988).

Another method of establishing the validity of a phonetic transcription is to use a consensus method, such as the ones described by Morris (2009) or Shriberg, Kwiatkowski and Hoffman (1984). In this method of validation, transcribers work independently to transcribe data, then transcriptions are compared, and discrepancies are listened to again by a third party until transcribers reach agreement on all sounds produced by the child. In cases where two transcribers disagree on a production, a third party listens to the data and contributes his or her perception to the discussion until consensus among transcribers is obtained. Phon, a phonological analysis program within CHILDES (see Corrigan, Chapter 18 this volume), contains a blind transcription mode and allows two independent transcribers to listen to a production and phonetically transcribe what they hear. Once both transcriptions are prepared, a validation mode allows transcribers to see any discrepancies between the transcribers, and to access the sound files for those productions to referee or validate the production. The validated transcription is the one used in final analyses. In this type of transcription validation, productions for which consensus is not possible can be eliminated from the analysis, providing for greater reliability of the phonological data.

Phonetic transcription may be supported by acoustic analysis to determine finer details of sound production, such as voicing or aspiration of a consonant. While acoustic analysis may support and aid transcription in many cases, many phonetic properties, such as voice onset time, are subject to influence from speaker variables, such as speech rate and stress patterns of the word or phrase, and acoustic analysis cannot be used to resolve all ambiguities in phonetic transcription (Rose, in press).

Analyses

There are two primary types of phonological analysis for spontaneous speech. The first is an *independent analysis*, which is typically used to report on the speech production abilities of very young children at the early stages of language development, from the onset of speech to about 24 months. The second is a *relational analysis*, which reflects how closely a child's production matches a target, and is used for children who are in later stages of phonological development, producing a variety of word shapes and sound combinations.

Independent Analyses

A *phonetic inventory* is the primary form of independent analysis. This measure is purely descriptive and reflects the sounds the child produces, usually organized by word position. The examiner listens to spontaneous speech produced by the child (usually during a toy play activity with a parent) and tallies the sounds the child produces in word-initial, -medial, and -final position. There is no decision on the part of the examiner as to whether the child's production is "correct" or accurate.

It is simply a report of the sounds heard. Typically, a sound must occur in two different words in order to be considered a part of the child's phonetic inventory. Phonetic inventories are typically reported in the number of phones a child produces (Dyson, 1988; Stoel-Gammon, 1985; Roberts *et al.*, 1998; Rescorla and Ratner, 1996). The number may be organized by word position (initial, medial, or final), or it may simply be a table containing all of the sounds a child uses by word position. Phonetic inventories generally report on consonants produced, but other inventories are possible as independent analyses as well – e.g., vowel inventories (the vowels produced by a child) or word shape inventories (the variety of phonotactic syllable and word shapes produced by a child). See Velleman (1998) for examples of inventory worksheets to aid in organization of the data.

Relational Analyses

A relational analysis relates a child's production to an intended target, usually an acceptable adult form of a word, and the goal is to measure accuracy and examine error patterns. Outcome measures can focus on individual sounds, such as percentage consonants correct (including consonant variants), percentage vowels correct, and percentage phonemes correct. They can also focus on word shape accuracy, like word shape match, or even whether whole words match the possible and accepted adult forms in measures like proximity of whole word production or percentage words correct. Investigators may also wish to report on a child's use of specific phonological patterns or phonological processes, particularly for clinical use, such as fronting or stopping. These are measured in percentage occurrence with respect to the opportunity for a process to occur (e.g., Williams and Elbert, 2003).

One problem researchers face in elicited tasks is whether utterances produced spontaneously or in imitation of an adult model should be analyzed as the same type of response. Researchers who have investigated differences between spontaneous and imitated productions found that children perform similarly under the two conditions and that the conditions are highly related and reflect roughly the same abilities in children, though for some children the imitated condition is more accurate than the spontaneous condition, and vice versa (Goldstein, Fabiano, and Iglesias, 2004; Wertzner *et al.*, 2006). There is little research addressing this question, so some researchers have chosen to use exclusively repetition tasks to avoid the possibility of having spontaneous and repeated productions, which may be produced differently by children (Edwards and Beckman, 2008b).

In imitation tasks, particularly in nonword repetition tasks that may be prone to more variability in production by adult speakers, a standard format for presentation may be helpful to make sure all children hear the same stimuli produced in the same way. Gathercole and Baddeley (1989) used pre-recorded stimuli presented at 3 second intervals in their study of nonword repetition. In our experience, younger children do not respond well to pre-recorded stimuli. In response to difficulty getting our data collection team to pronounce the nonword stimuli the same way each time, we tried to use a furry dog with a speaker in its hindquarter, and that made the children cry (see Ambridge, Chapter 8 this volume, for a similar experience). Instead, we had the examiner present the stimuli live, but in that case errors and inconsistency in presentation are inevitable, and thus both the examiner's presentation and the child's repetition need to be considered in the accuracy measure. In an imitation task, the child's production should be scored relative to the adult model that was presented. In our data, we found some dialectal variability in the children's productions, so when a child presented an acceptable variation of a consonant according to his/her dialect, it was scored as being correct. A good example of this was production of the palatal glide (the sound corresponding to the "ll") in "caballo" in Spanish. If a child produced the glide as a fricative because that is the sound that is standard in his dialect, we accepted it as a correct sound production.

Commonly used accuracy measures for individual sounds include percentage consonants correct, percentage vowels correct, and percentage phonemes correct. Percentage consonants correct (PCC) is widely used and has several variants (Shriberg and Kwiatkowski, 1982; Shriberg *et al.*, 1997). The basic metric is calculated by awarding a point value for each consonant a child produces correctly relative to the adult target, divided by the total number of consonants in a word.

A few researchers have proposed whole word measures to measure accuracy. The most widely reported whole word measure is Ingram's phonological mean length of utterance (PMLU), and the relational measure is proportion of whole word proximity (Ingram and Ingram, 2001; Ingram, 2002). PMLU is calculated as an independent measure of a child's word-level accuracy. Each word produced by the child receives a point value based on the number of sounds produced by the child and the number of consonants in the word produced accurately with reference to the adult target form. This measure is used to track the growth in a child's phonological ability over time, but there is little information available on the psychometric properties of this measure. The proportion of whole word proximity (PWP) is a ratio of the child's PMLU divided by the PMLU of the adult form of the target word.

Stoel-Gammon (2010b) reported on a word complexity measure and a proportional word complexity measure. Each word in a sample is awarded a complexity "score" based on word patterns, syllable structures, and sound classes. Complexity as a concept in phonological development is not well agreed upon, though in this case it relates to patterns of early productions by young children and normative data on sound acquisition. In general, developmental patterns observed in children with early-acquired sounds and patterns are described as less complex, and those with later-acquired sounds and patterns are described as more complex. The word complexity measure can be used as an independent analysis considering only the child's productions, or as a relational analysis by calculating a ratio of the complexity of a child's utterances to the corresponding adult forms of the same target words. Stoel-Gammon's measure is similar to the index of phonetic complexity, developed by Jakielski, Maytasse, and Doyle (2006) and described in Morris (2009).

For elicited tasks, one problem that arises is that a child might not produce a target word, even when prompted by the examiner, or in repetition. In order for an elicited task, such as a standardized test, to be scored the same way for all children, each child must produce all of the test items. Missing data in a closed dataset result in a dilemma for scoring. In the case of our real-word and nonword imitation tasks, we have scored nonresponses as 0, and this has been problematic because inaccurate responses may also be scored as 0 in some cases, yet nonresponsiveness is very different from poor accuracy in response. We have calculated PCC of items produced versus PCC of all items administered, including nonresponses. In analyses from our large database, the two measures were highly correlated, and the difference in mean values did not affect our analyses. But this is a good example of a case in which a weighted measure or a more complex accuracy measure, such as one of the complexity measures mentioned earlier, might be more robust, particularly for individual children or smaller groups of children.

Automated Analysis Programs

There are a few software programs that provide automated or semi-automated analysis of phonetically transcribed speech. The Logical International Phonetics Program (LIPP), developed by Kim Oller and colleagues, is a commercial software program for phonological analysis. It runs on Windows operating systems, and data are stored in a proprietary format. LIPP allows for a weighted accuracy measure, developed by Oller and colleagues (Oller and Ramsdell, 2006), as well as PCC.

Phon is an open-serve program designed for phonological research (Rose *et al.*, 2006). It is part of the CHILDES system and supports multimedia, and it allows for automated searches of large databases of phonological data. Phon has some unique attributes, such as the ability to link multimedia video and audio files directly to transcriptions. Phon's search feature allows users to design their own complex phonological queries based on sounds or features and to consider syllable or word position and stress patterns in data analysis. It allows users to track a child's productions over time for longitudinal studies, and it allows for group comparisons for cross-sectional studies, e.g., by age groups or populations. Data may be exported (as Unicode IPA symbols) in a spreadsheet and analyzed separately for accuracy.

Related Constructs

There are some psycholinguistic measures related to phonology which are also worth mentioning, given the frequency with which they are described in the literature on reading development and language disabilities. *Phonological processing, phonological awareness, phonological sensitivity*, and *phonological memory* are terms that refer to the psychological processing of speech sounds rather than to the production or direct knowledge of speech sounds. These measures of phonological knowledge are highly associated with literacy outcomes in young school-age children.

Phonological processing refers to a trio of skills that are related to literacy development. The three skills are phonological awareness, phonological memory, and rapid automatic naming. *Phonological awareness* refers to a set of metacognitive skills involving the manipulation of sounds and sound sequences in words. The term may refer to a number of different skills that address larger or smaller units of phonology, such as the word or the syllable, or individual phonemes. Most typically, phonological awareness refers to tasks that tap awareness of syllables, subsyllabic units (onsets and rimes), and individual phonemes. Syllable-level tasks are generally reported to be easier than onset/rime- or phoneme-level tasks, and phoneme-level tasks are the most difficult. Phoneme awareness refers to the ability to manipulate individual phonemes within a word and is usually measured by having a child delete word-initial or word-final phonemes from a word and say the remaining part of the word, or by identifying or naming sounds at the beginnings and ends of words. As with other measures of phonological knowledge, task type influences performance. For example, identifying matching rhymes is easier than producing or generating rhymes. The word position of a sound and the features of speech sounds can also affect performance. For example, it is easier to identify sounds in word-initial position than in word-final position (de Graaff *et al.*, 2008), and it is easier to delete a final obstruent than sonorant (Yavas and Core, 2006). There are several standardized measures of phonological awareness and phoneme awareness available.

Phonological sensitivity is a term proposed by Stanovich (1992) to encompass the set of related skills that are associated with phonological awareness at different levels of difficulty. In the reading research literature, phonological awareness is often referred to as phonological sensitivity, particularly when different phonological awareness tasks are used as a composite measure.

Phonological memory is also called verbal working memory, and it is generally assessed through nonword repetition. It has been proposed as the memory for speech sounds, though nonword repetition measures tap into other constructs as well, such as speech perception and the motoric aspects of speech planning and production. The most widely used nonword sets are from the CNRep (Gathercole and Baddeley, 1996), NRT (Dollaghan and Campbell, 1998), and Munson, Edwards, and Beckman (2005b). For a review of nonword repetition tasks, see Archibald and Gathercole (2006). There are also recently published nonword repetition tasks for Spanish (see Gutiérrez-Clellen and Simon-Cereijido, 2010; Girbau and Schwartz, 2008; Ebert *et al.*, 2008; Summers *et al.*, 2010).

Conclusion

This chapter reviewed assessment of phonology in young children and described ways that phonology is studied in language development. Phonology and phonology-based constructs such as frequency of sounds and sound combinations affect word learning, and the phonological properties of words may influence which words children say and how accurately they are able to produce them, and may influence which words children attempt to produce. Phonological information may be gathered through spontaneous language samples or elicited tasks, such as a standardized test of articulation. Both independent (qualitative) and relational (quantitative) measures can be used to analyze phonological data. Nonword repetition tasks are useful for investigating the lexical/phonological interface and phonological memory abilities in young children. There are several factors that can affect reliability of phonological (child speech) data, including elicitation methods, recording quality, and reliability of phonetic transcription. Recently, automated methods for data organization and analysis have become available, and these tools should enhance the productivity of research in phonological development and the role of phonology in language development.

Key Terms

Neighborhood density   The number of words that differ from a target word by a single phoneme.

Phoneme   The smallest unit of sound of a language that can be used to contrast meaning in that language.

Phonetics   The study of the production and perception of speech sounds, including acoustic and physiological descriptions of sounds.

Phonological awareness   The ability to identify and manipulate the sounds of a language in auditory tasks.

Phonological memory   Short-term working memory for speech sounds.

Phonological processing   A set of skills related to phonological coding, including phonological awareness, phonological memory, and rapid automatic naming.

Phonological sensitivity   Ability to analyze speech sounds at a variety of levels, including phonological and phonemic awareness skills.

Phonology   The study of sounds and sound patterns of a language, including the way sounds are put together to form words and change meaning. Phonology can include the study of syllables, stress patterns, prosody, and intonation.

Phonotactic probability   A measure of the likelihood of the occurrence of a sound sequence in a language.

Phonotactics   The possible sequences of sounds and syllable structures in the words of a language.

References

Archibald, L.M.D., and Gathercole, S.E. (2006) Nonword repetition: a comparison of tests. *Journal of Speech, Language, and Hearing Research*, 49, 970–983.

Bishop, D.V.M., North, T., and Donlan, C. (1996) Nonword repetition as a behavioural marker for inherited language impairment: evidence from a twin study. *Journal of Child Psychology & Psychiatry & Allied Disciplines*, 37, 391–403.

Carson, C.P., Klee, T., Carson, D.K., and Hime, L.K. (2003) Phonological profiles of 2-year-olds with delayed language development: predicting clinical outcomes at age 3. *American Journal of Speech–Language Pathology*, 12, 28–39.

De Graaff, S., Hasselman, F., Bosman, A., and Verhoeven, L. (2008) Cognitive and linguistic constraints on phoneme isolation in Dutch kindergartners. *Learning and Instruction*, 18 (4), 391–403.

Dispaldro, M., Benelli, B., Marcolini, S., and Stella, G. (2009) Real-word repetition as a predictor of grammatical competence in Italian children with typical language development. *International Journal of Language & Communication Disorders*, 44, 941–961.

Dollaghan, C., and Campbell, T.F. (1998) Nonword repetition and child language impairment. *Journal of Speech, Language, and Hearing Research*, 41, 1136–1146.

Dyson, A.T. (1988) Phonetic inventories of 2- and 3-year-old children. *Journal of Speech and Hearing Disorders*, 53, 89–93.

Ebert, K.D., Kalanek, J., Cordero, K.N., and Kohnert, K. (2008) *Communication Disorders Quarterly*, 29, 67–74.

Edwards, J., and Beckman, M.E. (2008a) Some cross-linguistic evidence for modulation of implicational universals by language-specific frequency effects in the acquisition of consonant phonemes. *Language Learning & Development*, 4 (2), 122–156.

Edwards, J., and Beckman, M.E. (2008b) Methodological questions in studying consonant acquisition. *Clinical Linguistics & Phonetics*, 22, 937–956.

Edwards, J., Beckman, M.E., and Munson, B. (2004) The interaction between vocabulary size and phonotactic probability effects on children's production accuracy and fluency in non-word repetition. *Journal of Speech, Language, and Hearing Research*, 47, 421–436.

Edwards, J., Munson, B., and Beckman, M.E. (2010) Lexicon–phonology relationships and the dynamics of early language development. *Journal of Child Language*, 38 (1), 35–40.

Eisenberg, S.L., and Hitchcock, E.R. (2010) Using standardized tests to inventory consonant and vowel production: a comparison of 11 tests of articulation and phonology. *Language, Speech, and Hearing Services in Schools*, 41, 488–503.

Elbers, L., and Ton, J. (1985) Play pen monologues: the interplay of words and babbles in the first words period. *Journal of Child Language*, 12, 551–565.

Fikkert, P. (1994) *On the acquisition of prosodic structure*. The Hague: Holland Academic Graphics.

Gathercole, S.E., and Baddeley, A.D. (1989) Evaluation of the role of phonological STM in the development of vocabulary in children: a longitudinal study. *Journal of Memory and Language*, 28, 200–213.

Gathercole, S.E., and Baddeley, A.D. (1990) Phonological memory deficits in language disordered children: is there a causal connection? *Journal of Memory and Language*, 29, 336–360.

Gathercole, S.E., and Baddeley, A.D. (1996) *The Children's Test of Nonword Repetition*. London: The Psychological Corporation.

Gathercole, S.E., Hitch, G.J., Service, E., and Martin, A.J. (1997) Phonological short-term memory and new word learning in children. *Developmental Psychology*, 33, 966–979.

Gathercole, S.E., Service, E., Hitch, G.J., *et al.* (1999) Phonological short-term memory and vocabulary development: further evidence on the nature of the relationship. *Applied Cognitive Psychology*, 13, 65–77.

Girbau, D., and Schwartz, R.G. (2008) Phonological working memory in Spanish–English bilingual children with and without specific language impairment. *Journal of Communication Disorders*, 41, 124–145.

Gnanadesikan, A. (2004) Markedness and faithfulness constraints in child phonology. In R. Kager, J. Pater, and W. Zonneveld (eds), *Constraints in phonological acquisition* (pp. 73–108). Cambridge: Cambridge University Press.

Goad, H., and Rose, Y. (2004) Input elaboration, head faithfulness and evidence for representation in the acquisition of left-edge clusters in West Germanic. In R. Kager, J. Pater, and W. Zonneveld (eds), *Constraints in phonological acquisition* (pp. 109–157). Cambridge: Cambridge University Press.

Goldman, R., and Fristoe, M. (2000) *Goldman–Fristoe Test of Articulation–Second Edition*. Circle Pines, MN: American Guidance Service.

Goldstein, B., Fabiano, L., and Iglesias, A. (2004) Spontaneous and imitated productions in Spanish-speaking children with phonological disorders. *Language, Speech, and Hearing Services in Schools*, 35, 5–15.

Gutiérrez-Clellen, V., and Simon-Cereijido, G. (2010) Using nonword repetition tasks for the identification of language impairment in Spanish–English-speaking children: does the language of assessment matter? *Learning Disabilities Research and Practice*, 25, 48–58.

Hoff, E., Core, C., and Bridges, K. (2008) Nonword repetition assesses phonological memory and is related to vocabulary development in 20- to 24- month-olds. *Journal of Child Language*, 35, 1–14.

Ingram, D. (2002) The measurement of whole-word productions. *Journal of Child Language*, 29, 713–733.

Ingram, D., and Ingram, K. (2001) A whole word approach to phonological analysis and intervention. *Language, Speech, and Hearing Services in Schools*, 32, 271–283.

Inkelas, S., and Rose, Y. (2008) Positional neutralization: a case study from child language. *Language*, 83, 707–736.

Jakielski, K., Maytasse, R., and Doyle, E. (2006) Acquisition of phonetic complexity in children 12–36 months of age. Poster presented at the convention of the American Speech–Language–Hearing Association, Miami.

Jusczyk, P.W., Luce, P.A., and Charles-Luce, J. (1994) Infants' sensitivity to phonotactic patterns in the native language. *Journal of Memory and Language*, 33 (5), 630–645.

Kent, R.D. (1982) Contextual facilitation of correct sound production. *Language, Speech, and Hearing Services in Schools*, 13, 66–76.

Kirk, C., and Demuth, K. (2006) Accounting for variability in 2-year-olds' production of coda consonants. *Language Learning and Development*, 2, 97–118.

Luce, P.A., and Pisoni, D.B. (1998) Recognizing spoken words: the neighborhood activation model. *Ear and Hearing*, 19, 1–36.

McLeod, S., Hand, L., Rosenthal, J.B., and Hayes, B. (1994) The effect of sampling condition on children's productions of consonant clusters. *Journal of Speech and Hearing Research*, 37, 868–882.

Miccio, A.W. (2002) Clinical problem solving: assessment of phonological disorders. *American Journal of Speech–Language Pathology*, 11, 221–229.

Morris, S.R. (2009) Test–retest reliability of independent measures of phonology in the assessment of toddlers' speech. *Language, Speech & Hearing Services in Schools*, 40, 46–52.

Munson, B., Edwards, J., and Beckman, M.E. (2005a) Phonological knowledge in typical and atypical speech–sound development. *Topics in Language Disorders*, 25, 190–206.

Munson, B., Edwards, J., and Beckman, M.E. (2005b) Relationships between nonword repetition accuracy and other measures of linguistic development in children with phonological disorders. *Journal of Speech, Language & Hearing Research*, 48, 61–78.

Munson, B., Edwards, J., Schellinger, S., *et al.* (2010) Deconstructing phonetic transcription: language specificity, covert contrast, perceptual bias, and an extraterrestrial view of vox humana. *Clinical Linguistics and Phonetics*, 24: 245–260.

Oller, D.K., and Ramsdell, H.L. (2006) A weighted reliability measure for phonetic transcription. *Journal of Speech, Language & Hearing Research*, 49, 1391–1411.

Parra, M., Hoff, E., and Core, C. (2011) Relations among language exposure, phonological memory, and language development in Spanish–English bilingually developing 2-year-olds. *Journal of Experimental Child Psychology*, 108, 113–125.

Pater, J. (1997) Minimal violation in phonological development. *Language Acquisition*, 6, 201–253.

Paul, R., and Jennings, P. (1992) Phonological behavior in toddlers with slow expressive language development. *Journal of Speech & Hearing Research*, 35, 99–107.

Pierrehumbert, J. (2003) Phonetic diversity, statistical learning, and acquisition of phonology. *Language and Speech*, 46, 115–154.

Preston, J.L., and Edwards, M.L. (2007) Phonological processing skills of adolescents with residual speech sound errors. *Language, Speech & Hearing Services in Schools*, 38, 297–308.

Pye, C., Ingram, D., and List, H. (1987) A comparison of initial consonant acquisition in English and Quiche. In K.E. Nelson and A. van Kleeck (eds), *Children's language* (pp. 175–190). Hillsdale, NJ: Erlbaum.

Pye, C., Wilcox, K.A., and Siren, K.A. (1988) Refining transcriptions: the significance of transcriber "errors." *Journal of Child Language*, 15, 17–37.

Rescorla, L., and Ratner, N.B. (1996) Phonetic profiles of toddlers with specific expressive language impairment (SLI-E). *Journal of Speech & Hearing Research*, 39, 153–165.

Robb, M., and Bleile, K. (1994) Consonant inventories of young children from 8 to 25 months. *Clinical Linguistics and Phonetics*, 8, 295–320.

Roberts, J., Rescorla, L., Giroux, J., and Stevens, L. (1998) Phonological skills of children with specific expressive language impairment (SLI-E): outcome at age 3. *Journal of Speech, Language & Hearing Research*, 41, 374–384.

Rose, Y. (in press) Corpus-based investigations of child phonological development: formal and practical considerations. In Jacques Durand, Ulrike Gut, and Gjert Kristoffersen (eds), *Handbook of Corpus Phonology*. Oxford: Oxford University Press.

Rose, Y., MacWhinney, B., Byrne, R., *et al.* (2006) Introducing Phon: a software solution for the study of phonological acquisition. In *Proceedings of the 30th Annual Boston University Conference on Language Development* (pp. 489–500).

Saffran, J.R., Aslin, R.N., and Newport, E.L. (1996) Statistical learning by 8-month-old infants. *Science*, 274, 1926–1928.

Sander, E. (1972) When are speech sounds learned? *Journal of Speech and Hearing Research*, 37, 55–63.

Schwartz, R.G., and Leonard, L.B. (1982) Do children pick and choose? An examination of phonological selection and avoidance in early lexical acquisition. *Journal of Child Language*, 9, 319–336.

Shriberg, L.D. (1993) Four new speech and prosody-voice measures for genetics research and other studies in developmental phonological disorders. *Journal of Speech and Hearing Research*, 36, 105–140.

Shriberg, L.D., Austin, D., Lewis, B.A., *et al.* (1997) The percentage of consonants correct (PCC) metric: extensions and reliability data. *Journal of Speech, Language, and Hearing Research*, 40, 708–722.

Shriberg, L.D., and Kwiatkowski, J. (1982) Phonological disorders III: a procedure for assessing severity of involvement. *The Journal of Speech and Hearing Disorders*, 47, 256–270.

Shriberg, L.D., Kwiatkowski, J., and Hoffmann, K. (1984) A procedure for phonetic transcription by consensus. *Journal of Speech and Hearing Research*, 27, 456–465.

Smit, A.B., Hand, L., Freilinger, J.J., *et al.* (1990) The Iowa articulation norms project and its Nebraska replication. *Journal of Speech and Hearing Disorders*, 55, 779–798.

Spencer, A. (1986) Towards a theory of phonological development. *Lingua*, 68, 3–38.

Stanovich, K.E. (1992) Speculations on the causes and consequences of individual differences in early reading acquisition. In P.B. Gough, L.C. Ehri, and R. Treiman (eds), *Reading acquisition* (pp. 307–342). Hillsdale, NJ: Erlbaum.

Stoel-Gammon, C. (1985) Phonetic inventories, 15–24 months: a longitudinal study. *Journal of Speech and Hearing Research*, 28, 505–512.

Stoel-Gammon, C. (1987) Phonological skills of 2-year-olds. *Language, Speech, and Hearing Services in Schools*, 18, 323–329.

Stoel-Gammon, C. (2010a) Relationships between lexical and phonological development in young children. *Journal of Child Language*. Available on CJO 18 October 2010. DOI:10.1017/S0305000910000425.

Stoel-Gammon, C. (2010b) The word complexity measure: description and application to developmental phonology and disorders. *Clinical Linguistics & Phonetics*, 24 (4–5), 271–282.

Stoel-Gammon, C., and Sosa, A.V. (2007) Phonological development. In E. Hoff and M. Schatz (eds), *Handbook of child language* (pp. 238–256). Oxford: Blackwell.

Summers, C., Bohman, T.M., Gillam, R.B., *et al.* (2010) Bilingual performance on nonword repetition in Spanish and English. *International Journal of Language and Communication Disorders*, 45, 480–493.

Tyler, A.A., Tolbert, L.C., Miccio, A.W., *et al.* (2002) Five views of the elephant: perspectives on the assessment of articulation and phonology in preschoolers. *American Journal of Speech–Language Pathology*, 11, 213.

Velleman, S. (1998) *Making phonology functional: what do I do first?* Boston: Butterworth-Heinemann.

Vihman, M.M., Macken, M.A., Miller, R., *et al.* (1985) From babbling to speech: a reassessment of the continuity issue. *Language and Speech*, 61, 395–443.

Wertzner, H.F., Papp, A.C., Camargo S., and Galea, D.E. (2006) Provas de nomeação e imitação como instrumentos de diagnóstico do transtorno fonológico. *Pró-Fono Revista De Atualização Científica*, 18, 303–312.

Williams, A.L., and Elbert, M. (2003) A prospective longitudinal study of phonological development in late talkers. *Language, Speech & Hearing Services in Schools*, 34, 138–153.

Wolk, L., Edwards, M.L., and Conture, E.G. (1993) Coexistence of stuttering and disordered phonology in young children. *Journal of Speech & Hearing Research*, 36, 906–917.

Yavas, M., and Core, C. (2006) Acquisition of #sC clusters in English speaking children. *Journal of Multilingual Communication Disorders*, 4, 169–181.

Zamuner, T., Gerken, L., and Hammond, M. (2004) Phonotactic probabilities in young children's speech production. *Journal of Child Language*, 31, 515–536.

Recommended Reading

Phonology

Johnson, W., and Reimers, P. (2010) *Patterns in child phonology*. Edinburgh: Edinburgh University Press.

Smith, N. (2010) *Acquiring phonology: a cross-generational case-study*. Cambridge: Cambridge University Press.

Vihman, M.M. (1996) *Phonological development: the origins of language in the child*. Chichester: Wiley-Blackwell.

Vitevitch, M.S., and Luce, P.A. (2004) A web-based interface to calculate phonotactic probability for words and nonwords in English. *Behavior Research Methods, Instruments, and Computers*, 36, 481–487.

Yavas, M. (2011) *Applied English phonology*. Chichester: Wiley-Blackwell.

Phonetics

Ladefoged, P., and Johnson, K. (2010) *A course in phonetics*. Cengage-Heinle.

Small, L. (2004) *Fundamentals of phonetics: a practical guide for students*. Allyn & Bacon.

Additional Resources

Phonotactic probability calculator: http://www.people.ku.edu/~mvitevit/PhonoProbHome.
   html.

Neighborhood density calculator (and phonotactic probability calculator): http://www.
   bncdnet.ku.edu/cgi-bin/DEEC/out_ccc.vi.

Logical International Phonetics Program: http://www.ihsys.com/site/LIPP.asp?tab=4.

The PhonBank Project and Phon: http://childes.psy.cmu.edu/phon/.

Praat Acoustic Analysis Software: http://www.fon.hum.uva.nl/praat/.

IPA fonts: Charis SIL font package, http://scripts.sil.org/cms/scripts/page.php?item_id=
   CharisSILfont.

7 Assessing Vocabulary Skills

Barbara Alexander Pan

Summary

This chapter begins by discussing why researchers, clinicians, or teachers might be interested in assessing children's vocabulary and considers the basic questions of what to measure and when. After briefly considering examples of commercially available standardized tests, the remainder of the chapter examines three other approaches to assessing children's vocabulary skills: parent report, analysis of spontaneous speech samples, and researcher-designed assessment. For each, we consider examples of the types of research questions the approach might be used to address, the ages and populations for which it is appropriate, as well as its relative advantages and limitations, both methodological and logistical. Studies from the research literature illustrating each approach are presented.

Why Study Vocabulary?

One of the milestones of early development is children's production of their first words. Indeed, the Latin origin of the word "infant" means "incapable of speech." Thus, the onset of intelligible speech marks the end of infancy and the emerging potential for more complex communication than is possible through typical nonverbal means. Although first words are initially often inconsistently produced and constitute only rough approximations of the adult form, they are typically accorded generous attention and interpretation by parents and other caregivers.

Vocabulary knowledge is also of keen interest to researchers. Words constitute the building blocks for language production and serve to index children's cognitive skills

Research Methods in Child Language: A Practical Guide, First Edition.
Edited by Erika Hoff.
© 2012 Blackwell Publishing Ltd. Published 2012 by Blackwell Publishing Ltd.

and understanding of the world. Vocabulary knowledge represents the nexus between children's language and cognitive development, and thus informs our theories of how children see and conceive the world. It is no surprise, then, that researchers in cognition and language alike look to vocabulary understanding and production as key developmental indices.

Assessing children's vocabulary development is also of interest to educational researchers who want to understand variability across children in rate of language development and how such variability relates to later academic achievement. Of the several domains of language, vocabulary is arguably the most sensitive to input and children's experiences (Hoff, 2005). Children learn words and meanings for concepts and referents to which they are exposed and which are of interest to them. In the absence of exposure, there is no vocabulary learning. Thus, to the extent that children's experiences and exposure to language in the world differ, their vocabulary can also be expected to vary. In contrast, variability in rate of phonological or syntactic development among typically developing children is relatively small. Perhaps in part because of the greater range of variability in vocabulary size and growth, associations between vocabulary size, reading comprehension, and academic achievement are robust and have been well documented in the literature (Snow, Burns, and Griffin, 1998). The assessment of vocabulary skills, then, is a mainstay of educational intervention and other applied developmental research, as well as basic developmental psycholinguistics.

What To Measure and When

One of the first questions that researchers must consider in assessing vocabulary is whether to measure receptive vocabulary, expressive (productive) vocabulary, or both. This decision is influenced not only by the tools available, but also by the age of the child, two factors that are themselves closely related. Of necessity, assessment before the age of 12–14 months is generally only undertaken for receptive vocabulary, for the obvious reason that most children are just beginning to produce their first words (Fenson *et al.*, 1994). Methodological advances such as the preferential looking paradigm (see Piotroski and Naigles, Chapter 2 this volume) have made it possible to assess very young children's understanding/learning of specific words in laboratory settings, but such methods are usually not practical for assessing the size or composition of children's overall vocabulary, particularly for large samples of children.

In toddlerhood (between ages 1 and 3 years), measuring children's productive vocabulary becomes more feasible and more meaningful, as differences in vocabulary size and growth rate across children begin to emerge. At the same time, however, the challenges of direct assessment of very young children remain a methodological consideration. Children's familiarity with the assessor, their behavioral states, and their interpretation of the task can all compromise the feasibility and validity of direct assessment, thus warranting researchers' consideration of some of the alternative approaches to be described below. As children enter the preschool years (after about 3 years of age), the range of available assessment tools and approaches changes yet again, with some earlier tools (e.g., parental report) losing their value, and others, such as direct assessment, becoming more useful and reliable.

In addition to child age, other considerations arise that influence the choice of assessment focus (expressive or productive vocabulary) and approach. For example, researchers who value ecological validity, and who are interested in children's actual *use* of vocabulary and how it varies by context, may prefer observation-based data collection and analysis (also to be considered below). Researchers of the social interactionist persuasion see children as active agents in influencing the input they receive, experience that in turn feeds children's further vocabulary acquisition. For those holding this theoretical view, it is important to document and measure the words children produce in interaction with others in various real-world (or simulated real-world) contexts.

For children exposed to more than one language, assessment becomes much more complex. Ideally, children's vocabulary in each language should be assessed in parallel fashion, so that total vocabulary knowledge is neither over- nor underestimated (Mancilla-Martinez, Pan, and Vagh, in press). Unfortunately, in practice, thorough assessment is often not possible, due primarily to the lack of appropriate measurement tools (see Hoff and Rumiche, Chapter 20 this volume). In the US, this lack is particularly acute for children acquiring English and a language other than Spanish.

A final consideration has to do with the researcher's interest in tracking or modeling vocabulary development over time. As is the case for other domains of child development, discontinuity in assessment tools over the infancy to preschool period is driven largely by the enormous qualitative changes in children's skills during this developmental period. The result is that repeated assessment over time using the same tool is often impossible, posing challenges for individual growth modeling and similar analytic approaches.

The remainder of this chapter describes an array of vocabulary assessment approaches, beginning with examples of standardized tests, but then moving on to describe in more detail methods that may be less familiar to the reader. For each, we will consider the age range over which it is applicable, its applicability to children acquiring more than one language, and the extent to which it lends itself to repeated use over time, as well as logistical considerations and constraints.

Standardized Tests of Vocabulary

Many researchers choose to rely on or to include in their study a widely used standardized measure of receptive or productive vocabulary such as the Peabody Picture Vocabulary Test (Dunn and Dunn, 2007) or the Expressive One Word Picture Vocabulary Test (Brownell, 2000). There are many such commercially available instruments and they are frequently updated periodically, so any review here would of necessity be selective, cursory, and potentially quickly outdated. Thus, we will focus here on some general issues researchers may want to consider in deciding to use such an instrument. For more detailed information on currently available standardized assessments, the researcher may wish to consult test compendia and reviews available in the reference department of most university libraries.

Commercially available standardized assessments have the advantage of a public track record. They have been normed on a population whose characteristics (age, ethnicity, socioeconomic status, etc.) are carefully documented, thereby providing some basis for deciding whether they are appropriate for one's own population of interest. There is publically available information about their reliability and validity. They often include alternate forms, to facilitate retesting, and there are usually copious instructions for those administering the test. A child's scores can be compared to those of peers in the norming sample to help determine whether the child is "on pace" relative to others of his/her age and gender. Because such instruments tend to be widely used, the resulting scores are easily interpretable by other researchers and lend themselves to cross-study comparison.

Some of the limitations of such instruments are the cost and the level of expertise required of assessors to properly administer and score them. Because such tests are generally updated every few years, materials can become outdated and comparison with earlier studies using previous versions may be compromised. On the other hand, some tests fail to be updated and renormed on more current populations. This can be particularly problematic for populations that may change over time as a result of immigration patterns, or when there are changes in diagnostic categories for certain atypical populations. Furthermore, more recently developed tests may come into favor in the research or policy arenas, again presenting difficulties for longitudinal research and/or comparability across studies. For very young children, standardized assessment frequently requires behavioral maturity that the child may not yet have attained (e.g., the ability to interact with an unfamiliar adult, to attend to test materials, to respond appropriately). Finally, of course, standardized assessments are often simply not available for the population one intends to study, because of the child's age, language, or disability status. In such cases, one must turn to other approaches such as those described below.

Parent Report

Parent report of young children's vocabulary knowledge and use builds on the tradition of clinicians' reliance on parents to report the onset of children's receptive and productive language, the emergence of multiword utterances, and other language and developmental milestones. Parents are typically children's closest and most consistent observers. Although parent report of children's *past* performance is sometimes suspect, they are generally considered accurate reporters of children's *current* behavior and accomplishments. As will be noted below, the accuracy of parental report of young children's vocabulary is borne out by laboratory studies (e.g., Dale *et al.*, 1989).

Potential research questions for which parental report might be the approach of choice include: what is the size and composition of a child's earliest receptive or productive vocabulary? How does it compare to that of other children of similar age? How does children's vocabulary grow over a period of weeks or months? How do the vocabularies of children acquiring both Spanish and English compare: do they know the same words in both languages, different words in each, or is there some overlap? Do bilingual children grow their vocabularies primarily by "filling in" labels in their second language for concepts they already know in the other? Are children with particular developmental delays slower in acquiring emotion words or other abstract terms? Do mothers and other caregivers report similarly about children's vocabulary?

For answering these and other similar questions, parent report may indeed be the tool of choice. In reporting about words infants and toddlers understand and/or produce, parents are drawing on a broad database of everyday interaction with the child. They thus enjoy considerable advantage over either an unfamiliar assessor or a transcriber/analyst of a speech sample when it comes to assessing vocabulary items that children may produce infrequently. Furthermore, parents tend to be familiar with their child's articulation patterns, and thus are likely to report words deemed unintelligible by unfamiliar assessors or transcribers. Reliance on parental report also avoids potential problems related to children's attentional/behavioral states, their unfamiliarity with the assessor or assessment context/procedure, the distraction of video cameras, and the effects of topic and interlocutor behavior. Depending on child age, parents can be queried about children's receptive as well as productive vocabulary. Parental reports in the form of checklists are efficient to administer and score, requiring minimal orientation to the instrument for parent reporters (parents need not, for example, establish basal or ceiling levels as is required by many standardized measures). The checklists are meant to be completed with paper and pencil by the parent, but can be administered orally when there is a concern about low literacy. Cost of the materials is generally modest.

Before discussing some of the limitations of parent report, we provide a description of the most widely used parent report instrument for assessing infant and toddler vocabulary, the MacArthur–Bates Communicative Development Inventories (CDI: http://www.sci.sdsu.edu/cdi/; Fenson *et al.*, 2007). The suite of checklist forms comprising the CDI is laid out in Table 7.1.

The concurrent and predictive validity and reliability of CDI parent reports have been well documented (Fenson *et al.*, 1994; Pan *et al.*, 2004) for both English and Spanish (Jackson-Maldonado *et al.*, 2003). A few studies have, however, noted questions about the accuracy of reports by less educated and low-income parents, especially for 1-year-olds (Feldman *et al.*, 2000), or have raised concerns about appropriateness for some minority populations (e.g., Roberts, Burchinal, and Durham, 1999). Researchers may want to annotate the standard list with dialect-specific alternative terms likely to be used by the particular population they are studying.

Authors of the CDI note that the checklists can be used for older children with developmental delays. Recent work has also demonstrated their utility for monolingual and bilingual children from low-income families at least through age 36 months

Table 7.1 The MacArthur–Bates Communicative Development Inventories for children acquiring English or Spanish

Form	Language	No. items	Recommended ages	Aspect of vocabulary
CDI: Words and Gestures	English	396	8–16 months	Expressive and receptive
CDI: Words and Gestures (short form)	English	89	8–16 months	Expressive and receptive
CDI: Words and Sentences	English	680	16–30 months	Expressive
CDI: Words and Sentences (short form)	English	100	16–30 months	Expressive
IDHC: Palabras y Gestos	Spanish	428	8–16 months	Receptive and expressive
IDHC: Palabras y Gestos (version breve)	Spanish	105	8–16 months	Receptive and expressive
IDHC: Palabras y Enunciados	Spanish	680	16–30 months	Expressive
IDHC: Palabras y Enunciados (version breve)	Spanish	100	16–30 months	Expressive

CDI refers to the MacArthur–Bates Communicative Development Inventories; IDHC refers to the Spanish Inventario del Desarrollo de Habilidades Comunicativas. Some forms include a small number of questions regarding topics such as gesture use and word combinations, in addition to the vocabulary checklists.
Source: http://www.sci.sdsu.edu/cdi/.

(Mancilla-Martinez, Pan, and Vagh, in press; Vagh, Pan, and Mancilla-Martinez, 2009). Lexical norms are available online for monolingual children acquiring English or Spanish.

As noted above, for children acquiring two languages simultaneously, it is advisable to assess vocabulary in each of the child's languages. Based on parental report from the English and Spanish forms of the CDI, Pearson and colleagues have proposed a method for examining the extent of overlap and unique contributions of words known in each language to the child's total vocabulary (see, for example, Pearson and Fernández, 1994). Pearson, Fernández, and Oller (1995) found approximately 30% overlap in the words bilingual children from middle-class families know in each language, suggesting that much of their vocabulary is known in only one language. In studying toddlers from low-income families, Mancilla-Martinez, Pan, and Vagh (in press) found the percentage of words known in both languages to be slightly lower (26%).

As to the accuracy of parental report for bilingual children, Marchman and Martinez-Sussmann (2002) found middle-class parents of 2-year-old Spanish–English bilingual children to be accurate reporters of their children's productive vocabulary in both languages, as did Mancilla-Martinez, Pan, and Vagh (in press) studying bilingual children from low-income families. It seems, then, that parent report using the CDI/IDHC toddler forms is appropriate for assessing the vocabulary development of young bilingual children from a range of socioeconomic backgrounds who are acquiring Spanish and English. The lack of bilingual norms remains a limitation, however.

Spontaneous Speech Samples

Suppose one's research questions are of the following nature: do children use some types of words more frequently than others? How varied is their early vocabulary use (that is, do they rely heavily on a small collection of words, or use each of a wide variety of words only occasionally)? How is their vocabulary production related to the talk parents or other caregivers address to them? Does the amount and/or diversity of vocabulary parents use with children affect children's rate of increase in vocabulary production? Does the vocabulary used by children and their parents differ by context, and if so, how (for example, is the vocabulary used in parent–child book reading richer than in toy play)? Do children who produce more varied vocabulary also use more complex sentences? How do words children use orally relate to their earlier or current use of gestures? How is children's early vocabulary use related to their phonological development (for example, do they favor certain sounds or sound patterns in their earliest production)? Are socioeconomic differences in children's vocabulary use apparent from very early ages, and do such gaps grow, diminish, or stay the same over time?

For researchers interested in pursuing these kinds of questions, the collection and analysis of spontaneous speech may be the most appropriate approach. Spontaneous speech samples are typically generated from video or audio recordings made in the child's home or in a semi-structured laboratory context (see Rowe, Chapter 13 this volume, for details of logistics involved). Such data collection may constitute longitudinal case studies, as in the classic study by Roger Brown (1973), or may involve larger groups of children, as in Hart and Risley's (1995) intensive study of 42 children and their families at home, or Pan and colleagues' (2005) study of 108 children from low-income families over the ages 14 to 36 months. The transcriptions generated from recorded spontaneous speech can provide a wealth of information about parents' verbal interaction with children, as well as the children's own talk and gestures. Hart and Risley, for example, found that children in the six welfare-eligible families they studied heard about a third as many words from their parents as children whose parents were professionals. Children who heard less talk themselves showed much slower growth in vocabulary use through age three, when the original study ended.

Spontaneous speech sampling offers a number of advantages over parental checklists or direct child assessments. Children's production can be observed in relatively natural, ecologically valid contexts, such as parent–child interaction at home or in a laboratory playroom. There are few to no "practice effects" or other limits on the frequency or spacing of data collection. The resulting transcripts can be analyzed not only for children's lexical use but for their phonological, syntactic, and pragmatic production, thus offering the possibility of examining congruence or divergence across domains of language development. As noted above, children's use can also be examined in relation to that of their conversational partner, so as to investigate, for example, the relationship of quantity and diversity of parental vocabulary use to children's concurrent or later vocabulary production and comprehension. Hoff's work (e.g., Hoff, 2003) has shown that socioeconomic differences in children's vocabularies are related to differences in maternal input. Similarly, Pan and colleagues have shown that although both quantity and quality of maternal talk contribute to differences *among* children from low-income families, the diversity of mothers' vocabulary use has a stronger effect than sheer quantity of talk (Pan *et al.*, 2005).

Sampling of spontaneous speech is less restricted in child age range than are parental reports. Although most of the existing data tend to focus on infants, toddlers, and preschoolers, there is in principle no reason why it could not be applied to older children in developmentally appropriate contexts. Likewise, most extant datasets involve dyadic interaction, but can also be used for multiparty conversation, such as dinner table or classroom talk. Work by Rowe and her colleagues (e.g., Rowe and Goldin-Meadow, 2009) demonstrates that analysis of videotaped interaction between mothers and very young children can reveal relationships between children's early use of gestures and their later oral vocabulary development. Their results showed that children who used gestures to express more different meanings (for example, pointing to more different objects) at 14 months had larger receptive vocabularies at age 54 months, even when their earlier oral vocabulary was taken into account. This work is important theoretically because it helps elucidate the connections between preverbal and verbal communication, but it is also of applied significance as it confirms the clinical utility of measuring children's use of gesture as an early indicator of later vocabulary development (see also Cartmill, Demir, and Goldin-Meadow, Chapter 14 this volume). Thus, "speech" sampling, perhaps something of a misnomer, offers the possibility of examining children's preverbal communicative development, as well as their oral vocabulary production.

Spontaneous speech sampling, however, has its share of drawbacks. In contrast to parental report or direct child assessment, speech sampling and analysis are highly time and labor intensive. They require good equipment, trained transcribers and coders, and familiarity with a software analysis system such as CHILDES or SALT (http://childes.psy.cmu.edu; http://www.languageanalysislab.com; see also Corrigan, Chapter 18 this volume; Rowe, Chapter 13 this volume). Audio- or videotaping in home or classroom settings is often plagued by ambient noise, unpredictable lighting conditions, the presence of unintended participants such as siblings of the target child, and other unanticipated interruptions. Furthermore, with infants and young toddlers, extended taping may be required to secure a large enough sample of child language. Transcribing 1 hour of taped interaction requires approximately 8–10 hours (or more, depending on the level of detail included in the transcript). Children's production in spontaneous speech is of course influenced by interlocutor, context, and topic – characteristics that are both speech sampling's greatest advantage and its potentially most serious disadvantage, depending on the researcher's goals and the level of analysis undertaken.

Over the last two decades, much of the cost of analyzing spontaneous speech samples has been ameliorated by the establishment of the Child Language Data Exchange System (CHILDES: MacWhinney, 2000). Researchers can access and download transcripts donated by other researchers, as well as a suite of automated analysis programs, both free of charge (http://childes.psy.cmu.edu). Proper citation of the data source in any resulting manuscript or presentation is of course expected. The database now includes transcripts of children acquiring English and many languages other than English, of children acquiring more than one language simultaneously, and of clinical populations. It is incumbent on the researcher wishing to utilize the data to become familiar with the characteristics of the population represented, the context in which taping was done, and project-specific decisions about level of transcription and coding detail undertaken by the donating research team (see Corrigan, Chapter 18 this volume, for a fuller discussion of the use of the CHILDES database). Several of the automated analysis programs available (e.g., CLAN) lend themselves to the study of vocabulary use, for example, by generating lists of word types produced by a particular speaker and with what frequency, or by automatically extracting for further examination and analysis the contexts of use for researcher-specified words. Longitudinal datasets in the database allow researchers to track children's increasing vocabulary production over time. Researchers may also collect their own data, transcribe them according to the CHILDES guidelines, and then utilize the CLAN analysis programs to address vocabulary questions of interest.

Researcher-Designed Vocabulary Assessment

Sometimes researchers are interested not so much in children's overall vocabulary use and growth as in their acquisition of particular vocabulary items introduced in the course of an intervention program. Does introducing new vocabulary in the context of classroom book reading to children by preschool teachers increase the likelihood that children will learn the target words? How does book reading exposure compare in efficacy to other types of interaction or activities involving use of the target words? How many exposures over what period of time are needed to insure that most children will learn the target words? Is more exposure needed for younger children or those with smaller vocabularies than those who already know more words? Is children's acquisition facilitated by already knowing words related to the target words?

For research questions of this nature, specially designed assessments are generally required. One cannot, for example, assume that children will spontaneously produce particular words, even if they have partially or fully learned them. Thus, spontaneous speech sampling is of little utility. Similarly, one cannot count on adult reporters to accurately judge children's knowledge, even with extensive exposure to or interaction with the child. Instead, researchers must design their own vocabulary assessments so as to evaluate children's learning of the target words.

There are several key considerations in designing such assessments, many of which have to do with study design. Children's knowledge of the target words must be assessed both before and after the intervention. Furthermore, it is highly desirable to have a control group of children who receive unrelated enrichment activities. Measuring any change in the target-word knowledge of children in the control group insures that whatever learning is observed by children receiving the intervention would not have occurred anyway in the natural course of things.

Researcher-designed assessments can take one of several forms, but the most frequently used are patterned on a standardized assessment of receptive vocabulary (such as the Peabody Picture Vocabulary Test–IV: Dunn and Dunn, 2007) or of expressive vocabulary (e.g., the Expressive One Word Picture Vocabulary Test: Brownell, 2000). The former presents the target word and three other choices and asks the child to point to the word the assessor says. The latter requires the child to name or label the picture of an object or a concept. An alternative to these assessments, which aims to measure the *depth* of children's knowledge of the target word, asks children to define a word or tell everything they know about its word meaning.

One example of research designed to evaluate the effectiveness of a vocabulary intervention is a series of studies by Wasik and colleagues (e.g., Wasik and Bond, 2001). Head Start classroom teachers were trained to expose children to the target words through read-alouds and other activities. Teachers were encouraged to use props provided by the researchers and to supplement book reading with strategies such as defining the target words, and to provide rich verbal interaction in general. Post-intervention assessment showed that children in the intervention classrooms scored higher on standardized assessment of receptive and expressive vocabulary (i.e., PPVT–R and Expressive One Word Picture Vocabulary Test–III) and learned more of the target words than children whose teachers read the same books but did not provide extensive explanation and exposure to the target words.

Researcher-designed vocabulary assessments are of course also useful for older children and those acquiring more than one language. For example, Carlo and colleagues (2004) designed an intervention to improve the academic vocabulary of fifth grade monolingual English and bilingual English–Spanish students. The meanings of targeted vocabulary words deemed important in the academic setting were taught directly and through repeated exposure in a variety of contexts. Native Spanish-speaking students were also given access to the words' meanings in Spanish, and all students were taught word-learning strategies to use on their own. At the end of the program, students in the intervention group showed greater increases in the depth of their knowledge of the targeted word (measured by asking students to provide multiple meanings of words such as *ring* or *check*), as well as growth in reading comprehension. Students who were English-language learners and received the intervention showed *growth* similar to that of their English-only peers, even though the level of their skills remained lower than their peers'.

One obvious limitation of researcher-designed assessments is that they do not index the size or makeup of children's overall vocabulary. Thus, they cannot show whether participation in a particular intervention has more generalized effects on vocabulary growth. Vocabulary words are by their very nature variable in complexity and occur with different frequencies in ordinary conversation or text. Given that researcher-designed vocabulary assessments are composed of particular items, such assessments do not lend themselves to use in other studies. Thus it is difficult to know whether children showing growth in knowledge about the set of items tested in a particular study would acquire other words at similar rates, given similar exposure.

Use of Multiple Measures

Whatever the vocabulary assessment method chosen by a researcher (parent report, speech sample analysis, researcher-designed tests), s/he often chooses to use more than one method so as to assess the validity of the vocabulary assessment. When scores from one measure are highly positively correlated with another, we have some indication that the two instruments are measuring the same thing (referred to as "concurrent validity"). Such a comparison is particularly useful if the second measure is one that has been rigorously evaluated earlier and has demonstrated solid psychometric properties (e.g., validity and reliability).

Key Terms

Expressive (productive) vocabulary   Words a child uses appropriately.
Parent report   An assessment method, often in the form of a checklist, that asks parents to identify words their child understands or says.
Receptive vocabulary   Words whose meaning or referent a child understands.
Speech sampling   The recording and transcribing of a sample of speech spontaneously produced by a child, usually in interaction with a parent or clinician/researcher, either at home or in the laboratory.
Vocabulary depth   How much a child understands about words s/he knows (e.g., their definitions, multiple meanings, contexts of appropriate use).

References

Brown, R. (1973) *A first language: the early stages*. Cambridge, MA: Harvard University Press.
Brownell, R. (2000) *The Expressive One Word Picture Vocabulary Test*. Academic Communications Associates, Inc.
Carlo, M.S., August, D., McLaughlin, B., *et al.* (2004) Closing the gap: addressing the vocabulary needs of English-language learners in bilingual and mainstream classrooms. *Reading Research Quarterly*, 39 (2), 188–215.
Dale, P.S., Bates, E., Reznick, J.S., and Morisset, C. (1989) The validity of a parent report instrument of child language at twenty months. *Journal of Child Language*, 16, 239–251.
Dunn, L.M., and Dunn, L.M. (2007) *Peabody Picture Vocabulary Test–Fourth Edition*. Minneapolis: Pearson Assessments.

Feldman, H.M., Dollaghan, C.A., Campbell, T.F., *et al.* (2000) Measurement properties of the MacArthur Communicative Development Inventories at ages one and two years. *Child Development*, 71 (2), 310–322.

Fenson, L., Dale, P., Reznick, J., *et al.* (1994) Variability in early communicative development. *Monographs of the Society for Research in Child Development*, 59 (5, serial no. 242).

Fenson, L., Marchman, V.A., Thal, D.J., *et al.* (2007) *MacArthur–Bates Communicative Development Inventories: user's guide and technical manual* (2nd edn). Baltimore: Brookes.

Hart, B., and Risley, T.R. (1995) *Meaningful differences in the everyday experience of young American children*. Baltimore: Brookes.

Hoff, E. (2003) The specificity of environmental influence: socioeconomic status affects early vocabulary development via maternal speech. *Child Development*, 74, 1368–1378.

Hoff, E. (2005) How social contexts support and shape language development. *Developmental Review*, 26, 55–88.

Jackson-Maldonado, D., Thal, D., Marchman, V., *et al.* (2003) *MacArthur Inventarios del Desarrollo de Habilidades Comunicativas: user's guide and technical manual*. Baltimore: Brookes.

MacWhinney, B. (2000) *The CHILDES Project: tools for analyzing talk*. Mahwah, NJ: Erlbaum.

Mancilla-Martinez, J., Pan, B.A., and Vagh, S.B. (in press) Assessing the productive vocabulary of Spanish–English bilingual toddlers from low-income families. *Applied Psycholinguistics*.

Marchman, V.A., and Martinez-Sussmann, C. (2002) Concurrent validity of caregiver/parent report measures of language for children who are learning both English and Spanish. *Journal of Speech, Language, and Hearing Research*, 45 (5), 983–997.

Pan, B.A., Rowe, M.L., Singer, J.D., and Snow, C.E. (2005) Maternal correlates of growth in toddler vocabulary production in low-income families. *Child Development*, 76 (4), 763–782.

Pan, B.A., Rowe, M.L., Spier, E., and LeMonda, C. (2004) Measuring productive vocabulary of toddlers in low-income families: concurrent and predictive validity of three sources of data. *Journal of Child Language*, 31, 587–608.

Pearson, B.Z., and Fernández, S.C. (1994) Patterns of interaction in the lexical growth in two languages of bilingual infants and toddlers. *Language Learning*, 44, 617–653.

Pearson, B.Z., Fernández, S.C., and Oller, D.K. (1995) Cross-language synonyms in the lexicons of bilingual infants: one language or two? *Journal of Child Language*, 22, 345–368.

Roberts, J.E., Burchinal, M., and Durham, M. (1999) Parents' report of vocabulary and grammatical development of African American preschoolers: child and environmental associations. *Child Development*, 70, 92–106.

Rowe, M.L., and Goldin-Meadow, S. (2009) Differences in early gesture explain SES disparities in child vocabulary size at school entry. *Science*, 323, 951–953.

Snow, C.E., Burns, S., and Griffin, P. (1998) *Preventing reading difficulties in young children*. Washington, DC: National Academy Press.

Vagh, S.B., Pan, B.A., and Mancilla-Martinez, J. (2009) Measuring growth in bilingual and monolingual children's English productive vocabulary development: the utility of combining parent and teacher report. *Child Development*, 80, 1545–1563.

Wasik, B.A., and Bond, M.A. (2001) Beyond the pages of a book: interactive book reading and language development in preschool. *Journal of Educational Psychology*, 93 (2), 243.

Further Reading and Resources

Bornstein, M., and Cote, L. (2004) Cross-linguistic analysis of vocabulary in young children: Spanish, Dutch, French, Hebrew, Italian, Korean, and American English. *Child Development*, 75 (4), 1115–1140.

Fenson, L., Dale, P., Reznick, J., *et al.* (1994) Variability in early communicative development. *Monographs of the Society for Research in Child Development*, 59 (5, serial no. 242).

Hart, B., and Risley, T.R. (1995) *Meaningful differences in the everyday experience of young American children*. Baltimore: Brookes.

Hoff, E. (2003) The specificity of environmental influence: socioeconomic status affects early vocabulary development via maternal speech. *Child Development*, 74, 1368–1378.

Huttenlocher, J., Haight, W., Bryk, A., *et al.* (1991) Early vocabulary growth: relation to language input and gender. *Developmental Psychology*, 27, 236–248.

Pan, B.A., Rowe, M.L., Singer, J.D., and Snow, C.E. (2005) Maternal correlates of growth in toddler vocabulary production in low-income families. *Child Development*, 76 (4), 763–782.

Pearson, P.D., and Hiebert, E.H. (2007) Vocabulary assessment: what we know and what we need to know. *Reading Research Quarterly*, 42 (2), 282–296.

Rowe, M.L., Özçalıskan, S., and Goldin-Meadow, S. (2008) Learning words by hand: gesture's role in predicting vocabulary development. *First Language*, 28, 182–199.

Child Language Data Exchange System (CHILDES): http://childes.psy.cmu.edu.

MacArthur–Bates Communicative Inventories: http://www.sci.sdsu.edu/cdi.

Systematic Analysis of Language Transcripts (SALT 2010): http://www.languageanalysislab.com.

8 Assessing Grammatical Knowledge (with Special Reference to the Graded Grammaticality Judgment Paradigm)

Ben Ambridge

Summary

This chapter briefly summarizes some of the most widely used experimental paradigms in the domain of grammatical development (elicited production, repetition, weird word order, priming, act-out, and preferential looking and pointing tasks) before focusing in more detail on a relatively new grammaticality judgment paradigm. This new paradigm allows children to provide graded acceptability judgments for sentences (e.g., *The magician disappeared the rabbit*) and individual lexical forms of both familiar (e.g., *unlock*, *unsqueeze*) and novel verbs (e.g., *rifed* and *rofe* as the past-tense form of *rife*). The paradigm is suitable for use with young children (*M* = 4:6 for the youngest group tested so far) and also with older children and adults (where it can be used to assess the relative unacceptability of errors that these speakers would not usually produce). The paradigm yields unambiguous numerical data that do not require scoring, recoding, or reliability checking, and that are suitable for most commonly used statistical analyses (e.g., ANOVA, regression). It is well suited to research questions for which competing theoretical accounts make quantitative predictions regarding the relative (un)acceptability of particular forms (including, for example, the retreat from argument structure overgeneralization and the English past-tense debate).

Research Methods in Child Language: A Practical Guide, First Edition.
Edited by Erika Hoff.
© 2012 Blackwell Publishing Ltd. Published 2012 by Blackwell Publishing Ltd.

Many different experimental paradigms have been used to assess children's knowledge of grammar (see especially McKercher and Jaswal, Chapter 10 this volume; Vasilyeva, Waterfall, and Gómez, Chapter 11 this volume). This chapter has two aims. The first is to briefly outline the most commonly used paradigms, along with their advantages and disadvantages, directing interested researchers to relevant articles (or other chapters in this volume). The second is to discuss in more detail grammaticality judgment paradigms that are suitable for use with children and, in particular, a new paradigm that my colleagues and I developed to obtained graded (as opposed to binary) judgments (Ambridge *et al.*, 2008).

Production and Comprehension Paradigms

Experimental paradigms for assessing children's knowledge of grammar can be broadly divided into three types: production, comprehension, and judgment. *Judgment paradigms* are discussed extensively later in this chapter, and we will say no more about them here. *Production paradigms* use various techniques to "persuade" children to attempt to produce particular sentence types (or individual word forms), often in the hope of eliciting a particular error that is of theoretical interest. In *comprehension paradigms*, children are not required to produce language. Instead, children demonstrate their comprehension of a sentence that is verbally presented to them by choosing a matching picture from a selection (either explicitly by pointing or implicitly by looking).

Elicited Production

Probably the most commonly used paradigm is *elicited production*, whereby the experimenter aims to elicit an attempt at a particular structure by placing the child in a discourse scenario in which the target response is particularly appropriate. There are three contexts (not mutually exclusive) in which elicited production studies of this type are particularly useful.

The first is where a researcher wishes to investigate whether children have abstract knowledge of a particular structure. For example, there is a debate in the syntax acquisition literature as to whether young children are in possession of an abstract SUBJECT VERB OBJECT construction that can be used with any verb, or a set of verb-specific templates (e.g., *KICKER kick THING-KICKED*; see Tomasello, 2000, for a review). Akhtar and Tomasello (1997) investigated this issue by teaching children a novel verb ("This is called *chamming*") to describe a particular novel action (e.g., one character bouncing another on a rope). At test, the experimenter used toys to enact a scenario such as Ernie chamming Big Bird and asked the child, "What's happening (with Ernie/Big Bird)?" Since the verb is novel, a response such as *Ernie's chamming him* (produced by 80% of 3-year-olds, but only 20% of 2-year-olds) constitutes evidence that the child has some type of verb-general knowledge. In addition to "live action" scenarios, children can also be asked to describe videos, animations, or still pictures (see Tomasello, 2000, and Ambridge and Lieven, 2011, for a summary of elicited production studies of this type).

A second scenario in which elicited production paradigms are particularly useful is when a researcher wishes to investigate children's acquisition of a structure that they rarely produce spontaneously, such as a complex question (e.g., *Is the boy who is smoking crazy?*) or the past-tense form of a low frequency verb (e.g., *rang*). One useful technique can be to engage children in a dialogue with a puppet or talking toy (who produces responses by means of a loudspeaker connected to a computer or mp3 player with pre-recorded responses). For example, Ambridge, Rowland, and Pine (2008) elicited attempts at complex questions (e.g., *Is the boy who is smoking crazy?*) by having children put questions to a talking dog toy who could "see" a picture illustrating the answer (hidden from view of the child). In some cases a "fill in the blank" technique is used. For example, in many past-tense studies (e.g., Marchman, 1997) children are presented with prompts such as, "Every day John likes to sing. Today he is singing. Yesterday he. ..." As these examples illustrate, the elicited production paradigm is really a family of related techniques that may differ in detail, but are united in their aim to persuade children to attempt to produce a particular utterance.

Finally, elicited production paradigms are useful for investigating the effect of one particular variable, whilst holding other factors constant. For example, one study of question acquisition (Ambridge *et al.*, 2006) used the talking dog procedure outlined above to investigate whether children produce fewer errors for questions with higher frequency auxiliaries (e.g., *can*) than lower frequency auxiliaries (e.g., *should*), whilst holding other aspects of the question constant (e.g., *What can/should Mickey eat?*).

The main advantage of elicited production studies is that the experimenter can exert a reasonable degree of control over what children are likely to say (though, of course, some children will not produce the intended utterances), and hence manipulate the variable(s) of interest. The main disadvantage is that elicited production tasks are probably the most difficult for children to complete. Hence children may fail not because they lack the required knowledge, but because they do not understand the nature of the task, or because one or more of the various task components (e.g., interpreting the scenario to be described, choosing the right words, planning the utterance) interferes with their ability to produce the correct form.

Repetition or Elicited Imitation

Repetition or *elicited imitation* tasks are useful when it is difficult to conceive of a discourse scenario that would restrict children to the particular structure of interest, or when this structure is sufficiently infrequent or complex that children will rarely produce it spontaneously in an elicited production task. For example, Kidd, Lieven, and Tomasello (2006) used a repetition task to assess children's ability to produce sentential complement clause constructions (e.g., *I hope she is making a chocolate cake*). The procedure is simply that the experimenter (or a puppet or cartoon character) produces an utterance, which the child is then asked to repeat. It may seem that this task is trivially easy, and that even young children would make few errors. In fact, errors (such as substituting *think* for *hope* in the study of Kidd, Lieven, and Tomasello, 2006) are relatively common (Ambridge and Pine, 2006, identified a number of children who consistently repeated such simple sentences as *She is playing football* as **Her is playing football*). It seems that such errors occur because, rather than storing the incoming sentence verbatim, children encode the "message" of the sentence and then construct a "new" sentence using their own grammar (Lust, Flynn, and Foley, 1996). Even when children do not make errors, the time taken to repeat a sentence can be used as a measure of the relative familiarity of particular strings (e.g., Bannard and Matthews, 2008). The main advantage of the paradigm is the high degree of control that it affords over the precise form and wording of the target utterance. The main disadvantage is that it cannot be used with older children, who – at some stage – will be able to repeat a sentence verbatim using a pure "parroting" strategy, whether or not they could produce it spontaneously.

Weird Word Order and Syntactic Priming

Somewhere in between the elicited production and imitation paradigms lies the *weird word order* paradigm (Akhtar, 1999). The experimenter and child take turns describing video clips (or live actions performed by puppets), often using novel verbs that describe novel actions. For some verbs, the experimenter uses conventional word order (e.g., *Fox meeked Bear*). For others, she uses a weird word order not found in the language (e.g., *Fox Bear tammed*). The aim (as in elicited production studies such as that of Akhtar and Tomasello, 1997) is to investigate whether children have verb-general knowledge of word order. If so, when asked to describe a new video using the novel verb presented in a weird word order, they should correct to the word order that is conventional for their language (e.g., *Duck tammed Snake*). If, on the other hand, children learn individual constructions for each verb (e.g., *TAMMER THING-TAMMED tam*) they will use this construction to produce a weird word order sentence such as *Duck snake tammed* (in fact, the 2-year-old children studied by Akhtar, 1999, produced both types of response at similar rates, suggesting some verb-general and some verb-specific knowledge). This paradigm has also been used to investigate verb frequency effects (Matthews *et al.*, 2004) and the intransitive construction (Abbot-Smith, Lieven, and Tomasello, 2001), and to compare word order acquisition crosslinguistically (Matthews *et al.*, 2007). The weird word order paradigm shares with the elicited production/imitation paradigms to which it is related the advantage of a high degree of control over the target structure. A disadvantage is that children (particularly older children) may mimic word orders that they know to be incorrect, either "for fun" or because they assume that this is what is required of them (though it is usually possible to control out this confound by using real verbs to estimate rates of deliberate weird word order responses). Like all other production paradigms, it is suitable for use only with children old enough to be able to produce the relevant sentence types (see below).

As the *syntactic priming* paradigm is discussed in detail in Vasilyeva, Waterfall, and Gómez (Chapter 11 this volume), I mention it here simply to point out that the findings of weird word order studies make the interpretation of syntactic priming studies less straightforward than is generally assumed. Syntactic priming refers to the phenomenon whereby hearing a particular construction (e.g., *The digger pushed the bricks*) increases the likelihood that the child will use the same construction (e.g., *The hammer broke the vase*) than a possible alternative (e.g., *The vase was broken by the hammer*) to describe a subsequently presented scene. Such findings are generally taken as evidence for prior knowledge of the construction (for this example, the SUBJECT VERB OBJECT transitive construction). The caveat from weird word order studies is that identical priming effects (though they are not usually described as such) are sometimes observed for constructions of which children cannot possibly have had prior knowledge (i.e., weird word order constructions). Thus care must be taken when interpreting syntactic priming as evidence for prior knowledge of a construction.

Comprehension Paradigms: Act-Out Tasks and Preferential Looking/Pointing

A problem shared by all production paradigms is that children may in principle have knowledge of a particular structure that is not sufficient to support production (which may be interrupted by the demands involved in utterance planning and formulation), but that is sufficient for comprehension. Comprehension tasks are used to investigate this possibility.

Act-out studies are primarily used to investigate children's knowledge of word order. As in the elicited production studies outlined above (e.g., Akhtar and Tomasello, 1997) children are taught a novel verb (e.g., *chamming*) to describe a novel action. Instead of describing an enactment performed by an experimenter, however, children are given a sentence and asked to enact it themselves (e.g., show me *Ernie chamming Big Bird*). As with the elicited production equivalent, the rationale is that if children can correctly enact the sentence (i.e., with Ernie as SUBJECT and Big Bird as OBJECT as opposed to vice versa), they must be in possession of some knowledge of word order that is verb general (SUBJECT VERB OBJECT). Act-out studies can also be used to investigate children's sensitivity to the different cues to SUBJECT (or AGENT) found crosslinguistically such as case marking (e.g., MacWhinney and Bates, 1989). In principle, the advantage of act-out studies is that they can be used with younger children than equivalent production studies (e.g., children who are not yet capable of producing three-word utterances with a novel verb). In practice, however, act-out tasks appear to be surprisingly demanding for young children: the study of Akhtar and Tomasello (1997) also included an act-out task, for which most children aged 2:10 showed at-chance performance.

Preferential looking/pointing paradigms (e.g., Naigles, 1990; Gertner, Fisher, and Eisengart, 2006) reduce task demands further (and hence generally show verb-general knowledge in younger children than act-out or production tasks). Children again hear a sentence such as *Ernie is chamming Big Bird* but, instead of enacting the sentence with toys, must "choose" from two video displays: one showing the scenario described, one with the roles reversed (e.g., Big Bird chamming Ernie). When a pointing task is used, children are taught to explicitly select the matching scene.

Preferential looking tasks make use of the fact that children generally spontaneously look for longer to the matching than the nonmatching image to infer comprehension.

The main advantage of the preferential looking paradigm (discussed in detail in Piotroski and Naigles, Chapter 2 this volume; and see also Golinkoff and Hirsh-Pasek, Chapter 5 this volume) is that it can be used with very young children (i.e., children who are too young to make any explicit response). Indeed, studies using the paradigm have demonstrated apparent verb-general knowledge in children aged as young as 1:9 (Gertner, Fisher, and Eisengart, 2006). The disadvantage is that, since children's looking behavior is not an unambiguous measure of their comprehension, the most appropriate interpretation of any given set of findings is not always clear, and is often controversial (see Ambridge and Lieven, 2011, Chapter 3; Chan *et al.*, 2010; Dittmar *et al.*, 2008). The pointing version of the paradigm produces unambiguous data, but presumably is suitable for use only with slightly older children (the youngest group studied so far had a mean age of 2:3; Noble, Rowland, and Pine, in press).

Grammaticality Judgment Paradigms

As we have already seen, there are many areas of investigation for which production and comprehension measures can be used to assess children's grammatical knowledge (indeed, for many research questions, these paradigms are more suitable than a judgment task). As we will see, however, the main advantage of the grammaticality judgment paradigm is that it allows the researcher to answer questions that cannot be directly addressed using production or comprehension measures, by investigating children's knowledge of grammar (both syntax and morphology) in a relatively explicit manner. The graded grammaticality judgment paradigm to be introduced here provides unambiguous, numerical data that do not require scoring, recoding, or checking for interrater reliability, and that are suitable for most commonly used statistical analyses (e.g., ANOVA, regression). As for many of the paradigms discussed above and elsewhere in this volume, novel items (usually verbs) can be created for use in the study, in order to test children's general syntactic or morphological knowledge independent of their knowledge of particular lexical items. The paradigm is relatively demanding, and hence is most suitable for use with relatively old children (we have not yet attempted to test children younger than 4). Generally speaking, grammaticality judgment tasks are also suitable for children with specific language impairment (e.g., Rice, Wexler, and Redmond, 1999; and see McGregor, Chapter 21 this volume) and second language learners (e.g., Mandell, 1999), though, of course, this may raise the minimum age further.

Research Aim

My own interest in developing a graded grammaticality judgment paradigm for use with children stems from my research on a topic that has become known as Baker's paradox (or the "no negative evidence" problem). Suppose that a child hears a particular verb (e.g., *break*) in both an intransitive sentence (e.g., *The stick broke*) and a transitive causative sentence (e.g., *The man broke the stick*). Through repeated encounters with other pairs that fit this pattern (e.g., for *roll* and *open*), the child will set up some kind of generalization or "rule" that (informally speaking) generates transitive causative sentences for verbs that have appeared only in the intransitive:

Intransitive sentence	*Transitive causative sentence*
[The stick] [broke]	[The man] [broke] [the stick]
[The ball] [rolled]	[John] [rolled] [the ball]
[The door] [opened]	[Louise] [opened] [the door]

Rule: [NP1] [VERB] → [NP2] [VERB] [NP1]

Suppose, for example, that the child hears *The cup smashed*. The child can use this rule to generate a sentence such as *Mummy smashed the cup*, even if no sentence of this type has been encountered in the input.

How do we know that children are forming generalizations of this type? One answer is simply that they must be, otherwise language would consist of nothing more than a set of rote-learned sentences, which is clearly not the case (Chomsky, 1959). A better answer is that many experimental studies (see Tomasello, 2000, for a review) have shown that, when taught a novel verb in intransitive sentences only (e.g., *The ball is tamming*), most children aged 3:0 and older are able to use this verb in a transitive causative sentence (e.g., *The mouse is tamming the ball*). Another source of evidence comes from children's overgeneralization errors. Many researchers (most notably Bowerman, 1988) have found that children produce utterances such as **The magician disappeared the rabbit*. Such utterances cannot have been learned by rote from the input (as adults do not produce them), and hence must have come from the application of a generalization process of the type outlined above. Errors of this type are termed *argument structure overgeneralization errors*, because a verb (*disappear*) has been used in an *argument structure construction* (sentence frame) in which it is not permitted in the adult grammar (here the transitive causative), through the *over*-application of a *general* rule.

Explaining how children learn not to make these errors turns out to be a very difficult problem. It cannot be simply that children avoid using verbs in sentence constructions in which they have not appeared in the input, or they would never make such errors in the first place (or be able to produce novel utterances such as *The mouse is tamming the ball*). Whilst implicit or explicit correction by parents and caregivers is no doubt useful (e.g., Chouinard and Clark, 2003), this cannot be the whole story, as adult speakers are able to reject as ungrammatical errors that they are extremely unlikely to have produced – and subsequently had corrected – during childhood (e.g., **The clown chuckled the man*).

The goal of the research program for which my colleagues and I developed the graded grammaticality judgment paradigm was to test various proposals for how, having begun to produce overgeneralization errors such as **The magician disappeared the rabbit*, children "retreat" from these errors. For example, one proposal, Braine and Brooks's (1995) *entrenchment hypothesis*, states that repeated presentation of a verb in particular constructions (e.g., *The rabbit disappeared*) gradually causes the child to probabilistically infer that the verb cannot be used in nonattested constructions (e.g., *The magician disappeared the rabbit*). Intuitively, the idea is that the child (not consciously of course) forms an "inference from absence" along the lines of "if *disappear* could be used in this way, surely I would have encountered it by now." The prediction from this account is that overgeneralization errors should be deemed more unacceptable for high frequency verbs than for semantically matched lower frequency verbs (e.g., *The magician disappeared/vanished the rabbit*), as this inference from absence is stronger for the former.

Choosing a Suitable Paradigm

In order to test this prediction, we need to obtain from children a measure of the relative (un)acceptability of different overgeneralization errors (and, as a control, correctly formed utterances). In fact, experimental tasks other than the grammaticality judgment paradigm do not provide a direct measure of the relative unacceptability of particular utterances.

An act-out, preferential looking/pointing comprehension task would provide information about the relative interpretability of a number of utterances, but there does not necessarily exist any correlation between interpretability and grammatical acceptability. Intuitively, it would seem that had we asked children to enact, for example, *The magician disappeared the rabbit* and *The magician vanished the rabbit*, they would have had little difficulty with either.

An elicited production task, in which the experimenter attempts to elicit each sentence from children, is more suitable (such a study was conducted by Brooks and Tomasello, 1999). Again, however, the paradigm does not provide a direct measure of grammatical acceptability. A child might produce an utterance that she considers to be ungrammatical (e.g., *He disappeared the rabbit*) if placed in a discourse scenario where such a response seems to be expected (e.g., *What did the magician do?*), particularly if she has not yet learned a suitable alternative formulation (e.g., *He made the rabbit disappear*). Conversely, the child's failure to produce a particular utterance does not constitute strong evidence that she considers it to be ungrammatical.

Consequently, any attempt to infer the relative unacceptability of two or more erroneous utterances from the relative rates at which they are produced is problematic. Suppose, for example, that a particular child produces five overgeneralization errors with *vanish* (e.g., *He vanished the rabbit*) and only two with *disappear* (e.g., *He disappeared the rabbit*). Is the correct conclusion (1) that the child deems the latter to be less acceptable or (2) that, having produced both utterances, the child considers both to be acceptable? After all, the normal assumption (assuming an idealized scenario with no pure "production errors") is that speakers' utterances reflect their grammars: if a speaker produces an utterance, she considers it to be grammatical.

It is also difficult to see how an elicited production task could be used to ask which of two alternative sentence constructions with the same verb children deem to be more grammatical. For example, if one wishes to test whether children know that

The rabbit disappeared is more acceptable than **The magician disappeared the rabbit*, one cannot simply compare the rates at which children produce each sentence in an elicited production task, as the sentences are not matched for difficulty. The second is longer and includes more participants (placing a higher load on memory) and is hence presumably more difficult for a child to produce, even if she considers it to be perfectly grammatically acceptable.

The best way to obtain a measure of the relative (un)acceptability of particular utterances is, of course, to ask children directly, using a grammaticality judgment task (though, in fairness, some of the children studied by Brooks and Tomasello, 1999, were probably too young for this to be feasible). We are by no means the first researchers to come to this conclusion. For example, Theakston (2004) investigated the entrenchment hypothesis using a *binary grammaticality judgment task*. Under this paradigm (discussed in more detail in McKercher and Jaswal, Chapter 10 this volume), children are asked simply to indicate whether or not each sentence is acceptable, as opposed to providing a graded judgment of the degree of (un)acceptability of a particular sentence. In this study, sentences containing overgeneralization errors (e.g., **I'm gonna disappear it*) were read aloud by an experimenter. The child's task was to help a toy animal decide whether each sentence was "OK" or "a bit silly" by moving the animal to a card showing a red cross or a green tick.

The advantage of a binary judgment task is that it can be performed by young children (Theakston's youngest group had a mean age of 5:9, though the task has been used with children as young as 4:1, e.g., Rice, Wexler, and Redmond, 1999). The disadvantage is that, for each child and each sentence, the task produces only a binary outcome measure (grammatical or ungrammatical). This means that to compare the judged grammaticality of two sentences (e.g., **I'm gonna disappear/ vanish it*) it is possible to compare only the *number of children* who judged each sentence to be ungrammatical. One consequence of this is that it is impossible to analyze the data using parametric statistical tests (e.g., ANOVA) which can be used to look for interactions between variables, and which can be run within subjects, hence increasing the power of the analysis (maximizing the likelihood of finding any effect that is present). A more serious problem is that, beyond a certain age, it will no longer be possible to compare the *relative* ungrammaticality of two ungrammatical sentences (e.g., **I'm gonna disappear/vanish it*), as both will be classified as ungrammatical by close to 100% of children.

It is for this reason that Theakston (2004) used a *graded grammaticality judgment task* with her adult participants. In a graded grammaticality judgment task, participants are asked to judge the relative (un)acceptability of utterances using a graded scale – in this case a seven-point Likert-type scale – ranging (for example) from "completely unacceptable" to "completely acceptable" (the precise wording varies between studies). Grammaticality judgment studies with adults often use more sophisticated measurements such as a visual analog scale, which is not divided into discrete ratings (participants indicate their judgment by making a mark on a continuous line), or magnitude estimation, in which participants' ratings are not confined to a particular scale (e.g., Bard, Robertson, and Sorace, 1996). Our goal, however, was to develop a graded grammaticality judgment paradigm that could be used in exactly the same format with adults and children.

Procedure

Smiley-Face Scale

Under the graded grammaticality judgment paradigm (Ambridge *et al.*, 2008), participants indicate their judgments using the five-point "smiley-face" scale shown in Plate 5 (reproduced with permission from Ambridge *et al.*, 2008, p. 105).

The scale consists of five cartoon faces and has a midpoint denoted by a neutral face, two "more acceptable" levels denoted by smiling green faces, and two "less acceptable" levels denoted by frowning red faces (the neutral face is split into red and green halves). The child has two counters – one red and one green – and indicates her judgment, first, by choosing either the red or the green counter (to indicate unacceptable/acceptable) and, second, by placing her chosen counter on one of the faces to indicate the *degree* of (un)acceptability (either counter can be placed on the middle face). We have never encountered a child who placed a red counter on a green face or vice versa. The goal of this "two-step" procedure is to ensure that any children who are unable to provide a graded judgment (by using the faces scale) still provide a binary judgment (by choosing the red or green counter). However, we have not yet found an age at which children are able to use the counters but not the scale (though we have only tested children aged 4 years and older). Testing can be conducted using either (1) a booklet with one scale for each test item (in which case the experimenter ticks or circles the relevant face after the child has made her selection) or (2) a single scale which is reused for each trial (in which case the experimenter notes down each judgment on a separate sheet). Note, however, that older children and adults generally prefer to mark their choice directly on the scale, necessitating option 1.

Training (Warm-Up) Procedure

Children are introduced to the use of the scale through a carefully constructed training procedure. First the experimenter explains the nature of the game: the "talking dog" (a soft toy containing a loudspeaker connected to a laptop computer or mp3 player) is "learning to speak English but, because he's only a dog, sometimes gets it wrong and says things a bit silly." The child's task is to help him by letting him know whether he "said it right" or "a bit silly." The use of a talking toy is designed to overcome any reluctance a child may have with regard to "correcting" an adult, and also to make the task more enjoyable for children. (Although most enjoy hearing the dog speak, very occasionally we encounter children who are too frightened to continue; and according to Core, Chapter 6 this volume, the talking dog is frightening to most 2-year-olds).

The experimenter then provides (via the dog) an example of a maximally acceptable sentence (e.g., *The cat drank the milk*) and places the green counter on the happiest face, explaining "when he gets it right, we're going to choose the green counter and put it here." Next, the experimenter provides an example of a maximally unacceptable sentence (e.g., *The dog the ball played with*) and places the red counter on the saddest face, explaining "when he says it wrong, we're going to choose the red counter and put it here. Don't worry about these other faces [*indicates the middle three faces*] for now." The child then completes two practice trials designed to provide further examples of maximally acceptable and unacceptable sentences (e.g., *The frog caught the fly*; *His teeth man the brushed*).

Taking the green counter, the experimenter then explains that "Sometimes he [indicates dog] says it right but it's not perfect. If it's good but not perfect, you can put the counter here [indicates second happiest face]. If it's a little bit right and a little bit wrong, or somewhere in between, you can put it here [indicates middle face]." Taking the red counter, the experimenter continues, "Sometimes he says it wrong but it's not really terrible. If it's wrong but not terrible, you can put the counter here [indicates second saddest face]. If it's a little bit wrong and a little bit right, or somewhere in between, you can put it here [indicates middle face]." The child then completes three further training trials designed to illustrate intermediate degrees of (un)grammaticality.

The sentences for these training trials need to be carefully chosen for the relevant study to ensure – on the one hand – that they exemplify the general type of error that will be judged in the main part of the study (e.g., argument structure overgeneralization errors as opposed to past-tense *-ed* overgeneralization errors) and – on the other – that they are not of exactly the same specific type (e.g., transitive causative overgeneralizations of intransitive verbs), to avoid providing hints that could affect responses in the main part of the study. For our study of transitive causative overgeneralization errors, the three intermediate training items involved overgeneralizations of prepositional-dative-only verbs into the double-object dative construction: *The woman said the man a funny story* (intended rating 2/5), *The girl telephoned her friend the news* (3/5 or 4/5) and *The man whispered his friend the joke* (4/5). By way of comparison, a study of the acceptability of various past-tense forms (Ambridge, 2010) used incorrect regular and irregular noun plurals as training items. Children's ratings are generally broadly in line with these target ratings but, if not, the experimenter can re-explain the procedure and give feedback. The child then moves on to the main part of the study, which proceeds in the same way (though with trials presented in random order).

Animations

For all training and test trials, a cartoon animation depicting the event being described by the dog is shown on a laptop screen, which both the child and the dog are "watching." This ensures that the truth value of the dog's description is never in doubt, and that the child is judging the sentence purely on the basis of grammatical acceptability. This also guards against misinterpretation of the sentences (for example, some of Theakston's, 2004, adult participants seemed to interpret the sentences *Don't laugh/giggle me* as *Don't laugh/giggle at me* rather than, as intended *Don't make me laugh/giggle*).

Control Sentences

Another important feature of the design is that, for every ungrammatical sentence (e.g., *The magician disappeared the rabbit*), a grammatical control sentence (e.g., *The rabbit disappeared* or *The magician made the rabbit disappear*) is included. This allows the researcher to control statistically for any general (dis)preferences that may exist for particular items by calculating *preference-for-grammatical-use* (or *difference*) scores (discussed in more detail below).

It is also prudent to avoid a scenario where every utterance of a particular type (e.g., transitive causative) is ungrammatical, whilst every utterance of another type (e.g., intransitive) is ungrammatical, to guard against the possibility of children developing a task-dependent strategy such as rating all transitive causative sentences as ungrammatical. Whilst this precaution was not followed in the study of Ambridge *et al.* (2008), subsequent studies that have included this control have yielded a similar pattern of findings (Ambridge *et al.*, submitted a; submitted b; Ambridge, 2010).

Because the task is relatively demanding and time consuming (young children are reluctant to complete more than about 40 trials, even if this is split over several sessions) we do not generally include any "filler" trials (i.e., trials where children rate unrelated sentence types). However, if particular study designs have trials "to spare," the inclusion of filler trials can only be beneficial.

Another difficult issue relates to the number of items per "cell" of the design. If a complex design with several variables is used, it may be difficult to include more than one or two trials per cell, whilst keeping the overall number of trials manageably low. For example, Ambridge *et al.* (2008) included only one transitive causative sentence with each verb (e.g., *The magician disappeared the rabbit*), whereas ideally one would take an average rating across several (e.g., *The witch disappeared the frog*, *The conjurer disappeared the card*, etc.). An approach followed in subsequent studies (e.g., Ambridge, 2010) is to have two (or more) versions of "the same" experiment with different items (e.g., half of the children would rate *The magician disappeared the rabbit* and half *The witch disappeared the frog*). This allows the number of items per cell to be doubled (or trebled, quadrupled, etc.) without increasing the time taken for an individual child to complete the study.

Data

As previously mentioned, an advantage of the graded grammaticality judgment paradigm is that it yields numerical data that can be analyzed using techniques such as ANOVA or regression: specifically a rating between 1 and 5 for each item (e.g., sentence) from each participant (where 5 represents the happiest face, i.e., the most acceptable). Technically, one might object that the data are not true interval-scale data (a requirement of parametric tests such as ANOVA) as we have no way of knowing whether an increase from (say) 2/5 to 3/5 on the scale represents the same increase in perceived grammaticality as (say) an increase from 4/5 to 5/5. However, the treatment of rating-scale data as interval data is so commonplace in psychology

Table 8.1 Some examples of children's judgments of grammatical and ungrammatical sentences on the five-point smiley-face scale (5 = happiest face = most acceptable)

	4–5 (N = 20)		5–6 (N = 27)		6–7 (N = 24)		Adults (N = 42)	
	M	SE	M	SE	M	SE	M	SE
Intransitive: *Bart disappeared*	3.15	0.39	4.63	0.14	4.92	0.06	5.00	0.00
Transitive: **The magician disappeared Bart*	2.25	0.31	3.26	0.26	2.92	0.23	2.60	0.14
Difference (intransitive minus transitive)	0.90	0.55	1.37	0.26	2.00	0.24	2.41	0.14
Intransitive: *Bart vanished*	4.25	0.23	4.70	0.12	4.92	0.06	4.95	0.03
Transitive: **The magician vanished Bart*	3.45	0.30	4.19	0.24	3.78	0.23	3.10	0.15
Difference (intransitive minus transitive)	0.80	0.34	0.52	0.25	1.13	0.26	1.86	0.15
Intransitive: *Bart blicked*	4.05	0.23	3.48	0.27	4.75	0.11	4.31	0.21
Transitive: **The magician blicked Bart*	3.70	0.34	3.48	0.30	4.00	0.22	3.67	0.18
Difference (intransitive minus transitive)	0.35	0.32	0.00	0.33	0.75	0.25	0.64	0.22

that, in practice, one will rarely encounter such an objection outside statistics textbooks (and, in many cases, a alternative nonparametric test is available). It is important to bear in mind, however, that the *absolute* values are almost certainly not particularly meaningful. Participants tend to rate the acceptability of one item with reference to another, meaning that the same sentence could receive very different absolute mean ratings in two studies with different items. The more meaningful comparison is between different items in the same study.

As an example of the type of data that the graded grammaticality judgment paradigm yields, Table 8.1 shows the mean scores for **The magician disappeared/ vanished/blicked Bart* (where *blick* denotes a novel type of disappearing action) and the control sentences *Bart disappeared/vanished/blicked* (for novel verbs, the claim is that children should be able to use the semantics of these verbs to determine the constructions in which they can and cannot appear; see Pinker, 1989). Note that this table shows both the raw scores and, for each grammatical/ungrammatical pair, the difference (preference-for-grammatical-use) score, calculated by subtracting the rating for the ungrammatical sentence from the rating for the grammatical sentence (on a pair-by-pair and child-by-child basis). Data for the three older groups are taken from Ambridge

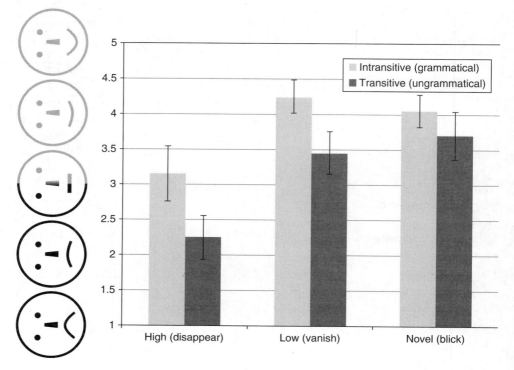

Figure 8.1 Four-year-olds' ratings for grammatical intransitive sentences (light bars) and ungrammatical transitive sentences (dark bars) for (from left to right) a high frequency, a low frequency, and a novel verb (*disappear/vanish/blick*). Error bars show standard error.

et al. (2008), and those for the younger group from a recent pilot study with 20 children aged 4:1–5:0 (*M* = 4:6). As an example of how data collected using this paradigm can be presented graphically, the scores for the youngest group only are also shown in Figure 8.1.

The data from the three older groups are analyzed in Ambridge *et al.* (2008), and hence will not be discussed in detail here. It will suffice to note that children aged 5–6 are clearly capable of completing the task, and give a pattern of judgments very similar to that shown by older children and adults.

For the younger children, there are two points to note. First, for the English verbs *vanish* and (marginally) *disappear*, 4–5-year-olds rated grammatical intransitive uses as significantly more acceptable than ungrammatical transitive causative uses (*vanish*, t_{19} = 2.37, *p* = 0.014; *disappear*, t_{19} = 1.63, *p* = 0.058, one-tailed test; for means see Table 8.1 and Figure 8.1). This finding is important, as it demonstrates, for the first time, that children aged 4–5 are able to use the scale to rate sentences appropriately (though the high standard error scores reflect considerable variation in this ability). Like the 5–6-year-olds, the youngest group do not appear to be able to use the semantics of the novel *disappearing* verb (or a novel *laughing* or *falling* verb, data for which are not shown) to determine the constructions in which it may and may not appear (though 5–6-year-olds can do so for a novel *laughing* verb).

Whether this is because the youngest children have yet to acquire the relevant semantics–syntax links or because the introduction of novel verbs makes the judgment task too difficult is unclear at this stage.

The second point relates to the importance of analyzing difference (preference-for-grammatical-use) scores in addition to raw scores. The entrenchment hypothesis predicts that ungrammatical transitive sentences should be rated as more acceptable for the low frequency verb (e.g., *vanish*) than for the high frequency verb (e.g., *disappear*). Looking again at the youngest group, if one compares the *raw* ratings for **The magician vanished Bart* ($M = 3.45$, $SE = 0.30$) and **The magician disappeared Bart* ($M = 2.25$, $SE = 0.31$), this prediction appears to be supported ($t_{19} = 2.60$, $p = 0.018$). However, this is misleading, because this difference is presumably a consequence – at least in part – of the fact that (for whatever reason) these children give higher ratings to sentences containing *vanish* than *disappear*, even when they are grammatical (*Bart vanished*, $M = 4.25$, $SE = 0.23$; vs *Bart disappeared*, $M = 3.15$, $SE = 0.39$). When one controls for this baseline preference by comparing *difference* scores, as opposed to raw scores, the preference for grammatical over ungrammatical uses (i.e., the dispreference for ungrammatical uses) is no longer significantly smaller for *vanish* ($M = 0.80$, $SE = 0.34$) than *disappear* ($M = 0.90$, $SE = 0.55$; $t_{19} = 0.15$, $p = 0.88$, n.s.).

Further Applications

Although the graded grammaticality judgment paradigm was initially developed to obtain ratings of verb argument structure overgeneralization errors (Ambridge *et al.*, 2008; 2009b; submitted a; submitted b), in subsequent work we have obtained judgments of past-tense forms of novel verbs (e.g., *rife* → *rifed*; *rife* → *rofe*; see Ambridge, 2010) and of grammatical and ungrammatical *un-* prefixed forms (e.g., *unlock*, *unwrap*; **unsqueeze*, **unfill*; see Ambridge *et al.*, 2009a; Ambridge, submitted). Beyond grammaticality, the smiley-face scale could also potentially be used to obtain judgments of familiarity (e.g., Ibbotson *et al.*, submitted), truth value, semantic plausibility, and so forth.

Conclusion

We end by summarizing the advantages and disadvantages of the graded grammaticality judgment paradigm introduced in this chapter. The primary advantage is that the paradigm can be used to address questions on which comprehension and production data bear only indirectly. For any domain in which the predictions of the competing theoretical accounts relate to the relative (un)acceptability of particular forms, a judgment task is – all other things being equal – more appropriate than a comprehension or production task. A related advantage is that the paradigm can be used with older speakers and adults to obtain ratings of the relative unacceptability of errors that these speakers would not produce themselves. For example, whilst adult speakers rate *The magician disappeared Bart* as less acceptable than *The magician vanished Bart*, it would presumably be impossible to tap into the knowledge that underlies these judgments using a production task, as adults would likely produce neither. Another advantage of this paradigm over many comprehension and production measures is that it produces an unambiguous response that does not require interpretation, coding, or reliability checking. The paradigm yields numerical data that can be analyzed directly using common statistical techniques such as ANOVA and regression. An advantage that the paradigm shares with most of the comprehension and production techniques discussed in this volume is that novel verbs (or nouns, etc.) can be used in order to test whether children are in possession of item-general knowledge (as opposed to lexically specific knowledge). Finally, the paradigm can be used to obtain acceptability judgments both for whole sentences and for individual lexical items, and the "smiley-face" procedure can potentially be extended into domains where graded judgments of factors other than grammatical acceptability are required.

One disadvantage of the paradigm is that it is presumably unsuitable for use on children much younger than 4. Although we have not attempted to test children younger than 4:6 (mean age), the considerable variation in performance observed at this age (which would be considered relatively old for many domains of acquisition) means that the paradigm is unlikely to work well for younger children. That said, it may well be that younger children are able to complete a binary version of the task. Clearly this is a question that requires future research. Another concern is that, compared to many comprehension or production tasks (and particularly naturalistic data collection), the paradigm is relatively artificial, in that children are being asked to do something that is far removed from their everyday experience and use of language. There is little that can be done to address this concern, except to seek to corroborate findings from judgment tasks using comprehension, production, and naturalistic data studies, where this would be appropriate.

Finally, it is important to note that there are many research questions for which a judgment task would be either altogether inappropriate, or considerably less appropriate than a comprehension or production task. For example, when the question relates to the age at which children have abstract item-general knowledge of a particular structure (e.g., the active SVO transitive), an elicited production (e.g., Akhtar and Tomasello, 1997), repetition (e.g., Kidd, Lieven, and Tomasello, 2006), weird word order (e.g., Akhtar, 1999), priming (e.g., Savage *et al.*, 2003), act-out (e.g., Akhtar and Tomasello, 1997), preferential looking (e.g., Gertner, Fisher, and Eisengart, 2006), or pointing (e.g., Rowland and Noble, 2011) task is more appropriate. Indeed, many of our own studies use an elicited production (e.g., Ambridge *et al.*, 2006; Ambridge, Rowland, and Pine, 2008; Ambridge and Rowland, 2009) or repetition paradigm (e.g., Ambridge and Pine, 2006) for precisely this reason (though always with the "talking dog," as an additional incentive for children to respond). However, for questions where the competing theories make predictions regarding the relative unacceptability of particular forms (as opposed to error rates,

rates of correct production, etc.), some kind of judgment paradigm is clearly the most appropriate. We hope that the paradigm outlined here will therefore inspire future research into such questions.

Acknowledgments

Thanks are due to Julian Pine and Caroline Rowland for their help both with this chapter and with the development of the judgment paradigm described herein. Thanks to Glen Goodliffe-Davies for collecting the pilot study data used in Table 8.1. This research was supported by grants RES-062-23-0931, RES-000-22-1540 from the Economic and Social Research Council.

Key Terms

Binary grammaticality judgment paradigm A grammaticality/acceptability judgment paradigm in which participants are asked to indicate simply whether a particular form is acceptable or unacceptable (see McKercher and Jaswal, Chapter 10 this volume).

Comprehension paradigm Any paradigm in which children are required not to produce language, but to demonstrate their comprehension (understanding) of a utterance produced by another speaker. Children can demonstrate comprehension via the ability to enact a sentence using toys (*act-out* task), or to "choose" a picture that matches the sentence, either implicitly by looking for longer at the target than a distracter (*preferential looking*) or explicitly by *pointing*.

Difference score A score calculated by subtracting the acceptability rating for one form (e.g., *The magician disappeared Bart*) from the acceptability rating for a related form (e.g., *Bart disappeared*), in order to control for any baseline preference that may exist, regardless of grammaticality (for this example, the extent to which participants "like" sentences that contain the noun *Bart* and the verb form *disappeared*). If the difference score is calculated by subtracting the rating for an ungrammatical form from the rating for a grammatical form (as in the above example), it may also be referred to as a *preference-for-grammatical-use score*. In some cases, it may be more appropriate to calculate the difference score by consistently subtracting the rating for one particular sentence type (e.g., irregular past-tense form) from the rating for another sentence type (e.g., regular past-tense form), regardless of which form is predicted to be more acceptable (e.g., rating for *rifed* minus rating for *rofe*).

Graded grammaticality judgment paradigm A grammaticality/acceptability judgment paradigm in which participants are asked to indicate *the extent to which* a particular form is acceptable or unacceptable, using some kind of linear (graded) scale (e.g., Likert scale, visual analog scale, or, as in the studies discussed here, smiley-face scale).

Grammaticality judgment, acceptability judgment A rating (either *binary* or *graded*) of the acceptability of a particular form. Although the terms have, on the whole, been used interchangeably here, the second, more general term is probably more appropriate when an individual word form (e.g., *Unsqueeze, rifed, rofe*) as opposed to a sentence (e.g., *The magician disappeared Bart*) is being judged. This is because, for individual word forms, it is debatable whether it is *grammatical* acceptability (as opposed to morphological or phonological acceptability) that is being rated. Whatever the domain, our written instructions to adult participants usually do not mention "grammaticality," in order to avoid participants basing their ratings on prescriptive rules.

Judgment paradigm   Any paradigm in which children rate the acceptability of a sentence or an individual word form (a *grammaticality/acceptability judgment* task), the truth value of an utterance (a truth value or *yes/no* judgment task), their confidence that a form has been previously encountered, etc.

Production paradigm   Any paradigm in which children are required to produce language. Commonly used production paradigms include *elicited production* (where the child describes or asks questions about a scene, often to a puppet or toy), *repetition* (where the child repeats an utterance produced by an experimenter, puppet, or toy), and *priming* (where the child and experimenter take turns to describe scenes, with the experimenter sometimes using a *weird word order* for some verbs).

Smiley-face scale   A five-point pictorial scale that can be used by children to give graded judgments of grammatical acceptability (or sentence familiarity, etc.) (see Figure 8.1).

References

Abbot-Smith, K., Lieven, E., and Tomasello, M. (2001) What preschool children do and do not do with ungrammatical word orders. *Cognitive Development*, 16 (2), 679–692.

Akhtar, N. (1999) Acquiring basic word order: evidence for data-driven learning of syntactic structure. *Journal of Child Language*, 26, 339–356.

Akhtar, N., and Tomasello, M. (1997) Young children's productivity with word order and verb morphology. *Developmental Psychology*, 33 (6), 952–965.

Ambridge, B. (2010) Children's judgments of regular and irregular novel past tense forms: new data on dual- versus single-route debate. *Developmental Psychology*, 46 (6), 1497–1504.

Ambridge, B. (submitted) Testing a probabilistic semantic account of the formation and restriction of linguistic generalizations: a grammaticality judgment study.

Ambridge, B., Freudenthal, D., Pine, J.M., *et al.* (2009a) Un-learning un-prefixation errors. Paper presented at the International Conference on Cognitive Modelling 2009, Manchester, UK.

Ambridge, B., and Lieven, E.V.M. (2011) *Child language acquisition: contrasting theoretical approaches*. Cambridge: Cambridge University Press.

Ambridge, B., and Pine, J.M. (2006) Testing the agreement/tense omission model using an elicited imitation paradigm. *Journal of Child Language*, 33 (4), 879–898.

Ambridge, B., Pine, J.M., Rowland, C.F., and Clark, V. (submitted a) The retreat from argument-structure overgeneralization errors: verb semantics, entrenchment or both? *Cognitive Linguistics*.

Ambridge, B., Pine, J.M., Rowland, C.F., and Clark, V. (submitted b) Restricting dative argument-structure overgeneralizations: a grammaticality-judgment study with adults and children. *Language*.

Ambridge, B., Pine, J.M., Rowland, C.F., and Young, C.R. (2008) The effect of verb semantic class and verb frequency (entrenchment) on children's and adults' graded judgements of argument-structure overgeneralization errors. *Cognition*, 106 (1), 87–129.

Ambridge, B., Pine, J.M., Rowland, C.F., *et al.* (2009b) A semantics-based approach to the "no negative evidence" problem. *Cognitive Science*, 33 (7), 1301–1316.

Ambridge, B., and Rowland, C.F. (2009) Predicting children's errors with negative questions: testing a schema-combination account. *Cognitive Linguistics*, 20 (2), 225–266.

Ambridge, B., Rowland, C.F., and Pine, J.M. (2008) Is structure dependence an innate constraint? New experimental evidence from children's complex question production. *Cognitive Science*, 32 (1): 222–255.

Ambridge, B., Rowland, C.F., Theakston, A.L., and Tomasello, M. (2006) Comparing different accounts of inversion errors in children's non-subject wh-questions: "What experimental data can tell us?" *Journal of Child Language*, 33 (3), 519–557.

Bannard, C., and Matthews, D. (2008) Stored word sequences in language learning: the effect of familiarity on children's repetition of four-word combinations. *Psychological Science*, 19 (3), 241–248.

Bard, E.G., Robertson, D., and Sorace, A. (1996) Magnitude estimation of linguistic acceptability. *Language*, 72 (1), 32–68.

Bowerman, M. (1988) The "no negative evidence" problem: how do children avoid constructing an overly general grammar? In J.A. Hawkins (ed.), *Explaining language universals* (pp. 73–101). Oxford: Blackwell.

Braine, M.D.S., and Brooks, P.J. (1995) Verb argument structure and the problem of avoiding an overgeneral grammar. In M. Tomasello and W.E. Merriman (eds), *Beyond names for things: young children's acquisition of verbs* (pp. 352–376). Hillsdale, NJ: Erlbaum.

Brooks, P.J., and Tomasello, M. (1999) How children constrain their argument structure constructions. *Language*, 75 (4), 720–738.

Chan, A., Meints, K., Lieven, E.V.M., and Tomasello, M. (2010) Young children's comprehension of English word order in act-out and intermodal preferential looking tasks. *Cognitive Development*, 25, 30–45.

Chomsky, N. (1959) A review of B.F. Skinner's *Verbal Behavior*. *Language*, 35 (1), 26–58.

Chouinard, M.M., and Clark, E.V. (2003) Adult reformulations of child errors as negative evidence. *Journal of Child Language*, 30 (3), 637–669.

Dittmar, M., Abbot-Smith, K., Lieven, E., and Tomasello, M. (2008) Young German children's early syntactic competence: a preferential looking study. *Developmental Science*, 11 (4), 575–582.

Gertner, Y., Fisher, C., and Eisengart, J. (2006) Learning words and rules: abstract knowledge of word order in early sentence comprehension. *Psychological Science*, 17 (8), 684–691.

Ibbotson, P., Theakston, A., Lieven, E.V.M, and Tomasello, M. (submitted) Prototypical semantics of the transitive construction: developmental comparisons.

Kidd, E., Lieven, E., and Tomasello, M. (2006) Examining the role of lexical frequency in the acquisition and processing of sentential complements. *Cognitive Development*, 21 (2), 93–107.

Lust, B., Flynn, S., and Foley, C. (1996) What children know about what they say: elicited imitation as a research method for assessing children's syntax. In D. McDaniel, C. McKee, and H. Cairns (eds), *Methods for assessing children's syntax*. Cambridge, MA: MIT Press.

MacWhinney, B., and Bates, E. (eds) (1989) *The cross-linguistic study of sentence processing*. New York: Cambridge University Press.

Mandell, P.B. (1999) On the reliability of grammaticality judgements tests in second language acquisition research. *Second Language Research*, 15 (1), 73–99.

Marchman, V.A. (1997) Children's productivity in the English past tense: the role of frequency, phonology and neighborhood structure. *Cognitive Science*, 21 (3), 283–304.

Matthews, D., Lieven, E., Theakston, A.L., and Tomasello, M. (2004) The role of frequency in the acquisition of English word order. *Cognitive Development*, 20, 121–136.

Matthews, D., Lieven, E., Theakston, A., and Tomasello, M. (2007) French children's use and correction of weird word orders: a constructivist account. *Journal of Child Language*, 34 (2), 381–409.

McDaniel, D., and Cairns, H. (1996) Eliciting judgments of grammaticality and reference. In D. McDaniel, C. McKee, and H. Cairns (eds), *Methods for assessing children's syntax*. Cambridge, MA: MIT Press.

Naigles, L. (1990) Children use syntax to learn verb meanings. *Journal of Child Language*, 17 (2), 357–374.

Noble, C.H., Rowland, C.F., and Pine, J.M. (in press) Comprehension of argument structure and semantic roles: evidence from infants and the forced-choice pointing paradigm. *Cognitive Science*.

Pinker, S. (1989) *Learnability and cognition: the acquisition of argument structure*. Cambridge, MA: MIT Press.

Rice, M.L., Wexler, K., and Redmond, S.M. (1999) Grammaticality judgments of an extended optional infinitive grammar: evidence from English-speaking children with specific language impairment. *Journal of Speech, Language and Hearing Research*, 42, 943–961.

Rowland, C.F., and Noble, C.H. (2011) The role of syntactic structure in children's sentence comprehension: evidence from the dative. *Language Learning and Development*, 7 (1), 55–75.

Savage, C., Lieven, E., Theakston, A., and Tomasello, M. (2003) Testing the abstractness of children's linguistic representations: lexical and structural priming of syntactic constructions in young children. *Developmental Science*, 6 (5), 557–567.

Theakston, A.L. (2004) The role of entrenchment in children's and adults' performance on grammaticality judgement tasks. *Cognitive Development*, 19 (1), 15–34.

Tomasello, M. (2000) Do young children have adult syntactic competence? *Cognition*, 74 (3), 209–253.

Further Reading and Resources

Because so little research has been conducted using this new paradigm, there is very little further reading to recommend. The paper that sets out the paradigm in detail (Ambridge *et al.*, 2008) is available from my website (http://pcwww.liv.ac.uk/~ambridge/). Theakston (2004) is a good example of a study that uses a binary judgment paradigm, whilst McDaniel and Cairns (1996) provide an interesting discussion of methodological considerations in child judgment studies. A comprehensive discussion of studies that have investigated children's grammatical knowledge using elicited production, repetition, weird word order, priming, act-out, and preferential looking and pointing tasks can be found in Ambridge and Lieven (in press, Chapters 5–7).

The smiley-face scale is reproduced here as Plate 5. We have reproduced the scale and cut-out counters in color, with the intention that readers can photocopy the scale for use in their own studies.

For the studies discussed here, animations were produced using either Adobe Flash Professional (http://www.adobe.com/uk/products/flash/), an educational version of which is available at a large discount, or (in most cases) Anime Studio (http://anime.smithmicro.com/). Sound files were recorded using the freeware Audacity program (http://audacity.sourceforge.net/). Animations created using these programs (with or without embedded sound files) can be played in most internet browsers and media software including VLC (http://www.videolan.org/vlc/), QuickTime (http://www.apple.com/quicktime/download/), and (for Flash animations) SwfMax (http://www.swfmax.com/).

9   Assessing Children's Narratives

Elaine Reese, Alison Sparks,
and Sebastian Suggate

Summary

We profile a story retell method of assessing young children's narratives that has been used with 3–8-year-old English-speaking children from a diverse range of cultural and socioeconomic backgrounds. In this method, a researcher reads a storybook to the child and then asks the child to retell the story back to the researcher or to a puppet. The stories children tell using this method are transcribed and can then be coded along a number of cognitive and linguistic dimensions. Our focus in this chapter is on children's memory for the story and on the structure and quality of their stories. These aspects of narrative development are linked to children's story understanding and to their later reading skill. Their narratives also contain information at the lexical and syntactic level that could be captured. The strengths of the method are its flexibility, its diverse applications, and its palatability to children.

Children's oral narratives offer a window into several domains of their learning and development. From a child's narratives, the researcher can acquire information about higher-order language use, such as mastery of story structure, the ability to connect events through cause and effect, and the child's grasp of character motivations and reactions. At the same time, the researcher can also access basic linguistic knowledge including expressive vocabulary, morphology, and sentence-level semantic-syntactic skills. Moreover, at a cognitive level, narratives based on previously experienced material can reveal important information about children's memory capabilities.

Narratives are viewed as a pragmatic skill because they are always told to someone for a reason (e.g., Berman, 1995). In other words, narrative is an authentic mode of communication and as such children are inherently motivated to participate.

Research Methods in Child Language: A Practical Guide, First Edition.
Edited by Erika Hoff.
© 2012 Blackwell Publishing Ltd. Published 2012 by Blackwell Publishing Ltd.

Narratives vary on a continuum of contextualization, from a highly contextualized narrative that is inserted into the flow of conversation, to a highly decontextualized narrative that is told in a school setting upon request; in short, narratives cannot exist without a context for telling. Narratives are a rich source for observing semantic skills, because they draw upon a child's lexical knowledge and knowledge of story structure. Narratives also reveal syntactic skills because they are built out of sentence-level constructions. Narratives thus provide a natural setting for observing multiple levels of linguistic, cognitive, and social-cognitive development, rendering them a useful tool for research and for diagnosing communication disorders (Bliss and McCabe, 2010; de Villiers and de Villiers, 2010).

A second advantage of narratives as a research and diagnostic tool is that most children readily engage in storytelling, given the slightest provocation, from as young as 2 or 3 years. Stories are, simply put, more fun for a child than participating in a standardized language assessment. A third advantage of narrative as a tool for understanding children's language and development is that storytelling appears to be a universal behavior. Children from all cultures studied thus far tell narratives of some sort (Miller *et al.*, 1990). Labov and Waletzky (1967/1997) defined a narrative as a minimum of two clauses joined by a temporal juncture. Using this definition, even 2-year-olds are capable of producing a story. Children's stories are, of course, shaped increasingly by the canonical story form offered in their culture (see Reese, in press, for a review).

The beauty of children's narratives as a research tool thus lies in their richness and their universal appeal. As usual, however, a tool's strengths also provide a clue to that tool's weaknesses. A rich source of data to one researcher is utter messiness and a lack of standardization to another. Can we have it both ways? Can we retain the richness of children's narratives while constraining the error variance that seems to be a natural result of asking a child to tell a story? Our quest has been to devise a method of eliciting children's narratives that reliably reveals aspects of their linguistic and cognitive development that cannot be gained from more constrained methods, but at the same time to limit the less informative sources of variability on children's narratives. In our research, we are especially interested in how children's narratives reveal their mastery of the story structure and story elements of their culture. How does narrative production reveal a child's comprehension of a story: of the main evaluative point of a story, of cause and effect, of characters' motivations and reactions, and of the sequence of story events? Our main focus has been on the implications of narrative for young children's literacy acquisition, although narratives can also be used to observe many other aspects of children's development, including the social-emotional domain (Hirsh-Pasek *et al.*, 2005; cf. Reese *et al.*, in press).

History of a Method

Our story begins in the early 1990s when I, the first author, was completing my PhD under the supervision of Dr Robyn Fivush. I was trained primarily as a researcher of children's memory, but the main way to access children's memory for everyday events is through their recounts of those events. Memory, language, and narrative are intertwined from nearly the beginning of speech (Sachs, 1983; Reese, 1999). My dissertation topic was the role of oral language in young children's literacy development. I had access to a rich longitudinal dataset on preschool children's personal narratives, or their stories about personally experienced events, which are a vital source of information for children's autobiographical memory development. I wished to supplement the existing dataset with narratives of children's fictional storytelling, both for stories they had heard and stories they produced from scratch. Understanding and reproducing fictional narratives is of hypothesized importance for children's reading development.

At this juncture in the field, a rich literature already existed on children's narrative development as revealed through their stories about wordless picture books (*The Frog Stories*, e.g., Bamberg and Damrad-Frye, 1991; later compiled in Berman and Slobin, 1994) and their stories of personal experience (e.g., Fivush, Gray, and Fromhoff, 1987; Peterson and McCabe, 1983), but neither of these research literatures had yet been linked to children's literacy development.

Drawing from the Home–School Study of Language and Literacy Development (Dickinson and Tabors, 2001; Snow *et al.*, 1995; see Dickinson, Chapter 17 this volume) and other sources (e.g., Morrow, 1989; Renfrew, 1969), I devised two new methods of storytelling for the children at the age 5 datapoint alongside the usual elicitation of their personal narratives (see Reese, 1995, for detailed information). The first was a method of *story retelling* in which a researcher read the child a picture book, then put the book away and asked the child to retell the story to her (*Tell me everything you remember about that story, from beginning to end*). The second was a method of *story production* in which the researcher showed the child a stimulus picture and then asked the child to make up a story about the picture.

All three methods produced usable data, but, somewhat like the story of *Goldilocks*, the personal narrative method produced data that erred a bit on the side of being too rich, the story production method erred a bit on the side of being too lean, and the story retelling method seemed to produce data that were just right. For instance, because all children have different experiences upon which to base their personal narratives, those narratives are by their nature more variable and less constrained. Personal narratives are the first stories that children tell, and they are essential for understanding autobiographical memory development (Reese *et al.*, in press). When we are trying to understand a child's mastery of story structure, however, personal narratives are in large part shaped by the event being narrated. If the event chosen for discussion is a positive one, such as going to the zoo, there may be no real problem to be solved and no high point or resolution – simply a series of fun and interesting actions and reactions. A child who is narrating a negative event such as a personal injury, however, has more opportunity to showcase his or her understanding of story structure (see Peterson and McCabe, 1983). Elicitation of personal narratives has the advantage of almost always producing some data from every child, but the problem is that the resulting variability in narrative structure is sometimes due to factors other than the child's mastery of story structure.

In contrast, story production from scratch, or even from stimulus pictures, is a difficult and demanding task for most 5-year-old children (Westerveld, Gillon, and Miller, 2004); thus, this method sometimes does not produce enough data, and thus underestimates a child's understanding of story structure. With story retelling, a child has the support of being provided with a story, but there is still plenty of scope for individual variability to emerge in the length and quality of the narrative that is retold.

This first attempt at devising a method of eliciting a story retell needed refinement. For some children, retelling a story that they had heard only once was too demanding. They needed more support. Also, some children balked at telling the story back to the researcher when they knew the researcher had just heard it too. So in our next longitudinal study with 5-year-old children in New Zealand, we made several modifications (see Trionfi and Reese, 2009). After reading the story, we let children look at the book during the retelling, with the researcher controlling the page turns and prompting the child to tell more of the story by asking "Now what's happening?" at each set of pages. To give the child a reason for retelling the story, thus rendering the storytelling more ecologically valid, the researcher pulled a Winnie-the-Pooh puppet out of her bag after the reading and told the child, "Pooh was inside my bag while I was reading that story and he didn't hear what happened. Could you please tell Pooh the story of that book from beginning to end?" The researcher then held Pooh so that he was "looking" at the book with the child, and delivered the prompts in Pooh's voice, along with general encouragement: "You're telling me a great story! What's happening here?" Even the shyer children could be engaged in the storytelling using this method. Coincidentally, Daniela O'Neill and colleagues (O'Neill, Pearce, and Pick, 2004) profiled a similar method of narrative elicitation, but we arrived upon this technique independently, having collected our data in 2000 before hearing of O'Neill and colleagues' technique.

Beginning in 2003, we used this modified technique successfully with 3- and 4-year-old children from diverse ethnic and linguistic backgrounds attending Head Start (see Reese *et al.*, 2010a). This study was an intervention that contrasted parent training in dialogic book reading with elaborative conversation techniques. We post-tested the children on a range of language measures, including their expressive vocabulary and phonological awareness, but the effects of the parent intervention were observed only on the story retelling measure. Children whose mothers had been trained in elaborative conversation demonstrated greater gains in the quality of their narratives than children whose mothers had been trained in dialogic reading techniques. Thus, the story retelling technique is sensitive enough to detect changes in children's narratives as a function of intervention. Table 9.1 contains a sample of the children's narratives at the end of the Head Start year, and shows the contrast between attenuated and elaborated narratives using the technique with children of similar age and schooling experience.

Back in New Zealand, the next step of our research program was to demonstrate that children's narratives using the story retelling method were predictive of their reading development, and in particular of their reading comprehension. Our goal here was to show the added value of a narrative assessment over and above simply

Table 9.1 Story retelling narratives for *Hemi's Pet*

(a) *Elaborated narrative, highest narrative quality (NQ) score*

Memory score 19, NQ score 14
Age 3 years 10 months, ethnicity Latino
She was looking in, in the door, and that's her brother.
And the teacher said, They're going to have a pet show.
And Rata said, What's a pet show? What's a pet?
And the brother said, A pet is what you look after and you play with it.
He helped her put on her clothes and he dressed her hair.
Her mother said, Why are you dressed up?
And the father said, Why you all dressed up? Where are you going?
The brother said, She's going to school.
They're laughing. They're laughing.
Cause they don't like the pet.
Then she doesn't have feet just like a
And then that bird doesn't have feathers to make a bird.
And neither does the cat.
The cat doesn't have a tail just like the fish.
And neither does the fish.
And then they gave her some chips.
And then the brother put the ribbon on her head.
And then the brother said, You can keep it forever and ever and ever and ever and ever.

Memory score 14, NQ score 15
Age 4 years 1 month, ethnicity African American
When he brings his sister to school, his teacher make her play for a little while.
When he was sad he didn't have a pet.
When he got home from school, he put on a, her brother put on the favorite clothes she like to wear.
And he mother said, She's going.
She's going to the thing.
When he said, There's a pet sister, the kids was laughing.
Woah, the bird has no four legs like the dog or fur.
And the cat didn't have fur too.
Cause the fish didn't have real fur or whiskers or nothing.
And the hamster didn't have fur.
And the mother gave her a red scarf and a piece of, a bag of potato chips.
And they went outside and her brother said she could keep it forever.

Memory score 13, NQ score 10
Age 4 years 2 months, ethnicity African American
Once there was a girl who went to school.
And her name was Hemi.
I remember she is three years old.
There is going to be a pet contest.

(continued)

Table 9.1 (cont'd)

The next morning he was washing her hands and he put on her favorite dress.
The mother said, Who's looking pretty?
He said, This is my pet sister.
But they were all laughing.
What? A pet sister? No!
It got hair! She don't have fur.
It doesn't look like a bird with wings.
Then they are the rest of the chips.

(b) *Attenuated narrative, lowest narrative quality (NQ) score*

Memory score 6, NQ score 0
Age 3 years 10 months, ethnicity African American
She goes to school.
And she brushed her hair.
And she goes to school to bring a pet.
Everybody laughed at her.
And she bring it to show and tell.
He has a snack and he eats snack.

Memory score 4, NQ score 0
Age 3 years 10 months, ethnicity Caucasian
They were washing themselves.
The girl's wearing a dress.
They were laughing.
And then she won a bag of potato chips.

Memory score 3, NQ score 1
Age 4 years 3 months, ethnicity Latino
He's brushing her hair.
Where are you going?
She won the prize.

Memory score 4, NQ score 2
Age 4 years 6 months, ethnicity Latino
Once upon a time there was a little girl.
And she said, Wanna be my puppet?
And then he does her hair.
Then she got a bag.

---

measuring oral language in terms of children's vocabulary development (see Dickinson *et al.*, 2003 for an extended version of this argument). After all, understanding and retelling a story require the narrator to formulate a narrative structure that delineates context and characters and conveys the characters' motivations, all of which cannot be captured by a measure of lexical knowledge. In New Zealand, children begin formal reading instruction on the day that they turn 5 years old. By about age 5½ or 6 years they are reading connected text, and by age 7 or 8 they are fluent readers. Our study focused on two age cohorts: those children who had been reading for one year on average ($M = 6$ years) and those who had been reading for two years on average ($M = 7$ years). With these school-age children, we collected their story retellings in a school setting as part of a larger battery of early literacy assessments (see Reese *et al.*, 2010b).

Children of this age in a school setting were capable of retelling the story without the additional supports of seeing the pictures, and without the aid of the puppet. One specific advantage of using the method without the support of a book is that the resulting stories are easier to transcribe and code, because the coder does not have to differentiate pictured information from nonpictured information in the retelling. As we detail later in the chapter, our coding for story memory is focused only on the text of the story, not on information that is only contained in the pictures and not also in the text. And, although the children's stories without these supports were shorter and less rich in terms of narrative elements, they still contained enough variability to detect many of the links we had predicted. Narrative performance predicted oral reading fluency, but for the 6-year-old cohort this was not above and beyond nonsense word reading (a purer measure of decoding). For the 7-year-old cohort, however, narrative quality predicted reading in the second and third years of school (ages 6 to 8) above and beyond both decoding and receptive vocabulary (Reese *et al.*, 2010b). With data recently collected, we have been able to demonstrate that both story memory and narrative quality uniquely predict 9-year-olds' reading comprehension, above and beyond decoding and receptive vocabulary at age 6 (Suggate, Schaughency, and Reese, 2011). These findings are consistent with a view of reading that sees a role for complex, higher-order language, such as narrative skill, as particularly important in reading comprehension.

Procedural Details

Given the findings to date, we recommend the story retelling elicitation method for researchers interested in assessing 3–8-year-olds' mastery of story structure and specific story elements such as references to context (time and place), cause and effect, characters' motivations and reactions, as well as their basic memory for a story. The technique can be modified depending on the age and developmental level of the child, and depending on the information that the researcher hopes to gain from the method. For younger children and those who are more difficult to engage, retelling the story to a puppet with the aid of a book provides the most supportive method for eliciting the story retelling. For older children, additional supports may not be necessary and may add unnecessary length to the data collection and to the transcription and coding process.

Choosing a Story to Retell

A common element to all of the variations in the story retelling elicitation method is that they are based on an existing story. The story can be one in a commercially available picture book, although it is best to choose one that is out of print or not readily available to control for children's previous experience with the story. We have used a range of commercially available books in the US and in New Zealand, such as *A Perfect Father's Day* (Bunting, 1991, in Reese, 1995; Trionfi and Reese, 2009); *Peter's Chair* (Keats, 1967, in Reese *et al.*, 2010a); *Hemi's Pet* (de Hamel, 1985, in Reese *et al.*, 2010a); and *Hemi and the Shortie Pyjamas* (de Hamel, 1996, in Reese *et al.*, 2010b). In our research in the US we often use books from New Zealand because children will not be familiar with them, and in New Zealand we often use US books that are not readily available to avoid the confound of previous experience with that book. The main requirement is that the book should contain a narrative line that reflects the canonical story structure of the culture. In Western cultures, for instance, the classic storyline is one in which characters are introduced and the listener is oriented to the time and place of the narrative. Shortly a problem presents itself to the main character, who then engages in a series of actions to solve the problem. Finally the problem is solved and the story ends with some sort of resolution, with the high point marked by an evaluation of the event and of the character (Labov and Waletzky, 1967/1997). Whether the stories are elicited with the help of the book, with a puppet, or simply at the request of the researcher, the resulting narratives must be transcribed verbatim and then coded for various elements. The basic instruction in all cases after reading the book is simply, "Wow, I'll bet you remember a lot about that story. Tell me (or a puppet) everything you remember about that story from beginning to end."

Coding

We have found that it is useful to rate the children's narratives along two dimensions: first for their memory of the story (adapted from Bishop and Edmundson, 1987; Mandler and Johnson, 1977), and second for the quality of their story (drawing upon Labov and Waletzky, 1967/1997; Peterson and McCabe, 1983). To code children's story memory, first the original text of the storybook is divided into propositions marked by a subject and a unique verb. Then the children's retellings are compared, utterance by utterance, against the actual story. This method guards against a child getting credit for simply describing pictures rather than narrating the story (cf. DeTemple, 2001). If a child recalls the exact words or the gist of a story proposition, he or she gets credit for recalling a unit of information about the story. We wished to create a system of coding that would be appropriate for children from linguistically diverse backgrounds, so in identifying propositions we concentrated on the content and we did not penalize for errors typically made by English language learners or dialect speakers, such as mistakes in the gender of pronouns or the absence of morphological endings on nouns and verbs (Sparks and Reese, 2011).

In this sense, the story memory coding is less concerned with children's acquisition of basic linguistic skills, and more focused on examining higher-order cognitive-linguistic knowledge. For each unit of information recalled, that unit is then evaluated along a dimension of *quality*. Quality is a measure of their skill at storytelling and also reflects their understanding of story structure. The two main categories of story quality are *orientations* (to time, place, person, and cause and effect) and *evaluations* (internal states of the characters or external judgments of the story or the characters). Retelling the story in the form of direct or indirect character dialogue is another aspect of story quality that we have sometimes included as an evaluative device, because it makes the storytelling more engaging to the listener and can highlight key plot developments (Trionfi and Reese, 2009).

Thus, the first pass of coding entails reviewing the transcript to identify all of the memory units, or propositions, from the text of the story. The second pass is to evaluate each memory unit for an instance of narrative quality. To avoid overestimating narrative quality, we allow the child to get credit for only one instance of each type of quality per proposition: orientations to time and to place; causal conjunctions; and descriptions and evaluations of story characters or events (see Trionfi and Reese, 2009, for more details). Character introduction is limited to a single point given for specific reference to each one of the story characters. Character introduction could easily be limited to a total of two points: one for mentioning the name of the main character and one for mentioning any supporting character by name or relationship.

To calculate reliability, two independent coders rate the same subset of transcripts, typically 25% of the sample. Reliability is then calculated separately via Cohen's kappas between the two coders on the number of memory units and on the number and type of narrative quality units. If desired, a composite score of total narrative quality as a function of the total number of memory units can be calculated for a measure of the *rate* of narrative quality per memory unit (see Trionfi and Reese, 2009). For younger children, however, the most robust measure of their narrative may simply be the total number of memory units, because their scores on narrative quality dimensions are still quite low (Sparks and Reese, 2011), so it is best to keep the memory and quality measures separate. Note that this "story memory" score is not simply a measure of narrative length, because all utterances that were mere picture descriptions are not a part of story memory. The main criterion for story memory is that the information is included in the text, based on the premise that the text of a story is privileged information in our literate society.

Narrative quality is also of great interest with respect to children's literacy, because it is via the quality variable that we gain access to children's understanding of story structure and their marking of important aspects of the story. Narrative quality is essentially a child's highlighting of the critical elements of the story for understanding: the time, place, and people, and the main point of the story, which is marked by evaluations. Griffin *et al.* (2004) identified narrative quality, especially in the form of evaluations, during children's fantasy narratives at age 5 as one of the main predictors of their reading comprehension 3 years later (cf. Westerveld, Gillon, and Miller, 2004, for another measure of narrative quality). Narrative quality can be subdivided into orientations and evaluations (with dialogue and description typically counted as evaluations; see Reese *et al.*, 2010b) or into the various subtypes of orientations and evaluations (Trionfi and Reese, 2009). For school-age children, the type of narrative quality may be of interest, depending on the precision of the research questions. For instance, if a researcher were particularly interested in the child's provision of characters' internal states, then because the reliability process has been conducted at the level of specific types of evaluations and orientations, this subcategory could be pulled out and analyzed separately. The only unacceptable measure of story retelling using our method would be a composite score of the memory units and the narrative quality units, because narrative quality is dependent upon the memory unit score: a child cannot receive credit for narrative quality unless he or she has first received credit for a memory unit.

Potential Pitfalls

We recommend that the researchers conduct pilot work to determine the right combination of support for the story retelling process with the target sample. The use of the puppet and the storybook during retelling can mean the difference between having a rich dataset versus no variation at all because children are not engaged in the storytelling process. However, if a researcher can get reasonable variation in the children's stories without the use of the puppet and the storybook during retelling, then we advise this more constrained option, because it will mean an easier time in transcribing, coding, and interpreting the data. For instance, in our study of children's storytelling as a function of whether or not they had imaginary companions (Trionfi and Reese, 2009), we used the puppet procedure to elicit children's story retellings. We found that children with imaginary companions created richer story retellings than children who did not have imaginary companions. If we had collected children's narratives only in this one context, we would have encountered the interpretive problem that children with imaginary companions are simply more comfortable in a storytelling situation that simulated pretend play with the use of a puppet. However, we also collected children's factual personal narratives without the puppet procedure and found the same pattern of effects, with children with imaginary companions telling richer personal narratives, so we were able to avoid this potential confound.

From time to time, children claim to already know the story that they are about to hear or be read. Before discontinuing the task because of the potential confound of the child's prior knowledge, we suggest a few probing questions. It usually turns out to be highly unlikely that the child has ever seen the story before, falling short at questions such as "Okay, so what is the story about?", "Where did you hear the story before?", or (after handing the child another book) "Do you know this one as well?" Because of the obvious advantage that prior knowledge of the story would give, we reiterate that the story be carefully chosen to eliminate this possibility.

Some children have trouble staying still during narrative tasks, be it during the listening or the retelling phase. Part of the beauty of this task is that, although remaining still may be ideal, it is not as necessary as it is in many standardized language and literacy tests. One of us (the third author) can remember reading a story to a child who was active the whole time, climbing under the table, over the chair, and constantly fidgeting. As I recall, his retell was still pretty good – at least about what would be expected, or perhaps slightly better, given his performance on language and other reading tasks. With younger and more active children, the puppet seems to have a calming and focusing effect. When children become restless, the puppet becomes the center of attention and a conversation ensues, which can be easily redirected by the researcher back to the story narration: the researcher, in the voice of the puppet, asks the child to keep telling the story. It is the authenticity of the communicative situation, a chat with a puppet, that helps the child to focus on the task. If the researcher simply directed attention back to the storybook, there would be less motivation for continuing the retell. The puppet thus provides a natural context for communication which fosters engagement.

Related to problems with excessive fidgetiness, some children interrupt the story reading with a stream of questions. In the interest of ensuring standard administration of the task, we suggest deflecting the questions as gently as possible, without discouraging the child from reflecting on the story (e.g., child asks, "Why did Hemi go to the hospital?", and researcher replies, "Well, if we read a little more, we might find out the answer").

New Directions in Narrative Assessment

One possibility for standardizing the story administration that we are trialing is delivering the story via headphones, and then the researcher pretends to be confused as to which story was played and asks the child to retell it (Struthers, Schaughency, and Reese, 2011; see Westerveld and Gillon, 2010, for a related procedure). The idea behind this adaptation is to reduce the likelihood that children will inhibit their story retell because they are aware that the researcher has heard it just as recently as has the child. We have also often wondered whether some children's performance is inhibited by shyness. Together, we think that it is important to find the optimal method for each age-group of children to ensure that children provide their best possible narratives.

We are also continuing to investigate how the kind of narrative procedure outlined in this chapter relates to other story retell procedures. One example of this is comparing story memory and narrative quality as predictors of reading fluency and comprehension in comparison to the story retell from the Dynamic Indicators of Basic Early Literacy Skills (DIBELS: Kaminski *et al.*, 2008). The DIBELS retell is a score of the number of words recalled in 1 minute from a passage previously read aloud by the student. DIBELS retell has the advantage of being quick and easy to score and administer but the disadvantages of not measuring narrative quality and of being dependent on children's reading ability.

In addition, we will be directly comparing the predictive validity of personal narratives versus story retellings for children's reading comprehension. As well, we will be comparing the narrative quality of children's narrations of wordless picture books (the *Frog* stories by Mercer Meyer) with their story retelling and personal narratives (see Westerveld and Gillon, 2010, for similar cross-context comparisons on linguistic measures). Given theoretical links between higher-order aspects of language and reading (Dickinson *et al.*, 2003), we think it is vital to also investigate relations between narratives and long-term reading achievement. Are children's early narratives as good or better at predicting later reading and language as their early vocabulary development (Cunningham and Stanovich, 1997)?

Buoyed by the findings of Reese *et al.* (2010a), in which narratives were sensitive to changes in maternal conversations whereas other child language measures were not, we have begun to use narratives to investigate curricular effects on language development. Specifically, we are interested in whether 5-year-old children in play-oriented kindergartens in Germany, or in Waldorf schools in New Zealand, develop different language profiles from children of the same age experiencing formal reading instruction in school (e.g., Suggate, Schaughency, and Reese, in press). We also note that a story retell called *Tell Me*, adapted in part from the story retelling in Reese (1995), is being used as part of the standardized school entry assessment in New Zealand (Ministry of Education, 1997). Teachers score the *Tell Me* for a range of linguistic features as children retell the story.

We are also continuing to explore and compare children's story retellings across cultures. For instance, we are recording narratives from 5–7-year-old children in Germany and New Zealand and will examine task performance both longitudinally and in relation to other measures of reading and language. One difficulty of this research is ensuring that the translation of the same story is similar across languages, such that each memory unit (the segments of the story for which children are awarded points when the gist thereof is correctly retold) in one language corresponds well to that in the other language, in terms of length and complexity of vocabulary and grammar, and pragmatic function.

Practical and Clinical Implications

The focus of the present chapter is primarily on methodological issues for researchers, but because this task has clinical relevance for assessing children with language delays, we briefly address these issues here. The second author, who is a speech–language pathologist as well as a researcher, has used the story retelling procedure in her clinical practice. The story retelling task can be a useful supplement to formal screening and evaluation tools designed to assess language competence and to identify children with language delay or disorder, especially in my work with 3–5-year-old children from linguistically diverse, low-income families attending preschool in urban schools.

Most norm-referenced batteries of language include molar measures of children's lexical knowledge and their semantic-syntactic skills using item formats such as identifying and naming pictures, imitation tasks, and cloze exercises in which the child must fill in the blank. These kinds of tasks are often less familiar to children from culturally diverse backgrounds whose families may not engage in the kinds of conversational routines that are typically observed in talk between teachers and students beginning in the preschool classroom (Michaels, 1981; Heath, 1983). Our story retelling, which is administered in a short period of time, can be used to supplement the information obtained by traditional testing and to provide a point of comparison when the clinician suspects that a child's language skills may have been under- or overestimated by formal testing. Because the task is situated in a natural communicative context, it may yield more valid information from children who are unfamiliar with a mainstream test-taking format.

The story retelling text can be used as an additional source of information about the range of a child's vocabulary knowledge, the diversity of verbs, and the use of morpho-syntactic markers. For clinicians who are trained in the practice and interpretation of discourse analysis, the story memory and narrative quality coding provides important information on children's complex, higher-order language processes. The retelling text can also be shared with the parent and/or teacher to see whether it accurately reflects the child's language at home or in the classroom.

Data Analysis

In preparing to conduct analyses on narrative data it is particularly important to view the distributions for narrative memory and quality. With young children in particular, it is possible that a significant proportion will be able to retell only a small portion of the story. As a result, there may be floor effects for memory and quality scores. In such circumstances we recommend using nonparametric analyses, such as logistic or Poisson regression (Aitkins and Gallop, 2007).

The good news is that there are strong theoretical reasons to believe that narrative memory and quality are conceptually unconstrained skills. Constrained skills are those that develop in short bursts and are quickly mastered, making only a limited contribution to development (e.g., naming of the letters of the alphabet, learning to count to 10 as quickly as possible). Thus, constrained skills can present problems of conceptual and measurement ceiling effects (see Paris, 2005, for a review). For instance, what would 9-year olds' letter naming skill tell you about their reading skill? However, the detail and richness with which it is possible to provide an oral narrative range from the first words of a toddler to the works of Shakespeare. Accordingly, we suggest that narratives are not one of the constrained skills that may plague research designs because the richness of language has a high ceiling at any point in development, as long as the narrative task is appropriate (e.g., ceiling effects would result if the story were developmentally too short or simple).

A third factor to consider is that a child has to first retell a story to be able to imbue the retelling with quality. Practically speaking, the narrative memory and narrative quality scores are not independent of each other because quality is derived from that which is retold. As a result, these two variables should be treated as being statistically dependent in analyses.

Conclusions

We offer our story retelling method as one way of capturing the richness and complexity of young children's higher-order language acquisition. We believe it will be especially useful for researchers who would like to measure semantic and pragmatic aspects of language development that go above and beyond children's lexical and conversational skills, and for clinicians wishing to supplement their use of standardized tests. We hope that researchers will test our story retelling method against their own preferred methods of assessing higher-order language so that we can gain a deeper understanding of its strengths and limitations with diverse populations of children.

Key Terms

Evaluation   Narrative clauses that elaborate upon events or highlight the meaning of the narrated events for the story characters or for the listener. These devices can include descriptive words (adverbs, adjectives), internal states (cognitive and/or emotional), character speech (direct or indirect), repetition of words for emphasis, and evaluations of story events or characters.

Narrative   Labov and Waletzky (1967/1997) defined a narrative as any two clauses joined by a temporal marker.

Narrative quality   Children's elaboration upon the basic story events through their use of orientation and evaluation elements.

Orientation   Narrative clauses that orient the listener to the time, place, and people in the narrative. Some researchers include causal conjunctions as an orienting device because they help clarify the order of events within a narrative for the listener.

Story memory   Children's memory for the text of the story.

References

Aitkins, D.C., and Gallop, R.J. (2007) Rethinking how family researchers model infrequent outcomes: a tutorial on count regression and zero-inflated models. *Journal of Family Psychology*, 21, 726–735.

Bamberg, M., and Damrad-Frye, R. (1991) On the ability to provide evaluative comments: further explorations of children's narrative competencies. *Journal of Child Language*, 18, 689–710.

Berman, R.A. (1995) Narrative competence and storytelling performance: how children tell stories in different contexts. *Journal of Narrative and Life History*, 5, 285–313.

Berman, R.A., and Slobin, D. I. (1994) *Relating events in narrative: a crosslinguistic developmental study*. Hillsdale, NJ: Erlbaum.

Bishop, D.V.M., and Edmundson, A. (1987) Language-impaired 4-year-olds: distinguishing transient from persistent impairment. *Journal of Speech and Hearing Disorders*, 52, 156–173.

Bliss, L.S., and McCabe, A. (2010) Personal narrative: cultural differences and clinical implications. *Topics in Language Disorders*, 28, 162–167.

Bunting, E. (1991) *A perfect Father's Day*. New York: Clarion.

Cunningham, A.E., and Stanovich, K.E. (1997) Early reading acquisition and its relation to reading experience and ability 10 years later. *Developmental Psychology*, 33, 934–945.

De Hamel, J. (1985) *Hemi's pet*. Boston: Houghton Mifflin.

De Hamel, J. (1996) *Hemi and the shortie pyjamas*. Auckland: Puffin.

DeTemple, J. (2001) Parents and children reading books together. In D.K. Dickinson and P.O. Tabors (eds), *Beginning literacy with language* (pp. 31–51). Baltimore: Brookes.

De Villiers, P.A., and De Villiers, J.G. (2010) Assessment of language acquisition. *Cognitive Science*, 1, 230–244.

Dickinson, D., McCabe, A., Anastasopoulos, L., *et al.* (2003) The comprehensive approach to early language and literacy: the interrelationships among vocabulary, phonological sensitivity, and print knowledge among preschool-age children. *Journal of Educational Psychology*, 95, 465–481.

Dickinson, D., and Tabors, A. (2001) *Beginning literacy with language: young children learning at home and school*. Cambridge: Brookes.

Fivush, R., Gray, J., and Fromhoff, F.A. (1987) Two-year-olds talk about the past. *Cognitive Develoment*, 2, 393–409.

Griffin, T., Hemphill, L., Camp, L., and Wolf, D.P. (2004) Oral discourse in the preschool years and later literacy skills. *First Language*, 24, 123–147.

Heath, S.B. (1983) *Ways with words: language, life, and work in communities and classrooms*. New York: Cambridge University Press.

Hirsh-Pasek, K., Kochanoff, A., Newcombe, N.A., and de Villiers, J. (2005) *Using scientific knowledge to inform preschool assessment: making the case for "empirical validity."* Society for Research in Child Development, Social Policy Report, XIX.

Kaminski, R.A., Cummings, K.D., Powell-Smith, K.A., and Good, R.H. (2008) Best practices in using Dynamic Indicators of Basic Early Literacy Skills for formative assessment and evaluation. In A. Thomas and J. Grimes (eds), *Best practices in school psychology* (vol. V, pp. 1181–1204). Bethesda: National Association of School Psychologists.

Keats, E.J. (1967) *Peter's chair*. New York: Harper and Row.

Labov, W., and Waletsky, J. (1967/1997) Narrative analysis: oral versions of personal experiences. In J. Helm (ed.), *Essays on the verbal and visual arts* (pp. 12–44). Seattle, WA: University of Washington Press.

Mandler, J., and Johnson, N. (1977) Remembrance of things parsed: story structure and recall. *Cognitive Psychology*, 9, 111–151.

Michaels, S. (1981) "Sharing time": children's narrative styles and differential access to literacy. *Language and Society*, 10, 423–422.

Miller, J.M., Potts, R., Fung, H., *et al.* (1990) Narrative practices and the social construction of self in childhood. *American Ethnologist*, 17, 292–311.

Ministry of Education (1997) *School Entrance Assessment*. Wellington, NZ: Ministry of Education.

Morrow, L.M. (1989) *Literacy development in the early years*. Englewood Cliffs, NJ: Prentice Hall.

O'Neill, D.K., Pearce, M.J., and Pick, J.L. (2004) Preschool children's narratives and performance on the Peabody Individualized Achievement Test–Revised: evidence of a relation between early narrative and later mathematical ability. *First Language*, 24, 149–183.

Paris, S.G. (2005) Reinterpreting the development of reading skills. *Reading Research Quarterly*, 40, 184–202.

Peterson, C., and McCabe A. (1983) *Developmental psycholinguistics: three ways of looking at a child's narrative*. New York: Plenum.

Reese, E. (1995) Predicting children's literacy from mother–child conversations. *Cognitive Development*, 10, 381–405.

Reese, E. (1999) What children say when they talk about the past. *Narrative Inquiry*, 9, 215–242.

Reese, E. (in press) Culture, imagination, and narrative. In M. Taylor (ed.), *Oxford Handbook of Imagination*. New York: Oxford University Press.

Reese, E., Haden, C.A., Baker-Ward, L., *et al.* (in press) Coherence of personal narratives across the lifespan: a multidimensional model and coding method. *Journal of Cognition and Development*.

Reese, E., Leyva, D., Sparks, A., and Grolnick, W. (2010a) Maternal elaborative reminiscing increases low-income children's narrative skills relative to dialogic reading. *Early Education and Development*, 21, 318–342.

Reese, E., Suggate, S., Long, J., and Schaughency, E. (2010b) Children's oral narrative and reading skills in the first three years of reading instruction. *Reading and Writing: An Interdisciplinary Journal*, 23, 627–644.

Renfrew, C. (1969) *The Bus Story: a test of continuous speech*. Oxford.

Sachs, J. (1983) Topic selection in parent–child discourse. *Discourse Processes*, 2, 145–153.

Snow, C.E., Tabors, P.O., Nicholson, P.A., and Kurland, B.F. (1995) SHELL: oral language and early literacy skills in kindergarten and first-grade children. *Journal of Research in Childhood Education*, 10, 37–48.

Sparks, A., and Reese, E. (2011) Exploring the role of narrative in children's emergent language and literacy skills. Manuscript in preparation.

Struthers, P., Schaughency, E., and Reese, E. (2011) Training parents to interact with beginning readers. Manuscript in preparation.

Suggate, S.P., Schaughency, E.A., and Reese, E. (2011) Children learning to read later catch up to children reading earlier. Manuscript in preparation.

Suggate, S.P., Schaughency, E.A., and Reese, E. (in press). The contribution of age and formal schooling to oral narrative and pre-reading skills. *First Language*. doi: 10.1177/0142723710395165

Trionfi, G., and Reese, E. (2009) A good story: children with imaginary companions create richer narratives. *Child Development*, 80, 1310–1322.

Westerveld, M.F., and Gillon, G.T. (2010) Oral narrative context effects on poor readers' spoken language performance: story retelling, story generation, and personal narratives. *International Journal of Speech–Language Pathology*, 12, 132–141.

Westerveld, M.F., Gillon, G.T., and Miller, J.F. (2004) Spoken language samples of New Zealand children in conversation and narration. *Advances in Speech Language Pathology*, 6 (4), 195–208.

Further Reading and Resources

Berman, R.A., and Slobin, D.I. (1994) *Relating events in narrative: a crosslinguistic developmental study*. Hillsdale, NJ: Erlbaum.

Guo, J., Lieven, E., Budwig, N., *et al.* (eds) (2009) *Crosslinguistic approaches to the psychology of language: research in the tradition of Dan Isaac Slobin*. New York: Psychology Press.

Nelson, K.E., Aksu-Koc, A., and Johnson, C.E. (eds) (2001) *Children's language: developing narrative and discourse competence* (vol. 10, pp. 1–30). Mahwah, NJ: Erlbaum.

New Zealand's School Entry Assessment, story retell procedure (*Tell Me*): http://toolselector.tki.org.nz/Assessment-areas/Cross-curricular/School-Entry-Assessment-SEA/%28back_to_results%29/Assessment-areas.

Stromqvist, S., and Verhoeven, L. (eds) (2004) *Relating events in narrative. Volume 2: Typological and contextual perspectives*. Mahwah, NJ: Erlbaum.

10 Using Judgment Tasks to Study Language Knowledge

David A. McKercher
and Vikram K. Jaswal

Summary

In this chapter, we discuss the truth-value judgment and grammaticality judgment tasks and how they are employed to study various aspects of children's knowledge of their language. In particular, we look at uses of these tasks for studying children's understanding of passive voice, imperative mood, scope of negation relative to quantifiers, the count/mass distinction in noun phrases, word meaning, category boundaries, verb transitivity, and plural and past tense morphology. The examples we review serve to illustrate how children's judgments of acceptability, whether based on accuracy relative to a given situation or conformity to grammatical rules, are informative and enlightening. In addition, the examples illustrate how truth-value judgments differ from grammaticality judgments.

Two Types of Judgment Task

In this chapter, we discuss the usefulness of two types of judgment task that can be used to assess multiple aspects of children's language knowledge: the truth-value judgment (TVJ) task and the grammaticality judgment (GJ) task. In a TVJ task, listeners compare a sentence (or a pair of sentences) with a situation and decide whether it is true (or which one of the two is true). In a GJ task, listeners are asked to judge whether an utterance is "good" or "silly," or to decide which of two utterances is the "right" way to say it. The utterance may be paired with a situation or presented in isolation. An important difference between the tasks is that the TVJ task only uses

Research Methods in Child Language: A Practical Guide, First Edition.
Edited by Erika Hoff.

grammatical utterances – some true and some false relative to the scenario – while the GJ task uses both grammatical and ungrammatical utterances. This means that in the GJ task, judgment of *no*, *false*, or *wrong* can be due to an utterance that violates some rule or convention of the language and not because it is untrue as a proposition. As Peter Gordon pointed out in his review of the TVJ task, "In grammaticality judgment tasks and other metalinguistic tasks, there is an implicit assumption that the child understands the notion of a sentence being 'good'/'right' or 'silly'/'wrong' as relating to intuitions about grammaticality. The TVJ task, on the other hand, makes no such assumptions" (1996, p. 212; see also McDaniel and Cairns, 1996, on the GJ task).

As an illustration of the difference, consider the following. A picture of a girl eating an apple is shown to an English speaker, child or adult. Two utterances are provided, either by the experimenter or by a pair of puppets:

(1)   A girl is eating an apple.
(2)   A girl is eating an orange.

The decision of which one is the correct description requires an understanding of the sentence: the meanings of each of the words and the contribution to the meaning from the particular order of the words, i.e., *a girl* is before the verb in subject position and *an apple/orange* follows the verb as a direct object. The hearer must parse the sentence, access word meanings, and decide whether it matches the scenario. If, however, utterance (1) were contrasted with utterance (3), the task would have an additional demand:

(3)   A girl is eating an apples.

This time, the decision of which one is right requires the same meaning extraction as in the TVJ task but also requires the speaker to assess each utterance with respect to the rules of grammar. In this example, determiner–noun agreement needs to be considered, and specifically that the indefinite article must occur with a singular form of a countable noun. In general, GJ tasks require participants to access metalinguistic knowledge, or knowledge about one's native language, in addition to what the utterance means.

There is certainly room for debate on whether a given task is a TVJ or a GJ task. Carrying on with our example from above, consider pitting the following two utterances against each other, for the same situation of a girl eating an apple:

(4)   A girl is eating an apple.
(5)   An apple is eating a girl.

Is the utterance in (5) wrong because it is false for the situation, or because it violates the subject–verb–object word order of English? It could be judged as wrong (specifically, false) because the apple is not doing the eating, or it could be judged as wrong (specifically, ungrammatical) because the undergoer of the eating action is not expressed as the direct object and the agent as the subject.

The contrast between sentence (4) and sentence (6) illustrates a different problem:

(6)   A girl is eating apple.

The utterance in (6) is true, though use of the mass noun as opposed to the count noun makes it ungrammatical relative to the situation of a girl eating a discrete apple. It is not ungrammatical in general, since it would be well formed and true if the girl were eating a bowl of mashed apple. In spite of these complications, most tasks are relatively easily classified as requiring judgments of truth, or judgments of grammaticality in addition to truth.

Uses of the Truth-Value Judgment Task

An early forerunner of the truth-value judgment task was the use of *yes/no* questions containing passive and cleft sentences with 3–5-year-old children (Abrams *et al.*, 1978). Before this study, children's understanding of reversible passive constructions in which either participant is a plausible agent, such as *The girl was pushed by the boy*, was mainly studied by an act-out method. The act-out method requires children to perform an action with dolls to demonstrate their comprehension of a given sentence (see Ambridge, Chapter 8 this volume). For example, de Villiers and de Villiers (1973) had 19–38-month-olds follow instructions of the sort *Make the horse kiss the cow* and *Make the cow be kissed by the horse*. For the 19–23-month-old group, about 30% of the responses involved the children *themselves* performing the action, such as the child kissing the cow, the horse, or both. Up to 15% of the responses by children in this group were refusals. In spite of these sorts of responses, the findings were informative: children's performance on active sentences was superior compared to performance on passives.

Abrams *et al.* (1978) pointed out a number of problems with the act-out method including these two: the observer must decide from the performance which doll has been assigned which role; and the requirement of an "extroverted performance that a doll action requires" (p. 339) may be too much to ask of some children, and may not lend itself easily to other cultures. To this end, Abrams *et al.* introduced a method in which 3–5-year-old children were asked to answer *yes* or *no* to questions about actions they had just seen performed by hand-puppets. For example, a boy puppet would push a girl puppet, and then the experimenter would give the instruction "Tell me 'yes' or no.' Was the boy pushed by the girl?" The *yes/no* questions included actives (e.g., "Did the boy push the girl?"), passives (as above), active subject clefts (e.g., "Was it the boy that pushed the girl?"), and passive object clefts (e.g., "Was it the girl that was pushed by the boy?").

The results showed that children were more accurate on active voice and active subject cleft questions, where the agent precedes the affected object, than on passive voice and passive object cleft sentences, where the affected object appeared before the agent in the sentence. In addition, performance on the affected object before agent sentences improved from the 3:0–3:3 group to the 5:0–5:3 group. Abrams *et al.*'s interpretation of the results was that children initially relied on a "first noun equals agent" strategy for interpreting the questions, and less so with increasing age. Another interesting finding of their study was that the differences in the comprehension of actives and passives were greater and the results clearer in the TVJ-like task than in the act-out task, which they also included for comparison.

Note that the Abrams *et al.* (1978) study used a TVJ-like task and found that the syntactic order of the noun phrases influenced children's understanding of the sentence in such a way that the agent was expected to come before the affected object. A similar finding in the domain of semantics is found in Lidz and Musolino's (2002) study of ambiguous sentences such as in (7):

(7)   The boy didn't pet two animals.

The sentence has two readings, paraphrased in (8) and (9). The reading in (8) can be called isomorphic in that the order of NOT and TWO in the interpretation follows the order in the sentence. The reading in (9) is nonisomorphic in that the numeral TWO has wide scope relative to NOT, unlike the order in the sentence.

(8)   It is not the case that the boy pet two animals. [NOT > TWO]
(9)   There are two animals that the boy didn't pet. [TWO > NOT]

Lidz and Musolino (2002) constructed stories with small toys and props so that a sentence such as (7) would be true on one reading and false on the other. One experimenter acted out the story while a second experimenter manipulated a puppet and had it say a sentence that was either true or false for the story. Children between 3:11 and 4:11 were given the task of rewarding the puppet for being right or punishing it for being wrong, and were also asked to say why the puppet was right or wrong.

Reminiscent of the better performance on actives than on passives in the Abrams *et al.* (1978) study discussed above, Lidz and Musolino (2002) found that children's performance was more adult-like on the isomorphic (NOT > TWO) interpretations than on nonisomorphic (TWO > NOT) interpretations. Adults were able to assign either scope interpretation, as required by the situation in the story, scoring 97% in isomorphic and 93% in nonisomorphic conditions. Children scored 81% in the isomorphic condition but only 33% in the nonisomorphic condition, rejecting the puppet's true statements two-thirds of the time. They justified their judgments with explanations such as "He did find two guys!" or "You're wrong, he did! He found two guys!" (Lidz and Musolino, 2002, p. 134).

Musolino and Gualmini (2004) extended this line of research, again using the TVJ task, with sentences of the form in (10) and (11):

(10)   Minnie didn't buy two of the rings. (partitive construction)
(11)   Minnie bought all the balloons but she didn't buy two rings. (nonpartitive construction with a preceding affirmative statement)

English-speaking adults and children aged 3:9 to 4:11 participated in a task in which short stories were acted out, each followed by a puppet saying a sentence of the sort in (10) and (11). The story that was acted out was true on the wide-scope reading of the numeral (the nonisomorphic interpretation) and false on the NOT > TWO interpretation. While adults almost always accepted the statements in both the partitive and the nonpartitive/preceding-context conditions, children rejected three-quarters of the nonpartitive statements, indicating a preference for the isomorphic interpretation. The partitive sentences, on the other hand, were accepted 75% of the time, possibly because the partitive "X of the Y" construction forces a wide-scope reading of the numeral. In short, the results of this study are important in that they demonstrate that the partitive construction helps children arrive at a nonisomorphic interpretation and also that a preceding affirmative context does not.

So far, we have seen use of the TVJ task for assessing comprehension of passives and scope of negation. A different use of the TVJ task is in the domain of word meanings. McKercher (2009) tested children's comprehension of the preposition *with* and whether or not the "together with," i.e., "accompaniment," sense of *with* was sufficient to license its occurrence, even when potential instruments that are unused are present. The question was whether children would accept a sentence such as "She's eating cake with a fork" for a situation in which a fork is present in the scene but is not used because the female participant instead uses her fingers to pick up and eat the cake. The design of the experiment was such that a given participant saw a photograph of a woman either using a fork to eat cake, or eating cake without use of a fork that was present in the scene. The critical test was the pairing of a situation in which the fork was not used but was simply present, and the statement "She's eating cake with a fork." If accompaniment is sufficient to license the use of *with*, then participants will judge the utterance as true for the situation. If use of the instrument is necessary, then participants will judge the utterance as false.

The materials included 10 different situations (e.g., drawing a circle in the sand with/without a stick, peeling an orange with/without a knife, wiping a table with/without a sponge) and the participants included 3-year-olds, 4-year-olds and adults. The surprising result was that 3-year-olds often judged statements of the form "X is VERBING Y with Z" as true even when the instrument Z was not being used. Out of a possible 40 judgments of this sort, 3-year-olds judged 18 (45%) as true, 4-year-olds judged 8 (20%) as true, and adults never did. It is quite possible that if 2-year-olds had been tested, an acceptance rate higher than 45% would have been found. In any event, the TVJ task as used here demonstrated a developmental trend in restricting the meaning of *with* in these situations from merely accompaniment to instrumentality.

As noted, by asking children to judge the truth or falsity of utterances, we can make inferences about their underlying knowledge. Although the responses most frequently associated with the TVJ task are *yes/no* answers by the child or reward/punishment of a puppet by the child, its basic structure can be extended to other responses as well. For example, building on a procedure by Gelman and Markman (1986), Jaswal (2004) presented 3- and 4-year-olds with pictures of animals that looked like members of one category, but which the experimenter claimed were members of a different category. For example, he referred to a cat-like animal as a "dog." The question was whether children would believe the adult, or whether they would discount what he said in favor of their own perceptually based hypothesis about what the animal was.

Rather than asking children whether the speaker was correct or using a puppet that could be rewarded or punished, Jaswal (2004) asked children to make an inference: in the case of the cat-like animal, to decide whether it chewed on bones (a property consistent with the label the adult used) or drank milk (a property consistent with the animal's appearance). This allowed children to judge the truth or falsity of the labeling event without having to explicitly contradict the experimenter.

Three-year-olds tended to go along with the unexpected label the adult used. But 4-year-olds often rejected the label, sometimes making comments like "That doesn't look like a dog" and pointing out reasons why the experimenter was wrong. Subsequent studies using the same basic procedure have addressed questions about the circumstances under which even 3-year-olds would be skeptical (e.g., if the speaker prefaced his assertion with "I think": Jaswal and Malone, 2007), and the circumstances under which even 4-year-olds would be credulous (e.g., if the speaker claimed to have some special knowledge about the labeled item: Jaswal, 2006).

The inference version of the TVJ can be useful, but it has its limits. Specifically, in the work just described, children could participate in only a few trials – between four and eight – because it took a fair amount of time to explain to children on each trial what the possible inferences were. Additionally, there was concern that 3-year-olds were merely complying with the labels the adult used – that they did not really believe that the cat-like animal was a "dog," for example. However, subsequent work suggested that they did indeed believe the unexpected labels in so far as they tended to use them when describing the objects to a different experimenter (Jaswal, Lima, and Small, 2009).

Uses of the Grammaticality Judgment Task

We turn now to the use of a task that adds the dimension of metalinguistic knowledge, i.e., an understanding of the rules of one's native language. In the GJ task, participants must access word meanings, parse the sentence into constituents, and construct a meaning, just as in the TVJ task. In addition, they must also consider whether or not the utterance conforms to the grammar of their language. In the realm of first language acquisition, the GJ task has been successfully used to study children's understanding of word order in imperative sentences, the count/mass distinction on nouns, verb transitivity, and irregular plural and past tense forms. We summarize each of these studies below to illustrate the utility of the method.

An early study in which judgments of acceptability were elicited from children is de Villiers and de Villiers' (1972) test of 2- and 3-year-olds' knowledge of correct word order and selectional restrictions in imperative sentences. This study was inspired by the earlier work of Gleitman, Gleitman, and Shipley (1972) in which three 2-year-old girls judged imperative utterances as "good" or "silly." Some of the utterances were well formed (e.g., "Bring me the ball"), some were reversed order (e.g., "Ball me the bring"), some were telegraphic (e.g., "Bring ball"), and some were telegraphic and reversed order (e.g., "Ball bring"). On average, the three girls judged the well-formed sentences, both full and telegraphic, as "good" 82% of the time, and the reversed order utterances, full and telegraphic, as "good" 60% of the time. De Villiers and de Villiers modified Gleitman, Gleitman, and Shipley's procedure and tested eight children aged 2:4 to 3:9 on the acceptability of imperative utterances. Their materials included reversed order imperatives such as "Teeth your brush" and semantically anomalous combinations such as "Throw the sky."

In the word order game, children whose mean length of utterance (MLU) scores were above 4.0 morphemes per utterance judged reversed order utterances as wrong 80% of the time and correct order as wrong 21% of the time. The four children with MLU scores below 4.0 were less successful and judged reversed order imperatives as wrong 29% of the time – not too different from the correct order imperatives, judged as wrong almost 20% of the time. Interestingly, this group was much better at the semantic game, judging semantically anomalous utterances as "wrong" 58% of the time. The more linguistically advanced group (MLU above 4.0) judged semantically odd sentences as wrong 89% of the time, a better performance than on the reversed word order materials. This finding is interesting in that judgments of semantic anomaly, such as "Drink the chair," need not draw on any grammatical rules; they could simply be truth-value judgments of something that would never be true. The word order materials such as "Cake the eat," on the other hand, require the more complex task of considering rules of grammar, and in fact children often judged these as fine.

Gordon (1981) used the GJ task to assess children's acquisition of the count/mass distinction on nouns, with a more elaborate design to elicit grammaticality judgments. Unlike the imperatives studies, where judgments were of utterances in isolation, Gordon used a doll-house and miniature props to present a scenario and then had each of two puppets say something. The children's task was to reward the puppet who said it "okay." The linguistic materials involved count and mass nouns and the quantifiers that appear with them. Count nouns, such as *dog* and *chair*, have plural forms that mean "more than one *X*" and can occur with quantifiers such as *few*, *many*, and *several* (as plurals) and with *each*, *every*, and *either* (as singulars). Mass nouns, such as *gold* and *information*, generally do not have plural forms unless the plural form signifies "type of *X*" (e.g., *golds* for "types of gold" or "shades of the color gold," among others). Mass nouns also occur with quantifiers such as *little* and *much*.

Gordon pointed out that errors in the domain of quantifier + noun constructions could be "selection failures" (e.g., *several water*, *much chairs*, *each information*) or "overpluralizations" (e.g., *every cars*, *either chairs*). Selection failures result from the incorrect co-occurrence of quantifier and noun. A quantifier such as *more* can occur with plural count nouns (e.g., *more books*) or singular mass nouns (e.g., *more water*). Other quantifiers only occur with plural count nouns (e.g., *several books*), with singular mass nouns (e.g., *much rice*), or with singular count nouns (e.g., *each book*). Overpluralizations only involve the quantifiers *each*, *every*, and *either* and occur when a plural count noun is used: though such a situation is semantically plural because it entails more than one instance of *X*, a singular form for *X* is the convention.

Children aged 3:3 to 5:10 were asked for their judgments on sentence pairs in a forced-choice task. For example, given a situation in which two chairs are at a table in a doll-house and the child is told that four people are coming for dinner, children were asked to reward one of two puppets with a gold star for saying a sentence "okay," one puppet saying "That's not enough chairs for four people," and the other saying the ungrammatical "That's not enough chair for four people." Other referents included cans, kettles, soup, corn, coffee, and sugar. Gordon (1981) reported percentage errors, and these correspond to choosing the ungrammatical utterance as the right way to say it. Error rates approached 40% for overpluralizations (e.g., *every chairs*) and selection failures (e.g., *much chairs*) combined when the nouns were count nouns. Error rates were lower with mass nouns. Overpluralization errors were also more likely to be endorsed than selection failure errors. In short, Gordon (1981) used the GJ task to study a complex set of distinctions in the domain of count and mass nouns and the appropriate quantifiers with which they occur.

Hochberg (1986) used the pair of puppets version in testing children's knowledge of a different aspect of syntax. She elicited judgments of transitive sentences with intransitive verbs, such as "I'm gonna jump the frog" and "I'm gonna fall the rock." Children were asked to judge three types of sentence pairs, each member of the pair said by one of the puppets: periphrastic causatives vs intransitives used as causatives ("innovative transitives"), as in (12); suppletive transitives vs innovative transitives, as in (13); and transitives vs innovative intransitives, as in (14).

(12) (a)   I'm gonna make the donkey dance.
      (b)   I'm gonna dance the donkey.
(13) (a)   I'm gonna take my toys to school.
      (b)   I'm gonna go my toys to school.
(14) (a)   Sally is drinking a cup of juice.
      (b)   A cup of juice is drinking.

Hochberg found an asymmetry in children's judgments: they were more likely to judge incorrect transitives as "okay" than they were for incorrect intransitives. In fact, no child over 3:8 chose the type of sentence illustrated in (14b) as the correct member of the pair. Overall, children favoured innovative transitives, more so when the choice was against periphrastic causatives, as in (12). Hochberg's findings are particularly important because analyses of diary data on the direction of errors were equivocal. Results from the GJ task showed a bias to form transitives from intransitives that was not apparent in diary data.

Jaswal, McKercher, and VanderBorght (2008) used a version of the GJ task to ask whether a speaker's history of accuracy played a role in children's willingness to entertain the possibility that the plural or past tense of a noun or verb is irregular. Most English nouns and verbs follow the regular paradigm (i.e., add -*s* for plural and -*ed* for past tense), and if you ask a 4-year-old to form the plural of a novel word like *wug* she will invariably say *wugs* (Berko, 1958). But of course, there are some exceptions to the regular paradigm: the plural of *mouse* is *mice* (not *mouses*), for example, and the past tense of *go* is *went* (not *goed*).

Given children's massive exposure to the regular paradigm and early developing expectations that nouns and verbs are regular, Jaswal, McKercher, and VanderBorght (2008) wondered how they deal with input that suggests a given noun or verb is irregular. Clearly, they do not dismiss it outright (because they end up learning some irregular words), but they also can be resistant to information that conflicts with their expectations (Naigles, Gleitman, and Gleitman, 1993). Jaswal, McKercher, and VanderBorght asked whether children may be willing to believe that a word is irregular if it comes from a speaker who they have reason to believe is a credible source.

Jaswal, McKercher, and VanderBorght used a credibility induction procedure in order to demonstrate to 3–5-year-olds that one speaker knew the names of familiar objects and a second speaker did not (e.g., one speaker referred to a shoe as a "shoe," and the other called it a "telephone"). Subsequently, and as in Koenig, Clément, and Harris (2004), children preferred the labels for novel objects from the speaker who had been correct in the past rather than the one who had been incorrect.

In the new part of the procedure, Jaswal, McKercher, and VanderBorght adapted Berko's (1958) "wug test" for use as a GJ task. On four novel plural trials, the experimenter showed children a picture of a novel animal, and explained, "This is a cra. Can you say cra? Now there are two. This friend [pointing to the formerly unreliable informant] says there are two cras, and this friend [pointing to the formerly reliable informant] says there are two cray. Which one of my friends is saying the right thing?" On four novel past tense trials, the experimenter showed children a picture of a person performing a novel action (e.g., swinging a ball on a rope), and explained, "This is a man who knows how to pim. Can you say pim? He pims every day. This friend [pointing to the formerly unreliable informant] says that yesterday, this man pimmed. This friend [pointing to the formerly reliable informant] says that yesterday, this man pame. Which one of my friends is saying the right thing?" Half of the children at each age had the plural trials first and half had the past tense trials first. Crucially, the formerly unreliable informant used the regular plural or past tense form – the one that matched the child's own expectation; the formerly reliable informant used the irregular form.

Results were unambiguous. Children at all ages tended to endorse the regular plural or past tense form of the novel word – even though that form was produced by a speaker who had been wrong in the past about the names of simple, familiar objects! This pattern of results was obtained when the data were analyzed in two different ways: first, by looking at the average number of selections of the form provided by the formerly accurate informant in plural and past tense trials, and second, by looking at results from the very first plural or past tense trial (whichever came earlier). The reason for looking at the very first trial is that children's responses on later trials can be influenced by feedback they receive or think they are receiving during the task (e.g., Diesendruck and Markson, 2001; Evey and Merriman, 1998). The very first trial may represent the purest response because it occurs before this kind of contamination could happen.

One concern about this procedure is that it pits two speakers against each other, and asks children to pick which one is correct. This, of course, forces children to make a selection – even if they may think that both (or neither) are correct.

Additionally, it is not a particularly ecologically valid procedure; it does not happen very often that children are presented with competing possibilities in quick succession. More likely, children may encounter one form and later, in a different context, another.

Finally, the particular procedure used by Jaswal, McKercher, and VanderBorght (2008) is what might be called a "hearsay" procedure: it adds an additional step above and beyond the normal TVJ or GJ procedure in that children heard the experimenter claim that each informant said X, but did not actually hear the informants themselves make these utterances. Part of the reason for this methodological choice was that it allowed the experimenters to quickly and easily conduct the study. It was not necessary to have multiple experimenters on hand every time a child came to participate or to videotape several clips with several actors; a single experimenter could simply present pictures of the two informants and attribute statements to them. Fortunately, the hearsay procedure replicated the finding that is often obtained with live or videotaped actors in the labeling phase (e.g., Koenig, Clément, and Harris, 2004): that is, children preferred novel labels from the informant who had been correct in the past rather than the one who had been incorrect. For this reason, Jaswal, McKercher, and VanderBorght were confident that the hearsay procedure was a valid one to address the question in which they were interested.

Data Analysis

One of the advantages of judgment tasks is that the data are straightforward, especially when compared with production data, where coding categories and criteria are required in the analysis of utterances. Data can simply be coded as acceptance and rejection of true or false statements (for TVJ tasks), or of grammatical or ungrammatical statements (for GJ tasks). Children's rewarding of a puppet counts as acceptance and punishment counts as rejection. A point can be awarded if children accept a true or grammatical statement or if they reject a false or ungrammatical one. The average number of points awarded in two or more conditions or at two or more ages can be compared using parametric statistics (e.g., analyses of variance, *t*-tests), and comparisons to chance can also be made using one-sample *t*-tests. Additionally, as noted earlier, it is often useful to consider responses on the first trial only. If, for example, children's average performance is higher in condition X than in condition Y, one might also expect that more children would respond correctly on the very first trial in condition X than in condition Y.

The main complications for purposes of data analysis on the TVJ or GJ tasks are when participants do not answer, when they accept and then reject a statement, or the reverse. For the case where they switch responses on a given trial, the researcher must decide whether to exclude these trials, count them according to the final answer, or count them as less than full accept/reject responses (e.g., assign 0.5 credit).

Conclusion

We conclude by noting that a number of important questions in language development can be addressed only by using technologically sophisticated procedures (see Kovelman, Chapter 4 this volume; and Trueswell, Chapter 12 this volume). But for other questions, low-tech procedures, including the TVJ and GJ tasks, can do the trick. We have seen how useful these tasks are for studying children's linguistic knowledge in domains of syntax (passives, word order, verb transitivity, and the count/mass distinction), semantics (scope of negation, word meaning, and category boundaries), and morphology (irregular plural and past tense forms). The most important thing is to not let the technology drive your questions; think about what your question is, and then consider which existing procedure (or new one) would be most effective and cost-efficient to answer it.

Key Terms

Grammaticality judgment (GJ) task   An experimental task in which participants indicate by various means whether or not a given statement is grammatically correct. The statement can be paired with a situation but need not be.

Imperative mood   Mood is part of the grammatical system of a language in which such things as possibility, probability, certainty, and wishes are expressed. Imperative clauses are typically used to express commands, as in *Clean up your room*. The unexpressed subject is understood as second person *you*, singular or plural.

Metalinguistic knowledge   An understanding that language can be treated as an object of analysis and that regularities and rules can be found. This sort of awareness is required for identifying an incorrect form in a language (e.g., an ungrammatical sentence), for correcting it, and for explaining why it is incorrect.

Passive voice   Voice is part of the grammatical system of a language in which the participants in an event are foregrounded or backgrounded in the description of it. In passive voice constructions, the undergoer of an action is expressed as the subject of the sentence and the agent of the action is optionally expressed. In English, the passive voice form of a sentence such as *The cat chased the mouse* would be *The mouse was chased by the cat*, or even *The mouse was chased*.

Truth-value judgment (TVJ) task   An experimental task in which participants indicate by various means whether or not they accept a statement as true for a given situation.

References

Abrams, K.H., Chiarello, C., Cress, K., *et al.* (1978) The relation between mother to child speech and word order comprehension strategies in children. In R.N. Campbell and P.T. Smith (eds), *Recent advances in the psychology of language: language development and mother–child interaction* (pp. 337–347). New York: Plenum.

Berko, J. (1958) The child's learning of English morphology. *Word*, 14, 150–177.

De Villiers, J.G., and de Villiers, P.A. (1973) Development of the use of word order in comprehension. *Journal of Psycholinguistic Research*, 2, 331–341.

De Villiers, P.A., and de Villiers, J.G. (1972) Early judgments of semantic and syntactic acceptability by children. *Journal of Psycholinguistic Research*, 1, 299–310.

Diesendruck, G., and Markson, L. (2001) Children's avoidance of lexical overlap: a pragmatic account. *Developmental Psychology*, 37, 630–641.

Evey, J.E., and Merriman, W.E. (1998) The prevalence and the weaknesses of an early name mapping preference. *Journal of Child Language*, 25, 121–147.

Gelman, S.A., and Markman, E.M. (1986) Categories and induction in young children. *Cognition*, 23, 183–208.

Gleitman, L.R., Gleitman, H., and Shipley, E.F. (1972) The emergence of the child as grammarian. *Cognition*, 1, 137–164.

Gordon, P. (1981) Syntactic acquisition of the count/mass distinction. *Papers and Reports on Child Language Development*, 20, 70–77.

Gordon, P. (1996) The truth-value judgment task. In D. McDaniel, C. McKee, and H.S. Cairns (eds), *Methods for assessing children's syntax* (pp. 211–231). Cambridge, MA: MIT Press.

Hochberg, J.G. (1986) Children's judgments of transitivity errors. *Journal of Child Language*, 13, 317–334.

Jaswal, V.K. (2004) Don't believe everything you hear: preschoolers' sensitivity to speaker intent in category induction. *Child Development*, 75, 1871–1885.

Jaswal, V.K. (2006) Preschoolers favor the creator's label when reasoning about an artifact's function. *Cognition*, 99, B83–B92.

Jaswal, V.K., Lima, O.K., and Small, J.E. (2009) Compliance, conversion, and category induction. *Journal of Experimental Child Psychology*, 102, 182–195.

Jaswal, V.K., and Malone, L.S. (2007) Turning believers into skeptics: 3-year-olds' sensitivity to cues to speaker credibility. *Journal of Cognition and Development*, 8, 263–283.

Jaswal, V.K., McKercher, D.A., and VanderBorght, M. (2008) Limitations on reliability: regularity rules in the English plural and past tense. *Child Development*, 79, 750–760.

Koenig, M., Clément, F., and Harris, P.L. (2004) Trust in testimony: children's use of true and false statements. *Psychological Science*, 15, 694–698.

Lidz, J., and Musolino, J. (2002) Children's command of quantification. *Cognition*, 84, 113–154.

McDaniel, D., and Cairns, H.S. (1996) Eliciting judgments of grammaticality and reference. In D. McDaniel, C. McKee, and H.S. Cairns (eds), *Methods for assessing children's syntax* (pp. 233–254). Cambridge, MA: MIT Press.

McKercher, D. (2009) *The polysemy of "with" in first language acquisition: psycholinguistic studies of children's understanding and use of a multi-functional preposition*. Saarbrücken, Germany: VDM Müller.

Musolino, J., and Gualmini, A. (2004) The role of partitivity in child language. *Language Acquisition*, 12, 97–107.

Naigles, L., Gleitman, H., and Gleitman, L.R. (1993) Children acquire word meaning components from syntactic evidence. In E. Dromi (ed.), *Language and cognition: a developmental perspective* (pp. 104–140). Norwood, NJ: Ablex.

Further Reading and Resources

Crain, S., and Thornton, R. (1998) *Investigations in universal grammar: a guide to experiments on the acquisition of syntax and semantics*. Cambridge, MA: MIT Press.

Gordon, P. (1996) The truth-value judgment task. In D. McDaniel, C. McKee, and H.S. Cairns (eds), *Methods for assessing children's syntax* (pp. 211–231). Cambridge, MA: MIT Press.

Lust, B. (2006) *Child language: acquisition and growth*. Cambridge: Cambridge University Press.

McDaniel, D., and Cairns, H.S. (1996) Eliciting judgments of grammaticality and reference. In D. McDaniel, C. McKee, and H.S. Cairns (eds), *Methods for assessing children's syntax* (pp. 233–254). Cambridge, MA: MIT Press.

Video of the truth-value judgment task:
http://www.ling.umd.edu/labs/acquisition/?page=methods.

11 Using Priming Procedures with Children

Marina Vasilyeva, Heidi Waterfall, and Ligia Gómez

Summary

The present chapter discusses the use of the syntactic priming paradigm in developmental research. This relatively new methodology has been used increasingly to explore questions fundamental to both psychology and linguistics. The key theoretical issues investigated within syntactic priming research with children include the nature of early syntactic knowledge, the relation between comprehension and production, and the mechanisms of language learning. The priming methodology has been applied in work with monolingual and bilingual children starting at 3 years of age, including typically and atypically developing populations. The chapter traces this technique from its origins in research with adults up to its current extensions, which explore children's syntactic representations over the course of development. Using examples from the literature, the chapter examines methodological issues arising in the context of syntactic priming studies. It concludes with a discussion of future directions for using this technique to explore new research questions.

Among the different techniques that have been used in the study of child language, syntactic priming methodology is relatively new. It was adopted by developmental psychologists less than a decade ago (Huttenlocher, Vasilyeva, and Shimpi, 2004; Savage *et al.*, 2003), yet it has already produced a wealth of empirical data concerning the nature of linguistic knowledge in children. In particular, priming methodology has been used to examine how children represent and process syntactic information. This line of inquiry is critical for understanding the mechanisms underlying children's production and comprehension of syntactic structures. In the present chapter, we

Research Methods in Child Language: A Practical Guide, First Edition.
Edited by Erika Hoff.
© 2012 Blackwell Publishing Ltd. Published 2012 by Blackwell Publishing Ltd.

discuss various procedures that involve syntactic priming and examine both empirical and theoretical contributions of this work.

Syntactic Priming: Basic Concepts

The term "priming" has been used to refer to a wide range of phenomena, in which exposure to a certain type of material increases people's ability to mentally access that material in their subsequent behavior. The increased access can manifest itself as a higher rate of production or as better comprehension of the primed material. In the linguistic domain, priming has been documented for different aspects of language processing, including phonological, lexical, syntactic, and pragmatic levels (e.g., Betjemann and Keenan, 2008; Brooks and MacWhinney, 2000; Savage *et al.*, 2003). The present chapter focuses specifically on syntactic priming (also known as structural priming), an area of significant interest to linguists and psychologists in recent decades (Pickering and Ferreira, 2008).

Syntactic priming in production refers to a tendency in speakers to repeat sentence structures that have been encountered earlier. The notion of syntactic priming in comprehension has been used in two different contexts. In the first context, it refers to an increased ability to understand sentences following exposure to other sentences with the same structure (Bencini and Valian, 2008). In the second context, syntactic priming in comprehension refers to a tendency to interpret an ambiguous utterance as having the same structure as the previously encountered sentence (Thothathiri and Snedeker, 2008). The majority of currently available studies that utilized the syntactic priming paradigm with children have examined priming effects in language production; only two studies so far have examined syntactic priming in children during comprehension (Bencini and Valian, 2008; Thothathiri and Snedeker, 2008). The focus of this chapter is on the analysis of methodological issues related to syntactic priming in production. For a discussion of syntactic priming during language comprehension, see Snedeker and Thothathiri (2008).

Syntactic Priming Research: from Adult to Developmental Studies

A systematic examination of syntactic priming in language production began with the work of Bock and colleagues carried out with adult speakers of English (Bock, 1986; Bock and Loebell, 1990). The goal of these investigations was to examine the nature of syntactic representation in mature speakers. The key research question was whether the speakers represented syntactic form independently of specific lexical items. To address this question, the investigators developed an experimental paradigm which examined the possibility of inducing syntactic priming. On each trial, the experimenter described a picture using a prime sentence of a particular form. Following the presentation of the prime, the participants were asked to describe another picture that involved different characters and actions. The results showed that adults were more likely to use a certain syntactic form if it had been just used by the experimenter. Since the experimenter's and participant's sentences involved different words, the observed effect indicated that adult speakers represented a syntactic structure in an abstract, lexically independent form; they were able to extract the structure of the prime and reproduce it with a new set of words.

Following the initial investigations by Bock and colleagues, syntactic priming has been used in numerous studies exploring the mental representation of syntax in adults (see Pickering and Ferreira, 2008, for review). At the same time, it has attracted the attention of developmental psychologists as a potentially effective tool for exploring the nature of children's syntactic representations at various points in development. The methodology originally used with adults has been adapted to work with children starting at preschool age; as of now, the youngest participants have been 3-year-olds (Bencini and Valian, 2008; Shimpi *et al.*, 2007). This methodology has been applied in developmental work with both monolingual and bilingual speakers as well as with atypically developing populations, allowing researchers to address a variety of questions concerning the nature of early syntax (Gámez *et al.*, 2009; Miller and Deevy, 2006; Van Beijsterveldt and Van Hell, 2009; Vasilyeva *et al.*, 2010).

Research Questions Addressed in Priming Work with Children

The Representation of Syntactic Structures

One of the key questions debated in the field of language development is how children represent the syntactic structure of sentences. Some investigators have suggested that early syntactic representations may be lexically based (Tomasello, 2000). According to this view, at the initial stages of syntactic development, children acquire the patterning of particular lexical items. After accumulating this lexically specific information, children start forming generalizations across different lexical items about common sentence structures. Thus, syntactic representations gradually become more abstract and independent of lexical content. Alternatively, it has been argued that even very young children possess abstract representations of syntactic structures (Fisher, 2002).

As indicated earlier, the priming technique has proven to be useful for investigating the lexical independence of syntactic representations in adults. Therefore, it is not surprising that the main use of this technique in developmental research has been to address the debate on the extent of lexical independence of children's syntax. By exploring whether children can reproduce the syntactic structure of the prime with a new set of lexical items, priming research yields information directly relevant to this debate. Indeed, the evidence of syntactic priming in children's performance would point to the existence of abstract syntactic representations. Such representations would enable children to extract a syntactic structure, independent of specific words, from the prime sentence and reuse this structure with different lexical items. In contrast, the lack of syntactic priming in children's performance would be indicative of lexically specific representations; such representations would not support generalizations across different lexical items, preventing children from reusing the structure of the prime sentence with new words.

Thus, by testing children of different ages, it is possible to determine how early lexically independent syntactic representations emerge. Furthermore, by presenting children with different types of prime sentences, it is possible to examine their sensitivity to specific syntactic forms at any given age. Certain sentence structures may be easier to generalize and therefore their abstract representations may emerge earlier than the representations of other structures. In this case, one would observe priming effects for some syntactic structures but not for others. Finally, researchers can also investigate whether syntactic priming is facilitated by nonsyntactic factors. For example, even if children's syntactic representations are lexically independent, the likelihood of syntactic priming may still vary depending on the extent of thematic similarity between the prime and the participant's own sentence. Thus, priming methodology can be used to explore a potential interaction between syntax and other aspects of language.

The Relation between Comprehension and Production

Another set of questions that can be addressed using the syntactic priming paradigm concerns the relation between processes involved in language comprehension and production. In particular, investigators have explored whether a person's use of a syntactic structure can be affected only by his or her earlier use of that structure (production-to-production priming) or also by mere exposure to that structure (comprehension-to-production priming). The possibility of comprehension-to-production priming would lend support to the view that a common representational system underlies both comprehension and production of syntactic forms.

In the original priming work with adults, it was assumed that syntactic priming depended on accessing processes uniquely associated with language production (Bock, 1986). Based on this assumption, participants were asked to repeat the experimenter's prime before producing their own response; this way, researchers could examine whether the participants' own use of a particular sentence form would prime their subsequent use of that form. Later studies established that repeating the prime was not necessary for obtaining a priming effect in adults; hearing the experimenter's sentence increased the likelihood of subsequent production of another sentence with the same structure (Branigan, Pickering, and Cleland, 2000). These findings indicate that processes involved in sentence comprehension influence sentence production in adults.

In the context of developmental research, the evidence points both to the links between comprehension and production and to the dissociations between them, especially at the early stages of language use (Hirsh-Pasek and Golinkoff, 1991; Huttenlocher *et al.*, 2002). Syntactic priming methodology offers a new tool for investigating the extent to which comprehension of a syntactic structure can affect the production of that structure in children. By examining the strength of comprehension-to-production priming and comparing it to the strength of production-to-production priming at different ages, one can identify potential developmental changes in the relation between comprehension and production of syntax.

Priming and Learning of Syntactic Structures

In addition to exploring the nature of syntactic representations underlying language production and comprehension, investigators use priming to examine the mechanisms of learning syntax. After the phenomenon of syntactic priming has been discovered in adults, questions have been raised as to whether it merely reflects a transient activation of the primed form or is part of the implicit language learning system (Bock and Griffin, 2000). The learning account would suggest that priming effects may accumulate over time or reflect longer-term changes within the utterance building system resulting from the learner processing the input. This learning mechanism may be particularly important for young children whose mastery of many syntactic forms, such as passives, is limited.

  The role of input in children's development of syntactic skills has been the subject of considerable debate among linguists and psychologists. Much of the empirical evidence has been based on examining spontaneous interactions between children and their caregivers (see Hoff, 2006, for review). While these studies provide important insight into the relation between children's skills and language exposure, priming methodology complements other available methods by exploring the role of input in the experimental context, which allows for a systematic manipulation of language exposure. To address the issues of learning, researchers examine the relation between experimentally controlled input and children's use of syntactic forms across different time lags (Huttenlocher, Vasilyeva, and Shimpi, 2004; Savage *et al.*, 2006; Vasilyeva, Huttenlocher and Waterfall, 2006). This type of investigation may allow us to better understand the timecourse and the conditions facilitating the learning of various syntactic structures.

Procedures Used in Syntactic Priming Research

The research questions presented above have been addressed in several studies investigating syntactic priming in children during language production (e.g., Gámez *et al.*, 2009; Hupp and Jungers, 2009; Huttenlocher, Vasilyeva, and Shimpi, 2004; Savage *et al.*, 2003; 2006; Vasilyeva *et al.*, 2010). The details of the method vary across studies, depending on the particular set of questions addressed. However, the basic characteristics of the priming procedure are similar. Generally, researchers present children with a task in which the experimenter and the child take turns describing pictures. The type of descriptions produced by the experimenter is carefully controlled: each experimenter's sentence has a predetermined syntactic structure. The child's utterances are recorded and later examined to determine whether they have the same structure as the previously encountered experimenter's sentence or an alternative structure. Below we provide an example of this approach, followed by an in-depth discussion of methodological issues that arise in syntactic priming research with children.

A series of studies conducted by Huttenlocher and colleagues (2004) illustrates the use of syntactic priming in developmental work. In one of these studies, the researchers examined whether the experimenter's use of passive voice affects the production of passives in 4–5-year-old children. Twenty pictures were designed to depict situations that could be described with either the passive or the active voice; 10 were used for the experimenter's sentences and the other 10 served as test pictures for children. On each trial, the experimenter described a picture; then the child was presented with a new picture and asked to describe it. Children were randomly assigned to either the active or the passive priming condition; the experimenter used only active or passive voice in each condition, respectively. Responses were coded to determine the proportion of utterances containing a passive relative to the total number of utterances produced by the child. Analysis of variance was conducted to examine whether children's production of passives was affected by the priming condition. Later in the chapter, we will summarize the findings of this and other priming research with children. Before discussing the findings, we address the key methodological issues that must be considered in designing a syntactic priming study.

Choosing the Target Syntactic Structure

One of the first issues to be addressed is the type of syntactic structure that the investigators are attempting to prime. The main requirement for the choice of a particular structure is that it can be expressed in one of two alternative forms. An example of such a structure is provided by the transitive construction, which can be expressed in either active or passive voice. Any scene depicting a transitive event can be potentially described with an active sentence (e.g., "The lightning struck the house") or a passive sentence (e.g., "The house was struck by lightning"). Another example of a syntactic structure that allows for alternative forms is the dative, which can be expressed with either a double-object sentence (e.g., "The teacher gave the boy the pencil") or a prepositional-object sentence (e.g., "The teacher gave the pencil to the boy"). In syntactic priming work conducted with children so far, investigators have tested the priming of transitive structures (e.g., Savage *et al.*, 2003), dative structures (e.g., Thothathiri and Snedeker, 2008), or both (e.g., Huttenlocher, Vasilyeva, and Shimpi, 2004). The availability of alternative forms enables investigators to manipulate the linguistic input provided by the experimenter (e.g., using passive voice on some trials and active voice on other trials). It also provides the participants with the freedom to choose one of the available syntactic alternatives in their own picture descriptions.

It should be noted that, in work with adults, investigators have tested a possibility of priming a wider variety of sentence forms. While many adult studies have used stimuli involving transitive and dative constructions, they also used other syntactic structures that allow for alternations of word order, including complex noun phrases and multi-clause sentences (Cleland and Pickering, 2003; Ferreira, 2003). This difference between adult and child priming research has to do with potential restrictions imposed by the child's developmental level. Investigators assume that it may be difficult for children to process more complex sentences and that processing limitations may influence their performance in the context of the priming paradigm. It would be important to test this assumption in future research and examine whether it is possible to induce in children the priming of a wider range of syntactic structures. This type of investigation may allow us to compare children's sensitivity to different sentence forms.

Designing Pictorial Stimuli

Once the investigators determine which syntactic structure will be primed, they have to create pictorial stimuli that may elicit this type of structure. For example, to elicit the active or passive form of the transitive, the stimuli must depict a transitive event, involving an agent and a patient, such as a car hitting a fence or a ball breaking a window. As shown in the Huttenlocher, Vasilyeva, and Shimpi (2004) example, one set of pictures is designated as the experimenter's set (to be described with a prime sentence); the other set of pictures is for the child to describe. In designing the pictures, several methodological considerations must be taken into account. First, the characters and actions involved in the pictures must be easily identifiable by children. It is useful to pilot the stimuli prior to testing to ensure that all the objects and actions depicted can be recognized by children of the target age (Savage *et al.*, 2003). In addition, or as an alternative to piloting, investigators may include a lexical warm-up at the beginning of the priming study, in which children are asked to name each object in the picture (e.g., Bencini and Valian, 2008).

Second, in designing the pictures for the experimenter's and the child's sets, researchers have to ensure that the two sets do not vary in the likelihood of eliciting a particular syntactic form. For example, some depictions of transitive actions may be more likely to elicit a passive rather than an active sentence. In particular, the animacy of the characters involved in the action has been shown to influence the choice of syntactic form: actions involving animate patients and inanimate agents are more likely to be described in passive voice than actions in which the characters' animacy is reversed (Lempert, 1989). Thus, controlling the animacy of the characters is one of the ways to increase the comparability of the two sets in terms of the likelihood of eliciting a certain type of sentence. In some studies, this is done by ensuring that all the pictures in both sets contain characters of the same animacy (e.g., all inanimate characters, as in Bencini and Valian, 2008, and Savage *et al.*, 2003). In other studies, researchers create a pool of pictures containing a mix of animate and inanimate characters and randomly divide them into the experimenter's and the child's set (e.g., Huttenlocher, Vasilyeva, and Shimpi, 2004).

In addition to animacy, researchers should pay attention to other features of the pictorial stimuli that may increase the likelihood of producing one of the alternative forms over the other. Potentially relevant factors include the size of the objects depicted and their relative positioning in the picture. For example, children may be more likely to start their description by mentioning the most prominent (largest) object in the picture. Thus, if the patient of the transitive action is much larger than the agent, children may be tempted to start the sentence by naming the patient, which will result in the passive structure. Balancing the experimenter's and the child's sets with respect to such factors as animacy, size, and relative positioning of objects should ensure that any observed variability in children's utterances reflects the variability in the input provided by the experimenter (i.e., the form of the prime sentence) rather than the particular characteristics of the picture that the child is describing.

Whereas the structural similarity of the pictures in the experimenter's and the child's sets should be maximized, the similarity of individual objects depicted in the two sets is generally minimized. In other words, to reduce the likelihood that children may describe their pictures with the same words that were used by the experimenter, the characters and actions depicted in the child's pictures should be different from those in the experimenter's pictures. This is critical if the investigator's goal is to determine whether children can reuse the syntactic structure of the experimenter's sentence with a new set of words (i.e., whether children have lexically independent syntactic representations). To further reduce reliance on nonsyntactic cues, the pictures in the two sets not only should differ in terms of individual objects depicted but, more generally, should be thematically unrelated.

It must be noted, however, that particular research questions may require the designing of two sets of pictures that are not completely unrelated. For example, in one of the studies, investigators hypothesized that syntactic priming may be influenced by semantic factors (Goldwater *et al.*, 2011). To address this question, they designed pictorial stimuli so that in one condition the experimenter's pictures were semantically related to the child's pictures (e.g., both sets depicted sports scenes), whereas in the other condition they were unrelated (e.g., the experimenter's pictures showed sports scenes and the child's pictures showed food scenes). The researchers compared priming effects across conditions to determine whether syntactic priming was facilitated by semantic similarity. Thus, the ultimate decision on whether the pictures included in the experimenter's and the child's sets should display unrelated or related events and characters depends on the specific research question addressed in the study.

Manipulating Verbal Input Provided by the Experimenter

When children are presented with the experimenter's picture, they simultaneously receive verbal input – the description of that picture. As noted above, the key manipulation in syntactic priming studies concerns the sentence form used in the experimenter's description. Given the availability of two alternative forms (e.g., active versus passive), the experimenter uses one of these forms in each priming condition. An important issue arising in the design of the priming study is whether the priming condition should be tested within or between subjects. In contrast to the priming research with adults, most studies with children utilize a between-subject design, in which participants are randomly divided into two groups and each group receives only one type of prime sentence (Bencini and Valian, 2008; Goldwater *et al.*, 2011; Hupp and Jungers, 2009; Huttenlocher *et al.*, 2002; Shimpi *et al.*, 2007; Thothathiri and Snedeker, 2008). In one study using a within-subject design, where all participants received both active and passive primes, the trials were blocked by the priming condition, and each condition (active versus passive priming) was tested on separate days (Savage *et al.*, 2003). This manipulation, as well as the general trend to use a between-subject design, reflects the investigators' attempts to reduce a potential interference of different types of primes across trials.

In addition to varying the experimenter's sentences according to the priming condition, researchers can manipulate input along other dimensions. For example, Savage and colleagues (2003) varied the degree of lexical overlap between the experimenter's sentence and the child's potential response. In the "low lexical overlap" condition, the experimenter described transitive actions using nouns when referring to the agent and patient of the action (e.g., active prime, "The digger pushed the bricks"; passive prime, "The bricks got pushed by the digger"). The nouns used by the experimenter had a low probability of being repeated by the child because the child's and experimenter's pictures involved different objects. In the "high lexical overlap" condition, the experimenter described the same actions using pronouns (e.g., active prime, "It pushed it"; passive prime, "It got pushed by it"). The pronouns used by the experimenter could potentially be repeated by the child when describing a different picture. The manipulation of lexical overlap is directly relevant to the issue of lexical independence of syntactic representations. Indeed, an interaction between the priming and the lexical overlap conditions would indicate that lexical factors affect syntactic priming. In particular, if children reuse sentence forms previously used by the experimenter in the high lexical overlap condition but not in the low overlap condition, this would support the view that early syntactic representations are influenced by lexical factors.

In sum, when conducting a syntactic priming study, investigators always manipulate the syntactic structure of priming sentences provided to participants. In work with children, the priming condition is usually varied between subjects. Further, investigators may cross the priming condition with other experimental conditions in which the input provided to the child is systematically manipulated. This is done to identify factors that may facilitate or inhibit syntactic priming. Savage and colleagues (2003) have manipulated only the experimenter's sentences while using the same pictures in the high and low lexical overlap conditions. Other researchers, as discussed earlier (Goldwater *et al.*, 2011), have also manipulated pictures presented across conditions (high versus low semantic similarity) to determine whether nonsyntactic cues affect syntactic priming.

Eliciting Children's Responses

Once the child receives a picture description from the experimenter, the child's task is to describe his or her own picture. The participant's responses are usually prompted by a simple instruction (e.g., "Tell me about this picture"). To draw the child's attention to the depicted action, the experimenter may formulate the instruction as, "Tell me what happened/what's happening in this picture," which increases the likelihood that the child will produce a sentence containing a verb. Most children tested so far (with the youngest participants at 3 years of age) find this task relatively easy and produce very few nonresponses. However, even with the instructions focusing the child's attention on the action, it cannot be assured that the child's response will be a full sentence. Some children, especially younger participants (3- and 4-year-olds), may describe the picture simply by naming one or two characters involved in the action. To convey the idea that the picture descriptions should be sentence-like and to familiarize children with the turn-taking procedure, most priming studies involve practice trials. During the practice, if the child responds in a single word, the experimenter can provide an additional prompt (e.g., "Tell me more").

There are two additional methodological factors that must be considered with respect to eliciting children's responses. The first consideration is whether or not the child is required to repeat the experimenter's sentence before providing his or her own picture description. As indicated earlier, it has been established in adult research that repeating a prime is not necessary to induce priming. Yet, in work with children, asking participants to repeat the experimenter's sentence may serve to ensure that the child is paying attention to the verbal input. Thus, in many priming studies with children, participants are required to repeat the prime (e.g., Bencini and Valian, 2008; Savage *et al.*, 2003). Other researchers have tested children with and without repetition to examine whether repetition facilitates syntactic priming (Huttenlocher, Vasilyeva, and Shimpi, 2004; Shimpi *et al.*, 2007). By exploring the possibility of comprehension-to-production priming (i.e., eliciting priming effects in production through exposure to experimenter's sentences), investigators address questions concerning the relation between comprehension and production at different ages.

Another methodological consideration concerns the way in which the turn-taking procedure is organized. In most priming studies, the child's response is elicited on each trial. That is, the child is prompted to describe a picture after receiving a single picture description from the experimenter. In several studies, investigators have blocked the priming sentences together so that, rather than taking turns on each trial, children first hear all the sentences provided by the experimenter and then proceed to describe all of their own pictures (Huttenlocher, Vasilyeva, and Shimpi, 2004; Shimpi *et al.*, 2007). This variation in the design has been introduced to determine whether the effect of the experimenter's input would last over the entire set of test trials in which children do not receive any further exposure to the primed form. To examine how long the primed syntactic structure is retained by the child, the researchers compare the strength of the priming effect in the first half versus the second half of the test trials. One potential problem with this approach is that children's own responses may prime their subsequent responses. To address the possibility of self-priming, researchers may determine, during data analysis, whether children are more likely to produce a primed form given that they had produced it on the previous trial.

Data Analysis

The data provided by the syntactic priming technique consist of children's utterances that they produce when describing pictures. Each utterance is recorded (usually through audiotaping) and later transcribed and coded. The coding involves categorizing each utterance according to its syntactic structure. Generally, all of the child's utterances get divided into three categories; the first two categories correspond to the alternative forms of the primed syntactic construction, and the third category ("other") includes all remaining responses. For example, when children describe pictures of transitive actions, their utterances are coded as passive or active. The "other" category is reserved for incomplete sentences (e.g., the naming of one of the objects), and for complete sentences whose syntactic structure is different from either of the two alternative forms primed (e.g., intransitive sentences). It should be noted that there are differences in how strict the coding of syntactic structure across studies is. In some studies, investigators apply the same coding scheme that is used in adult research. For example, Savage and colleagues (2003) coded as "passive" only the utterances containing a full passive, which explicitly included the *by*-phrase (e.g., "The flower was eaten by the bunny"). In contrast, Huttenlocher, Vasilyeva, and Shimpi (2004) included in the "passive" category both full passives and truncated passives, in which the *by*-phrase was omitted (e.g., "The flower was eaten").

Based on the coding of the child's picture descriptions, investigators compute the dependent variable, capturing the frequency with which the child produced a particular syntactic form. As in the case of syntactic coding, there are different ways in which researchers can go about determining this frequency. One way is to compute the proportion of utterances containing one of the alternative forms (e.g., passive) over the total number of utterances produced by the child (passive + active + other). Another way is to eliminate all the "other" utterances from the analysis and focus on the utterances containing one of the alternative forms. For example, to determine the frequency of using passives, one can divide the number of child's utterances with passives by the number of all transitive utterances (passive + active). Thus, the values of the dependent variable may differ quite significantly depending on how they are calculated. This is especially true of child research because young children tend to produce a particularly large number of "other" utterances. Such variability in the analytical approach, as well as in experimental methodology, must be taken into account in examining the findings across studies that utilize somewhat different versions of the priming paradigm.

Key Findings and Future Directions

The findings of priming research provide a complex picture of the developing syntactic representations in children. The key question concerns the level of abstractness, or lexical independence, with which children of different ages represent syntactic structures. The evidence obtained with the youngest participants tested

(3- and 4-year-olds) is somewhat mixed. Savage and colleagues (2003) found that 3- and 4-year-old children show priming effects only when the prime sentences have high lexical overlap with children's own sentences, whereas 6-year-olds demonstrate priming even with a low lexical overlap between primes and targets. These findings suggest that early syntactic representations may be lexically based. However, several subsequent studies demonstrated syntactic priming in children younger than 6. For example, Huttenlocher, Vasilyeva, and Shimpi (2004) showed that 4.5-year-olds increased the use of the primed structure in their own picture descriptions, which involved different lexical items than the prime sentences.

Recent studies have demonstrated syntactic priming in production in 3-year-olds (Bencini and Valian, 2008; Shimpi *et al.*, 2007). It should be noted though that such young children show priming effects only under restricted conditions. In particular, repeating a prime serves as a prerequisite for their ability to reuse the primed structure with a new set of lexical items, whereas older children demonstrate comparable priming with and without repeating the experimenter's sentence. Combined with the evidence from priming studies in comprehension (e.g., Thothathiri and Snedeker, 2008), it appears that children as young as 3 years old have the ability to form abstract representations of syntactic structures (even though they may require favorable circumstances, such as repeating the prime, to access these structures). In the course of development, syntactic representations become sufficiently robust to produce consistent evidence of priming by the age of 5 or 6 years.

In sum, the priming methodology provides a valuable research tool allowing researchers to explore the developing nature of syntactic representations in experimental settings. At present, several significant research directions have been identified in priming work with children, providing guidance for further investigations. One of these directions involves the study of possible interactions between syntactic and nonsyntactic information in sentence production. For example, recent studies have shown that syntactic priming can be enhanced by the similarity of semantic roles across sentences (Goldwater *et al.*, 2011) and that pragmatic cues may play a role in explaining some of the observed priming effects (Gámez *et al.*, 2009). More work is needed to understand how these nonsyntactic factors affect children's production of particular sentence forms. Another research direction focuses on the issues related to the learning of syntactic structures. Several studies have documented longer-term priming effects in children, but only one study so far (Savage *et al.*, 2006) has used the priming paradigm to examine conditions facilitating the learning of syntactic forms – the issue that needs to be systematically addressed in future investigations.

Finally, a potentially productive research direction has been identified in several studies examining priming phenomena in non-English-speaking children (Gámez *et al.*, 2009; Vasilyeva *et al.*, 2010). Work with monolingual children from different language backgrounds allows researchers to examine how specific aspects of the child's language (e.g., the availability of multiple alternative forms of the passive) affect sentence production in the context of priming. At the same time, work with bilingual children allows researchers to explore the relation between syntactic representations across languages. Thus, the priming paradigm enables psychologists to pursue a wide range of questions concerning language development in diverse populations.

Key Terms

Abstract syntactic structure　A sentence form that is represented independently of lexical items (words).

Active voice　A type of sentence structure in which an agent of a transitive action is the syntactic subject of the sentence (e.g., *The lightning broke the tree*).

Animacy　A semantic property of nouns based on whether their referent objects are living/ sentient being (e.g., animate nouns, *girl*, *cat*, *engineer*; inanimate nouns, *hat*, *chair*, *road*).

Passive voice　A type of sentence structure in which a patient (or recipient) of a transitive action is the syntactic subject of the sentence (e.g., *The tree was broken by the lightning*).

Syntactic priming in production　A tendency to repeat a syntactic structure that has been encountered earlier.

Syntax　Aspect of language that governs the arrangement of words in sentences.

References

Bencini, G.M.L., and Valian, V. (2008) Abstract sentence representation in 3-year-olds: evidence from comprehension and production. *Journal of Memory and Language*, 59, 97–113.

Betjemann, R.S., and Keenan, J.M. (2008) Phonological and semantic priming in children with reading disabilities. *Child Development*, 79, 1086–1102.

Bock, K. (1986) Syntactic persistence in language production. *Cognitive Psychology*, 18, 355–387.

Bock, K., and Griffin, Z.M. (2000) The persistence of structural priming: transient activation or implicit learning? *Journal of Experimental Psychology: General*, 129, 177–192.

Bock, K., and Loebell, H. (1990) Framing sentences. *Cognition*, 35, 1–39.

Branigan, H., Pickering, M., and Cleland, A. (2000) Syntactic coordination in dialogue. *Cognition*, 75, 13–25.

Brooks, P., and MacWhinney, B. (2000) Phonological priming in children's picture naming. *Journal of Child Language*, 27, 335–366.

Cleland, A.A., and Pickering, M.J. (2003) The use of lexical and syntactic information in language production: evidence from the priming of noun-phrase structure. *Journal of Memory and Language*, 49, 213–230.

Ferreira, V.S. (2003) The persistence of optional complementizer production: why saying "that" is not saying "that" at all. *Journal of Memory and Language*, 48, 379–398.

Fisher, C. (2002) The role of abstract syntactic knowledge in language acquisition: a reply to Tomasello (2000). *Cognition*, 82, 259–278.

Gámez, P.B., Shimpi, P.M., Waterfall, H., and Huttenlocher, J. (2009) Priming a perspective in Spanish monolingual children: the use of syntactic alternatives. *Journal of Child Language*, 36, 269–290.

Goldwater, M.B., Tomlinson, M.T., Echols, C.H., and Love, B.C. (2011) Structural priming as structure-mapping: children use analogies from previous utterances to guide sentence production. *Cognitive Science*, 35 (1), 156–170.

Hirsh-Pasek, K., and Golinkoff, R. (1991) Language comprehension: a new look at some old themes. In N. Krasnegor, D. Rumbaugh, R. Schiefelbusch, *et al.* (eds), *Biological and behavioral determinants of language development* (pp. 301–320). Hove: Psychology Press.

Hoff, E. (2006) How social contexts support and shape language development. *Developmental Review*, 26, 55–88.

Hupp, J.M., and Jungers, M.K. (2009) Speech priming: an examination of rate and syntactic persistence in preschoolers. *British Journal of Developmental Psychology*, 27, 495–504.

Huttenlocher, J., Vasilyeva, M., Cymerman, E., and Levine, S. (2002) Language input and child syntax. *Cognitive Psychology*, 45, 337–374.

Huttenlocher, J., Vasilyeva, M., and Shimpi, P. (2004) Syntactic priming in young children. *Journal of Memory and Language*, 50, 182–195.

Lempert, H. (1989) Animacy constraints on preschool children's acquisition of syntax. *Child Development*, 60, 237–245.

Miller, C.A., and Deevy, P. (2006) Structural priming in children with and without specific language impairment. *Clinical Linguistics and Phonetics*, 20, 387–399.

Pickering, M.J., and Ferreira, V.S. (2008) Structural priming: a critical review. *Psychological Bulletin*, 134, 427–459.

Savage, C., Lieven, E., Theakston, A., and Tomasello, M. (2003) Testing the abstractness of children's linguistic representations: lexical and structural priming of syntactic constructions in young children. *Developmental Science*, 6, 557–567.

Savage, C., Lieven, E., Theakston, A., and Tomasello, M. (2006) Structural priming as implicit learning in language acquisition: the persistence of lexical and structural priming in 4-year-olds. *Language Learning and Development*, 2, 27–49.

Shimpi, P.M., Gámez, P.B., Huttenlocher, J., and Vasilyeva, M. (2007) Syntactic priming in 3- and 4-year-old children: evidence for abstract representations of transitive and dative forms. *Developmental Psychology*, 43, 1334–1346.

Snedeker, J., and Thothathiri, M. (2008) What lurks beneath: syntactic priming during language comprehension in preschoolers (and adults). In I.A. Sekerina, E.M. Fernandez, and H. Clahsen (eds), *Developmental psycholinguistics: on-line methods in children's language processing* (pp. 137–167). Amsterdam: Benjamins.

Thothathiri, M., and Snedeker, J. (2008) Syntactic priming during language comprehension in three- and four-year-old children. *Journal of Memory and Language*, 58, 188–213.

Tomasello, M. (2000) Do young children have adult syntactic competence? *Cognition*, 74, 209–253.

Van Beijsterveldt, L.M., and Van Hell, J.G. (2009) Structural priming of adjective-noun structures in hearing and deaf children. *Journal of Experimental Child Psychology*, 104, 179–196.

Vasilyeva, M., Huttenlocher, J., and Waterfall, H. (2006) Effects of language intervention on syntactic skill levels in preschoolers. *Developmental Psychology*, 42, 164–174.

Vasilyeva, M., Waterfall, H., Gámez, P., *et al.* (2010) Cross-linguistic syntactic priming in bilingual children. *Journal of Child Language*, 37, 1047–1064.

Further Reading and Resources

Hartsuiker, R.J., Pickering, M.J., and Veltkamp, E. (2004) Is syntax separate or shared between languages? Cross-linguistic syntactic priming in Spanish–English bilinguals. *Psychological Science*, 15, 409–414.

Pickering, M.J., and Ferreira, V.S. (2008) Structural priming: a critical review. *Psychological Bulletin*, 134, 427–459.

Snedeker, J., and Thothathiri, M. (2008) What lurks beneath: syntactic priming during language comprehension in preschoolers (and adults). In I.A. Sekerina, E.M. Fernandez, and H. Clahsen (eds), *Developmental psycholinguistics: on-line methods in children's language processing* (pp. 137–167). Amsterdam: Benjamins.

Whitehurst, G., Ironsmith, M., and Goldfein, M. (1974) Selective imitation of the passive construction through modeling. *Journal of Experimental Child Psychology*, 17, 288–302.

The study by Whitehurst, Ironsmith, and Goldfein (1974) provides an early example of using an experimental technique that was later adopted by syntactic priming researchers in work with children. The chapter by Snedeker and Thothathiri (2008) can be viewed as complementary to the present chapter, in that it addresses syntactic priming methodology, focusing on comprehension rather than production measures. The article by Hartsuiker, Pickering, and Veltkamp (2004) has introduced a new direction in syntactic priming research by applying the priming methodology cross-linguistically to investigate the relation between syntactic representations across languages in bilingual speakers. Pickering and Ferreira (2008) present a comprehensive review of syntactic priming, discussing both conceptual and methodological issues arising in work with diverse populations, including monolingual and bilingual speakers, children and adults, and typically and atypically developing individuals.

12 Studying Language Processing Using Eye Movements

John C. Trueswell

Summary

This chapter evaluates the use of child eyetracking methods to study spoken language production and comprehension. A summary of the available methods and data analyses is provided. An emphasis is placed on understanding the chain of inferences, or linking assumptions, researchers commonly make when going from measurements of eye position to conclusions about attention, reference, and sentence parsing. It is concluded that to a large extent these assumptions are valid, though care is needed when disentangling developmental changes in visual attention from developmental changes in language processing abilities.

Research Aim

Over the past decade, there has been a renewed interest in understanding how children process speech in real time and how they dynamically construct an utterance despite their linguistic and cognitive limitations. Recent interest in this topic stems in part from concurrent methodological advancements; it is now possible for instance to record children's eye movements as they carry out relatively natural tasks involving language, such as following spoken instructions, inspecting images that are being described, and even engaging in a spoken conversation with interlocutors. The resulting eye movements, when linked with linguistic events, provide researchers with a record of each child's moment-by-moment

Research Methods in Child Language: A Practical Guide, First Edition.
Edited by Erika Hoff.
© 2012 Blackwell Publishing Ltd. Published 2012 by Blackwell Publishing Ltd.

consideration of possible referents in the world, and thus tell us in some detail about the process the child is going through when deriving meaning from linguistic forms.

Here I provide an evaluation of this "visual world" method (Tanenhaus *et al.*, 1995) and focus especially on how it has been applied to sentence processing research with toddlers and children.[1] My emphasis will be on understanding the linking assumptions necessary to use eye movements to study language development. I will explore the chain of inferences researchers usually make when going from measurements of "darting eyes" to conclusions about attention, reference, and even sentence parsing. The plan is to step through these linking assumptions and explore the extent to which each is valid and how each might interact with known developmental changes in attention.

I hope to convince you that the conclusions drawn from developmental research using the visual world paradigm require careful consideration of how certain attentional skills develop, in particular, the ability to engage in the control of information collection from the world (attentional control) and information recharacterization (a component of cognitive control). I will discuss how these two kinds of attentional abilities change over development, and how these changes might bear upon the interpretation of eye movement research in psycholinguistics. With respect to information collection, it is well known that the eye movements generated during the visual interrogation of the world are driven by both exogenous and endogenous factors (i.e., by both bottom-up visual factors and experience-related goals set by the individual). With respect to information recharacterization, it is well known that humans routinely characterize perceptual input along several different dimensions at several levels of abstraction. Language is perhaps the parade example of this: we characterize linguistic input acoustically, phonologically, syntactically, semantically, and referentially, with each characterization having its own representational dimensions. Adult listeners must be able to control the content of these characterizations in real time and override certain characterizations when conflicting evidence arises within and across these levels. Indeed, the skill of dealing with conflict turns out to be important in the development of sentence comprehension abilities.

With this broader understanding of how attentional and cognitive control abilities develop, researchers are likely to make, and are already making, significant advances in understanding how the dynamics of language comprehension and production emerge in the young child. It is my hope that touring these facts here will allow others to take advantage of the visual world method, and that it will facilitate theoretical advancements in understanding language acquisition as the development of a dynamic information processing skill.

As should become apparent below, this method is well suited for a large number of typical and atypical populations because overt responses are not necessarily required. Indeed, the method is currently being applied to children with language impairments and patients with brain damage, and it can even be used with infants who are only a few months old. In this latter case, the method is often described as "looking while listening" (see Swingley, Chapter 3 this volume).

Procedure: the Visual World Paradigm for Psycholinguistics

Cooper (1974) was the first to use eye movements as a real-time measure of adults' spoken language processing abilities. In a series of eyetracking experiments, it was observed that adult listeners rapidly fixate pictures depicting the referents of heard speech, often mid-word, prior to the completion of the utterance. This work received fairly limited discussion in the psycholinguistic community until the reintroduction of this method by Tanenhaus and colleagues, who explored the eye gaze of listeners in the natural setting of following spoken instructions to move about objects in the world (Tanenhaus *et al.*, 1995). Tanenhaus *et al.* demonstrated that when adult participants follow spoken instructions to manipulate objects in a task-relevant visual context, fixations to these objects are also closely time-locked to the elements present in the unfolding utterance that signal abstract representational units. It was therefore possible from this work to infer a great deal about the lexical (e.g., Allopenna *et al.*, 1998) and syntactic (e.g., Spivey *et al.*, 2002) hypotheses that adults consider as the speech is perceived. Since publication of this seminal work, a growing body of research has demonstrated that eye movements can be used to trace the timecourse of adult language comprehension, production, and even dynamic conversation (see the edited volumes of Henderson and Ferreira, 2004, and Trueswell and Tanenhaus, 2005).

Eyetracking Techniques for Use with Children and Toddlers

The development of accurate head-mounted and remote eyetracking systems has made it possible to conduct similar visual world studies with young children, toddlers, and even infants. Head-mounted systems (Figure 12.1A) use highly miniaturized cameras and optics mounted on a visor (two cameras, one trained on the eye and the other on the surrounding visual world). In these systems, the video output from the eye camera is analyzed in real time to calculate the current location of the pupil (i.e., the central position of all the darkest pixels) and the center of the corneal reflection (i.e., the central position of the brightest pixels). During an initial calibration procedure, these coordinates are mapped onto coordinates in the scene video. This is typically done by asking the participant to look at locations in the world that correspond to particular pixel coordinates in the scene video. For each location, the pupil and corneal reflection coordinates in the eye camera are sampled and paired with a coordinate position in the scene camera. Informally, the computer is being told that the participant's eyeball looks like this when the participant is looking here and it looks like this when the participant is looking over here, etc. The resulting matrix of coordinates (triplets of pupil, corneal reflection, and position coordinates) is then analyzed. This analysis creates a multi-dimensional linear or nonlinear regression equation that reflects the best fit between the eye calibration coordinates and the scene calibration coordinates. This equation can then be applied

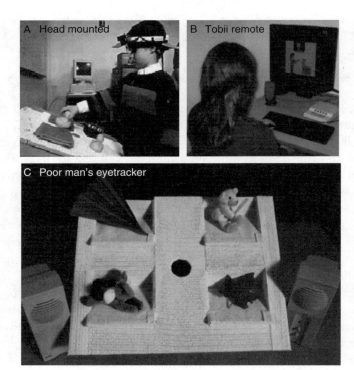

Figure 12.1 Examples of eyetracking systems.
Source: J.C. Trueswell (2008). Using eye movements as a developmental measure within psycholinguistics. In I.A. Sekerina, E.M. Fernández, and H. Clahsen (eds.), *Language Processing in Children*. Copyright © 2008, John Benjamins.

in real time throughout the experiment, such that for any pupil and corneal coordinates, the corresponding scene coordinate is generated and plotted on top of the scene video, usually as a moving dot or crosshair.

This calibration procedure can be difficult to use with children because it requires the child to hold his/her head still while fixating a target location in the world. However, some calibration procedures eliminate this problem. For instance, in the point-of-light calibration procedure, the experimenter holds a small light (such as a small LED) while the participant follows the light around with his/her eyes. The eyetracking calibration software then samples the position of this bright light in the scene video and pairs it with the pupil and corneal coordinates from the eye video, thereby creating a calibration matrix. This procedure does not require the child to hold still, and substantially decreases calibration time and increases calibration accuracy.

Remote eyetracking systems (Figure 12.1B) work like head-mounted systems except the optics are housed off the head, requiring no visor. These systems require tracking of the head as well, either via video-based methods (e.g., the Tobii 1750 and the Eyelink 1000 remote) or by magnetic head tracking (e.g., the ASL and ISCAN systems). Remote systems are becoming increasingly popular because they can be easier to use with toddlers and even infants (e.g., Aslin and McMurray, 2004; Johnson, Slemmer, and Amso, 2004). Most remote systems map direction of gaze directly onto the coordinates of a computer video display, rather than a scene camera, allowing for simple automatic coding of eye position. It is also possible to use such systems to generate a three-dimensional vector of the participant's gaze in the physical world rather than a virtual world.[2]

Finally, several labs, including my own, sometimes use a system that we affectionately call the "poor man's" eyetracker (Figure 12.1C). In a modified preferential looking procedure, a video camera is located in the center of a platform that has been placed in front of the child. This camera is trained on the child's face and eyes. Objects are placed on the platform, usually in four different quadrants around the camera. Direction of gaze toward each quadrant can be coded from the video of the child's face; a trained coder can use a digital video editing system to step through the video frame by frame, recording shifts in gaze. Hand coding of this sort is quite time consuming; it takes approximately an hour to code 10 to 15 experimental trials when each trial consists of one or two utterances. However, no calibration procedure or expensive eyetracking equipment is required. This hand coding procedure also tolerates considerable head movements without substantial loss in coding accuracy. We have found that intercoder reliability is usually 90–95% on a frame-by-frame basis (Snedeker and Trueswell, 2004). Similar hand coding procedures are used in looking-while-listening tasks (e.g., Swingley, Pinto, and Fernald, 1999; Swingley, Chapter 3 this volume).

Data Analysis

Regardless of the data collection technique used by the experimenter, similar analyses can be performed on the resulting gaze record. For each trial of interest, the child's direction of gaze is linked to the onset of critical speech events (e.g., the onset of words in a sentence) and then averaged across trials and participants. For example, Trueswell *et al.* (1999) evaluated the timecourse with which 5-year-old children visually inspect a set of four possible referents, relative to critical word onsets in a sentence. The children were instructed to look at a centrally located "smiley-face" sticker and then to follow instructions to move some of the objects. For purposes of illustration, consider a hypothetical trial in which participants heard: *Look at the smiley face. Now put the frog that's on the napkin into the box.*

A photograph of a sample scene for this item is presented in Figure 12.2. Objects include the target (a frog on a napkin), the competitor (a frog on a plate), a correct goal (an empty box), and an incorrect goal (an empty napkin). The upper right panel of Figure 12.2 shows the eye gaze records from five hypothetical trials. The zero time point (where the x and y axes meet) indicates the onset of the spoken word *put*. In addition, the onsets of the nouns are marked (*frog*, *napkin* and *box*). On trial 1, the hypothetical participant initiated a look to the target about 400 ms after the onset of the word *frog* and then launched a look to the correct goal later in the sentence. On trial 2, the fixation on the target begins a bit later. On trial 3, the first fixation is on the competitor, followed by a fixation on the target and then the correct goal. On trial 4, the fixation sequence is target, incorrect goal, and

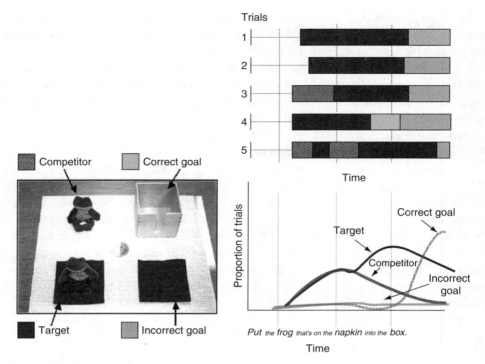

Figure 12.2 Calculating gaze proportions over time.
Source: Modified from Tanenhaus and Trueswell (2005).

correct goal. Trial 5 shows another trial where the initial fixation is on the competitor. The lower right panel of Figure 12.2 provides a plot of the proportion of looks over time for the four regions, averaged across trials for this hypothetical participant. These fixation proportions are obtained by determining the proportion of looks to the alternative objects at each time slice (as derived from the trial samples) and show how the pattern of looks to objects changes as the sentence unfolds. The probabilities do not sum to 1.0 because most participants were initially fixating on the smiley face, which is not plotted here. If it were plotted, looks to the smiley face would steadily drop over time while children begin to inspect the task-relevant objects.

Researchers often define a time window of interest. For example, one might want to focus on the looks to the target and competitor in a time region starting 200 ms after the onset of the word *frog* and ending 200 ms after the onset of the word *napkin*. This 200 ms offset is designed to take into account that it takes about 200 ms for a participant to program an eye movement to a target (e.g., Matin, Shao, and Boff, 1993; though see below). The proportion of looks to objects, the time spent looking at the alternative objects (essentially the area under the curve, which is a simple transformation of proportion of looks), and the number and/or proportion of looks generated to objects in this time region can then be analyzed. These different measures are all highly correlated but in principle offer slightly different pictures of what is happening in the eye movement record.

The hypothetical data in Figure 12.2 (lower right) are quite similar to what was actually observed by Trueswell *et al.* (1999). Focusing only on the looks to the target and the competitor, one can see that these looks are fairly well time-locked with the onset of words; first, looks to both the target and the competitor (the two frogs) rise sharply upon hearing the first noun, *frog*, and remain equally distributed between these two objects until *napkin*, at which time participants begin to look more at the target (*the frog on the napkin*). Similarly, looks to the correct goal rise upon hearing *box*.

It is not the case that the eyes simply dart to objects that best match the nouns mentioned in the input. For instance, at the onset of the noun *napkin*, gaze proportion does not split between the two napkins in the scene like it did for the two frogs when hearing *frog*. Rather, looks to the target (that has the napkin under it) prevail over looks to the incorrect goal (the empty napkin). Why would this be? The most plausible explanation is that this is due to the syntactic position of the noun *napkin* in the sentence; this noun is part of a relative clause that unambiguously modifies the NP *the frog* (i.e., *the frog that's on the napkin*) and, as such, the NP *the napkin* must refer to the napkin under the frog, not the empty napkin. Similar timecourse data have been reported for adults (e.g., Spivey *et al.*, 2002; Tanenhaus *et al.*, 1995; Trueswell *et al.*, 1999) and replicated in other children (Hurewitz *et al.*, 2001; Snedeker and Trueswell, 2004), all of which suggests that gaze direction is tightly related to the linguistic events in complex sentences and that reference is being computed by the child and adult listener in real time.

Evaluation of Data and Linking Assumptions

It is crucial to consider the linking assumptions, or chain of inferences, that we just rapidly ran through when evaluating data like those in Figure 12.2. How can we confidently go from eye gaze patterns to the conclusion that child listeners compute referential hypotheses in real time? In order to answer this question, there are at least three crucial linking assumptions worth evaluating further:

1   Eye position indicates the child's current attentional state, and attention is driven by properties of the world and by the goals of the child.
2   In tasks requiring the linking of speech to a visual referent world, visual attention can be used as an indication of referential decisions.
3   Referential decisions can in turn be used by the researcher to infer the child's parsing decisions, in so far as these parsing decisions were necessary to determine the referent.

Here I unpack each of these linking assumptions and examine the current experimental literature for validation.

Assumption 1: Eye Position Is a Real-Time Measure of Spatial Attention in Infants, Children and Adults

Adults rapidly shift their eyes from location to location approximately one to five times per second. During these rapid eye movements, or saccades, the eye is in motion for 20 to 100 ms, and can reach speeds up to 700 degrees per second (see Land and Tatler, 2009). Saccades allow for the repositioning of visual input onto the fovea, a small central region of the retina that, because of its higher density of cone photoreceptors, has considerably better image resolution than peripheral retinal regions. Each saccade is followed by a fixation, during which the eye holds essentially still for 150 ms or more depending on the task. For the normally developing newborn, most of these anatomical properties of the retina are in place at birth or develop rapidly during the first months of life. Basic fundamental oculomotor abilities are also in place quite early; saccades, fixations, and even the ability to smoothly pursue a slowly moving object all emerge quickly during the first 6 months of life and are known to be well in place by the child's first birthday (for a review, see Colombo, 2001).

It is important to know however that developmental changes in eye movement abilities do occur well after the first birthday. For instance, several studies have demonstrated that the latency to launch a saccade to a visual target decreases systematically well into the age ranges studied by most psycholinguists (e.g., Yang, Bucci, and Kapoula, 2002). However, these developmental differences become quite small when there is some warning given to the child that a target is about to be presented (e.g., Cohen and Ross, 1978). This latter finding may be particularly relevant to the psycholinguistic visual world method because ample response "warning" is given in this task, via linguistic input (*Look at the smiley face. Now put…*). Children (5-year-olds) in visual world tasks appear to show only modest delays in their latency to find a target (Snedeker and Trueswell, 2004). And toddlers (18 months) show a 150 ms benefit in targeting a visual referent when the referential expression is preceded by a linguistic carrier phrase (Fernald and Hurtado, 2006).

It is also the case that there are well documented developmental changes in the attentional procedures involved in how a viewer selects an object for fixation. For instance, children up to the age of 3 years continue to have some trouble overriding exogenous contributions to attention (e.g., flashing lights, moving objects) in favor of task-relevant endogenous factors (Scerif *et al.*, 2005). It is not the case that 3-year-olds are completely unable to override exogenous factors; rather they are slightly delayed and slightly less accurate at doing this as compared to older children and adults.

It is difficult to draw straightforward connections between the developmental attention literature and the developmental psycholinguistic literature because most psycholinguistic experiments use very different experimental settings. However, if the relative influence of exogenous and endogenous factors changes over developmental time, it becomes quite important for psycholinguistic researchers to control for visual factors known to capture attention (e.g., motion, sudden onsets). Otherwise, developmental changes that are simply due to general attentional development might instead be misinterpreted as developmental changes related to spoken language understanding.

Assumptions 2 and 3: Eye Movements Can Be Used to Infer Children's Referential and Syntactic Decisions

I asserted above that if a task requires linking speech to a visual referent world, the eye movements of a child performing this task can be used to uncover the child's ongoing referential decisions and, by inference, his/her ongoing syntactic parsing decisions. Note that this does not mean that, at all times, where the child is looking is what the child is considering as the referent. Eye movements in visual selection tasks reflect goal-directed behavior and, as such, studies in which reference is necessary to achieve some goal (such as acting on spoken instructions) permit a researcher to infer referential and syntactic decisions.

Is there evidence supporting this linking assumption? Let us return for a moment to the eye movement record illustrated in Figure 12.2, which involved the utterance *Put the frog that's on the napkin into the box*. Recall that upon hearing *frog*, gaze probability was split equally between the two frogs in the scene. In contrast, upon hearing *napkin*, looks did not split between the two napkins but instead converged only on the target (the frog and the napkin underneath it). It was suggested that this eye pattern for the napkin reflected a particular syntactic parse that children were pursuing for the phrase *that's on the napkin*: it was parsed as a relative clause modifier of the NP *the frog*, and hence required the NP *the napkin* to refer to the napkin under the frog.

One could however argue that this eye movement pattern is not reflecting structural and referential decisions. For instance, it could simply be a reflection of a simple conjunction heuristic: the child has heard *frog* and *napkin* and hence he/she looks to the only quadrant that contains both a frog and a napkin. There are however several ways to design a study that would rule out this possibility and lend further support to the assumption that eye patterns are reflecting the referential implications of parsing choices. For instance, the Trueswell *et al.* (1999) study also contained target utterances like the following:

(1)   *Put the frog on the napkin into the box.*

The absence of the *that's* in this sentence makes *on the napkin* temporarily ambiguous between being a modifier of the NP *the frog* (i.e., a property of a frog) or a goal of the verb *put* (i.e., where to put a frog). Essentially all theories of human sentence processing predict that listeners should initially parse this ambiguous prepositional phrase (PP) *on the napkin* as a goal rather than a modifier (only to have to revise this parse upon hearing *into the box*). Some theories predict this preference based on lexical facts: the verb *put* tends to take a goal, usually in the form of a PP. If the child knows this fact, he/she will parse the PP *on the napkin* as a goal. Other theories predict this goal preference on the grounds of structural simplicity: linking a PP to a verb is claimed to be computationally simpler than linking it to an NP. For either of these parsing reasons, our linking assumptions lead us to predict that children (if they parse in one of these manners) should under these conditions start considering the empty napkin (the incorrect goal) as a possible referent of *the napkin*. This is because the most plausible goal for putting a frog in this case is the empty napkin (not the napkin that already has a frog on it). If a simple conjunction heuristic were at work, the result should be similar to the unambiguous sentence (i.e., we should again see increased looks to target – the only quadrant that has both a frog and a napkin).

Consistent with the parsing/reference linking assumptions, Trueswell *et al.* (1999) found that looks to the incorrect goal do in fact increase soon after hearing *napkin* in this condition, a pattern that is reliably different from that in Figure 12.2 when the phrase was unambiguously a modifier. It was also found that as a consequence of interpreting *on the napkin* as a goal rather than a modifier phrase, children had considerable trouble distinguishing between the two frogs; they looked equally often at both the target and the competitor frogs for a much more extended period of time well after the end of the sentence. This additional pattern is also expected under the parsing and reference assumptions; if *on the napkin* isn't parsed as a modifier (but rather as a goal), then this phrase is no longer informative for distinguishing between the two frogs.

Since the publication of Trueswell *et al.* (1999) numerous other studies have been conducted that also use children's eye movement patterns during spoken language comprehension to infer ongoing syntactic and referential decisions. A complete review of this literature is beyond the current chapter (see instead, e.g., Trueswell and Gleitman, 2007).

Before closing this discussion of using eye movements to infer parsing and referential decisions, it is important to explore for a moment the possibility that facts about general cognitive development might also interact with our visual world measures. For instance, the adult ability to dynamically and flexibly reconsider possible interpretations of a sentence "on the fly" over the course of the sentence no doubt requires some skill to execute in a timely manner. What general cognitive skills, if any, might be needed to achieve this? And do children have these prerequisite cognitive abilities, or do they show a protracted developmental profile? It is well known, for instance, that for nonlinguistic tasks, children 12 years of age and younger show difficulties overriding a rule that they have recently learned for characterizing a stimulus, as in the Wisconsin Card Sorting task, where children continue to sort based on the original rule while normal adults can switch rules with relative ease. (For discussion of these and related experimental findings see Davidson *et al.*, 2006, and references therein.)

Put another way, children are "cognitively impulsive." Automatic and/or highly learned responses to stimuli are often difficult for a child to rescind and revise. This behavioral pattern over development follows nicely from what is known about the development of frontal lobe brain systems that support "cognitive control" of this sort. Interestingly, this cognitive impulsivity was also observed for the 5-year-olds in the Trueswell *et al.* (1999) "put" study. Consider the temporary ambiguity in (1). Children never consistently converged on the intended target frog (looking just as often at the competitor), suggesting that they never realized that *on the napkin* could be a modifier of the NP *the frog*. In fact, children's ultimate actions suggested they had not fully recovered from their garden path: children were at chance selecting between the two frogs, and frequently (60% of the time) moved the selected frog to the incorrect goal – placing the frog on the empty napkin, or placing the frog on the empty napkin and then into the box. This difficulty was clearly related to ambiguity, since these same children made essentially no errors in response to unambiguous versions (*that's on the …*).

Researchers who are not predisposed to thinking of child language use as an emerging dynamic process might interpret such child failures as indicating an age range at which children lack some knowledge; perhaps they have not yet acquired the restrictive (NP modifying) PP structure. However, similar parsing failures in comprehension have recently been seen in a special population of adults – specifically, an individual with a focal lesion to frontal lobe regions known to be responsible for cognitive control (Novick, Trueswell, and Thompson-Schill, 2005). This surprising association between specific frontal lobe deficits and garden path recovery bodes well for dynamic processing accounts of child language development. Given that frontal lobe neural systems are some of the last regions of the brain to fully mature anatomically, it is completely plausible that children's dynamic processing systems are hindered by delayed development of systems responsible for engaging cognitive control, specifically the ability to recharacterize otherwise supported interpretations of linguistic input.

Conclusions

This chapter has reviewed the so called "visual world" studies of child language processing, in which the eye movements of young children are recorded as they hear or produce spoken linguistic material. An evaluation of the linking assumptions necessary to interpret findings from this methodology suggests that these assumptions are valid, making this a promising way to study the dynamics of child language processing. However, caution and care are necessary when performing such research because developmental changes in attentional control and cognitive control can in principle interact with observations from this method. It is important to note that this concern is true of any experimental method when applied to the study of development; the onus falls on the developmental researcher to understand and even seek out these interactions in their experimental findings. Otherwise, developmental observations can be easily misattributed to the researcher's theoretical topic of interest. In particular, the present evaluation of the visual world methodology suggests that care must be taken in understanding how general attentional control and cognitive control change with age. Developmental shifts were identified in the relative contribution of exogenous and endogenous factors when it comes to the direction of spatial attention, particularly in younger children (3 years of age and younger). In addition, developmental shifts exist in general cognitive control abilities well into a child's 10th year of life. Children show a domain-general difficulty overriding initial characterizations of stimuli. This same difficulty is also manifested in language processing: children sometimes have difficulty overriding their initial characterization of a sentence and hence sometimes fail to recover from garden paths.

There is no doubt that as we increase our understanding of the development of visual attention and cognitive control, significant advances will simultaneously occur in our understanding of language learning and language processing, particularly in the relatively natural setting of discussing visually co-present referents. The visual world method serves as an important new way of evaluating the dynamics of language use in the young child.

Key Terms

Attentional control   The ability of an observer to engage in the control of information collection from the world. Typically this refers to the rapid and dynamic ability to select visual information that is task relevant *just in time* to carry out actions or to satisfy goals.

Cognitive control   The ability to flexibly control thoughts, be they characterizations of the world or plans of action. Relevant components of cognitive control are believed to include inhibition and/or excitation in the service of biasing abstract representations of the world.

Endogenous factors   Internal (mental) factors that contribute to attentional control. These include immediate and longer-term plans and the general goals of the observer.

Exogenous factors   External (environmental/sensory) factors that contribute to attentional control. These include the sudden appearance and motion of objects.

Fixation   The brief halting of the eye to allow for the visual processing of a region of space. Fixations last on the order of 100 to 1000 milliseconds, and can be used to infer recognition time in some experimental settings.

Fovea   A small region of the retina that has an unusually high density of cone photoreceptors, leading to high visual acuity in this region. The fovea processes the central 2–3 degrees of a visual scene. Visual acuity falls off rapidly "para-foveally" and into the periphery.

Saccade   The sudden jerking of the eye to a new position to allow for a repositioning of visual input on the fovea. Saccades usually last on the order of 20 to 80 milliseconds and can reach speeds up to 700 degrees per second.

Notes

1   Portions of this chapter also appeared in: Trueswell, J.C. (2008) Using eye movements as a developmental measure within psycholinguistics. In I.A. Sekerina, E.M. Fernández, and H. Clahsen (eds), *Language processing in children*. Copyright 2008 John Benjamins Publishing.

2   Eyetracking companies (see "Further Reading and Resources") usually provide software for calibration and stimulus presentation. Several third-party software packages are also available, particularly for stimulus presentation. For example, freeware from the Aslin lab (Smart-T) and commercial software from E-Prime are currently the most popular options, and are especially useful for complex experimental designs.

References

Allopenna, P.D., Magnuson, J.S., and Tanenhaus, M.K. (1998) Tracking the time course of spoken word recognition: evidence for continuous mapping models. *Journal of Memory and Language*, 38, 419–439.

Aslin, R.N., and McMurray, B. (2004) Automated corneal-reflection eye-tracking in infancy: methodological developments and applications to cognition. *Infancy*, 6, 155–163.

Cohen, M.E., and Ross, L.E. (1978) Latency and accuracy characteristics of saccades and corrective saccades in children and adults. *Journal of Experimental Child Psychology*, 26, 517–525.

Colombo, J. (2001) The development of visual attention in infancy. *Annual Review of Psychology*, 52, 337–367.

Cooper, R.M. (1974) The control of eye fixation by the meaning of spoken language. *Cognitive Psychology*, 6, 84–107.

Davidson, M.C., Amso, D., Anderson, L.C., and Diamond, A. (2006) Development of cognitive control and executive functions from 4–13 years: evidence from manipulations of memory, inhibition, and task switching. *Neuropsychologia*, 44, 2037–2078.

Fernald, A., and Hurtado, N. (2006) Names in frames: infants interpret words in sentence frames faster than words in isolation. *Developmental Science*, 9, F33.

Henderson, J.M., and Ferreira, F. (eds) (2004) *The interface of language, vision, and action: eye movements and the visual world.* New York: Psychology Press.

Hurewitz, F., Brown-Schmidt, S., Thorpe, K., et al. (2001) One frog, two frog, red frog, blue frog: factors affecting children's syntactic choices in production and comprehension. Journal of Psycholinguistic Research, 29, 597–626.

Johnson, S.P., Slemmer, J.A., and Amso, D. (2004) Where infants look determines how they see: eye movements and object perception performance in 3-month-olds. *Infancy*, 6, 185–201.

Land, M.F., and Tatler, B.W. (2009) *Looking and acting: vision and eye movements in natural behavior.* Oxford: Oxford University Press.

Matin, E., Shao, K.C., and Boff, K.R. (1993) Saccadic overhead: information processing time with and without saccades. *Perception and Psychophysics*, 53, 372–380.

Novick, J.M., Trueswell, J.C., and Thompson-Schill, S.L. (2005) Cognitive control and parsing: re-examining the role of Broca's area in sentence comprehension. *Journal of Cognitive, Affective, and Behavioral Neuroscience*, 5, 263–281.

Scerif, G., Karmiloff-Smith, A., Campos, R., *et al.* (2005) To look or not to look? Typical and atypical development of oculomotor control. *Journal of Cognitive Neuroscience*, 17, 591–604.

Snedeker, J., and Trueswell, J.C. (2004) The developing constraints on parsing decisions: the role of lexical-biases and referential scenes in child and adult sentence processing. *Cognitive Psychology*, 49, 238–299.

Spivey, M.J., Tanenhaus, M.K., Eberhard, K.M., and Sedivy, J.C. (2002) Eye movements and spoken language comprehension: effects of visual context on syntactic ambiguity resolution. *Cognitive Psychology*, 45, 447–481.

Swingley, D., Pinto, J.P., and Fernald, A. (1999) Continuous processing in word recognition at 24 months. *Cognition*, 71, 73–108.

Tanenhaus, M.K., Spivey-Knowlton, M.J., Eberhard, K.M., and Sedivy, J.C. (1995) Integration of visual and linguistic information in spoken language comprehension. *Science*, 268, 1632–1634.

Tanenhaus, M.K., and Trueswell, J.C. (2005) Eye movements as tool for bridging the language-as-product and language-as-action traditions. In J.C. Trueswell and M.K. Tanenhaus (eds), *Approaches to studying world-situated language use: bridging the language-as-product and language-as-action traditions.* Cambridge, MA: MIT Press.

Trueswell, J.C., and Gleitman, L.R. (2007) Learning to parse and its implications for language acquisition. In G. Gaskell (ed.), *Oxford handbook of psycholinguistics.* Oxford: Oxford University Press.

Trueswell, J.C., Sekerina, I., Hill, N.M., and Logrip, M.L. (1999) The kindergarten-path effect: studying on-line sentence processing in young children. *Cognition*, 73, 89–134.

Trueswell, J.C., and Tanenhaus, M.K. (eds) (2005) *Approaches to studying world-situated language use: bridging the language-as-product and language-as-action traditions.* Cambridge, MA: MIT Press.

Yang, Q., Bucci, M.P., and Kapoula, Z. (2002) The latency of saccades, vergence, and combined eye movements in children and adults. *Investigative Ophthalmology and Visual Science*, 43, 2939–2949.

Further Reading and Resources

Recommended reading for understanding eye movements in natural tasks generally:

Land, M.F., and Tatler, B.W. (2009) *Looking and acting: vision and eye movements in natural behavior.* Oxford: Oxford University Press.

Recommended reading for the development of child language processing abilities:

Sekerina, I.A., Fernández, E.M., and Clahsen, H. (eds) (2008) *Language processing in children.* Amsterdam: Benjamins.

Trueswell, J.C., and Gleitman, L.R. (2007) Learning to parse and its implications for language acquisition. In G. Gaskell (ed.), *Oxford handbook of psycholinguistics*. Oxford: Oxford University Press.

Recommended reading for the visual world paradigm in adults:

Henderson, J.M., and Ferreira, F. (eds) (2004) *The interface of language, vision, and action: eye movements and the visual world.* New York: Psychology Press.

Trueswell, J.C., and Tanenhaus, M.K. (eds) (2005) *Approaches to studying world-situated language use: bridging the language-as-product and language-as-action traditions.* Cambridge, MA: MIT Press.

Information about MatLab-based Smart-T software for Tobii Eyetracking can be found at: http://smartt.wikidot.com/.

Some popular manufacturers of eyetrackers:

Applied Scientific Laboratories (ASL): http://asleyetracking.com/site/.

ISCAN: http://www.iscaninc.com/.

SR Research (Eyelink): http://www.sr-research.com/.

Tobii: http://www.tobii.com/scientific_research.aspx.

Part III Capturing Children's Language Experience and Language Production

13 Recording, Transcribing, and Coding Interaction

Meredith L. Rowe

Summary

This chapter discusses the process involved in collecting child language data by recording children's language use during interactions with others, transcribing those interactions, and coding the transcripts for specific measures of child language production. This approach is useful for obtaining production measures in a variety of domains including, but not limited to, gesture, phonology, pragmatics, vocabulary, and syntax. However, both the domain studied and the particular research questions of interest affect the specifics of the method as described in more detail below. In general, the approach presented here can be used with children from a wide range of populations, including typically and atypically developing children, children learning more than one language, children from diverse cultures and backgrounds, and children of all ages interacting with a range of interlocutors.

Research Aim

Observations of children's language production offer a window into children's language abilities and a glimpse of their typical language experiences. Documenting child language production originated with parents' diaries of their children's language use. One of the first notable diaries of this kind was that kept by Charles Darwin of his son's first words and utterances (Darwin, 1877). In time, researchers adopted this approach to collect data on groups of children. Over the years, and with the introduction of audio and video recorders, the methods employed to record,

Research Methods in Child Language: A Practical Guide, First Edition.
Edited by Erika Hoff.
© 2012 Blackwell Publishing Ltd. Published 2012 by Blackwell Publishing Ltd.

transcribe, and code spontaneous speech have become more streamlined and widespread. The approach is considered ecologically valid because the child is observed in a naturalistic situation, and it can be used with children of all ages and populations, and in various settings.

Capturing observations of children's language can address a wide variety of questions about children's language production, including developmental questions about the range of verbal and nonverbal communicative abilities that children exhibit at different ages. Depending on sampling choices made by the researcher, these abilities can be examined across individuals from similar or different backgrounds, or across groups that differ in various ways (gender, minority status, impaired development, language spoken, and interlocutor). The approach also allows for examining the language production of others as a potential correlate of child language skill. That is, researchers adopt this approach if they are interested in examining the quantity or quality of language that parents or teachers (or others) address to young children in relation to child language development. To better illustrate the types of questions that can be addressed with this approach, I provide a summary of three studies which used recording, transcribing, and coding interaction to examine children's morphological, lexical, and pragmatic development, respectively.

Example 1: Studying Morphological Development

One of the first (nondiary) studies to record samples of spontaneous speech was conducted by Roger Brown and his research team at Harvard University in the 1960s (Brown, 1973). This project focused primarily on the morphological development of three children known as Adam, Eve, and Sarah. The researchers visited these three children in their homes and audiorecorded approximately 2 hours a month of the child's interaction with his/her parent (usually mother). Observations occurred repeatedly over a 10 month to 4 year timespan, depending on the child. The process required two researchers: one audiotaped children's and parents' speech, while the other took notes about the setting and context of the interaction. For two of the children (Adam and Eve), the microphone was set in a fixed location and effort was made to keep the child in the general area near the microphone for the duration of the visit. For the third child (Sarah), the microphone was sewn into a garment which she wore during the interactions. This was done to get a higher fidelity recording which could subsequently be used for phonological analyses.

The same researchers who were at the home visit transcribed the audio recordings. Having a memory of the scene and the events that took place aided the researchers with their transcription. The transcriptions were done by hand on mimeograph paper so copies could be shared (a sign of the technology at the time). The transcripts were then hand coded to study the children's morphological development. For example, the mean length of utterance (MLU), measured in morphemes, was calculated for each child at each session following the researchers' very specific rules regarding what counts as a morpheme and as a usable utterance. The specific morphemes produced (e.g., plural –s) at each session were also coded. This detailed morphological coding

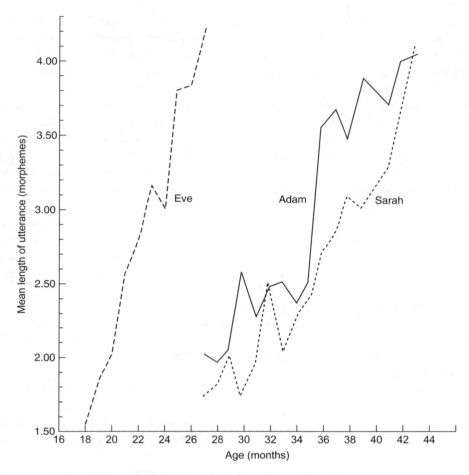

Figure 13.1 The relation of MLU to age for Adam, Eve, and Sarah.

Source: Reprinted and adapted by permission of the publishers from R. Brown, *A first language: the early stages*, p. 55. Cambridge, MA: Harvard University Press. Copyright © 1973 by the President and Fellows of Harvard College.

of the transcription allowed Brown and his colleagues to calculate and report analyses of the children's MLU growth over time and the order of morpheme acquisition for these three children. The MLU growth for Adam, Eve and Sarah is displayed in Figure 13.1. After further analyzing these data, Brown proposed five specific stages of morphological development and a mapping of the general order in which morphemes are learned by children learning English as a first language (Brown, 1973).

Example 2: Studying Lexical Development

About two decades after Brown's seminal study, the methodological approach of recording, transcribing, and coding children's language production had become more widespread. One noteworthy study that adopted this approach to look at children's lexical development was a longitudinal study conducted in the 1980s by Betty Hart and Todd Risley (1995). Hart and Risley were interested in the everyday language experiences of American children from families that differed in socioeconomic status. They followed 42 children longitudinally from approximately 10 months to 3 years of age. The children were selected to represent three general social class groups: children from families on welfare ($n = 6$), children from working class families ($n = 23$), and children from professional families ($n = 13$). Like Brown and colleagues, Hart and Risley audiotaped children's interactions in the home and supplemented audiotapes with trained observers taking copious notes. They observed each child once a month for an hour, and typical sessions involved the child's interactions with parents and other family members. Effort was made to keep observers consistent with families to help put families more at ease, thus resulting in more naturalistic interactions on tape. Since families differed in ethnicity in addition to social class, the observer's race was matched to the race of the family when possible. The observers followed the children around for the 1 hour period, not limiting them to any particular room or task, and doing their best to point the microphone in the direction of the child and minimize background noise.

As in the Brown studies, the observers transcribed their own tapes, relying on their notes and memory to help decipher what was captured on audiotape. The study resulted in 1318 hours of observation, which were all transcribed, spell-checked, and coded for parts of speech, syntax, and discourse function. I direct the reader to Hart and Risley's (1995; 1999) books for a detailed account of their findings and will only mention the primary findings here. From the analysis of their transcripts, Hart and Risley found extreme average social class differences in the amount (and types) of talk that parents directed to their children: professional parents produced the most talk (487 utterances an hour, on average) and parents on welfare the least (178 utterances an hour, on average). Furthermore, these differences in quantity of parent input were related to differences in the children's vocabulary growth across the period studied. Thus, the children of the professional families produced more vocabulary words themselves than the children from the working class and welfare families, on average. The average vocabulary growth trajectories for the three groups of children are displayed in Figure 13.2. This was one of the first studies to emphasize the importance of socioeconomic status in parent–child interaction and child language development, and it could not have been accomplished without adopting this methodological approach of recording, transcribing, and coding children's spontaneous language production.

Example 3: Studying Pragmatic Development

Using video to record child language production allows for measurement of even more fine-grained aspects of children's language abilities such as gesture and pragmatics. The final example presented here comes from a study examining children's development of the expression of communicative intents (e.g., Snow *et al.*, 1996). In this longitudinal study, parent–child dyads were observed in a laboratory setting interacting with a set of toys at child ages 14, 20, and 32 months (for more

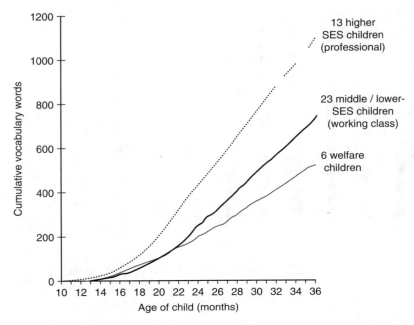

Figure 13.2 The widening gap in the vocabulary growth of children from professional, working class, and welfare families across their first three years of life.
Source: Reprinted by permission from B. Hart and T. Risley, *Meaningful differences in the everyday experience of young American children*, p. 47. Baltimore: Paul H. Brookes Publishing Co. Inc. Copyright © 1975.

on the sample, see Snow, 1989; Dale *et al.*, 1989). The researcher brought the parent and child into the playroom, gave them some time alone to become accustomed to the setting, and then instructed the parent to play with the child using, in sequence, the contents of four boxes (each containing a different toy: Snow *et al.*, 1996). The duration of the videotaped sessions varied, as they were terminated only when the parent had tried to engage the child with all four toys.

These videos were then transcribed following the CHAT conventions of the Child Language Data Exchange System (MacWhinney, 2000; see Corrigan, Chapter 18 this volume, for more detail on CHILDES; this is the New England sample in the CHILDES database). Transcripts were then coded for communicative intent using a coding system the authors called the Inventory of Communicative Acts–Abridged (INCA–A), which was a modified version of a previous speech-act coding system (Ninio and Wheeler, 1984). This modified coding system involved coding each communicative attempt by parent or child in the transcripts at two levels: the level of the verbal interchange and the level of the utterance. Some examples of verbal interchange codes include: directing the hearer's attention (DHA), negotiating the immediate activity (NIA), and discussing a joint focus (DJF). Some examples of speech-act types at the utterance level include: state or make a declarative statement (ST), repeat/imitate other's utterance (RT), and ask yes/no question (YQ). It was often necessary for coders to rely on children's nonverbal acts to determine coding at the interchange level, thus requiring the use of videotapes to accurately apply this

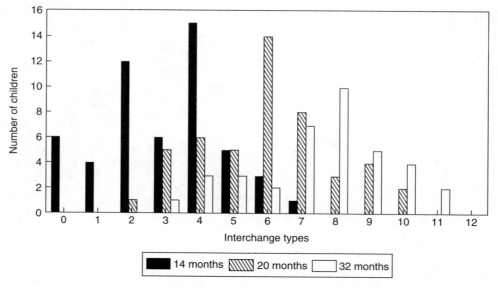

Figure 13.3 Number of interchange types used by children at three ages.
Source: Snow *et al.* (1996).

coding system. Importantly, coders became reliable on the coding scheme, and codes were integrated into the CHAT transcripts for automated analyses using the CLAN program (see Corrigan, Chapter 18 this volume). The study resulted in a very detailed developmental account of the number and types of social interchanges and communicative intents that children produce between 14 and 32 months (Snow *et al.*, 1996). For example, Figure 13.3 displays the number of different interchange types used by children at the three different ages.

Should You Use This Method?

As the above examples illustrate, there are many types of questions that can be answered by recording, transcribing, and coding children's language production. However, there are also some questions for which this approach is not ideal. The first are questions about comprehension, as we cannot be sure what one understands by observing what is said. In addition, some questions about language production are also hard to examine using this approach. If you are interested in the morphological errors children make (e.g., producing "breaked" instead of "broke") or other aspects of language that occur very infrequently, the approach might not be best because it would require recording many hours of child language production to get enough data to examine the phenomenon. In those cases, the researcher needs to consider the sampling plan carefully (e.g., Rowland, Fletcher, and Freudenthal, 2008; Tomasello and Stahl, 2004) or choose a different approach. In general, recording, transcribing, and coding children's language production is a time-consuming method, yet the amount of data generated can be great.

Procedure

If you have decided that recording, transcribing, and coding language production data is the appropriate way to address your research question, how do you go about doing this? The answer is that there is not one best approach, but rather a range of issues to consider and choices to make along the way. Below, I outline some important things to take into consideration when using this method of data collection and analysis. A summary of these issues is presented in Table 13.1.

Recording Interactions

Before collecting or recording data, you need to decide on your sample population and size. This approach can be used to conduct very detailed qualitative analyses or case studies with few individuals, or it can also generate large amounts of data for sophisticated statistical analyses. If the latter is your aim, think carefully about how many children you need in your sample to find the effects you are looking for. As with all research, having enough statistical power to detect effects is very relevant here. It would be a shame to spend a year (or more) recording, transcribing, and coding 20 videotaped parent–child interactions, only to realize you do not have enough variation in your data to see your desired results!

In addition to determining sample size, you need to establish the setting and length of your recorded sessions. Will children be playing at home with a parent? Will they be coming into the lab and interacting with a researcher? Will they be on the playground with their friends? Once the setting and participants are decided, you'll need to determine whether you want them to play with particular toys or engage in specific activities. Many studies have used the approach of having several different toys in bags or boxes so that the dyad uses one at a time and so that you can compare across participants more evenly because they all use the same toys (e.g., Vandell, 1979; Snow *et al.*, 1996; Pan *et al.*, 2005). This approach can be used in the home as well. Alternatively, you can be more liberal and allow the participants to interact as they normally would. This is an important decision because some aspects of language (e.g., pragmatics) are found to differ based on activities (Yont, Snow, and Vernon-Feagans, 2003) and thus you may want to control for this depending on your research questions. Similarly, you need to decide if you will restrict the participants to a specific location (e.g., a blanket with a fixed camera as in the Snow *et al.*, 1996 example above) or if you will let them roam around (e.g., follow them around with a hand-held camera, as in Hart and Risley, 1995). In general, studies which bring specific toys or activities often restrict the use of those toys to a single room or location, while studies that allow participants to do what they wish often allow more freedom to roam. The advantage of allowing children to roam is that you get a good idea of what they typically do with their time. One disadvantage is that it is often hard to keep the child and the interlocutor on video at the same time, and the researcher needs to make online decisions about what to film.

Table 13.1 Things to consider when recording, transcribing, and coding interactions

Recording	Transcribing	Coding
Determine sample size and number of sessions (cross-sectional or longitudinal)	Choose an existing transcription program	Will you use an existing coding scheme or create your own?
Who will participate (child and parent, sibling, researcher, teacher, friend)?	Who will transcribe (native speaker of language, person who did recording, etc.)?	What level will you be coding at (word, utterance, conversational topic, etc.)?:
Determine session length to record	Decide what you care about capturing and make sure all relevant information gets transcribed	If developing your own coding scheme, review transcripts and devise codes that capture what you are interested in
Determine session location (home, school, lab, etc.)	Make clear rules about transcription	Will you need just transcripts to code, or transcripts and video?
Is mobility allowed or will child be restricted to area?	Make sure transcribers are reliable in the things that matter to your research	Good idea to incorporate the codes into the transcript, rather than coding on a separate sheet
Will the activity be structured? If so, how (bring toys, or allow free play)?	Recheck reliability to watch for decay	Teach someone else the coding scheme and check reliability (agreement and kappa)
Audio or video?	Often helpful to have one person transcribe and then a separate person verify transcription	Analyze codes!
What equipment?	Be patient, transcribing is time consuming.	
Who will record data?	Back up work!	
Make copies of recordings!		

Further, how much time will you record? Will you need 30 minutes or several hours of interaction? The answer depends on your research questions and the measures of communication you wish to study. Generally speaking, the minimum time for recording in the field seems to be about 10 minutes, with the maximum up to several hours (although see Naigles, Chapter 16 this volume, on getting it all). Using the available transcripts from the CHILDES online database (see Corrigan, Chapter 18 this volume) can give you a good estimate about how much data you might want to collect. The database contains transcripts of different durations; one can download and analyze them for various aspects of language production and get an idea for what duration might be necessary to capture different types of data.

Finally, what equipment will you use? Most studies now use video recordings. However, if you are gathering discourse data from a child (e.g., narratives) that do not require contextual information, audio recordings should suffice. Or, if video is not necessary for your research questions and you think it might be threatening to a teacher and/or parent, then you might choose audio recordings. The quality of equipment changes so rapidly that instead of recommending specific equipment, I direct you to the Talk Bank website (currently http://talkbank.org/) within CHILDES which has an information section containing the most up-to-date recommendations for video and microphone equipment.

Think carefully about who will do the recording as well. If you plan on observing in the child's home, you want a person who will make the parent and child feel as comfortable as possible. Studies often try and match the ethnicity of the person recording to the ethnicity of the parent or child. If conducting multiple visits it, helps to keep the same researcher assigned to a family; this consistency gives the family a sense of stability, resulting in more naturalistic interactions and potentially less attrition. As noted earlier, it is preferable to have the person who recorded the interaction also transcribe the interaction, and it is preferable to have the transcriber be a native speaker of the language(s) spoken by the child and parent.

There are some potential pitfalls you will want to avoid. First, be sure to try out and become familiar with your equipment beforehand, and watch your recordings soon after you collect them to make sure your microphone is working and your video angle is capturing everything you need. You may need to make decisions about who to get on video if mother and child are in different rooms, or you may need to move your camera angle to be sure to capture gesture if there are toys in the way. Make sure you have the clock or time counter visible on the video for coding. Make copies of recordings as backup. Technical difficulties are always possible; therefore, you are better off overestimating your sample size a bit just in case you run into trouble.

Transcribing Interactions

It is a good idea to transcribe your data as they are collected so that details of the interaction are not forgotten. I highly recommend choosing an existing transcription program rather than developing your own. There are many to choose from, including SALT (Miller, 2010), ELAN (Max Planck Institute, 2010), and the CHAT transcription conventions in the CHILDES system (MacWhinney, 2000; see Corrigan, Chapter 18 this volume). Each system has its own rules for how to transcribe what you see and hear on your recording. At first it may seem like a daunting task to learn all the transcription rules, but, as noted by MacWhinney (2010), we also find that those new to transcription can successfully learn the CHAT conventions in about 30–40 hours. The program has a built-in check procedure to find errors, which helps in the learning process.

Transcription programs have conventions for how to go about transcribing all aspects of child language production you might encounter. However, this does not mean you need to incorporate everything into your transcript. The rules you choose to apply to your transcripts should follow from your research questions. For example, if you are studying phonological development in infants, there are rules for how to accurately transcribe the babbling children produce. However, if you are interested in lexical development in 2-year-olds, you will place more emphasis on accurately capturing the words that are spoken and you might decide not to phonetically transcribe the babbling. Thus, before you begin transcribing, think about your research questions and envision all the information you want your completed transcripts to contain. Some questions to ask yourself include: Will you transcribe all adult talk or just child-directed speech? How will you decide what counts as a word (does the child need to produce the entire word correctly or just attempt to produce the word)? Will you transcribe gestures and nonverbal actions? Will you include contextual information in your transcripts?

While you do not need to incorporate every single aspect of the interaction into your transcript, getting it transcribed in as detailed a way as possible will be helpful in the long run. Transcribing is a very time-consuming process: MacWhinney (2010) estimates a ratio of 15:1 for speech transcription, and thus a 10 minute tape would take an estimated 2.5 hours to transcribe. In my lab we estimate about 23:1 to transcribe both speech and gesture in an interaction that is easy to see and hear. If only transcribing speech, using audio chunking systems (e.g., Blitzscribe) is found to decrease transcription time slightly (Roy and Roy, 2009). Once recordings are transcribed, they are valuable data sources that can be tapped for additional coding and future analyses. In sum, choose wisely what information you want to incorporate in your transcripts. You do not want too much extra information that you will never examine, nor do you want too little to gather the data you need.

Reliability is important in transcription and should be tailored to the level of analysis. If you plan lexical and syntactic analyses, you need to be sure transcribers are reliable at both the word and the utterance levels. The first step is to develop clear rules for what counts as a word and for how to determine utterance boundaries.

In regard to what counts as a word, some questions to consider include: will you transcribe fillers such as "um"? Will you transcribe animal sounds such as "moo" and "baa"? If the child repeats the adult's utterance verbatim, will you count that as productive and transcribe it? If you don't understand what the child says, but the parent does and repeats it, will you give the child credit for that word? There are no right answers to these questions. You need to decide based on your theoretical stance and your research questions as to what should count as productive language, and once you make some rules you should document them and stick to them.

If you plan to use mean length of utterance (MLU) as a measure of child language production, or if you are going to code your transcripts further at the utterance level, it is important to ensure that all transcribers are consistent in how they determine utterance boundaries. Pauses, acoustic markers, interruptions, and speaker and topic changes are some cues used to determine utterance termination. Nonetheless, there remain situations where you create your own rules and apply them consistently. For example, if a child repeats the same word several times as in "milk" "milk" "milk" (e.g., MacWhinney, 2000), will you count that as one utterance or three? Your choice will not make a difference for lexical analyses, but for MLU and other coding at the utterance level the difference can be great.

We establish transcription reliability by having an experienced transcriber and a novice transcriber compare their transcripts of the same recording. We calculate agreement on utterance boundaries with a goal of having 95% of the utterances match. The process usually involves (1) comparing transcripts, (2) discussing the utterances that do not match, and (3) having the novice transcribe another tape until his/her level of agreement on utterance boundaries is acceptable. From that point forward we still always have one person transcribe a tape and then a second person "verify" the transcript to double-check for utterance boundaries and any portions of speech or gesture that might have been missed. Often utterances don't match because two different individuals hear different words in the recording. When that happens we always have both individuals (and sometimes a third) relisten to try and come to an agreement about what was said. At the word level, we do not calculate reliability *per se*, but we use other methods to check the transcript. In addition to having the verifier watch the video and read over the transcript to be sure nothing is missing, we also run a frequency analysis (FREQ in CLAN) to get a list of the words spoken in the transcript. We then spell-check this list and also scan it for words that we did not want to be transcribed. Thus, a transcript is considered ready for further analysis and coding once (1) a reliable transcriber has transcribed it, (2) the CHECK program has been run successfully, (3) the FREQ program has been run and typos have been fixed, and (4) the verifier has gone over it as a second pair of eyes, and any discrepancies have been discussed and ratified between verifier and transcriber.

If you pay attention to all of the above-mentioned issues in transcribing, there are few potential pitfalls. One thing I've learned is that it is important to include the time in your transcript along the way so that you notice if some recordings are shorter or longer than planned. Perhaps the child got sick, or the interaction was so cute that the research assistant just kept recording. If the recordings are long you can always stop at a certain time, but if they are short you should consider pro-rating the data to try and make the sessions equivalent. If the sessions vary widely in length, you can opt to use proportions (in minutes or in utterances depending on unit of analysis) rather than counts in your analysis. In addition, always back up your transcripts, and keep your backups in a different location from the originals.

Coding Interactions and Generating Data

Are you interested in coding your transcripts further to glean more information? To answer this question, you need to ask yourself what type of data you need to accomplish your research objectives. Many types of data can be generated from transcripts, and they fall into three main categories. The first are data that can be automatically generated as a function of the transcription analysis program, including word tokens (total number of words spoken), word types (number of different words spoken), and mean length of utterance (MLU). The second category of data are those that can be automatically generated from the transcripts but need some additional coding. For example, a recent study looked at parents' use of number talk with their children in relation to children's later mathematical skill (Levine, Suriyakham, Rowe, *et al.*, 2010). To examine number talk, we automatically extracted all uses of the numbers 1–10 produced by parents during parent–child interactions in the home. This can be done in different ways depending on the program; in CLAN, you can use an "include file" to search for the words of interest. We then had to do some extra checking of the number words to be sure they were used numerically: for example, the word "one" can be used in various ways ("which one" versus "one more"). But after that level of checking was complete, we were able to accurately quantify parent number talk. You can imagine how this type of approach can be applied to other types of words as well (emotion words, color words, mental state verbs, etc.).

The third category of data generated by coding is with the use of a coding scheme. This scheme may already exist, or it may be developed by you. The coding system gets incorporated into the transcript and is often applied to the entire transcript (or to one speaker). The use of this method requires that the coding scheme is one that can be learned and that coders are reliable in their application of the coding scheme. The Snow and colleagues (1996) speech-act coding scheme (INCA–A) presented earlier in this chapter is an example of this type of coding. If there is no existing coding scheme that captures what you are looking for, you can create your own. I will explain this process by walking you through an example of a coding scheme we developed to compare features of maternal and paternal talk to toddlers. I will not describe the entire rationale of the study or all the results here, but will focus on the development and application of the coding scheme (for more information please see Rowe, Coker and Pan, 2004).

Our interest was in understanding similarities and differences in how low-income mothers and fathers communicate with their 2-year-old children. Based on our review of the previous literature in this area, we were interested in generating data which would fall into all three of the above-mentioned data categories. First, we automatically analyzed the transcripts for parent and child word tokens, word types, and MLU so that we could compare the quantity, diversity, and linguistic complexity of maternal and paternal talk. Second, we were interested in the questions that parents posed to their children, and we were able to automatically pull out questions by searching for all parent utterances that ended in a question mark. This type of analysis highlights how crucial it is to accurately transcribe the data. The questions were then further coded as to whether or not they were wh- questions or yes/no questions. Finally, in addition to questions, we were interested in other pragmatic aspects of parents' speech. Thus, we developed a coding scheme to capture directives, prohibitions, and requests for clarification.

We chose to code at the utterance level. If your transcript is based at the utterance level (as most transcripts are these days) your coding will often be at that level as well. Of course you can code data at the word level (as noted above in the number talk example) or you can chunk your data based on some other unit (i.e., clauses) and code accordingly. Nonetheless, the first decision is to determine the unit or level of coding.

Table 13.2 Pragmatic speech coding system for maternal and paternal talk to toddlers

Type of speech act	Definition	Example
Request for information	Wh-questions framed with who, what, when, where, why, or how	"What are you doing?", "Where does the cat go?"
Request for clarification	Explicit request for child to repeat/revise utterance	"What?", "Say that again," "Huh?"
Direct prohibition	Prohibition expressed in the imperative	"No," "Stop," "Don't," "Wait a minute," "Be careful"
Indirect prohibition	Prohibition expressed indirectly	"You're not going anywhere"
Direct directive	Command expressed through the imperative	"Give me the ball," "Look" (unless it is clear the child is already looking)
Indirect directive	Command expressed indirectly as a question or suggestion	"Would you give me the ball?", "What are you doing?"

Source: reprinted with permission from M.L. Rowe, D. Coker, and B.A. Pan (2004) A comparison of fathers' and mothers' talk to toddlers in low-income families. *Social Development*, 13 (2), 278–291.

We started with three codes and, after reading through a few transcripts, realized that the directives and prohibitions could be broken down further into "direct" or "indirect" categories. Thus, we ended up with five mutually exclusive final coding categories, presented here in Table 13.2. For this coding, we found that we had to watch the videos and read the transcripts as we coded to reliably code the data. As we watched videos and read every parent utterance in the transcript, we incorporated our codes into the transcripts on additional coding lines when the parent produced utterances that fell into one of our five categories in the coding scheme.

For coding reliability, we had two independent raters code 15% of the transcripts (half mother–child and half father–child). We calculated percentage agreement and Cohen's kappa. Percentage agreement is the percentage of all utterances that the coders agreed on (gave the same code or noncode to) in their coding. Cohen's kappa is a more stringent reliability measure that corrects for the possibility of coding the same by chance. Cohen's kappa can be calculated by hand, by using an online kappa calculator, or by using the crosstabs function in the SPSS program (SPSS, 2001). When calculating reliability of observational coding schemes it is often useful to present both reliability measures (see Bakeman and Gottman, 1997, for more information).

Automated analyses of the codes we inserted into the transcripts resulted in counts for each code that we incorporated into our dataset and analysis. Our results did not show any differences between mothers and fathers in the quantity, diversity, or complexity of talk to children (word tokens, word types, and MLU). However, fathers produced more wh-questions and explicit clarification requests than mothers, leading us to conclude that the fathers were more challenging communicative partners for their children because these specific pragmatic functions require a verbal response from the child.

The Data

This procedure provides both quantitative and qualitative data. Quantitatively, you can generate counts such as the number of child word types per 10 minute interaction or the proportion of parental utterances that are directives, and these counts can be merged with other background data on the participating families (e.g., child age, gender, SES). Sample sizes using this approach are never very large because recording, transcribing, and coding is time consuming. However, the amount of data you obtain in terms of words and utterances can be enormous and the variation wide. For example, Hart and Risley (1995) had enough variation with 42 families to find group (SES) differences, and significant relations between parents and children. Qualitatively, incorporating codes into transcripts allows you to identify and pull out chunks of transcript (e.g., examples of clarification requests) to use as evidence when making a claim.

In sum, the disadvantages to this methodological approach include the amount of time and manpower it takes to record, transcribe, and code data. The advantages include the ability to document and analyze naturalistic child language production, and the wealth of data that can be generated.

Key Terms

Coding   The process of categorizing transcribed speech or gestures/actions for analysis. The type of coding system used depends upon the intended goal of the analysis.
Ecologically valid   The methods, materials and setting of the research study closely approximate the real-life situation that is under investigation.
Language production   The use of spoken words to communicate.
Naturalistic interactions   Naturalistic interactions are meant to capture language that a child uses in an everyday situation, such as during dinner or while playing with his/her own toys. They usually occur at a child's home or school, and are less structured than experiments.
Parent–child interaction   Occurs when parent and child cooperate to accomplish a task, or when each understands what the other is communicating, and they take turns responding to one another. This can be verbal (e.g., a conversation) or nonverbal.
Transcription   The process of writing down words spoken (and, optionally, nonverbal gestures and actions that occur) during a set period of time.

References

Bakeman, R., and Gottman, J.M. (1997) *Observing interaction: an introduction to sequential analysis* (2nd edn). Cambridge: Cambridge University Press.
Brown, R. (1973) *A first language: the early stages*. Cambridge, MA: Harvard University Press.

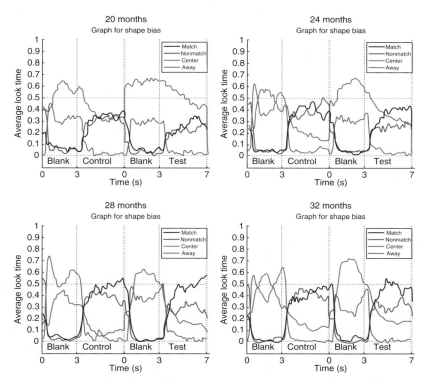

Plate 1 (*Chapter 2*) Timecourse of children's looking patterns during a shape bias task, at four different ages, showing total conglomerate graph.

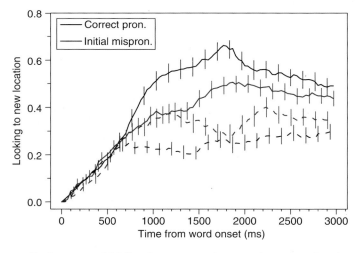

Plate 2 (*Chapter 3*) One-year-olds' fixation to named target pictures on hearing ordinary pronunciations of words and mispronunciations of words. Time from the acoustic onset of the target word is plotted on the *x*-axis. The *y*-axis reveals the proportion of children (*n* = 60) who, at each moment, were no longer fixating the image they had been fixating when the target word began. Solid lines indicate trials on which children happened to be fixating the distracter when the target word began; dashed lines indicate trials on which children were already fixating the target. Black lines show responses on correct pronunciation trials, red lines mispronunciation trials. Vertical bars show standard errors of the mean computed over children.

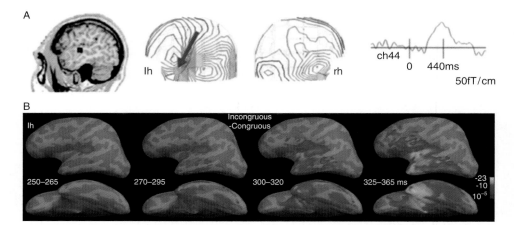

Plate 3 (Chapter 4) N400m MEG response to congruous and incongruous final words in visual sentences. (A) Left to right: equivalent current dipole modeling (ECD) localization, MEG field maps, and timecourses to incongruous minus congruous words. ECDs on sagittal MR images are consistently localized in or near the superior temporal sulcus in all subjects in the study. In the next column, MEG fields at the peak response latency of 400 ms are illustrated as contour maps, with the step between lines set at 20 fT, and current entering the brain as blue. The green arrow indicates the direction of the current generating the magnetic field (within the apical dendrites of pyramidal cells). Dipolar field patterns are most apparent over the left hemisphere and are consistent across individual subjects. In this participant, the MEG signal in sensor 44 shows greater response amplitude to incongruous versus congruous words at about 440 ms. (B) Distributed source modeling method results: averaged cortical activity patterns to sentence-terminal incongruous minus congruous words in four latency windows prior to 400 ms. Activation is exclusively left hemisphere. It is estimated to begin in Wernicke's area at 250 ms; it spreads to anterior temporal sites at approximately 270 ms and to the prefrontal cortex by 300 ms, and becomes increasingly widespread by approximately 325 ms. Activation is averaged across subjects and shown as significance levels on the average inflated cortical surface.

Source: Reprinted from Halgren *et al.* (2002).

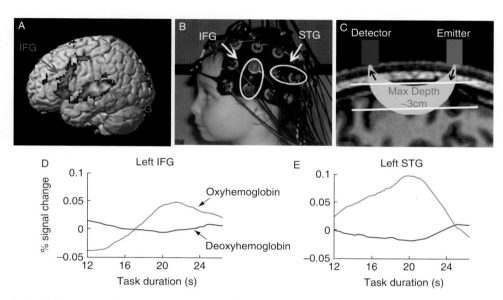

Plate 4 (*Chapter 4*) Brain activation to a rhyme task relative to rest, as measured with hemodynamic methods. (A) fMRI method: children ($n = 12$, ages 6–13) show significant increase in BOLD response in left inferior frontal and superior temporal gyri ($p < 0.005$, extent threshold > 15). (B–E) fNIRS method showing data for one representative participant: (B) 3 × 5 probe placement on a child, using probe set which overlays left hemisphere IFG and STG/parietal regions; (C) brain tissue in which hemodynamic response is being measured, or the "banana" curve, which lies on the intersection of near infrared light emitted by the laser emitter and light absorbed by the detector; increase in oxy-hemoglobin and decrease in deoxy-hemoglobin during the task in (D) left IFG and (E) left STG brain regions of interest.

Plate 5 (Chapter 8) The "smiley-face" scale used by adults and children to rate acceptability.
Source: Reproduced with permission from Ambridge *et al.* (2008), p. 105.

Dale, P., Bates, E., Reznick, S., and Morisset, C. (1989) The validity of a parent report instrument. *Journal of Child Language*, 16, 239–249.

Darwin, C. (1877) A biographical sketch of an infant. *Mind*, 2 (7), 285–294.

Hart, B., and Risley, T. (1995) *Meaningful differences in the everyday experience of young American children*. Baltimore: Brookes.

Hart, B., and Risley, T. (1999) *The social world of children learning to talk*. Baltimore: Brookes.

Levine, S.C., Suriyakham, L.W., Rowe, M.L., *et al.* (2010) What counts in the development of young children's number knowledge? *Developmental Psychology*, 46 (5), 1309–1319.

MacWhinney, B. (2000) *The CHILDES project: tools for analyzing talk* (3rd edn). Mahwah, NJ: Erlbaum.

MacWhinney, B. (2010) Introduction to CHILDES and TalkBank. Powerpoint presentation on website: http://childes.psy.cmu.edu/intro/.

Max Planck Institute (2010) EUDICO Linguistic Annotator (Version 3.9.0). Computer software. Nijmegen: Max Planck Institute for Psycholinguistics.

Miller, J.F. (2010) Systematic Analysis of Language Transcripts (Version 9). Computer software. Madison, WI: University of Wisconsin–Madison.

Ninio, A., and Wheeler, P. (1984) *A manual for classifying verbal communicative acts in mother–infant interaction*. Working Papers in Developmental Psychology, no. 1. Jerusalem: Hebrew University. Reprinted as *Transcript Analysis*, 1986, 3, 1–82.

Pan, B.A., Rowe, M.L., Singer, J.D., and Snow, C.E. (2005) Maternal correlates of growth in toddler vocabulary production in low-income families. *Child Development*, 76 (4), 763–782.

Rowe, M.L., Coker, D., and Pan, B.A. (2004) A comparison of fathers' and mothers' talk to toddlers in low-income families. *Social Development*, 13 (2), 278–291.

Rowland, C.F., Fletcher, S.L., and Freudenthal, D. (2008) How big is enough? Assessing the reliability of data from naturalistic samples. In H. Behrens (ed.), *Corpora in language acquisition research* (pp. 1–24). Amsterdam: Benjamins.

Roy, B.C., and Roy, D. (2009) Fast transcription of unstructured audio recordings. In *Proceedings of Interspeech*, Brighton, UK.

Snow, C.E. (1989). Imitativeness: trait or skill? In G. Speidel and K.E. Nelson (eds), *The many faces of imitation in language learning*. New York: Springer.

Snow, C.E., Pan, B.A., Imbens-Bailey, A., and Herman, J. (1996) Learning how to say what one means: a longitudinal study of children's speech act use. *Social Development*, 5, 56–84.

SPSS (2001) SPSS for Windows, Release 11.0.1. Chicago: SPSS Inc.

Tomasello, M., and Stahl, D. (2004) Sampling children's spontaneous speech: how much is enough? *Journal of Child Language*, 31, 101–121.

Vandell, D.L. (1979) Microanalysis of toddlers' social interaction with mothers and fathers. *Journal of Genetic Psychology*, 134 (2), 299–312.

Yont, K.M., Snow, C.E., and Vernon-Feagans, L. (2003) The role of context in mother–child interactions: an analysis of communicative intents expressed during toy play and book reading with 12-month-olds. *Journal of Pragmatics*, 35 (3), 435–454.

Further Reading and Resources

The CHILDES website: http://childes.psy.cmu.edu/.
The Talk Bank Website: http://talkbank.org/.
Information on SALT: http://www.saltsoftware.com/.
Information on ELAN: http://www.lat-mpi.eu/tools/elan/.

14   Studying Gesture

Erica A. Cartmill, Özlem Ece Demir, and Susan Goldin-Meadow

Summary

To gain a full understanding of the steps children follow in acquiring language, researchers must pay attention to their hands as well as their mouths – that is, to gesture. We first define our methodology for studying gesture. We then describe different types of gestures and their typical uses, and the methods by which meaning can be attributed to gesture. We stress the importance of characterizing the relationship between gesture and speech, and illustrate how that relationship changes over time as children's spoken language develops. Importantly, the methods for coding and analyzing gesture in relation to speech also change over time, and we provide examples of these changes. We end by discussing gesture's role in language learning and later stages of cognitive development.

Introduction

The spontaneous gestures that speakers produce when they talk constitute a rich and multifaceted phenomenon, one that has generated a field of research dedicated solely to its study (e.g., McNeill, 1992). The term "gesture" has been used to describe a variety of body and facial movements, both rehearsed and spontaneous. Studies of gesture are wide-ranging and focus on, for example, gesture's role in language production and comprehension (Alibali, Kita, and Young, 2000; Goldin-Meadow, 1999), including its neural correlates (Kelly, Kravitz, and Hopkins, 2004) and how it varies across languages (Kita and Özyürek, 2003); gesture's role in teaching and learning (Goldin-Meadow and Wagner, 2005); and gesture when it takes over as the primary mode of communication in children who do not have a conventional language

Research Methods in Child Language: A Practical Guide, First Edition.
Edited by Erika Hoff.
© 2012 Blackwell Publishing Ltd. Published 2012 by Blackwell Publishing Ltd.

(Goldin-Meadow, 2003; 2009) and in adults who do (Goldin-Meadow *et al.*, 2008). We focus here on the spontaneous gestures that children produce when communicating with others. Recent work suggests that this type of gesture plays a role in language development, and that important insights can be gained about language learning by examining not only what children say with their words, but also what they say with their gestures. This chapter outlines a general framework for studying gesture in relation to language learning. We first provide guidelines for identifying and categorizing gestures at different stages of language development. We then give a brief description of insights already gained from including gesture in the study of language development. We conclude with a picture of where the field may take us in the future.

Gesture is an integral part of children's communicative repertoires. Before they are able to produce any words at all, children use gesture to communicate (Bates, 1976). Gesture thus provides a window onto the meanings and concepts that children at the earliest stages of language learning are not yet able to convey in speech. Moreover, children eventually grow not only into adult speakers but also into adult gesturers, and the period between children's first gestures and their acquisition of a fully fluent language presents a rich and changing landscape of communicative development. It is in this landscape that gesture plays its most significant role by supplementing, predicting, and perhaps even facilitating the development of spoken language. Using gesture as a variable in studies of language learning, researchers are able to ask more targeted questions about predictors of vocabulary, syntax, and narrative development. We suggest that it is only by examining speech and gesture together that language acquisition researchers can gain a full understanding of a child's communicative intentions and abilities.

Gesture can be studied in children of all backgrounds, all ages, and all abilities. Comparing gestures used during language acquisition across speakers of different languages not only reveals similarities in the way gesture accompanies and adds to speech across languages, but can also reveal which aspects of gesture are shaped by the language-specific constraints of the accompanying speech (So, Demir, and Goldin-Meadow, 2010). Comparing gestures across age groups is useful in revealing the changing roles of speech and gesture during the acquisition of spoken language. Comparing gestures across children whose language trajectory is likely to be atypical (e.g., children with autism, Down syndrome, or early brain injury) is useful in understanding the nature of the child's delay. Moreover, gesture has been shown to be an early indicator of language delay (Iverson, Longobardi, and Caselli, 2003; Sauer, Levine, and Goldin-Meadow, 2010; Thal and Tobias, 1992), raising the possibility that gesture can be used for early diagnosis and intervention when language learning goes awry (LeBarton and Goldin-Meadow, under review).

Methods

The first step in including gesture in a study of language acquisition is to isolate gesture from the ongoing stream of motor behavior. We define gesture as a movement that is *part of an intentional communicative act* but is not a functional act in the real world

(Goldin-Meadow and Mylander, 1984). For example, actively trying to twist the lid of a jar while looking at mother, although part of a communicative act, is a direct manipulation of an object and therefore not a gesture. In contrast, producing a twist-like movement removed from the jar while eyeing mother would constitute a gesture. Once isolated, gestures must be characterized in terms of their form and meaning.

Gesture Form

Gestures can be described in terms of the three parameters typically used to code conventional sign languages: (1) the shape of the hand, (2) the movement of the hand, and (3) the location of the hand in space. In principle, several gestures can be concatenated into a single string; if the hands do not relax and there is no pause between the gestures, the gestures constitute a string. However, in reality, typically developing hearing children rarely concatenate gestures into strings (Goldin-Meadow and Mylander, 1984).

Gestures are often classified on the basis of their form and function into one of the following four categories (McNeill, 1992). All of these gesture types convey some aspect of meaning and, in this sense, are distinct from manual movements that serve as self-adaptors (e.g., scratching or adjusting clothing: Ekman and Friesen, 1969) or that are associated with speech failures (Butterworth and Hadar, 1989).

1   *Deictic* gestures direct attention toward a particular object, person, or location in the surrounding environment (Figure 14.1A). Deictics are typically produced with an index finger point, but any part of the body may be used and, indeed, some cultures point predominantly with the whole hand or by inclining the head (Wilkins, 2003).
2   *Conventional* gestures have an agreed meaning and form within a given community and are therefore culturally shared symbols. They can be arbitrary in form (e.g., the OKAY or THUMBS-UP gestures) or ritualized from a frequent action (e.g., infants' PICK-ME-UP arm raise) (Figure 14.1B).
3   *Representational* (*iconic* and *metaphoric*) gestures reference objects, actions, or relations by recreating an aspect of their referent's shape or movement. Iconic gestures represent physical objects or events (Figure 14.1C). Metaphoric gestures represent abstract ideas or concepts (e.g., moving the hands forward when talking about the future).
4   *Beat* gestures are movements (typically of the hands or head) that correspond to and highlight the prosody of the accompanying speech. Beats do not have an easily discernible semantic meaning, but typically reflect the speaker's understanding of narrative or discourse structure (Figure 14.1D).

It is important to note that a single gesture may have deictic, representational, and discourse-marking beat elements. Take, for example, a gesture produced while saying, "You need to put them in order." The speaker extends her open, flat hand towards a messy bookshelf, with the palm turned sideways (in the orientation of a book), and makes three chopping downward motions while moving her hand to the

Figure 14.1 Examples of gestures produced by children in the early stages of language learning. (A) Point gesture: an 18-month-old child points at a marker without talking. (B) Conventional gesture: a 46-month-old child produces a conventional STOP gesture while saying "stop." (C) Iconic gesture: a 46-month-old child moves his hand across the table wiggling his fingers while saying "he crawled over." (D) Beat gesture: a 46-month-old child says "milk and brown sugar" and beats his hand downwards on "brown" and "sugar."

side; each chop is produced with a different word ("put," "them," "in order"). The gesture indicates the books (the deictic element), represents how the books should be arranged (the iconic representational element), and highlights the prosody of speech by accenting the words with which it occurs (the beat element). Given that it is often difficult to classify a gesture according to type (i.e., as solely deictic, conventional, representational, or beat), it is often more revealing to know the gesture's meaning in relation to the speech it accompanies than to merely know its type.

Gesture Meaning

The meaning assigned to a gesture is derived not only from its form, but also from the physical environment and linguistic context within which it is produced. However, the relative importance of form, environment, and context in determining a gesture's meaning differs across gesture types. The meaning of a deictic gesture is determined by the object, person, or place toward which it is directed (e.g., a point at a dog is taken to mean *dog*) and is thus heavily dependent on its physical environment. The meaning of a conventional gesture is determined by the culture within which it is used (e.g., the THUMBS-UP gesture means *things are good* in American culture). The meaning of a representational gesture is determined by its form in relation to its linguistic and discourse context (e.g., a hand rotating in the air might mean *twirl* when describing a ballerina dancing, or *twist open* when requesting mom to open a bubble jar).

Importantly, the role that gesture plays in relation to speech changes over the course of language acquisition. In adult speakers, gesture is produced in the context of speech more than 90% of the time (McNeill, 1992). At the earliest stages of language learning, infants use gesture on its own, although even these early gestures are usually accompanied by meaningless vocalizations (Iverson and Thelen, 1999). Interestingly, at the same time that children begin to produce meaningful words along with their gestures, they also begin to synchronize their vocalizations (both meaningful and meaningless) with those gestures (Butcher and Goldin-Meadow, 2000), thus integrating gesture with speech semantically and temporally.

Once gesture begins to be routinely produced with speech, communicative acts can be examined from the perspective of both gesture and speech. A communicative act is defined as a string of words or gestures that is preceded and followed by a pause, a change in conversational turn, or a change in intonational pattern. Communicative acts can be classified into three categories. (1) *Gesture-only* acts are gestures produced without speech, either singly (e.g., point at cookie) or, much less frequently, in combination (e.g., point at cookie + point at mother). (2) *Speech-only* acts are words produced without gesture, either singly (e.g., "cookie") or in combination ("mommy cookie," "baby drink juice"). (3) *Gesture–speech combinations* are acts containing both gesture and speech (e.g., "nice doggie" + point at dog; "mommy" + point at cookie).

For gesture–speech combinations, the meaning gesture conveys must be interpreted in relation to the meaning conveyed in the accompanying speech. Gesture often conveys information that is, for the most part, redundant with speech ("ball" + point at ball). But gesture can also convey information that is different from the information conveyed in the accompanying speech ("ball" + point at the location where the ball belongs, used to mean *ball goes there*). One of the best ways to determine whether a gesture is conveying information that goes beyond the information found in the accompanying speech is to turn off the video component of the tape and listen to the speech without gesture. In this case, all we would hear is "ball," suggesting that the sentence-like *ball goes there* meaning comes from integrating information from the two modalities.

Gesture's Changing Role over Language Development

Gesture is sensitive to a child's developmental stage. The types of meanings conveyed in gesture, and the information gesture adds to speech, change over development as the child's speech skills develop. We therefore need to take the child's level of language development into account when analyzing gesture. Here we outline the early periods in language development. For each period, we discuss how gesture's role changes as speech becomes more adult-like, and how the approach to gesture analysis must also change as a result. We also describe the information gesture typically adds to speech, and the changes gesture signals with respect to future language development.

Pre-linguistic Period (Approximately 6–10 Months)

Characteristics

This stage is characterized by a dominance of gesture over speech. Infants have few, if any, words during this period and communicate primarily through gesture – typically pointing gestures, hold-up gestures in which an object is held up and displayed to another, or palm extended GIVE gestures (Bates, 1976). Although not accompanied by words, gestures at this stage often co-occur with meaningless vocalizations (Iverson and Thelen, 1999). At this age, infants in the US are often taught to communicate using "baby signs" (Acredolo, Goodwyn, and Abrams, 2002); if possible, when transcribing a child's gestures, it is a good idea to distinguish learned baby signs from naturally occurring gestures.

Coding and analyses

During this early period, the most interesting aspect of gesture is the nature and diversity of the meanings it conveys. Assigning meaning to gesture during the pre-linguistic period involves paying attention to the physical environment in which the gesture is produced, the ongoing social interaction, and the linguistic discourse context provided by parents and other communication partners. The number of different meanings children convey in gesture at this stage of language development (e.g., the number of different types of objcts a child points to) has been found to predict the size of the child's vocabulary later in development (Rowe and Goldin-Meadow, 2009a). The number of meanings conveyed in gesture can also be used to distinguish children with brain injury who are likely to continue to be delayed with respect to word learning from those who are able to acquire words at a typical rate (Sauer, Levine, and Goldin-Meadow, 2010). In studies of this sort, the number of gesture meanings early in development is correlated with the number of different words the child produces (as measured by word types in spontaneous specch) or understands (as measured by the Peabody Picture Vocabulary Test, PPVT: Dunn and Dunn, 1997) at a later time point.

When assigning meaning to deictic gestures, the tendency is to assume that the infant is referring to a physically present object. However, Liszkowski and colleagues (2009) have shown that even very young children can point to the place where an object was in order to refer to the now-absent object (see also Butcher, Mylander, and Goldin-Meadow, 1991). Thus, it is important for researchers to allow for the possibility that early communication refers to objects and people outside the immediate environment. Overall, pre-linguistic gesture provides a unique opportunity to assess communicative development before the onset of spoken language and to predict upcoming changes in speech.

One-Word Period (Approximately 10–24 Months)

Characteristics

In this period, children begin to build a spoken vocabulary and to communicate using one-word utterances. However, those words are often accompanied by gesture.

Coding and analyses

Once gestures are routinely accompanied by a spoken word, it is important to code the relation between the information conveyed in gesture and the information conveyed in the accompanying speech. Gesture can be used to *reinforce* the information conveyed in speech (e.g., a point to a book accompanied by the word "book"; a side-to-side head shake accompanied by "no"). Gesture can also be used to *disambiguate* the information conveyed in speech; these gestures typically co-occur with nonspecific demonstrative or pronominal forms (e.g., a point to a particular location accompanied by "there"; a point to a toy accompanied by "it"). Finally, gesture can *add* information to the information conveyed in speech (e.g., a point to ball accompanied by "want"; a palm extended in a conventional GIVE gesture accompanied by "cookie"). Keeping track of gestures that add information to speech not only provides a more complete picture of a child's communicative skills, it also gives us a way to predict the onset of two-word speech. The age at which a child first produces combinations in which gesture and speech together convey sentence-like information (e.g., point at box + "open") reliably predicts the age at which the child will produce her first two-word utterance ("open box") (Goldin-Meadow and Butcher, 2003; Iverson and Goldin-Meadow, 2005).

Gestures that add information to speech can be further categorized according to the type of information they contribute. For example, gesture may add noun-like information to a spoken adjective (e.g., point to flower + "pretty"). In these gesture–speech combinations, gesture adds information about an object and, in this sense, the process is like building a noun phrase. In other gesture–speech combinations, gesture adds subject or object information to a spoken verb (e.g., point to mother + "dance"; point to bottle + "give") or action information to a spoken noun (e.g., an iconic OPEN gesture + "box"). In these cases, the process is like building predicate structure. Identifying and classifying sentence-like gesture–speech combinations is important because their prevalence early in development can be used to predict overall syntactic complexity at later stages of language learning (Rowe and Goldin-Meadow, 2009b). More specifically, multiple regression analyses show that the number of gesture–speech combinations children produce at 18 months predicts grammatical complexity (as measured by the Index of Productive Syntax, IPSyn:

Scarborough, 1990), although not vocabulary size, at 42 months. Interestingly, the number of gesture meanings produced at 18 months shows the reverse pattern: it predicts vocabulary size, but not grammatical complexity, at 42 months, demonstrating that gesture selectively predicts language learning.

Moreover, the particular constructions expressed in these gesture–speech combinations can be used to predict the emergence of the same constructions in speech later in development (Özçalışkan and Goldin-Meadow, 2005). Chi-square analyses can be used to compare the number of children who express a particular construction first in speech + gesture to those who express the construction first in speech alone. Interestingly, although children seem to rely on gesture to produce the first instance of a construction (e.g., a predicate plus one argument: "give" + point at cookie), once the construction is established in their repertoire, children are no more likely to use gesture to flesh out the construction than they are to use speech. For example, they are just as likely to produce a predicate plus three arguments entirely in speech ("you see my butterfly on my wall") as they are to use a combination of gesture and speech ("Daddy clean all the bird poopie" + point at table) (Özçalışkan and Goldin-Meadow, 2009). Gesture thus acts as a harbinger of linguistic steps only when those steps involve new constructions, not when the steps merely flesh out existing constructions.

Later Language Development and Early Discourse (Starting at Approximately 24 Months)

Characteristics

During this period, children acquire many different linguistic features: they speak in multi-word utterances; acquire prepositions, determiners, demonstratives; conjugate verbs; and begin to use multi-clausal utterances. Children also increase their use of iconic gestures (Özçalışkan and Goldin-Meadow, in press) and begin to produce discourse-marking gestures such as beats (McNeill, 1992).

Coding and analyses

As children's speech increases in complexity, and as they produce more iconic representational gestures, the relationship between gesture and speech becomes more complex. Representational gestures can convey many different aspects of an object, event, or idea simultaneously, and thus can have multiple relationships to the surrounding speech. For example, a child might accompany the utterance "put it on top" with a gesture in which a curved hand is lowered onto an imaginary surface as if setting down a glass. In this case, the action and path of movement are *reinforced* by the gesture, but the characteristics of the moved object are conveyed only in gesture and are thus *added* by gesture. Coding the particular information that is either reinforced or added by gesture becomes particularly important as iconic gestures become more frequent in a child's repertoire and metaphoric gestures begin to emerge.

As in earlier periods of language development, gesture is used to express more complex structures than children express in speech alone. The range of information gesture adds to speech increases with children's communicative complexity. For example, where gesture would add an argument or a predicate to a single-word utterance in the one-word stage, it can now add a new predicate to a single clause utterance, thus creating a multi-clausal utterance. For example, the child says, "I like it," while producing an iconic EAT gesture, in effect conveying two predicates. Or the child says, "me try it," while producing a conventional GIVE gesture.

Thus, the information conveyed in gesture needs to be coded for the semantic relation it holds to the information conveyed in the accompanying speech. These gesture–speech relationships grow more complex and subtle as speech becomes more proficient. For example, when children begin to express causal relationships in speech (e.g., "he broke the window"), they use gesture to convey information about agents, patients, or instruments. Three-year-olds use gesture primarily to reinforce the goal of an action, but 5-year-olds use gesture to add information about the instrument or direction – information that is often not found in the accompanying speech (e.g., producing an iconic THROW gesture that adds information about the instrument to the utterance "he broke the window": Göksun, Hirsh-Pasek, and Golinkoff, 2010). As another example, when children begin to describe motion events in speech (e.g., "it went under there"), gesture is often used to reinforce or add information about manner, path, source, and endpoint. The type of information children choose to convey in gesture reflects not only their understanding of the event, but also the linguistic framing of the language they are learning (Özyürek *et al.*, 2005; Özyürek and Özçalışkan, 2000). Crosslinguistic studies of gesture's relation to speech can thus provide insight into how children come to describe events in the manner typical of their language.

In addition, as children begin to engage in extended discourse with others, the relationship between children's gestures and the ongoing social context can become a window onto their understanding of shared reference. When children introduce into the conversation a referent not previously known to their conversation partner, they often produce a gesture along with their speech, thus marking the referent as new. For example, children are more likely to point at a toy if the toy has not been mentioned earlier in the conversation than if it has been mentioned (So, Demir, and Goldin-Meadow, 2010).

Narrative Development (Starting at Approximately 4 Years)

Characteristics

As children become more comfortable with the basic aspects of language such as vocabulary and syntax, they start to engage in larger stretches of discourse. When producing extended discourse structures, children are required for the first time to pay attention to the macro-level structure of these larger units. The way in which gesture relates to speech changes during these later stages as gesture begins to add metalinguistic information (e.g., gestures highlight events that form the plotline of a narrative). With the emergence of discourse skills, children's gestures begin to structure the accompanying speech, mirroring the gesture–speech relation observed in adults.

Coding and analyses

During this period, gesture can be studied in relation to how it helps construct or support narrative structure. For example, children's iconic gestures reveal information about the perspective they take *vis-à-vis* the event they are describing. Iconic gestures can be produced from two different perspectives: character viewpoint and observer viewpoint. In character viewpoint gestures, the gesture portrays an event from the character's point of view (e.g., pumping the arms as though running to describe a character who is moving quickly; moving a closed hand away from the torso to describe a character giving something away). In observer viewpoint gestures, the gesture portrays the event from the observer's point of view (e.g., moving the two fingers of an upside-down V-hand back and forth, representing the moving legs of a character in a running event; or moving an index finger up to represent the ascent of the character in a climbing event).

The viewpoint of a child's gestures reveals if and when the child is able to take the perspective of different characters in a story. At initial stages of narrative development, being able to produce character viewpoint gestures is associated with better developed narrative skills in speech at that moment and in the future (Demir, 2009). Multiple regression analyses reveal that producing character viewpoint gestures when retelling a cartoon story at age 5 predicts narrative complexity (as measured by number of plotline events mentioned, and overall story structure) at age 6. How children use character vs observer viewpoint gestures also reveals their understanding of the central events in a narrative. Character viewpoint gestures tend to accompany events that are central to narrative structure (e.g., the main goal of the protagonist); observer viewpoint gestures tend to accompany events that are more peripheral to the main plotline (McNeill, 1992). Being able to use character viewpoint gestures for important events emerges around 6 years of age, and is associated with narratives that are better structured (i.e., children who use character viewpoint gestures to highlight important events produce stories with significantly higher complexity scores than children who do not use these gestures: Demir, 2009).

As a second example of how gesture can be used to structure discourse, recurring gestural features (hand configuration, location, and orientation) can be used to refer back to a character and, in this way, enhance the cohesion of a narrative (McNeill, 1992). As their narrative skills develop, children begin to use the shape and placement of the hand to keep track of characters. For example, in describing a cartoon, a child consistently uses a gesture shaped like a beak produced in front of his torso to refer to a bird. This gesture is used exclusively for the bird throughout the narrative and thus serves to mark the bird as a recurring character in the story. Narrative cohesion can also be enhanced by the use of space. In telling a narrative, adults produce a gesture for a character in a particular location and then gesture toward this location whenever they refer back to the character (So, Demir, and Goldin-Meadow, 2005).

Children do not appear to use gesture space systematically to refer back to previously introduced characters in their early narratives, and we do not yet know when children first begin to use this gestural device to enhance the cohesion of their narratives. Beat gestures also play an important role in adult narrative production. Adults use beats when they suspend talking about the narrative plotline to make a metanarrative comment or repair lexical items (McNeill, 1992). Beats thus serve to mark events as on or off the narrative line. Children occasionally use beats for emphasis around age 5, but the age at which beats take on a functional metalinguistic role in narrative is currently unknown.

Summary of Gesture's Changing Role over Language Development

When adding gesture to a language learning study, researchers must carefully consider the child's stage of language development, simply because gesture starts to take on new roles as speech becomes the preferred modality of communication. In pre-linguistic children, gesture assumes the primary burden of communication, but, as children pass through the one-word stage, gesture is combined with speech and, as such, often forms sentence-like utterances. During this period, gesture can be used to elaborate noun phrases or to construct single- or multi-clausal utterances. When children begin to use narrative, gesture helps to structure language on the macro level, and researchers must then consider the role that gesture is playing in relation to the overall discourse structure. Table 14.1 illustrates how gesture can play different roles at different points in development, and what types of questions researchers can ask about gesture at each of these points.

Gesture as a Potential Mechanism of Language Learning

Thus far, we have been discussing how gesture can be studied in relation to children's speech as a way to gain insight into the cognitive and communicative processes that underlie language learning. However, the fact that child gesture correlates with, and predicts, subsequent language learning suggests that gesturing may be playing a role in *facilitating* language development, not just *reflecting* it. To explore this possibility, we must move beyond naturalistic data and experimentally manipulate gesture, as has been done in older children learning mathematical concepts (e.g., Broaders *et al.*, 2007; Goldin-Meadow, Cook, and Mitchell, 2009). In these cases, gesturing brings about learning by altering the child's cognition.

Child gesture can also play a role in language learning by altering the child's communicative situation; in particular, by eliciting from communication partners a linguistic input that is targeted to the child's needs at the moment. For example, a child points at an unknown object and her mother provides the label for the object, "that's a giraffe"; the child is hearing the label at a moment when her attention is focused on the object and may therefore be particularly ready to learn the label. Or a child may say "nap" while pointing at a sleeping bird, and mother responds with the sentence, "yes, the bird is napping," thus providing a way to translate the child's gesture–speech combination into an English sentence (Goldin-Meadow *et al.*, 2007). The responses children receive to their own gestures may thus help them acquire linguistic constructions.

In addition, adult gesture, and specifically, the gestural input that children receive from either their parents or their teachers, may also play a role in language learning. Others' gestures might draw a child's attention to particular objects, making the child more likely to learn the labels for those objects. Or the gestures others produce might help the child acquire vague or abstract language by relating abstract speech to the physical environment. Past work has found that parents who use gesture to communicate a greater range of meanings have children who subsequently develop larger vocabularies (Rowe and Goldin-Meadow, 2009b). In addition, the gestures that others produce along with specific types of language have been found to facilitate a child's acquisition of that language. For example, parent gesture that is produced along with spatial language predicts children's subsequent spatial language development (Cartmill *et al.*, 2010).

Gesture thus has the potential to play a role in a child's language development when it is produced or observed by the child, and when it is produced or observed by a parent or other communication partner.

Gesture's Changing Role in Cognition

An important question for future work is whether gesture's role in communication and cognition changes over time and, if so, when the change occurs. Proficient language users, like beginning language learners, convey information in gesture that is different from the information conveyed in speech and often do so when describing tasks that they are on the verge of learning (Goldin-Meadow, 2003). As we have described here, the learning task facing the young child is language itself. When gesture is used in these early stages, it is used as an assist into the linguistic system, substituting for words that the child has not yet acquired. But once the basics of language have been mastered, children are free to use gesture for other purposes – in particular, to help them grapple with new ideas in other cognitive domains, ideas that are often not easily translated into a single lexical item.

As a result, although gesture conveys ideas that do not fit into speech throughout development, we might expect to see a transition in the kinds of ideas that gesture conveys once children have become proficient language users. Initially, as seen in many of the examples described here, children often use gesture as a substitute for the words they cannot yet express. Later, once they have mastered language and other learning tasks present themselves, they begin to use gesture in more adult ways, expressing in their gestures ideas that do not fit neatly into word-like units. From a

Table 14.1 Examples of gesture coding at different stages of language development

Period	Utterance	Gesture	Gesture's relationship to speech	Interpretation of gesture meaning	Possible research question
Pre-linguistic	"Da!"	Point to bear	No meaningful speech	Bear	Does the range of objects indicated by deictic gesture relate to future vocabulary acquisition?
One-word stage	"Pretty"	Point to flower	Adds argument	Gesture adds an argument to speech thus building a noun phrase (*pretty flower*)	Do children convey noun phrases in speech plus gesture before conveying them in speech alone?
	"You"	Iconic HIT gesture (open hand sweeps downwards quickly)	Adds predicate	Gesture adds a predicate to speech thus building a simple sentence (*you hit*)	Do children convey sentential relations in speech plus gesture before conveying them in speech alone?
Later language development	"It went under there"	Point to chair	Disambiguates argument	Gesture disambiguates the referent of the deictic "there"	Does gesture precede and predict talk about spatial relationships?

"You gotta see them"	Iconic SPREAD gesture (spread both hands apart over surface of table)	Adds predicate	Gesture adds a predicate to speech, creating a multi-clausal sentence (*you gotta spread them out so you can see them*)	Do children use gestures to create multi-clausal utterances?
Narrative development				
"She talked to her"	One point to the right side of the gesture space and another point to the left side of the gesture space	Disambiguates referent	Gesture refers to a location previously associated with a referent and thus disambiguates it	Do children use gesture to disambiguate referents in speech and to provide cohesion to their narratives?
"The mouse gave a cracker to the bird"	Iconic GIVE gesture (move closed hand away from the torso)	Adds perspective information	Gesture depicts act of giving from the character's perspective	Do individual differences in the perspective of children's gestures relate to narrative outcomes in their speech?

Note: Each example is accompanied by a hypothetical research question. The underlining in the utterance column reflects the fact that the gesture was produced simultaneously with the speech, and indicates where in the speech stream the gesture occurred.

methodological point of view, the important point is that coding systems for each new task need to be designed with that task in mind. Although the guidelines we have provided for describing gesture *form* can be usefully applied to any task, when the goal is to assign *meaning* to gesture we need to construct categories that are appropriate to the task at hand. For example, coding the meaning of gestures in a mathematical equivalence task is done in terms of problem-solving strategies (Broaders *et al.*, 2007; Goldin-Meadow, Cook, and Mitchell, 2009) rather than the word-like and sentence-like units we have described here for language learning.

Pitfalls

Gesture can provide insight into many different types of information (communicative intent, semantic structure, discourse, etc.), but the interpretation of the gesture depends on the developmental stage of the children studied and, to some extent, on the research question asked. This flexibility means that each study will require a coding system that is tailored to the particular question and population under study. Thus, the first step in any study involving gesture is to devise a coding system that captures information relevant to the question. In addition, because coding relies on human judgment and observation, it is important to establish inter-observer reliability between coders. The final step is, of course, to code the data, which is typically done from videotapes because gesture coding is usually too detailed to be performed in real time.

Gesture coding is a time-consuming process. Each step of the process – developing a coding system, training coders to use the system, establishing reliability between coders, and finally coding the data – takes time. The result, however, is a look into the mind of the language learning child that is often importantly different from the view provided by speech alone.

Acknowledgments

All authors contributed equally to this work. The studies and methodologies described in this chapter were supported by grant numbers P01HD40605, R01DC00491, and R01 HD47450 to Goldin-Meadow.

Key Terms

Beat gesture   Movement (typically of the hands or head) that corresponds to and highlights the prosody of the accompanying speech.

Conventional gesture   Culturally shared symbol with a stable form and meaning used within a community.

Deictic gesture   Used to direct attention toward a particular object, person, or location in the surrounding environment; typically produced with an index finger point, but may involve any part of the body or holding up an object.

Gesture–speech relationship The relationship between a gesture's meaning and the meaning of the speech it accompanies; gesture can reinforce, disambiguate, or add information to the meaning conveyed in speech.

Iconic representational gesture Represents a physical object or event by recreating an aspect of the referent's shape or movement.

Linguistic context The spoken context in which a gesture is produced, and may include the word, utterance, or discourse.

Metaphoric representational gesture Represents an abstract idea or concept by adding an iconic element to abstract ideas conveyed in speech.

Narrative cohesion The linguistic, local, micro-level relations that tie the span of idea units in the narrative together and create a text; cohesive devices include inter-clausal conjunction and pronominal reference.

Perspective The perspective from which iconic gestures are produced: first-person or "character viewpoint" gestures are made from the perspective of the gesturer; third-person or "observer viewpoint" gestures are made as if the gesturer is describing a scene from the outside.

References

Acredolo, L., Goodwyn, S., and Abrams, D. (2002) *Baby signs: how to talk to your baby before your baby can talk*. New York: McGraw-Hill.

Alibali, M.W., Kita, S., and Young, A.J. (2000) Gesture and the process of speech production: we think, therefore we gesture. *Language and Cognitive Processes*, 15, 593–613.

Bates, E. (1976) *Language and context: the acquisition of pragmatics*. New York: Academic.

Broaders, S., Cook, S.W., Mitchell, Z., and Goldin-Meadow, S. (2007) Making children gesture brings out implicit knowledge and leads to learning. *Journal of Experimental Psychology: General*, 136 (4), 539–550.

Butcher, C., and Goldin-Meadow, S. (2000) Gesture and the transition from one- to two-word speech: when hand and mouth come together. In D. McNeill (ed.), *Language and gesture* (pp. 235–257). Cambridge: Cambridge University Press.

Butcher, C., Mylander, C., and Goldin-Meadow, S. (1991) Displaced communication in a self-styled gesture system: pointing at the nonpresent. *Cognitive Development*, 6, 315–342.

Butterworth, B., and Hadar, U. (1989) Gesture, speech, and computational stages: a reply to McNeill. *Psychological Review*, 96 (1), 168–174.

Cartmill, E., Pruden, S.M., Levine, S.C., and Goldin-Meadow, S. (2010) The role of parent gesture in children's spatial language development. In K. Franich, K.M. Iserman, and L.L. Kei (eds), *Proceedings of the 34th Annual Boston University Conference on Language Development* (pp. 70–77). Somerville, MA: Cascadilla.

Demir, Ö.E. (2009) A tale of two hands: development of narrative structure in children's speech and gesture and its relation to later reading skill. Doctoral dissertation, The University of Chicago, 2009. ProQuest Dissertations and Theses 3369323.

Dunn, L.M., and Dunn, L.M. (1997) *Peabody Picture Vocabulary Test (3rd edn)*. Circle Pines, MN: American Guidance Service.

Ekman, P., and Friesen, W. (1969) The repertoire of nonverbal behavioral categories. *Semiotica*, 1, 49–98.

Göksun, T., Hirsh-Pasek, K., and Golinkoff, R.M. (2010) How do preschoolers express cause in gesture and speech? *Cognitive Development*, 25, 56–68.

Goldin-Meadow, S. (1999) The role of gesture in communication and thinking. *Trends in Cognitive Science*, 3, 419–429.

Goldin-Meadow, S. (2003) *Hearing gesture: how our hands help us think*. Cambridge, MA: Harvard University Press.

Goldin-Meadow, S. (2009) Homesign: when gesture becomes language. In R. Pfau, M. Steinbach, and B. Woll (eds), *Handbook on sign language linguistics* (pp. 145–160). Berlin: Mouton de Gruyter.

Goldin-Meadow, S., and Butcher, C. (2003) Pointing toward two-word speech in young children. In S. Kita (ed.), *Pointing: where language, culture, and cognition meet* (pp. 85–107). Mahwah, NJ: Erlbaum.

Goldin-Meadow, S., Cook, S.W., and Mitchell, Z.A. (2009) Gesturing gives children new ideas about math. *Psychological Science*, 20 (3), 267–272.

Goldin-Meadow, S., Goodrich, W., Sauer, E., and Iverson, J. (2007) Young children use their hands to tell their mothers what to say. *Developmental Science*, 10 (6), 778–785.

Goldin-Meadow, S., and Mylander, C. (1984) Gestural communication in deaf children: the effects and non-effects of parental input on early language development. *Monographs of the Society for Research in Child Development*, 49 (3, serial no. 207).

Goldin-Meadow, S., So, W.-C., Özyürek, A., and Mylander, C. (2008) The natural order of events: how speakers of different languages represent events nonverbally. *Proceedings of the National Academy of Sciences*, 105 (27), 9163–9168.

Goldin-Meadow, S., and Wagner, S.M. (2005) How our hands help us learn. *Trends in Cognitive Science*, 9, 234–241.

Iverson, J.M., and Goldin-Meadow, S. (2005) Gesture paves the way for language development. *Psychological Science*, 16, 367–371.

Iverson, J.M., Longobardi, E., and Caselli, M.C. (2003) Relationship between gestures and words in children with Down's syndrome and typically developing children in the early stages of communicative development. *International Journal of Language and Communication*, 38 (2), 179–197.

Iverson, J.M., and Thelen, E. (1999) Hand, mouth and brain: the dynamic emergence of speech and gesture. *Journal of Consciousness Studies*, 6, 19–40.

Kelly, S.D., Kravitz, C., and Hopkins, M. (2004) Neural correlates of bimodal speech and gesture comprehension. *Brain and Language*, 89 (1), 253–260.

Kita, S., and Özyürek, A. (2003) What does cross-linguistic variation in semantic coordination of speech and gesture reveal? Evidence for an interface representation of spatial thinking and speaking. *Journal of Memory and Language*, 48, 16–32.

LeBarton, E.S., and Goldin-Meadow, S. (under review) Experimentally induced increases in early gesture lead to increases in spoken vocabulary.

Liszkowski, U., Schäfer, M., Carpenter, M., and Tomasello, M. (2009) Prelinguistic infants, but not chimpanzees, communicate about absent entities. *Psychological Science*, 20, 654–660.

McNeill, D. (1992) *Hand and mind: what gestures reveal about thought*. Chicago: University of Chicago Press.

Özçalışkan, S., and Goldin-Meadow, S. (2005) Gesture is at the cutting edge of early language development. *Cognition*, 96, 101–113.

Özçalışkan, S., and Goldin-Meadow, S. (2009) When gesture–speech combinations do and do not index linguistic change. *Language and Cognitive Processes*, 24 (2), 190–217.

Özçalışkan, S., and Goldin-Meadow, S. (in press) Is there an iconic gesture spurt at 26 months? In G. Stam and M. Ishino (eds), *Integrating gestures: the interdisciplinary nature of gesture*. Amsterdam: Benjamins.

Özyürek, A., Kita, S., Allen, S., Furman, R., and Brown, A. (2005) How does linguistic framing of events influence co-speech gestures? Insights from crosslinguistic variations and similarities. *Gesture*, 5 (1), 219–240.

Özyürek, A., and Özçalışkan, S. (2000) How do children learn to conflate manner and path in their speech and gestures? Differences in English and Turkish. In E.V. Clark (ed.), *Proceedings of the Thirtieth Child Language Research Forum* (pp. 77–85). Stanford, CA: CSLI.

Rowe, M.L., and Goldin-Meadow, S. (2009a) Differences in early gesture explain SES disparities in child vocabulary size at school entry. *Science*, 323, 951–953.

Rowe, M.L., and Goldin-Meadow, S. (2009b) Early gesture selectively predicts later language learning. *Developmental Science*, 12, 182–187.

Sauer, E., Levine, S.C., and Goldin-Meadow, S. (2010) Early gesture predicts language delay in children with pre- and perinatal brain lesions. *Child Development*, 81, 528–539.

Scarborough, H.S. (1990) Index of Productive Syntax. *Applied Psycholinguistics*, 11, 1–22.

So, W.C., Demir, Ö.E., and Goldin-Meadow, S. (2010) When speech is ambiguous gesture steps in: sensitivity to discourse-pragmatic principles in early childhood. *Applied Psycholinguistics*, 31, 209–224.

Thal, D.J., and Tobias, S. (1992) Communicative gestures in children with delayed onset of oral expressive vocabulary. *Journal of Speech and Hearing Science*, 35 (6), 1281–1289.

Wilkins, D. (2003) Why pointing with the index finger is not a universal (in sociocultural and semiotic terms). In Kita S. (ed.), *Pointing: where language, culture, and cognition meet* (pp. 171–215). Hillsdale, NJ: Erlbaum.

Further Reading

Goldin-Meadow, S. (2003) *The resilience of language: what gesture creation in deaf children can tell us about how all children learn language*. New York: Psychology Press.

Hostetter, A.B., and Alibali, M.W. (2008) Visible embodiment: gestures as simulated action. *Psychonomic Bulletin and Review*, 15, 495–514.

Kendon, A. (2004) *Gesture: visible action as utterance*. New York: Cambridge University Press.

McNeill, D. (2005) *Gesture and thought*. Chicago: University of Chicago Press.

15 Dense Sampling

Elena Lieven and Heike Behrens

Summary

This chapter describes the methods used to develop much denser samples of children's naturalistic speech than have previously been available. Most longitudinal corpora capture an estimated 1–2% of children's speech. Depending on the exact sampling regime, the new dense corpora capture an estimated 7–15%. Dense sampling is important in assessing the productivity of children's grammars and in the collection of rarer structures. It also allows much more reliable quantitative comparisons between the input and the child's developing system as well as the use of computational and modeling methods that cannot be used with corpora of smaller sizes. The collection and transcription of these denser corpora is complete or under way for English, German, Polish, Japanese, Estonian, and Finnish. The limitations of the method are the extensive resources that are required and, given this, the fact that corpora can only be collected from a very small number of children.

Research Aim

Naturalistic recordings of children's speech are an essential part of the study of child language development. Experiments, of their very nature, control what it is the child has to either understand or produce, and diary studies can only focus rather narrowly either in time and/or on a particular construction or phenomenon. Therefore periodic longitudinal recordings of children talking have always had a central place in the study of language acquisition, especially since they provide

Research Methods in Child Language: A Practical Guide, First Edition.
Edited by Erika Hoff.
© 2012 Blackwell Publishing Ltd. Published 2012 by Blackwell Publishing Ltd.

information not only about the children's own language production (arguably an insufficient cue for the assessment of their competence) but also about the input the child receives as the basis for the generalization over language, and the interactional processes that may help the child to identify the relevant information in adult speech. Thus a corpus, once transcribed, can serve as the resource for addressing many different research questions, including the interaction between different strands of development, whereas an experiment needs to reduce the number of variables involved. The main constraint in setting up a corpus is the time involved in transcription, especially when the children are young and their speech is not very clear. This has meant that almost all longitudinal corpora can only capture a very small proportion of a child's waking life, typically 1–2 hours every 2–3 weeks at best. Dense databases (DDBs) aim to achieve a much higher sampling level (of between 5% and 20%).

Although DDBs also collect only a proportion of the child's active and passive linguistic experience, they can fulfill an important role in dealing with the problem of thin sampling. Thin sampling presents two major problems. First, there is the possibility that the absence of a structure in the child's transcribed speech is due to its rarity rather than to the fact that the child has not yet acquired that structure. Clearly researchers could radically underestimate the child's developmental level in these circumstances. A second problem acts in the opposite direction: the rare appearance of a complex utterance in the child's corpus could be taken as evidence of acquisition when in fact it is partially or wholly rote learned, but there are not enough data from either child or interlocutors to check this possibility (Rowland and Fletcher, 2006; Rowland, Fletcher, and Freudenthal, 2008; Tomasello and Stahl, 2004). Of course the ideal would be to collect everything that a child says, but this is an even more resource intensive undertaking which only the *Human Speechome Project* has realized (Roy, 2009; see Naigles, Chapter 16 this volume).

For What Population Is It Suited?

Dense databases can be collected for all populations and types of language acquisition. For practical reasons (see below), dense sampling is easier and timewise better if children spend more time at home rather than full-time nursery or school. It could be particularly suited to the longitudinal study of children who talk and communicate little: they will familiarize to the recording situation, and dense sampling will yield a better picture of their communicative and linguistic profile than thin sampling. Another application is the recording of children growing up multilingually, if the sampling was well distributed over the various linguistic environments. However, collecting DDBs, especially continuous ones, requires a deep commitment by the families involved. Thus when recruiting families, attention has to be paid to the stability of life circumstances. The requirements of such a study self-select families who take an intense interest in the development of their children and are willing to arrange their lives according to the requirements of the study.

What Can Be Learned from the Application of This Technique?

DDBs make possible a number of analyses that cannot be obtained with experiments or thinner samples. Obviously, DDBs are extremely useful for tracing the acquisition of infrequent structures such as relative clauses or complement clauses (e.g., Brandt, Diessel, and Tomasello, 2008; Brandt, Lieven, and Tomasello, 2010). They provide the data necessary for good descriptive accounts and fine-grained analyses of developmental processes.

DDBs also allow one to check the conclusions of previous studies based on much thinner sampling. Apart from just providing more extensive data, DDBs are needed to assess hypotheses derived from linguistic and developmental theory. A long-standing debate in acquisition theory concerns the interpretation of first and single occurrences. While researchers from a nativist perspective argued that a limited number of instances were sufficient evidence of the child's competence to produce the underlying structure, developmental psychologists and usage-based linguists claimed that more evidence is needed to support such far-reaching conclusions: in terms of development, it was observed that children generalize to new structures only very carefully such that early instances do not automatically provide evidence for a full-fledged adult-like representation. Here, the distributional analyses possible with DDBs allow for a fine-grained assessment of productivity, because we can not only identify first usages of a particular linguistic structure, but also assess whether a structure develops in a lexically specific fashion or in a more general fashion. Of particular interest are the changing representations within individual children (not just averages over different groups): only dense data allow us to analyze whether a particular development takes place across the board or where it starts. Regular corpora soon become surprisingly thin once the level of analysis reaches a certain fine-grainedness (e.g., correlation of morphology and lexicon) and this makes it difficult to produce reliable quantitative assessments of the relative frequency of different forms.

Results showing the lexical specificity of child language are in line with findings from usage-based and corpus linguistics in which actual language use is studied based on "real-world" texts (e.g., newspapers, internet, conversations). First, usage-based theories of language claim that language structure is shaped by language use (e.g., Bybee, 2010). This implies that the input data available to the child should provide the necessary positive and indirect negative evidence for the structures of the target language. Second, findings from corpus linguistics show that, for many linguistic structures, we find a skewed distribution of lexical items, and it has been argued that this is important for the process by which children develop a particular structure. For instance, the verb *get* allows multiple syntactic frames, so-called alternations of argument structure, and Goldberg, Casenheiser, and Sethuraman (2005) found that *get* predominantly occurs as verb–object–locative construction when the meaning is "caused motion" (*Bob got the ball over the fence*), but as verb–object–object construction when the meaning is "transfer" (*Bob got him a cake*).

Such statistical skewings may facilitate learning and, indeed, studies show that children's early production relies on such frequency information. Training studies support the conclusion that children learn constructions best when trained with skewed input (Goldberg, 2006). The interrelationship between the lexicon and the form–meaning correspondences of syntactic constructions and their effect on children's acquisition of such constructions cannot be revealed with thin samples.

Dense databases will give a much more accurate assessment of the relationship between types and tokens in the child's speech. An example is the issue of "blocking" in the debate on morphological overgeneralization in English. Do children stop over-generalizing irregular verbs in the past tense (e.g., *goed* for *went*) as soon as they have learned the correct form – an essential part of the "dual route" model (Marcus, 1995) – or do instances of the over-regularization slowly reduce, which is more compatible with the "single route" model (Marchman, Plunkett, and Goodman, 1997)? On the basis of estimates from "thin" longitudinal corpora on CHILDES, Maratsos (2000) calculated that the latter was more likely to be the case. Using the Thomas-Brian DDB, Maslen *et al.* (2004) were able to show that Maratsos's hypothetical calculations were correct. Also relevant to this debate is the issue of whether German has a single "default" plural (governed by a rule in the "dual route" model). Using the Leo DDB, Behrens (2002) showed that the child's error patterns as well as their frequency changed over time, reflecting gradual abstraction over the phonotactic factors that determine the choice of the plural allomorphs rather than the acquisition of a "once and for all" rule or rules. This provided detailed support for previous studies with less dense data such as that of Köpcke (1998) and Szagun (2001).

Denser data also allow us to investigate the relationship between different strands of development and between the child's speech and the input. This makes an interesting comparison with the "getting it all" topical diary approach (Naigles, Chapter 16 this volume). Topical diaries are exhaustive for the items that parents are asked to record and this may allow for the assessment of productivity across that particular group of items. However they are probably of limited use for identifying the mechanisms of development in terms of the mutual influence of lexical items and constructions on one another, let alone any influences of the input which, of course, is not recorded. A good example is the use of growth curves in determining the relationship between the learning of constructions. Ruhland and van Geert (1998) point out that densely sampled data are essential for this. Abbot-Smith and Behrens (2006) used the Leo corpus to investigate the question of how learning one construction may support or hinder the learning of another – the construction conspiracy hypothesis (Morris, Cottrell, and Elman, 2000). Abbot-Smith and Behrens investigated Leo's development of German passive and future constructions containing a lexical verb and the auxiliaries with *sein* (to be) or *werden* (to become). Because Leo had acquired *sein* in the copula construction months earlier than he started using the passive, the authors predicted that the *sein*-passive would develop earlier and faster than the *werden*-passive, and this was found to be the case. Leo became (morphologically) productive with the *sein*-passive earlier than *werden*-passives, according to the criteria of higher cumulative type frequency, type/token ratios, and active–passive alternation, and his rate of assimilation of new verb types into the former was twice that of the latter. When investigating patterns of development, the authors predicted that the form of a "nonsupported" construction should be exponential (with a slow start and the child showing an increasing ability to use the construction the more it has been previously used). By contrast, a supported construction should demonstrate sudden acquisition and a subsequently linear function, similar to that of adult baseline in which cumulative frequency grows linearly to a point where it tails off when the mother has said most of the verb types most frequent in the particular construction. Again this is what was found.

A major issue in child language is the extent to which children are innovative and productive with language. How much of what they say is simple repetition of what they have heard others say, how much of it is novel, and what is the basis of this novelty? With dense sampling the researcher has a much better chance of discovering whether there are prior instances of an utterance and, therefore, assessing the child's level of productivity. Lieven and colleagues examined this issue in a number of studies using the English DDBs with a method they called "traceback" (Dąbrowska and Lieven, 2005; Lieven, Salomo, and Tomasello, 2009). Each 6 week DDB was divided into a "test corpus" of the last 2 hours of recording in the 6 weeks and a "main corpus" consisting of the previous 28 hours. All multiword utterance types were collected from the test corpus and their relationship to utterances in the main corpus was then examined. This involved identifying possible "component units" from the main corpus that could have been used to construct the utterances in the test corpus. Two types of component units were defined: "fixed strings" and "schemas with slots." Fixed strings were fully lexically specific, while schemas contained slots as well as fixed lexical material (e.g., *There's an X, I'm X-ing it*). Slots could be identified in schemas only if they were semantically coherent, and the single or multiword strings that filled the slots also had to match the semantics of the slot. All possible matches were identified using a computer program. The program output was then used to identify semantically coherent strings and slots and to derive the potential tracebacks. Lieven, Salomo, and Tomasello (2009) were able to trace back a very large proportion (58–92%) of the four 2-year-olds' utterances in the test corpus either to exact repetitions in the main corpus or to schemas that required only one substitution into a slot. The vast majority of these substitutions were of single nouns into "referent" slots. With developing mean length of utterance (MLU), the range of other semantic slots developed, as did the variety of strings. Some of these schemas seemed highly productive, but the schemas themselves were fairly simple and the scope of that productivity was, at first, limited both semantically and structurally.

In a related study Bannard, Lieven, and Tomasello (2009) used a computational method to generate grammars from the main corpora for two of the same children at 2:0 and 3:0 (Thomas-Brian and Annie). The grammars consisted of lexically specific constructions, with or without slots, and contained no fully abstract rules. They were extracted by aligning all strings that overlapped in their lexical content. This resulted in potential slots in the alignments and the process was repeated until no further alignments were possible. The result was a large set of alternative candidate analyses which were probabilistically sampled and used to parse all the unique multiword utterances in the test corpora. At 2:0, the mean performance of these sampled grammars showed wide coverage and good predictive fit as compared with fully abstract grammars, with the children showing radically limited productivity. The researchers also added more abstract categories such as "noun" and "verb" to the grammars. At 2:0 only the addition of the category of noun improved coverage. At 3:0, the children's productivity had sharply increased and the addition of abstract linguistic information over verbs as well as nouns markedly improved performance. Another important finding came from parsing the different corpora with the different grammars. Not surprisingly the 2:0 grammars show poor coverage and fit when parsing the 3:0 grammars. In addition, when one child's grammar was used to parse the other child's corpora, much better results were found for the 3:0 data than for the 2:0 data, suggesting that initially the children's grammars were very idiosyncratic but that by 3:0 they were starting to converge on the adult system. The important point to note is that the larger the corpora over which this procedure operates, the more reliable the results.

Procedure

The DDBs were collected and transcribed by staff of the Max Planck Institute for Evolutionary Anthropology in Leipzig and associated scientists. Families were recruited through advertisement and/or informal contacts. The sampling regimes vary in terms of both the periods covered and the number of hours of recording, though in all cases the aim was to record for at least 5 hours per week over the period of the study. We have done this for a number of English-speaking children as well as for children learning German, Estonian, Polish, Japanese, and Finnish. In the case of the last four of these languages, we collaborated with researchers working on language development in these languages (for details, see Table 15.1). The most extensive in terms of time and age range cover 5 hours per week of one German and one English boy from ages 2:0 to 3:0. Table 15.1 shows all the DDBs that have been collected and their current status in terms of hours and ages covered and transcription. The aim, eventually, is to deposit them all with the open-source CHILDES database (see Corrigan, Chapter 18 this volume).

DDBs can be combined with other means of assessment. For example, tests of the children's language development can be made (this was done at the onset of the English studies, but not for the other languages as standardized tests were not available). For the Thomas-Brian, Annie, and Leo corpora, the parents also kept a daily diary with the most precocious utterances of the day. Thus the emergence of new structures on the tape-recorded sequences can be checked against the parental notes.

Implementation

In order to avoid intervention in regular family life, dense recording regimes work best when parents can carry out the recordings themselves. The families participating in the Max Planck DDBs were equipped with a recording device and two high-quality

Table 15.1 The Max Planck dense databases

Child	Language	Age	No of hours	Status of data	Principal investigators
Annie	English	2:0–2:1:14	5 per week	Transcribed	Lieven/Goh
		3:0–3:1:14	5 per week		
Thomas-Brian[a]	English	2:00:12–3:00:12	5 per week	CHILDES	
		3:03:02–4:11:20	5 in 1 week/month		
Eleanor	English	2:0–2:01:08	10 per week	Transcribed	
		2:2:01–2:11:09	10 in 1 week/month		
		3:0–3:01:15	10 per week		
Fraser	English	2:0–2:01:10	10 per week	Transcribed	
		2:2:01–2:11:06	10 in 1 week/month		
		3:0–3:01:11	10 per week		
Cathy	English	3:0–3:1:14	5 per week	In progress	
		3:01:15–3:11:29	5 in 1 week/month	In progress	
		4:0–4:1:14	5 per week	In progress	
		4:01:15–4:11:29	5 in 1 week/month	In progress	
		5:0–5:1:14	5 per week	In progress	
Hannah	English	3:0–3:1:14	5 per week	In progress	
		3:01:15–3:11:29	5 in 1 week/month	In progress	
		4:0–4:1:14	5 per week	In progress	
		4:01:15–4:05	5 in 1 week/month	In progress	
Leo	German	2:0–2:11:29	5 per week	CHILDES	Behrens
		3:1:14–5:0	5 in 1 week/month		

Marysia	Polish	2:0–2:1:14	5 per week	Transcribed and glossed	Dąbrowska
		3:0–3:1:14	5 per week	Transcribed, glossing in progress	
Julia	Polish	2:0–2:1:14	5 per week	Transcribed, glossing in progress	
		3:0–3:1:14	5 per week	Transcribed, glossing in progress	
Andreas	Estonian	2:0–2:1:12	5 per week	CHILDES	Vihman/Vija
		2:3:26–2:8:13	≈ 1 per month		
		3:0–3:1:13	5 per week		
Child J	Japanese	2:0–2:01:14	5 per week	In progress	Matsui
		2:01:15–2:11:29	1 per week	In progress	
		3:0–3:01:14	5 per week	In progress	
Piia	Finnish	1:07:21–4:00:13	3 per week	In progress	Kirjavainen

[a] "Brian" is this child's pseudonym, but just before the corpus was deposited with CHILDES, the family gave permission for the use of the child's real name, "Thomas," and for the deposition of sound files as well as transcriptions.

wireless microphones that could be situated wherever the activity took place. This mobility makes a flexible schedule possible, as the recordings can be interrupted when the child is no longer willing to engage in the situation or wishes to change location. For the English and German DDBs, one recording in each week was videotaped. Experience showed that 1 hour recordings are very exhausting for 2-year-olds, and parents often sampled half an hour in the morning and half an hour in the afternoon. To guarantee privacy, parents were given the right to withhold recordings of family situations they did not feel comfortable with making publicly available. Families were paid the equivalent of 50% of a clerical salary.

In addition to sampling density, a choice about the time frame has to be made. Continuous dense recordings constitute the most labor intensive sampling regime, but provide a clear developmental picture as the development can be traced over time. Continuous recording is especially valuable if it covers a time frame of several years in order to be able to analyze later stages of development as well. The pitfall of case studies – lack of inter-individual reliability checking – can be overcome if the language development of the child in question is compared to the development of other children's data.

Dense databases can also be implemented with temporal gaps. For a number of the DDBs, 6 week periods of dense (5 h/week) or double dense (10 h/week) recordings were followed by intervals without recordings. Short periods of dense data can be analyzed for purposes of testing the productivity and distribution of particular structures.

The quality of the settings is also very important. For practical reasons, the families participating in the DDBs were asked to refrain from noisy activities, to avoid background noise, and to keep the television, radio, and other "noisy" appliances off during recording. This means that we mainly covered dyadic, sometimes triadic play situations within the families or with a few, usually well-known visitors.

Are There Any Likely Pitfalls?

The biggest pitfall is that the original scheme for transcribing and coding the data is too ambitious given the amount of time and personnel available. Thus careful choices have to be made regarding the degree of detail of the transcription (phonetic or orthographic) and the amount and detail of coding. Recent technological advances provide (partial) solutions for all these issues: if the transcripts are linked to the digitized sound file or video, a standardized orthographic transcription can always be amended with a more detailed transcription when needed. Regarding the coding of data, for English the morphosyntactic annotation program has been completed. It provides part-of-speech tagging and lemmatization (providing the "base form" of the word to facilitate lexical searches, e.g., "walk" for "walked," "walking," and "walks": MacWhinney, 2008). For other languages or other areas of linguistic interest, the situation is less good, though we are well advanced with glossing the Polish data and are starting on the Finnish and Japanese data. Standardized orthographic transcription seems to be the only choice for dense databases, as the size of the database makes searches by reading through the transcripts impossible (Behrens, 2008).

Developments in speech and speaker recognition technology will probably help in the future to identify those segments in the recordings where speech occurs, and it may even be possible to identify the speaker. This would speed up and facilitate the transcription process (see Roy, 2009, for the implementation of such ideas). Currently, such technology is most advanced when only a limited number of speakers is present. The future will probably lie in a smart mix of automated speech recognition and perhaps partial automatic transcription and coding, combined with additional manual detailed transcription and annotation of the relevant sequences for the research question at stake.

Because of the high investment in recording and transcribing the data, the collection, transcription, and glossing of DDBs impose unique requirements in terms of sources of support, and often only more permanent institutions like the Max Planck Institutes can back such a long term investment. However, support might be more readily available from funding programs for the collection of DDBs from children who are in one way or another atypical, or for languages other than English.

It could be argued that the demands on the family of DDB recording limit the types of social and family backgrounds represented in DDBs. Despite the fact families were paid the equivalent of a 50% clerical position, there are bound to be sociological factors involved in the self-selection of parents for such a project. While this is true, it is also not obvious how it can be remedied. Again, it is always possible to check the data obtained from DDBs against corpora from other children to identify possible biases and test these experimentally.

Finally, recordings usually took place inside the house during play, book reading, or snack time. As a consequence we know little about how the child performs in unknown situations or with unknown interlocutors. Eisenbeiss (2009) argues that recording the same situations may emphasize the impression that children's linguistic performance is largely stereotypical and formulaic, and suggests that researchers bring in new stimulus material (interesting new and complex objects, new games) to stimulate talk about unfamiliar objects or situations.

Interrater Reliability

Transcribing dense databases requires a team of transcribers who must be trained and supervised throughout, as the child's language development may lead to new transcription problems. For the DDBs we opted for orthographic, not phonetic transcription and linked the utterances to the sound wave. Linking is an option in the Child Language Data Exchange System (CHILDES: see Corrigan, Chapter 18 this volume). The main problems remaining were establishing standards for domains without standardized orthography (interjections, discourse markers, but also multi-word units like compounds and proper or brand names: see MacWhinney, 2008).

Before the databases were published in the CHILDES archive (again see Corrigan, Chapter 18 this volume), word lists were created to check for spelling variants. A domain that proved to be notoriously difficult to gain agreement on is the demarcation of utterance boundaries because spoken language tends to be continuous, and the speech stream does not always signal clause or sentence boundaries. Contrary to the CHILDES recommendation to transcribe in clauses (defined by the presence of a finite verb), we decided to represent the flow of the discourse and transcribed in turns rather than in clauses.

If one wants to indicate imitations and self-repetitions in order to exclude them from further analyses, criteria for what counts as repeated – just whole utterances or partial utterances (chunks), within a range of how many utterances – have to be developed, implemented, and checked thoroughly.

In case of the Leipzig–Manchester databases, the principal investigator or an experienced lab coordinator supervised the project over the whole period and made sure that standards did not change implicitly. As they were also familiar with the families and the typical topics of conversation, they helped resolved ambiguities the transcribers might have.

Future Directions for the Use of DDBs

As can be seen from Table 15.1, there is still a long way to go in the transcription and glossing of many of the DDBs. Thus the research reported here gives only an initial idea of the ways in which they can be used. In comparing adult and child it is often important to control the adult data down to the level of the child, for instance in terms of the types used and the number of tokens, otherwise one is inevitably likely to end up with the child looking less productive than the adult. DDBs allow us to do this without reducing the amount of data to almost nonexistence (Aguado-Orea, 2004; Krajewski, Lieven, and Theakston, submitted). Similarly, large corpora can be used to derive frequency and distributional information when designing stimuli for experiments, with the frequency counts much more closely matched to the ages of the children in the proposed experiment. Computational linguists are also starting to make use of the DDBs to build and test probabilistic and algorithmic models of various aspects of language learning (Bannard, Lieven, and Tomasello, 2009; Chang, Lieven, and Tomasello, 2008).

Since dense databases cover not only the child's productions but also large portions of the input in a naturalistic setting, we can study the effect of input and interaction on the emerging child language directly. A particular child's development can be studied against the backdrop of the input s/he received up to that point in time, and we can also study the effect of interaction on acquisition. For example, the role of variation sets (small adaptations of the utterances that highlight and contrast the formal properties of a particular structure: Küntay and Slobin 2002) could be explored and the size of the database would allow for more control and quantitative testing.

Another potentially important direction is that of children's semantic and pragmatic development, where thinner data may only record the most frequent usage of a word or structure. Thus Cameron-Faulkner, Lieven, and Theakston (2007) were able to analyze Thomas-Brian's uses of multiword negation in great detail and compare it to his mother's use of negation, even though some form–function mappings were quite rare. Another example is Steinkrauss's (2009) study of Leo's development of *wh*-questions. While his analysis by and large confirmed previous findings that the emergence of *wh*-word–auxiliary pairings is item based and reflects the distribution in the input, he also found that some high-frequency question types were not picked up by the child because, from the child's point of view, they were pragmatically irrelevant (e.g., rhetorical questions using mock-surprise tone).

In sum, DDBs take corpus-based studies on language acquisition to a new level because they provide the richness of data necessary to assess current hypotheses on learning processes in light of new insights from developmental and linguistic theories.

Key Terms

Corpus linguistics In corpus linguistics, samples of spoken and/or written naturalistic language use are analyzed to characterize properties of the language system and aspects of language change. This is by contrast with the method of introspection, where competent speakers judge whether linguistic structures are acceptable or not.

Crosslinguistic studies In crosslinguistic studies, a linguistic phenomenon is compared across languages to assess aspects like cognitive complexity and processability and their effect on language development.

Linguistic productivity Productive structures can generate more types of the same underlying structure. For example, in English morphology, the affix -*ly* can be used to make adjectives into adverbs. In child language, productivity measures are used to assess whether the child reproduces forms from memory or is able to create new forms based on knowledge about the underlying structure. Productivity is typically assessed by contrast within the morphological paradigm, by percentage of correct utterances in obligatory context, or by experimental studies that test children's productivity with nonce words, i.e., words they have not heard before and cannot have memorized.

Longitudinal corpora Data samples that track the development of individuals or groups over time. The sampling rate can vary from daily recordings to recordings every couple of weeks or months.

Usage-based theory Usage-based theories assume that language structure is shaped by communicative processes in so far as all linguistic units are considered to be symbolic, i.e., form–function pairings of varying degrees of abstraction. In acquisition, usage-based theories assume that language is acquired from the language use the child is exposed to.

References

Abbot-Smith, K., and Behrens, H. (2006) How known constructions influence the acquisition of other constructions: the German passive and future constructions. *Cognitive Science*, 30, 995–1026.

Aguado-Orea, J. (2004) The acquisition of morpho-syntax in Spanish: implications for current theories of development. Unpublished PhD dissertation, University of Nottingham.

Bannard, C., Lieven, E., and Tomasello, M. (2009) Modeling children's early grammatical knowledge. *PNAS*, 106, 17, 284–17, 289.

Behrens, H. (2002) Learning multiple regularities: evidence from overgeneralization errors in the German plural. In A.H.J. Do, L. Domínguez, and A. Johansen (eds), *Proceedings of the 26th Annual Boston University Conference on Language Development* (pp. 72–83). Somerville, MA: Cascadilla.

Behrens, H. (2008) Corpora in language acquisition research: history, methods, perspectives. In H. Behrens (ed.), *Corpora in language acquisition research: finding structure in data* (pp. xi–xxx). Amsterdam: Benjamins.

Brandt, S., Diessel, H., and Tomasello M. (2008) The acquisition of German relative clauses: a case study. *Journal of Child Language*, 35 (2), 325–348.

Brandt, S., Lieven, E., and Tomasello, M. (2010) Development of word order in German complement-clause constructions: effects of input frequencies, lexical items, and discourse function. *Language*, 86, (3), 583–610.

Bybee, J. (2010) *Language, usage, and cognition.* Cambridge: Cambridge University Press.

Cameron-Faulkner, T., Lieven, E., and Theakston, A. (2007) What part of *no* do children not understand? A usage-based account of multiword negation. *Journal of Child Language*, 34, 251–282.

Chang, F., Lieven, E., and Tomasello, M. (2008) Automatic evaluation of syntactic learners in typologically-different languages. *Cognitive Systems Research*, 9, 198–213.

Dąbrowska, E., and Lieven, E. (2005) Towards a lexically specific grammar of children's question constructions. *Cognitive Linguistics*, 16, 437–474.

Eisenbeiss, S. (2009) Contrast is the name of the game: contrast-based semi-structured elicitation techniques for studies on children's language acquisition. *Essex Research Reports in Linguistics 57*. http://www.essex.ac.uk/linguistics/publications/errl/errl57-7.pdf.

Goldberg, A.E. (2006) *Constructions at work: the nature of generalization in language.* Oxford: Oxford University Press.

Goldberg, A.E., Casenhiser, D., and Sethuraman, N. (2005) The role of prediction in construction learning. *Journal of Child Language*, 32, 407–426.

Köpcke, K.-M. (1998) The acquisition of plural marking in English and German revisited: schemata vs. rules. *Journal of Child Language*, 25, 293–319.

Krajewski, G., Lieven, E., and Theakston, A. (submitted) Productivity of a Polish child's inflectional noun morphology: a naturalistic study. *Morphology*.

Küntay, A.C., and Slobin, D.I. (2002) Putting interaction back into child language: examples from Turkish. *Psychology of Language and Communication*, 6, 5–14.

Lieven, E., Salomo, D., and Tomasello, M. (2009) Two-year-old children's production of multiword utterances: a usage-based analysis. *Cognitive Linguistics*, 20, 481–508.

MacWhinney, B. (2008) Enriching CHILDES for morphosyntactic analysis. In H. Behrens (ed.), *Corpora in language acquisition research: finding structure in data* (pp. 165–197). Amsterdam: Benjamins.

Maratsos, M. (2000) More overgeneralizations after all: new data and discussion on Marcus, Pinker, Ullman, Hollander, Rosen and Xu. *Journal of Child Language*, 27, 183–212.

Marchman, V., Plunkett, K., and Goodman, J. (1997) Overregularization in English plural and past tense inflectional morphology: a response to Marcus (1995). *Journal of Child Language*, 24 (3), 767–779.

Marcus, G.F. (1995) Children's overregularization of English plurals: a quantitative analysis. *Journal of Child Language*, 22, 447–459.

Maslen, R., Theakston, A., Lieven, E., and Tomasello, M. (2004) A dense corpus study of past tense and plural overregularization in English. *Journal of Speech, Language and Hearing Research*, 47, 1319–1333.

Morris, W.C., Cottrell, G.W., and Elman, J.L. (2000) A connectionist simulation of the empirical acquisition of grammatical relations. In S. Wermter and R. Sun (eds), *Hybrid neural symbolic integration* (pp. 175–193). Berlin: Springer.

Rowland, C., and Fletcher, S. (2006) The effect of sampling on estimates of lexical specificity and error rates. *Journal of Child Language*, 33, 859–877.

Rowland, C., Fletcher, S., and Freudenthal, D. (2008) How big is enough? Assessing the reliability of data from naturalistic samples. In H. Behrens (ed.) *Corpora in language acquisition research: finding structure in data* (pp. 1–24). Amsterdam: Benjamins.

Roy, D. (2009) New horizons in the study of child language acquisition. *Proceedings of Interspeech 2009*. Brighton, UK.

Ruhland, R., and van Geert, P. (1998) Jumping into syntax: transitions in the development of closed class words. *British Journal of Developmental Psychology*, 16 (part 1), 65–95.

Steinkrauss, R. (2009) Frequency and function in wh-question acquisition. Doctoral dissertation, University of Groningen (GRODIL 75).

Szagun, G. (2001) Learning different regularities: the acquisition of noun plurals by German-speaking children. *First Language*, 21, 109–141.

Tomasello, M., and Stahl, D. (2004) Sampling children's spontaneous speech: how much is enough? *Journal of Child Language*, 31, 101–121.

Further Reading and Resources

The read.me files for the DDBs already deposited in the CHILDES database (see Table 15.1) are a useful source of information.

16 Not Sampling, Getting It All

Letitia R. Naigles

Summary

Diary methods allow researchers to record all of the utterances that a given child produces. Such methods allow researchers to make assessments of that child's state of linguistic knowledge that are more accurate than those relying on sampled speech; if the diary is collected over a span of time, it can also reveal the shape and nature of the child's changes in knowledge of language. Three types of diary methodologies are reviewed, including a "pen-and-paper" diary that targets only specific lexical or grammatical items but tracks children's usage in micro scale; the LENA system, which collects day-long audio recordings of children's vocalizations and their language environments; and the Speechome Recorder, which collects continuous audio *and* video recordings of children and their home environments on a daily basis for months. These methods are particularly suitable for assessing the speech of children at the beginnings of their language acquisition, including typically developing children and children with speech or language delays, as well as children learning one or multiple languages.

Research Aim

Language development is a process whose outcomes change with the age of the child. Every text on language development notes that children produce their first word around 12 months of age, add words one at a time over the next 6 months or so, combine words into two- and then three-word phrases over the next 6 months, add grammatical items either concurrently with their multi-word utterances or shortly

Research Methods in Child Language: A Practical Guide, First Edition.
Edited by Erika Hoff.
© 2012 Blackwell Publishing Ltd. Published 2012 by Blackwell Publishing Ltd.

thereafter (depending on which language is being learned), and generally begin producing full and complete grammatical sentences around 2.5 years of age (e.g., Hoff, 2009). Some of the outcome changes undoubtedly occur because language development relies on linguistic input and older children have experienced more of this input than younger children. Some outcome changes also likely occur because older children make different uses of their input than younger children. The existence of changes with age in children's linguistic productions is not disputed; however, what is not obvious is what the changes indicate about the child's linguistic knowledge state, and the extent to which the changes are discrete and qualitative changes as opposed to more continuous. Because numerous theories of children's language acquisition depend on characteristics of the nature and trajectory of the child's linguistic knowledge state (e.g., Ambridge and Lieven, in press; Chomsky, 1972; Fisher, 2002; Gleitman, 1984; Tomasello, 2000), it is critical to have at hand accurate and precise descriptions of these changes.

Studies of children's language production have investigated questions about children's changing language already, of course, but almost all have employed some kind of sampling methodology (see Rowe, Chapter 13 this volume; Lieven and Behrens, Chapter 15 this volume) in which the children are recorded in conversation with their caregivers – and/or siblings and experimenters – while engaged in specific activities for specific amounts of time at specific intervals. These studies have yielded a wealth of valuable data, but are less informative concerning the questions of discrete vs continuous change in general, and "What does Johnny know about language now?" in particular. This is because the very act of sampling will always yield findings of more or less discrete change: a specific word or grammatical construction was not observed at visit 1, but was observed at visit 2, so therefore a change occurred between visits such that that word or construction was (at least beginning to be) acquired. But what if the word or construction began to be learned and/or used on the day after visit 1? Moreover, the very act of sampling will always miss some child utterances: a specific word or construction may not have been used because the context wasn't appropriate, or the child's desired addressee wasn't present, or the relevant objects weren't the topics of the conversation. In a different developmental domain, Adolph and her colleagues (2008) have demonstrated that changes in children's locomotor activity during the first 2 years of life seem discrete and qualitative if the data are considered on a monthly basis; however, data capturing children's daily activities reveal gradual and incremental changes. Likewise with language development, ideally, we want to capture *everything* that the child says, so as to get a better idea of what s/he knows about language at any given time, as well as to capture the *real* patterns of change in language production with age. We call this, "getting it all."

There exists a venerable methodology for capturing everything that a child says: keep a diary. That is, enlist a parent or caregiver in the task of recording every child utterance and noting the relevant aspects of its context. Parents or caregivers are needed to do this, because they are in the child's presence whenever s/he is awake and talking. And in fact, the earliest studies of child language were all diaries, including those of Darwin (1877/1974) and the Sterns (1907); more modern examples include Dromi (1987) and Tomasello (1992). These latter diaries, especially, were Herculean efforts, yielding extremely rich datasets which are still being analyzed today (e.g., Dromi, 2009; Naigles, Hoff, and Vear, 2009). But I am not necessarily advocating here the use of this "complete" diary method because it is extremely labor intensive, because a given adult can keep a language diary for only one child at a time, and because the task of recording exactly what the child says and discerning exactly what s/he means, in real time, becomes increasingly challenging as the child develops. For example, with just a few hours of training, caregivers who are easily literate are certainly able to write down children's isolated words, and even their two/three-word utterances that only include content words, if noted immediately after production. However, children's earliest multi-word utterances are usually grammatically fragmentary (e.g., *want juice, play in pool, no want bath*), and if they are not recorded immediately, caregivers may remember such utterances in more grammatical forms (e.g., *I want juice, playing in the pool, don't want a bath*). But researchers need to know if the child actually produced a subject or not, if s/he actually produced the "-ing" suffix and the "a" determiner, and if the negated form was "no" or "don't." So as the child's grammar develops, caregivers without specific training in linguistics may not record utterances as accurately as needed.

The art of meaning discernment should not be minimized, either, as it is not always clear exactly what a child means when s/he says something. For example, when a child looks at a ball and says "ball," or looks at a cracker and says "eat it," is she making a request or a comment? (Gestures certainly help make this call – see Cartmill, Demir, and Goldin-Meadow, Chapter 14 this volume – but add yet another form for the caregivers to record.) Does she use "ball" to refer to all balls, or just one special one? Does she use "eat it" with all types of eaters and eatables, or just one or two? Unless specifically instructed, caregivers may not report which ball was the referent – which would be important to know for questions about children's ability to extend words to new objects – or what were the intended agents and patients of the utterance "eat it," which would be important to know for questions about how lexically specific vs grammatically abstract are children's early sentences. Ideally, children's utterances would be recorded in such a way that their manifestations and contexts could be reviewed and coded by the researchers themselves. The final clincher is that as children talk more, parents and caregivers become more interested in the purpose of the interaction and less interested in recording its exact content and form. This pretty much precludes the follow-your-child-around-and-write-down-everything-s/he-says diary for anything but the earliest words.

What I am going to describe here are three newer ways to implement the diary method, two of which are reliant on state-of-the-art technology: (1) the targeted diary, (2) day-long audio recordings using the LENA system (Xu *et al.*, 2008), and (3) months-long audio/video recordings using the Speechome Recorder (Roy *et al.*, 2006).

The Targeted Diary

The targeted diary still involves recruiting the parent or caregiver as data recorder, but it restricts the child utterances to be recorded to a smaller but well-defined, theoretically motivated, and well-specified set. For example, in our recent "verb diary" study (Naigles, Hoff, and Vear, 2009), my colleagues and I asked eight mothers to record the first 10 times their child used each of 34 specified verbs. By specifying the verbs, the mothers only needed to listen for specific utterances rather than write down all. By asking for only the first 10 instances of each verb, mothers were freed from actively listening for each verb once the 10-instance mark had been reached. Thus, requiring the caregiver to record only a targeted subset of utterances made the task more tractable, as did specifying when the recording could cease. Yet the most important aspects of the diary method were preserved: mothers recorded their children's utterances wherever and whenever these occurred, so that we obtained data on the children's flexibility vs conservatism of verb use – pragmatic, semantic, and syntactic – from its very beginnings.

Two primary findings were most notable. First, early flexibility rather than conservatism was the norm. That is, the eight children in our study used 38% of their verbs with reference to appropriately diverse actions (e.g., *come* used for both going downstairs and going outside; *open* used for both opening bags and opening jars) and 50% of their verbs while describing actions by different actors (e.g., *eat* used for both dog and father eaters). And contrary to previous reports in the literature (e.g., Huttenlocher, Smiley, and Charney, 1983), they did *not* primarily use their first instances of their first verb self-referentially: about 50% of their very first verb uses were about the actions of others. Finally, they used 89% of their verbs while describing actions on different affected objects (e.g., *wash* used for washing dishes and washing clothes). In sum, by using records of children's talk all day, in all contexts, and with all available co-conversationalists, we can see that 1-year-olds very quickly extend their verbs in myriad ways. Because the diary records included time outside, at the mall, and/or in the car, children had the opportunity (seldom enabled by just recording mother–child play sessions with toys) to talk to and about their pets (frequent actors and addressees), to talk about actions seldom carried out at home (e.g., going on an escalator), and to talk about actions with a variety of affected objects (e.g., flowers, swings, egg rolls). All of these types of flexibility were observed, on average, by the child's sixth production of a given verb. Thus, as documented by Adolph *et al.* (2008) for infant locomotion, the onset of "new" aspects of verb use is early – and gradual – rather than late and sudden.

Our second major finding was that there was considerable variability among the children – and the verbs – in the flexibility they evidenced. For example, while early grammatical flexibility was also the norm across all eight children (i.e., children used their verbs in different (but appropriate) syntactic frames), three of the children (Carrie, Heather, Elaine) produced their verbs in multi-word utterances with multiple frames within the first 6 weeks of verb use, whereas two others (Carl and Mae) did not demonstrate this level of grammatical flexibility until about 10 months after they began to produce verbs at all (showing flexibility around 28 and 25 months of age, respectively). Moreover, whereas most of the children demonstrated most of their early grammatical flexibility via their use of subject and object NPs rather than verbal morphology (e.g., saying "drop," "I drop," "I drop something" rather than "dropped" or "dropping"), Sam demonstrated grammatical flexibility in his use of verb particles, producing five of his verbs with at least two particles each (e.g., "push in," "push down") and two particles with at least two different verbs. Verb variability could be seen in that six of the children produced their first SVO frames with *want*, whereas *look* elicited the first V + locative frames ("look at me," "look my shoe," "look here") with three children. Moreover, children who began producing verbs *earlier* showed *more* semantic flexibility, whereas verbs whose onsets of use were *later* showed *more* grammatical flexibility.

The targeted diary method thus can reveal much more flexibility in the child's spontaneous speech than would be evident from speech sampled in specific contexts at specific intervals. By obtaining records of speech whenever and wherever it is produced, researchers can demonstrate that children use their very first verbs – and possibly other words as well – with reference to a variety of actions, actors, and affected objects, and in a variety of sentence frames. The targeted nature of the diary (specific lexical items to listen for, specific numbers of instances to record) makes record keeping tractable for the caregiver. However, the targeted diary, by definition, omits a lot of the child's speech: we do not know, for example, whether these children learned and extended nouns in the same way as verbs. Furthermore, it does not provide much, if any, information about two additional critical components of children's earliest speech experiences: namely, the language used by others in their environment (i.e., linguistic input), and details about the visual-spatial and social situations in which the child speaks.

The visual-spatial and social situations in which a child produces language tell researchers, for example, how narrow vs general are his/her mappings between words and meanings, how much the caregiver and child engage in joint attention, and how context specific are his/her uses of different grammatical forms. Our verb diarists were able to track some aspects of context because these were specifically built into the diary; however, other aspects, including joint attention between speaker and addressee, use of gesture, and exact form of the actions the verbs referred to, were not captured. No diary keeper can note every aspect of the context; those aspects that seem irrelevant to the focus of the study will be ignored. Thus, what would be ideal would be to have a video and audio record of the child's speech, including the context, which could be coded for any number of situational aspects, afterwards.

The child's linguistic environment also tells researchers about the child's degree of generalizability. Has s/he produced something that she has never heard before? Did she use "ball" for a completely new and so-far-unlabelled ball? Did she use "open" with completely new actor, affected object, and/or overt direct object? If her first words and/or sentences are identical to those already in her linguistic environment (i.e., produced by adults or older children in her hearing), how slowly, steadily, or suddenly do they manifest the creativity that is such an important characteristic of human language (Chomsky, 1959)? There is an abundance of evidence that the sentence frames of preschoolers, older children, and adults can be primed by previously heard forms (e.g., Fisher, 2002; Shimpi *et al.*, 2007); to what extent are the constructions used by beginning speakers similarly primed by their linguistic environment? Even the best-kept conventional diary cannot record all of the speech a child hears; the targeted diary method sketched above does not even try because the skills of recording adult speech in real time are beyond those of nonspecialist caregivers. Below, I discuss two new ways to collect and analyze ecologically valid corpora of children's speech and home environment.

Language Environment Analysis (LENA)

The LENA system is a commercial product that allows researchers to audio record a given child's speech and language environment for one entire day at a time. The recorder is a small, battery-operated device that fits into a pocket of the child's clothing and can record for 16 hours straight. A LENA recorder, then, can capture a child's speech in all of her varied daily activities; moreover, it can also capture the speech of others in the vicinity – her input. Automated analyses of LENA recordings can provide separate vocalization tallies for the target child and ancillary children, separate word token tallies for male and female adults, a tally of the conversational turns in which each participated, and even the duration of electronic media (e.g., television) playing in the vicinity. These tallies can be organized by time of day and/or across the entire day. Concordance of LENA automated tallies and human transcriber tallies has been reported to be 70% (Christakis *et al.*, 2009).

The LENA system is currently being used to record the speech and language environments of children who are typically developing and children with specific language impairment, autism, and other language disorders (http://www.lenafoundation. org). Published studies include the following. Zimmerman *et al.* (2009) used the LENA system to record children (2–4 years of age) for 12 hours/day, one day a month, for either 6 or 18 consecutive months. The children were administered a standardized language assessment during the first 6 months and (where applicable) at the end of the 18 month period. Concurrent analyses of the first 6 month phase revealed that the adult word count from the recording and the child test scores were significantly and positively correlated; moreover, children whose recordings included longer spans of television had lower test scores and participated in fewer conversational turns (see also Christakis *et al.*, 2009). Longitudinal analyses revealed that adult word counts and number of conversational turns during the first 6 months were both significant and positive predictors of child test scores after the 18 month phase. These positive concurrent and longitudinal correlations between amount of adult input and child language are not new findings (e.g., see Hoff, 2006), but these new studies extend the findings to hundreds of children engaged in a wider range of activities than had ever been accessible before.

Warren and colleagues (2010a; 2010b) replicated this finding with 29 preschool-aged children with autism, based on eight day-long recordings from each child across 7 weeks. Warren *et al.* also found that, whereas the recordings of ASD children did not differ from developmental-age-matched controls on adult word count, child vocalizations, or conversational turns, the children with ASD did produce more vocalizations in monologues (i.e., which were not responded to by adults) than the controls.

Finally, Oller (2010) compared a trilingual child's input and output in her three languages (German, Spanish, English) during her second year of life. The child produced more words in the two languages which were usually addressed to her (i.e., German and Spanish, from her mother and nanny) than in the language (English) which she usually experienced as overheard adult-directed speech between her parents (Oller, 2010), although she also produced more words in Spanish than would be predicted based solely on relative input frequency. Oller categorized the language of each word manually, as the LENA system does not include ways to distinguish languages. The LENA system also does not provide complete transcripts of the recordings; these must be carried out by human transcribers much as with conventional recordings (see Rowe, Chapter 13 this volume). But it seems clear that transcripts of such densely collected linguistic input and output – from large numbers of children – have the potential to address many of the questions raised above.

Human Speechome Project

What the LENA system lacks, though, is a way to capture the child's social and visual/spatial environments while she and others are talking. That is, there is no camera that could film what the child is looking at, the child him/herself, the surroundings, etc. A device for making a comprehensive audio/video record of a given child's speech and home environment is under development by Deb Roy and his colleagues at the MIT Media Lab (Roy *et al.*, 2006). The original implementation set up camera lenses and microphones throughout a house, connected to continuously operating recorders and vast amounts of storage. This was carried out in Roy's own house, recording the speech and home environment of his son; however, the amount of renovation needed to install and then remove the hardware made this system ungeneralizable to other households. Roy and his colleagues have since developed a single device, which can be installed in one corner of a room in any residence, and which has the capability of video and audio recording all of the activities in that room for a period of 3 months. This Speechome Recorder has the potential to prove very useful to child language researchers.

Physically, the Speechome Recorder resembles an arching floor lamp with a friction-fit ceiling brace for stability; it plugs into an electrical outlet. It includes a high-quality camera (fish-eye lens) and microphone (boundary layer) hardware built into its overhead mast, plus a second camera is incorporated into the base of the unit, which is horizontally oriented to capture more detailed facial and gestural observations. The Speechome Recorder contains sufficient computational power and disk storage to record, compress, and store approximately 3 months of data. A touch display is used to turn recording on and off. Privacy measures include a one-button controller to start and stop recording and a second button to delete recorded data retroactively.

Published findings using this method thus far come from the case study of Roy's son, based on 72 days of 9 hours/day recordings when the boy was 9–24 months of age (an additional 372 days were recorded and are currently being transcribed). Transcribing such a corpus necessitated the development of a specialized system called Blitzscribe, in which

> automatic audio processing algorithms are used to robustly detect speech in the audio and split speech into short, easy to transcribe segments. Sequences of speech segments are loaded into a specially designed transcription interface that enables a human

transcriber to simply listen and type, obviating the need for manually finding and segmenting speech or explicitly controlling audio playback. As a result, playback stays synchronized to the transcriber's speed of transcription ... Transcribers using this system can obtain average transcription times of less than twice the audio duration. (Roy, Frank, and Roy, 2009, p. 2)

Roy and his colleagues have tracked the child's *word births* – the first time this word, spoken by the child, appeared in the transcripts – per week and found a smooth and highly accelerating increase up to about 20 months of age (there were 100 word births in that month alone). They categorized those words by form class, finding that across the second year, the modal or majority category of word births was common and proper nouns. Moreover, the frequency with which the child's three caregivers used a given word was negatively related to the age of acquisition or word birth of that word; this effect was particularly strong for nouns. That is, words used more frequently by caregivers had earlier onsets/births by the child (Roy, Frank, and Roy, 2009). Previous studies (e.g., Goodman, Dale, and Li, 2008) had reported similar findings based on checklist data; their use of frequency across children as a proxy for age of acquisition is now corroborated by this more reliable word birth data.

Vosoughi *et al.* (2010) have further analyzed the caregiver speech for its prosodic emphasis, measured by the duration, relative fundamental frequency, and relative intensity of each word. They report similar effects for all three prosodic measures, in that words spoken with more prosodic emphasis by adults have earlier word births by the child. This finding corroborates long-standing theories that the prosody of speech assists the child in the task of speech segmentation (e.g., Gleitman and Wanner, 1982). Incorporation of analyses of the visual/spatial and social contexts is still in progress (DeCamp and Roy, 2009; Roy, 2009); such analyses could reveal, for example, the relative importance of different kinds of activity contexts that co-occur with linguistic exposure in predicting a given word's birth.

In sum, diary methods can reveal everything – with some qualifications – that a child and/or his/her caregivers say and do. Such a comprehensive record of child speech, adult speech, and context can address foundational questions about just what a child knows about language at a given point in time, and how this knowledge changes over time. The targeted diary method is most feasible when a child is not producing speech all the time; the task of diary keeping is tractable for a caregiver when there isn't that much speech to record. The task of *transcribing* all of the speech recorded via innovative technologies (LENA, Speechome Recorder) may only become tractable for researchers by using additional innovative technology (e.g., Roy and Roy, 2009). Diary methods are also suitable if researchers are interested in children's use of multiple languages; however, the researchers and diary keeper(s) would need to be fluent and easily literate in all of the languages their child used. Diary methods could also be both relevant and informative for researchers interested in early language impairments, as diary keepers, LENA devices, and/or Speechome Recorders are likely to record language uses that are not evident in clinical or research settings.

Procedures

Targeted Diary

To carry out a targeted diary study, researchers need to (1) select the words, (2) select the child participants, and (3) train the caregiver/mother participants. Possible words can be gleaned from published lists of children's early word use (e.g., Dromi, 1987; Goldin-Meadow, Seligman, and Gelman, 1976; Tomasello, 1992); a newer resource comes from the norming study performed with the MacArthur Communicative Development Inventories (MCDI), whose results for English learners are presented at http://www.sci.sdsu.edu/lexical/ (Dale and Fenson, 1996). The number of words to include might range from 20 to 50: Naigles, Hoff, and Vear's (2009) verb diary included 34 verbs, and most mothers were able to keep the diary long enough to complete entries for 30 of these. Two mothers attempted to track the first 10 uses of *all* of their child's first verbs, delivering completed diary sheets to us for an additional 10–20 verbs. The number of words to include should also be motivated by the range of words and word meanings of interest. That is, if the study concerns learning names for animals, fewer words might need to be targeted than if the study concerns learning nouns or verbs in general.

Creating a hard-copy version of the diary for the mothers to fill in made the task easier for them; spaces for all 10 instances for each word fit on a single page, and the pages were alphabetized by word. Obviously, each instance should be written down verbatim, and its date of utterance noted. Contextual features to be recorded will vary depending on the specific purposes of the study. Because we were interested in children's first verbs, we wanted to know the actor/agent of each action the child was describing by a target verb, as well as the patient or affected object when relevant. To select our child participants, we first sent out a recruitment letter to parents of children who were 15–19 months of age; such children are unlikely to have produced verbs yet, if learning English. When we followed up with a phone call, we asked all interested mothers if their children had produced any verbs yet, and went through the list of action words on the CDI to see if any of the verbs had been produced. Additional criteria for selection included (1) mothers acting as primary caregiver at home with the target child, (2) mothers willing to contribute the time and persistence to carry out the study for at least several months, and (3) mothers comfortably literate such that transferring their child's speech to the written word would not pose any challenges. Any mothers who are uncertain about their willingness to participate should not be recruited.

Once mothers agree to participate, we set up a "home visit" to train them and verify the verbless/wordless status of the children. A completely accurate verification is not possible (unless a LENA device or Speechome Recorder had been in use since birth!), of course; however, a 20 minute mother–child play session and another discussion of the (action) words on the CDI should elicit most if not all of the words/ verbs the child has already produced, if she has produced any. Training involves showing the diary pages to the caregiver and describing multiple possibilities of how to fill them out. We gave at least five examples of ways to fill out each contextual category. Moreover, a point of consistent emphasis must be that the mother is to include *every single utterance*, unless it is *a direct repeat* of an adult's or older child's utterance. Child self-repetitions must be included, though (else, how can one determine the onset of flexible use?) and some of the how-to-fill-out-the-diary examples should include children's repetitions of their own earlier words. Training also included the request/mandate that the mothers carry the diary wherever they go with the target child, so that his/her speech could be recorded as soon as it is produced.

After training, each mother was contacted by telephone every two weeks, and asked about whether the child had begun to produce verbs. Such frequent calls are needed to keep the diary study fresh in the mothers' minds, so that they begin recording utterances as soon as these are produced. Once the first utterances of the first target verbs are produced, mothers are called on a *weekly basis* for the duration of the study, reminding them to keep the diary, how to enter the utterances, and how to code the context. These reminders are absolutely critical to enable the mothers to maintain the diary accurately. After 1–2 months, some mothers may ask to withdraw because the demands of keeping the diary were more than they realized; usually this occurred with children who were already fluent talkers, and who were thus producing recordable utterances at high rates. Another set of mothers may ask to withdraw after 3–6 months during which their child has not produced any verbs at all; this may be indicative of a child with a language delay and the child may need to be referred to developmental services.

The LENA and Speechome Recorders

Implementing a diary study using the LENA or Speechome recorders involves, of course, first procuring these devices. Information on purchasing LENA Pro systems can be found at http://www.lenafoundation.org/; the Speechome Recorder is not yet commercially available (but see http://web.media.mit.edu/~dkroy/index.html for more information). Another crucial step, though, is to secure project approval from your institution's internal review board (IRB) for the protection of human subjects. This is because the very act of recording children – and their caregivers – *all the time* frequently leads to recording during what may be conventionally or culturally private situations – bathtime, bedtime, conflicts, therapy time, homework time, etc. Moreover, the act of recording a child during all of his/her activities in a given day, week, or month frequently leads to recording other people who are not the child's primary caregiver(s), and who may not realize they are being recorded. Both of these raise key issues of consent and confidentiality which must be addressed for the responsible conduct of research (see http://www.hhs.gov/ohrp/humansubjects/guidance/belmont.htm and http://www.hhs.gov/ohrp/humansubjects/guidance/45cfr46.html). Useful inclusions in the IRB protocol are (1) explicit descriptions of how the caregivers can turn the recorders off and on, and how they will be trained to do so; (2) explicit descriptions of how the caregivers can delete or withhold selections from the recording, and how they will be trained to do so; and (3) forms for securing consent from the caregivers for recordings of themselves, the target child, and/or any relevant siblings, forms for securing assent from siblings who are old enough to require this (usually above the ages of 8–10 years), and forms for securing consent from adults who are regular visitors to and/or interactors with the target child, such as other family members or family friends. I recommend, in addition, that researchers planning to use these recorders meet with the relevant members of their institution's IRB before submitting a protocol for approval, to discover what their unique concerns might be. As with the targeted diary method, it is important for researchers to keep in close contact with the families who are using the LENA or Speechome recorders, to make sure they continue to use the recorders to address any questions or issues that may arise.

Data

Targeted Diary

The targeted diary method yields data about children's age of onset of whichever lexical or grammatical category is under investigation, plus the age of onset of each individual lexeme. Thus, some indication can be provided about which lexical items are easier or harder to learn – and the extent to which these vary across samples and across populations. For example, Naigles and Hoff (2006) reported considerable variation in verb acquisition, based on sampled speech, which depended on the contexts recorded, how the mothers chose to play with the toys provided, and the individual children as well. Our verb diary (Naigles, Hoff, and Vear, 2009) was able to shed light on these findings because the context specificity was no longer an issue. What we found was that, across eight children, there was a core set of verbs that seven or eight of the children acquired within the span of the study (*bite*, *come*, *cry*, *cut*, *eat*, *go*, *jump*, *look*, *open*, *run*, *sit*, *walk*, *want*, *wash*), as well as another set of verbs that were acquired by only two or three of the children within the span of the study (*clap*, *bring*, *move*, *wave*). Thus, both generality and idiosyncrasy are attested in early verb acquisition.

The diary also reveals the timing of the onset of flexibility of use; that is, the number of (identical) instances produced before the first different usage occurs. This measure can be captured by number of instances, or by the number of days since the first use. Other measures are dependent on the way(s) the utterances are coded by the diary keeper: the more information that the diary keeper can record, the more measures can be analyzed by the researcher. For example, we coded the children's utterances after the fact for their grammatical form (verb alone, verb + subject, verb + object, SVO, verb + inflection, verb + particle), but asked the caregivers to record the verb referent's actor and affected object; all of these became dependent measures in our analyses. We also included a variety of verbs (transitive and intransitive, heavy and light), so these became independent variables whose differences in verb onset and various types of flexibility were tested via *t*-tests, carried out both by items and by participants. Correlations between lexical and grammatical measures, for example, are also of interest.

The LENA and Speechome Recorders

The LENA Pro system provides tallies of the adult words (separated by gender of adult if desired), conversational turns, and child vocalizations (separated by target vs ancillary child) in the recordings, on an hourly to daily basis. Parent data collectors can send their recorders to the researcher for data analysis, or can view the analyses themselves if they have obtained the custom software. The recordings themselves can also be reviewed for more detailed transcription as well as for acoustic analysis. These transcriptions can then be analyzed for the same sorts of measures as used in other assessments of spontaneous speech.

The Speechome Recorder holds up to 3 months of speech (audio) and situation (visual) data, the sheer volume of which has prompted numerous innovations for transcription and video analysis (e.g., DeCamp and Roy, 2009; Roy and Roy, 2009). Once transcribed, the speech can likewise be subjected to any of the myriad sorts of analyses available to assessments of spontaneous speech; the video record enables additional analyses concerning the situational and social context.

It is important to point out, though, that the comprehensive nature of these recordings opens up additional types of analyses, including variability analyses (how the child's use of specific words with respect to referents, or referents with respect to words, varies or becomes consistent over time: e.g., Adolph *et al.*, 2008), microgenetic analyses (what tracking the changes in usage over time of specific lexical or grammatical items reveals about bigger patterns of developmental change: e.g., Siegler, 2006), and growth curve analyses (what pattern of use over time of a given lexical category, grammatical category, or combination thereof is revealed: e.g., Singer and Willett, 2003).

We don't know, in the field of child language acquisition, the extent to which the processes of learning language are best captured by macro or micro changes in children's knowledge of language, their ability to produce speech, and/or their ability to understand and interact with their physical and social worlds. These diary methods provide some ways to find out.

Key Terms

LENA   Language Environment Analysis, an audio recording system that captures an entire day of a child's speech and language environment in a variety of contexts.

Speechome   Speech-at-home, an audiovisual recording system that captures several months' worth of a child's speech and language environment in the home.

Targeted diary   A daily record of a child's usage of specific words in a variety of contexts.

References

Adolph, K.E., Robinson, S.R., Young, J.W., and Gill-Alvarez, F. (2008) What is the shape of developmental change? *Psychological Review*, 115, 527–543.

Ambridge, B., and Lieven, E. (in press) *Child language acquisition*. Cambridge: Cambridge University Press.

Chomsky, N. (1959) Review of Skinner's *Verbal behavior*. *Language*, 35, 26–58.

Chomsky, N. (1972) *Language and mind*. New York: Harcourt Brace.

Christakis, D., Gilkerson, J., Richards, M., *et al.* (2009) Audible television and decreased adult words, infant vocalizations, and conversational turns. *Archives of Pediatrics and Adolescent Medicine*, 163, 554–558.

Dale, P.S., and Fenson, L. (1996) Lexical development norms for young children. *Behavioral Research Methods, Instruments, and Computers*, 28, 125–127.

Darwin, C.R. (1974) A biographical sketch of an infant. In H.E. Gruber and P.H. Barrett, *Darwin on man* (pp. 464–474). New York: Dutton. Reprinted from *Mind: A Quarterly Review of Psychology and Philosophy*, 2, 285–294, 1877.

DeCamp, P., and Roy, D. (2009) A human–machine collaborative approach to tracking human movement in multi-camera video. In *Proceedings of the 2009 International Conference on Content-Based Image and Video Retrieval*, Santorini, Greece.

Dromi, E. (1987) *Early lexical development*. Cambridge: Cambridge University Press.

Dromi, E. (2009) Old data – new eyes: theories of word meaning acquisition. In V. Gathercole-Muller (ed.), *Routes to language: in honor of Melissa Bowerman* (pp. 39–59). Hillsdale, NJ: Psychology Press.

Fisher, C. (2002) The role of abstract syntactic knowledge in language acquisition: a reply to Tomasello (2000). *Cognition*, 82, 259–278.

Gleitman, L. (1984) Biological predispositions to learn language. In P. Marler and H. Terrace (eds), *The biology of learning* (pp. 553–584). New York: Springer.

Gleitman, L., and Wanner, E. (1982) The state of the state of the art. In L. Gleitman and E. Wanner (eds), *Language acquisition: the state of the art* (pp. 3–48). Cambridge: Cambridge University Press.

Goldin-Meadow, S., Seligman, M.E., and Gelman, R. (1976) Language in the two-year old: receptive and productive stages. *Cognition*, 4, 189–202.

Goodman, J., Dale, P., and Li, P. (2008) Does frequency count? Parental input and the acquisition of vocabulary. *Journal of Child Language*, 35, 515–531.

Hoff, E. (2006) How social contexts support and shape language development. *Developmental Review*, 26, 55–88.

Hoff, E. (2009) *Language Development* (4th edn). Belmont, CA: Wadsworth, Cengage Learning.

Huttenlocher, J., Smiley, P., and Charney, R. (1983) The emergence of action categories in the child: evidence from verb meaning. *Psychological Review*, 90, 72–93.

Naigles, L.R., and Hoff, E. (2006) Verb learning at the very beginning: parallels between comprehension and input. In K. Hirsh-Pasek and R. Golinkoff (eds), *Early verb learning: action meets words* (pp. 336–363). New York: Oxford University Press.

Naigles, L.R., Hoff, E., and Vear, D. (2009) Flexibility in early verb use: evidence from a multiple-*n* diary study. *Monographs of the Society for Research in Child Development*, 74 (2).

Oller, D.K. (2010) All-day recordings to investigate vocabulary development: a case study of a trilingual toddler. *Communication Disorders Quarterly*, 31 (4), 213–222.

Roy, D. (2009) New horizons in the study of child language acquisition. In *Proceedings of Interspeech 2009*, Brighton, UK.

Roy, D., Patel, P., DeCamp, P., *et al.* (2006) The Human Speechome Project. Presented at Twenty-Eighth Annual Meeting of the Cognitive Science Society.

Roy, B., Frank, M., and Roy, D. (2009) Exploring word learning in a high-density longitudinal corpus. In *Proceedings of the 31st Annual Meeting of the Cognitive Science Society*, Amsterdam.

Roy, B., and Roy, D. (2009) Fast transcription of unstructured audio recordings. In *Proceedings of Interspeech 2009*, Brighton, UK.

Shimpi, P.M., Gamez, P., Huttenlocher, J., and Vasilyeva, M. (2007) Syntactic priming in 3- and 4-year-old children: evidence for abstract representations of transitive and dative forms. *Developmental Psychology*, 43, 1334–1346.

Siegler, R.S. (2006) Microgenetic analysis of learning. In D. Kuhn and R.S. Siegler (eds), *Handbook of child psychology. Vol. 2: Cognition, Perception, and Language* (6th edn, pp. 464–510). New York: Wiley.

Singer, J.D., and Willett, J.B. (2003) *Applied longitudinal data analysis: modeling change and event occurrence*. New York: Oxford University Press.

Stern, C., and Stern, W. (1907) *Die Kindersprache: Eine psychologische und sprachtheoetrische Untersuchung*. Liepzig: Barth.

Tomasello, M. (1992) *First verbs*. Cambridge: Cambridge University Press.

Tomasello, M. (2000) Do young children have adult syntactic competence? *Cognition*, 74, 209–253.

Vosoughi, S., Roy, B., Frank, M., and Roy, D. (2010) Effects of caregiver prosody on child language acquisition. In *Proceedings of the 5th International Conference on Speech Prosody*, Chicago.

Warren, S., Gilkerson, J., Richards, J., *et al.* (2010a) What automated vocal analysis reveals about the vocal production and language learning environment of young children with autism. *Journal of Autism and Developmental Disorders*, 40 (5), 555–569.

Warren, S., Gilkerson, J., Richards, J., *et al.* (2010b) Using LENA to map the language learning environments and vocal behavior of young children with ASD. Presented at LENA Users Conference, Denver, CO.

Xu, D., Yapanel, U., Gray, S., *et al.* (2008) Signal processing for young child speech language development. Presented at Workshop on Child, Computer, and Interaction, Chania, Crete, Greece.

Zimmerman, F., Gilkerson, J., Richards, J., *et al.* (2009) Teaching by listening: the importance of adult–child conversations to language development. *Pediatrics*, 124, 342–349.

Further Reading and Resources

http://www.lenafoundation.org.
http://www.sci.sdsu.edu/lexical/.
http://web.media.mit.edu/~dkroy/index.html.
http://www.hhs.gov/ohrp/humansubjects/guidance/belmont.htm.
http://www.hhs.gov/ohrp/humansubjects/guidance/45cfr46.html.

17 Approaches to Studying Language in Preschool Classrooms

David K. Dickinson

Summary

Approaches to studying the language used by teachers and 3- and 4-year-old children in preschool classrooms are discussed. After a brief framing of the historical and intellectual context for my work, I discuss three distinct approaches to describing language use in classrooms. First I discuss my early and current work which relies on audio- or videotaping interactions that are then transcribed in a way that allows for computerized analysis. Varied methods of coding and analyzing transcriptions are reviewed. Time sampling approaches that code for some of the same features as the transcribed speech are discussed. Rating systems are also considered, one that focuses on the specifics of teacher–child interaction and one that takes a global approach. Illustrative findings are reported, and the merits and shortcomings of the methods presented are discussed.

There are three widely accepted points of view that provide strong support for the importance of studying language use and support in preschool classrooms: (1) language plays a central role in reading comprehension (Snow, 1991; Dickinson and Porche, in press); (2) preschool classrooms can foster children's language development and associated reading success (Dickinson and Porche, in press); and (3) strong early childhood classrooms can increase the chances of long-term educational success (e.g., Reynolds, Ou, and Topitzes, 2004). But there was a time when these perspectives were not widely accepted and we are only beginning to understand the role of preschool classrooms in fostering language development; indeed, we have limited knowledge of the patterning of language use in classrooms.

Research Methods in Child Language: A Practical Guide, First Edition.
Edited by Erika Hoff.
© 2012 Blackwell Publishing Ltd. Published 2012 by Blackwell Publishing Ltd.

In this chapter I use my personal line of investigation of classrooms as language environments because over the past 20 years I have examined classrooms using a variety of methods. To understand why different methods were adopted it is helpful to understand the intellectual climate from which they emerged and the questions they were developed to address. I begin by providing a historical and conceptual context for my first major study of language use in classrooms and then discuss other methods. Methods to be discussed include multiple ways of analyzing transcripts of audio- and videotaped interactions, time sampling methods, real-time language coding, and live coding using checklists and rating tools.

Historical Framing

To understand the methods I have devised and used to study the relationships between classroom experiences and the language and literacy development of young children it is helpful to travel back to the 1980s, the originating point for my work. What follows is a simplified overview of theoretical and associated methodological trends prevalent in the 1980s that set the stage for a series of studies using language-focused methodologies.

In the late 1970s, child language researchers were transcribing and analyzing audio and video recordings of adult–child interactions in an effort to describe patterns in children's language use to uncover their linguistic competences (e.g., Brown, 1973; see Rowe, Chapter 13 this volume). The focus was on the timing of children's acquisition of structures hypothesized as universal, with mothers providing the data children use to construct linguistic knowledge. Typically middle class mothers were observed in their homes as they conversed with one child during naturally unfolding events or when using props provided by researchers. In a landmark study, Wells (1985) identified book reading as making particularly important contributions to language development. That study is noteworthy because book reading is a context shared by homes and classrooms. During this same period cognitive psychologists also were in search of evidence of universal narrative structures (e.g., Mandler and Johnson, 1977).

Reading researchers interested in early reading and reading problems were discovering the power of phonemic awareness as an explanatory mechanism for reading failure, an important insight that began to bridge the divide between reading and language (Stanovich, 1986). Typically they studied correlations among children's performances on tasks, with a narrow focus on associations between phonemic awareness and reading. Occasionally measures of vocabulary were used as control variables to adjust for verbal IQ.

Meanwhile, following the lead of child language researchers, other reading researchers began to describe the origins of children's understanding of print. The resulting emergent literacy research focused on child–print interactions, with studies of children's writing being used to identify universal patterns in writing development (Harste, Woodward, and Burke, 1984), and analyses of children's emergent reading of books revealing features of literate ways of using language (Purcell-Gates, 1988). Similar to language researchers, the dominant thrust was to describe how universal developmental patterns were manifest across cultures.

Anthropologists, long interested in the interplay between literacy, culture, and thought, provided another theoretical perspective and associated methods. Anthropologists had long been interested in the interpenetration of printed and spoken language, and in the 1970s and 1980s two major studies were reported that examined cultural variability in how language and literacy are used and explored the implications of cultural variation on cognition and ways of using print and language (Heath, 1983; Scribner and Cole, 1981).

Sociolinguists, like anthropologists, were interested in understanding the manifestation of culture in interaction, with a particular interest in language (Cazden, John, and Hymes, 1972). Similar to anthropologists, they called attention to the powerful role of context in shaping the structure, content, and interpretation of interaction. Using videotaping, audio recording, and written observations, ethnographers and sociolinguists began describing patterns of interaction in classrooms in an effort to understand how classroom participation was structured (Mehan, 1975). This work dealt with differences at the level of groups – cultures, classrooms – and one thrust of it was to highlight structural differences between the language practices of majority and minority cultural groups. Some researchers reported in detail the interactions between a teacher and a particular child and described how they led to a child being excluded from full participation in classroom instruction such as reading groups (McDermott and Hood, 1982). Others described how classroom routines that required children to display knowledge in a way that made them stand out from the group, and that was discrepant from the child's culture, created conditions that contributed to educational failure (Phillips, 1972). Still other studies noted the mismatch between the narrative practices of children from African-American homes and the practices typically seen among middle class Caucasian children (reviewed in McCabe and Bliss, 2003). Researchers did not seek to find if the educational failure of children from different demographic groups was related to language abilities that, in turn, resulted from differential exposure to language in homes and classrooms.

Two methodological insights of importance for later studies of language in classrooms emerged from work done from an anthropological perspective. First, language is organized at the discourse level and the structure and interpretation of discourse are shaped by social context and attendant beliefs and values. A complete understanding of what children are learning and of the factors affecting learning requires attention to the social context. Second, sociolinguists demonstrated that the frequency of a particular linguistic form, such as the frequency of deleting or contracting a copula (Labov, 1972), is important. This attention to the frequency with which a child uses a given structure may be as important to consider as the child's competence to use a form at one point in time.

A new brand of thinking and research began to emerge along the boundaries between language, reading, and linguistic anthropology as researchers examined book reading between mothers and children from different backgrounds. Ninio's (1980) work on mother–child book reading drew attention to the variability in interaction that is associated with different levels of income and maternal education. The importance of these issues was later driven home by experimental work (Whitehurst *et al.*, 1988) which showed that reading that encouraged children to participate resulted in superior language growth. Examination of mother–child book reading also provided evidence of the impact of literacy practices on children's emerging understanding of how meaning is derived from books (Snow, 1983) and demonstrated that children with considerable exposure to book reading can adopt ways of using language that include patterns of language use found in books (Purcell-Gates, 1988; Snow, 1983).

Thus, by the mid 1980s several themes characterized the study of language that had implications for studying language in classrooms:

1 Interest in universal patterns of development at the level of the sentence and culture-specific patterns of interacting at the discourse level.
2 Efforts to describe mismatches between the language use required in schools and that in homes and communities among children from racial and ethnic minority groups, but limited interest in identifying language-based sources of reading failure for children from low-income homes.
3 The assumption that language learning occurs as children interact with parents in the home and neglect of classrooms as a potential source of linguistic input for fostering language development.
4 Clear boundaries between child language researchers and most reading researchers, with reading researchers being interested in the phonemic level and child language researchers having little interest in how language ability relates to reading.
5 A blurring of boundaries between language, reading, and writing among emergent literacy researchers and anthropologists interested in studying language use in classroom settings.

Starting Points for Examining Language in Classroom Settings

It was against this backdrop that Catherine Snow and I launched a longitudinal study in which we sought to understand factors that support literacy development among children from low-income homes (Dickinson and Tabors, 2001; Snow, 1991). We surmised that, while children universally display the ability to acquire sophisticated language-using abilities, the language competencies associated with literacy success (that we referred to as "decontextualized language") might be differentially distributed in the population, with low-income children coming up short due to limitations in language exposure in their homes and classrooms. Because prior work by Snow and colleagues had suggested that the early childhood years might hold a key to understanding later problems (Snow, 1991), we started the Home–School

Study of Language and Literacy Development (HSSLLD) with 3-year-olds as they entered formal child care settings. Key assumptions were:

1   While some language abilities may emerge in a universally determined sequence and rate, those that are especially important for later reading are differentially supported in children's homes and classrooms.
2   Children acquire skill using these structures through frequent exposure and use; fluency using language is more important for reading skill than is demonstration of competence in a selected setting.
3   Language ability is fundamental to reading comprehension, and understanding of the contribution of early experience to reading requires a long-term view because early language competencies may not translate into improved reading skill until children have mastered basic decoding.
4   Richly textured yet brief samples of behavior can provide information about enduring patterns that play a role in shaping children's development.

These hypotheses drove our methodological decisions. First, we decided to study language environments in both homes and classrooms, focusing primarily on adult–child interactions (Dickinson and Tabors, 2001). Like reading researchers, we were interested in differential patterns of learning and sought generalizable knowledge. We tested children's language and literacy abilities using standardized tools and worked with a sample that was large enough to merit use of parametric statistics. However, like child language researchers and classroom ethnographers, we wanted to describe patterns of interaction that we hypothesized would foster learning of literacy-related language skills. Snow focused on homes, the setting with which she was familiar, and I led our investigation of classrooms.

Audiotaping and Transcribing Interactions

When we launched the HSSLLD we immediately found ourselves faced with daunting methodological challenges associated with the sheer enormity of the potential data. As one schooled in the ways of child language researchers and classroom ethnographers, I wanted to capture the language experiences of children in as much detail as possible. But we were collecting data in roughly 85 classrooms scattered across eastern Massachusetts. The solution we chose was to capture as much detail in as short a time as possible and hope that finely textured linguistic information would reveal patterns of interaction that were sufficiently stable to enable us to predict later learning (Dickinson and Tabors, 2001). This leap of faith led us to audio record teachers and children throughout an entire classroom day and to videotape book readings while taking field notes about their activities. The result was a room filled with video- and audiotapes collected over two years. Ultimately we analyzed over 222 hours of classroom interaction.

Methods

We took different approaches to examining the tapes that we made of teachers and the children. Audio- and videotapes of teachers were transcribed verbatim; to reduce transcription time, the audiotapes made of individual children were coded directly from the tapes without transcription. A critical decision that we made as we coded our data, one that was consistent with the admonitions of anthropologists and sociolinguists, was to analyze interactions in a context-specific manner. We coded all tapes by setting, creating separate files for each of the classroom settings (book reading, free play, small groups, large groups, lunch time). All the data were transcribed into CHAT format to allow for automated analysis of the transcripts and of subsequent codes (see Corrigan, Chapter 18 this volume; Rowe, Chapter 13 this volume). Every tape was verified by a second person, who listened to the audio or video recording while reading the transcript. This step adds considerably to the time required, but we believe it is essential given the difficulty of understanding children's voices and the need to transcribe the language and add important contextual information from field notes. The importance of coding in a context-specific manner was made clear by the finding of reversed effects depending on context. For example, extended topic conversations were positively associated with kindergarten outcomes when they occurred in one-to-one conversations during free play but negatively related to outcomes when they occurred during group times.

The transcripts of teachers' talk were coded exhaustively. We coded each utterance, with adults referred to as "teacher" and children combined and coded as "child." This decision reflected our goal of describing the lexical environment in the classroom and our belief that the identities of the individual speakers were not important; we sought to detect patterns of teacher–child exchange. Besides, it is impossible to distinguish individual children's voices from audiotapes; so, while theoretically motivated, this decision also reflected acknowledgment of the limits of our transcription capacity. Our coding was driven by our hypotheses regarding the kinds of interactions that we anticipated would give rise to the linguistic skills that nurture long-term literacy. We expected that the type of discourse of interest to us would occur during teacher–child interactions that were information rich, included varied vocabulary, encouraged analytic thinking, and included children as active participants. Each utterance was coded for context, speaker, content, and conversational function:

1 *Context.* Based on the content of the activity and the number of participants involved, we assigned a classroom setting code (e.g., lunch, book reading, small group).
2 *Speaker.* Speakers were either child, adult, or unknown (a rarely used code).
3 *Content.* We applied codes designed to described variability in the cognitive challenge level of the comment. Content was deemed to have high-level cognitive challenge if it required analysis of actions, events, or words, involved prediction, or reflected links between children and texts being discussed. Low-challenge interactions were those requiring labeling, recall of factual details, or, in the case of book reading, chiming in to complete familiar phrases, reciting rote information (e.g., counting).

4   *Function.* Comments were coded for how they functioned in the conversation, such as giving (or requesting) information, requesting (or giving) attention, clarifying, and giving feedback. These codes provided information about the relationship between one utterance and another.

Audiotapes that we made of our target children's conversations were coded using transcription machines that displayed elapsed time in seconds. This timing feature allowed us to calculate how many seconds children spent talking with teachers, talking with other children, or in silence, how long they spent in different activity settings (e.g., lunch, free play), and how much time they spent talking about different types of content. Content was coded using categories similar to those employed for coding the teacher transcripts. This approach to coding did not allow us to determine how interactions were structured (e.g., if a child initiated or responded).

Two other variables that proved to be important were created using the automated analytic capabilities provided by the CHAT program (MacWhinney, 1991; see Corrigan, Chapter 18 this volume). The first was the frequency with which sophisticated or "rare" words were used. This variable was created by using an automated "filter" to screen out words likely to be known by children, leaving us information about the variety of less common words used (types) and the frequency of their use (tokens). This variable was created because we assumed that a critical feature of literate-style discourse is its relatively rich concentration of novel words and associated conceptual information. The second variable created using CHAT procedures was the ratio of teacher talk relative to child talk.

Results

Possibly the most noteworthy finding was that it was possible to carry out this type of intensive and detailed study of classrooms even though it required thousands of hours to transcribe, verify, code, and analyze the data. Our approach yielded detailed descriptions of children's classroom experiences and surprisingly clear support for our initial hypotheses. We found that variables describing classroom interactions that were consistent with our hypotheses enabled us to predict later language and literacy (Dickinson and Tabors, 2001). For example, analysis of book reading in preschool when children were 4 years old revealed that analytic talk that included children as participants predicted vocabulary and story comprehension at the end of kindergarten after controlling for other measures of classroom quality (Dickinson and Smith, 1994). Recent analysis of data from the full day revealed associations between preschool conversations and end-of-fourth-grade language and reading competencies after controlling for home support for literacy and children's early language abilities (Dickinson and Porche, in press). The effects of preschool were mediated by first-grade reading and language skills. Variables that proved to be especially strong predictors included two that were created using CHAT, namely the frequency of use of rare words and the ratio of teacher to child talk (with less teacher talk being better), and two that described the content of talk during book reading, namely analytic talk and comments designed to hold children accountable for attending. The latter finding may indicate that children benefited from having teachers who helped them learn to maintain attention in group settings. That unexpected finding was possible because our exhaustive coding had required us to code even passing brief comments designed to capture children's attention.

It also is important to note what did not bear fruit. Our analyses of the audiotapes we made of children's conversations yielded detailed descriptions of classroom life from the perspective of our target children, but those variables were weak predictors of later performance. This failure to find consistent associations could mean that individual children's experiences are so subject to moment-to-moment and day-to-day fluctuations that measuring their experience on any single day provides limited information about their overall classroom experiences. It also suggests that the content of interactions between teachers and children may be of primary importance. Thus our findings supported our core hypotheses:

1 Language abilities that are especially important for later reading are differentially supported in classrooms attended by children from low-income homes.
2 Children acquire skill using language through frequent exposure and use.
3 A long-term view is necessary because competence with literacy-related language may not translate into improved reading skill until children have mastered basic decoding.
4 Richly textured yet brief samples of behavior can provide information about patterns of language use in classrooms that may play a role in shaping children's development.

The final point is the most surprising and the one most in need of verification. Our ability to find these associations is contrary to the results of multiple studies that have used large samples and more global measures of classrooms and have either failed to find predictive relationships between process measures and child outcomes or found relatively weak associations (Dickinson and Darrow, in press).

Time Sampling

The view of classrooms provided by the HSSLLD transcripts made it apparent that far too often children from low-income homes receive relatively limited intellectual stimulation and less than optimal support for acquisition of the kind of language skills that support later reading comprehension. This observation led me to seek to improve classrooms by creating a professional development intervention designed to inform preschool teachers about language and literacy development and help them improve the quality of supports they provide children (Dickinson and Caswell, 2007). For such a study our energy had to go into developing and delivering the intervention; we could not take on the exhaustive data collection methods used for the HSSLLD. The solution was to create a time sampling tool that allowed us to code interaction on site, describing as many features of the interaction as possible.

The first time sampling tool, the Teacher–Child Verbal Interaction Profile (TCVI: Dickinson, Howard, and Haine, 1998), was designed to provide information about features of teacher–child interaction that the HSSLLD had indicated were likely to be related to enhanced development. In addition, since we were physically present it was possible to describe potentially important aspects of the situation that were invisible to someone coding an audiotape, such as teachers' relative degree of engagement with children, the number and gender of children in her immediate vicinity, and physical positioning (e.g., sitting, moving) or location in the classroom. Content and conversational structure were coded in ways designed to be comparable to the HSSLLD methods. Interactions grounded in the immediate present that represented limited cognitive challenge were coded as "ongoing activity" and accounted for much of the coded time. Topics of particular interest because they represented talk more likely to foster language growth included the following: pretending, talk about nonpresent events, general knowledge, and talk about literacy and math (instructional talk). We also were interested in structural aspects of the interaction, so we coded for the relative balance of talk between teachers and children (teacher dominant vs balanced between teacher and child) and for whether or not the conversation stayed on and elaborated a single topic. Using this tool, researchers observed for 30 seconds and then spent 30 seconds coding. While it took some effort, we achieved and maintained good levels of interrater reliability (83% or better for dichotomous codes, and Cohen's kappa scores of 0.85 or better for variables with more than two codes).

Observations carried out in 61 classrooms yielded textured descriptions of children's language experiences that, once again, were generally disappointing (Dickinson, McCabe, and Clark-Chiarelli, 2004). In general, during the 30-second intervals, teachers rarely extended and deepened topics (14% during free play, 19% during meal times) and rarely discussed or explained the meanings of new words (less than 1% of all coded intervals). The vast majority (79% at 3 years, 72% at 4) of teacher talk during book reading was devoted to issues that make few cognitive demands of the children. Mostly teachers focused on organization of the task, simple feedback, and naming activities. Higher cognitive demands were not common (17% at 3, 26.6% at 4). Thus, the features of conversations most predictive of later growth were those least commonly observed.

Even though we were able to use the TCVI system reliably and it allowed collection of data in many classrooms without the burden of transcribing and coding, sometimes we had to spend four or more sessions in classrooms in order to achieve reliability. In a subsequent study that examined the effectiveness of a small-scale professional development intervention, Sarah Fanelli (now Sarah Ngo) and I created a somewhat streamlined tool, Teacher–Child Discourse Analysis, to code interaction (Dickinson et al., 2009). This tool once again was designed to capture features of classroom discourse that the HSSLLD work had found to be important contributors to children's language development: attention to vocabulary, cognitively enriching topics of conversation, and extended stretches of talk that stayed on a single topic. Context again was important because we studied the effects of our intervention on teachers' book reading and their conversations during meal times. Distinct content codes were necessary for each setting. This tool was sensitive to changes in patterns of book reading and lunch time conversation that occurred as a result of professional development and use of scripted guidance for reading books in the manner required of teachers using the preschool curriculum, *Opening the world of learning* (Schickedanz and Dickinson, 2005).

Our time sampling systems have been used to code interactions between particular teachers and whatever children they happen to be talking with. This approach makes it possible to focus either on the lead or on the assistant teacher, providing a more comprehensive picture of classroom lexical environments. Global rating tools such as the Early Language and Literacy Classroom Observation (ELLCO: Smith *et al.*, 2002) and the Early Childhood Environment Rating Scale (Harms, Clifford, and Crye, 1998) do not allow for this degree of precision.

Time sampling methods are appealing because they yield readily grasped descriptions of exactly what is happening between teachers and children. However, reliability can be challenging to achieve if distinctions are too fine or codes too numerous. Also, data analysis can be daunting when using typical statistical programs because there are multiple distinct codes for each interval. This database barrier reduced the utility of TCVI data collected as part of our program evaluation effort. In a subsequent small-scale study we used a less complex system of tallying and were able to quickly determine patterns for different codes. In a further extension of time sampling methods I sought to devise a system that could run on a hand-held PDA, using its built-in timing capabilities. I was not able to arrive at a workable system, but Meador, Vorhaus, and Wilson (2009) have created a system that runs on a tablet computer for on-site data collection and enables observers to capture considerable detail in real time. Such approaches hold considerable promise for finding a way to strike a balance between intensive data collection that relies on audiotape and transcriptions and global rating systems.

Rating Tools

Rating tools are a third general method we have explored for describing preschool classrooms. The most noteworthy tool is the ELLCO, developed by Miriam Smith with assistance from others (Smith *et al.*, 2002). It was created at the request of state officials in Connecticut who wanted a tool for describing classrooms from an emergent literacy perspective to assist them in their efforts to improve the quality of support for emergent literacy in preschool classrooms. The ELLCO was created to describe classrooms in a more general manner than the approaches that had emerged from the Home–School Study. It has scales to describe the language environment and others that describe the physical environment, behavior management, and the nature of support for using print. It has been widely used in evaluations of Early Reading First programs and in many other early childhood settings. Its popularity, in part, derives from the fact that it is easy to understand and use, and provides staff with concrete, objective descriptions of classroom practice that can be the starting point for coaching conversations. It gives teachers clear descriptions of valued ways of organizing their material and rooms, but provides only limited information about patterns of language use. While teachers and program directors report finding the ELLCO useful as part of professional development efforts, its ratings have been no more potent at predicting growth in children's language and literacy than other global rating systems.

An even simpler rating tool has yielded interesting descriptions of teacher support for learning in classrooms. The first iteration, Adult Roles (Dickinson, 1996), was created when I was evaluating our emerging professional development intervention and was frustrated by how some teachers spent classroom time. In particular, I noted that some lead teachers spent nearly half of the time when children were free to engage in activities around the room supervising children as they brushed their teeth. Based on emerging HSSLLD findings suggesting that teacher–child interactions during centers time could make measurable contributions to children's learning, I was concerned that teachers were totally missing opportunities to verbally interact with children. Similarly, I noted disengagement during meal times, another setting our data suggested holds potential for fostering learning. Adult Roles proved to be easy to use; and later, when I was engaged in another large evaluation project and wanted to augment the ELLCO with a tool that described more of the interactional environment, I created a refined instrument, Teacher Engagement. Designed for simplicity, this tool requires observers to apply one score for each of 10 codes after observing an activity (e.g., lunch, meal time, book reading). During the activity period observers make notes about the interactions occurring between the lead and assistant teachers and the children and record their codes when the activity period ends. This rating approach retains core assumptions about beneficial features of classrooms and adult–child interaction: active engagement in conversations with adults, especially when a single topic is developed and the conversation has a focus on vocabulary. Negative codes are included because I surmised that things that were clearly detrimental to adult–child interaction might be as diagnostic as positive features.

The Teacher Engagement rating tool has been relatively easy to use and yielded interesting results when used as part of a study carried out in 52 classrooms (Dickinson *et al.*, 2009). We used it to code three settings: book reading, meal times, and centers time. In addition, we coded videotapes of book reading and small group instruction for many of the same features of interaction. Across approaches, we coded when teachers told children the meanings of words. When we combined results for that single item from these two data sources we had a five-point scale describing teachers' attentiveness to vocabulary across the day. When this simple scale was used as part of HLM analyses that controlled for fall scores, demographic factors, and other statistical confounds, we found a statistically significant effect for talk about vocabulary. Interestingly, the effect appears to be carried by the high-end teachers. That is, a boost in vocabulary learning may not occur unless a relatively high level of support is attained. This is a message that is consonant with other recent studies and may help explain why many interventions fail to achieve noteworthy success (Burchinal *et al.*, 2010). It also carries a methodological caution: researchers need to be sure their scales are sensitive to high-end teaching and alert for nonlinear relationships between environmental input and children's growth.

Thus, rating tools can be devised that capture some of the same core elements of interaction that seem to be related to enhanced language learning. They have appeal to practitioners because they are relatively easy to use and can yield concrete descriptions of interaction. They may appeal to researchers for the same reasons.

Concluding Thoughts

Beginning early this century there have been increasing numbers of interventions designed to enhance the quality of preschools, but interventions delivered as part of full curriculum or programmatic interventions typically have had only limited impact on measures of language (Dickinson and Darrow, in press). This is a challenge we are grappling with as we evaluate the effectiveness of a curriculum-based intervention that was delivered in 52 classrooms. When we designed the study we built in plans to videotape classrooms three times during the year. These tapes enabled us to code fidelity of delivery of the curriculum in distinct activity settings. The codes include information about whether specified activities were done and how they were carried out. For example, during book reading teachers are directed to read particular books, to define selected words, and to engage children in thought-provoking conversations. Our coding draws on the data-intensive data collection methods favored by child language researchers and classroom ethnographers in that we attend to the details of teacher–child interactions; thus we can create a nuanced picture of the implementation of the curriculum. Also, undaunted by the time-intensive nature of audio-based examination of classrooms, we have transcribed over 70 hours of selected classroom settings (book reading, group literacy instruction, centers time, small groups) into CHAT format and we are analyzing these transcripts for the percentage of talk by teachers (an easier way to capture the ratio of teacher relative to child talk), the density D of talk tokens relative to talk types, the overall amount of talk, and the use of rare words using an updated version of the list used for the HSSLLD project. We also are coding these tapes for complex syntax using a system modeled on that of Washington and Craig (1994) and for content, function, and topic development in a manner parallel to the HSSLLD. (See Table 17.1 for an illustration of these multiple approaches.) Analyses are ongoing. We have found that transcribing from videotapes, while still time consuming, is less arduous than coding from audiotapes and that technology that enables use of a foot pedal to stop and slightly rewind tapes in the same manner as for audiotape transcribing machines greatly facilitates transcription (see also the video-linked transcript function of CHILDES, described in Core, Chapter 6 this volume).

The time may be ripe for those interested in the nuanced details of language use in classrooms to collaborate with field researchers who are struggling to evaluate the fidelity of implementation of interventions and to identify critical features of classrooms that account for differential growth. After all, it is widely acknowledged that much of the learning that occurs for a child in a preschool classroom happens when she is engaged in conversations. Perhaps more robust strategies for describing the structure, content, and frequency of these interactions will lead to deeper understanding of how classrooms can contribute to language acquisition and enhanced conceptual knowledge.

Table 17.1 Example of CHAT transcription and coding for topic construction, social function and semantic content of a small group transcript[a]

Context
Activity involving moving objects with air after reading *Gilberto and the Wind*.

Rare words
12 (in full transcript); 4 in this segment indicated by boldface.

Content coding

*TCH: $TOP:SPC $FUN:GIVE $CON:BO and then the wind was blowin(g) um the **pillowcases** outside.
*TCH: $TOP:T00 $FUN:GIVE $CON:SW so _we're gonna see what can air move.
*TCH: $TOP:T00 $FUN:GIVE $CON:SW we're gonna see if this stuff is too heavy or is it just right for the wind to move it.
*TCH: $TOP:T00 $FUN:ATTN $CON:OA ok?
*TCH: $TOP:NTO $FUN:ASKA $CON:OA everybody pick an **item**.
*TCH: $TOP:SPC $FUN:ASKA $CON:OA let's see what we got first.
*TCH: $TOP:SPC $FUN:QUKN $CON:VO what is this?
*CHI: $TOP:TN2 $FUN:RESP $CON:VO a block.
*TCH: $TOP:TN3 $FUN:CORR $CON:VO a unifix **cube**.
*TCH: $TOP:NTO $FUN:QUKN $CON:VO what's this?
*CHI: $TOP:TN2 $FUN:RESP $CON:VO a dice.
*TCH: $TOP:TN3 $FUN:EXPD $CON:VO a dice, a number dice.
*TCH: $TOP:NTO $FUN:QUKN $CON:VO what is this?
*CHI: $TOP:TN2 $FUN:RESP $CON:VO feet thing.
*TCH: $TOP:TN3 $FUN:CORR $CON:VO **cotton+ball**.
*CHI: $TOP:TN4 $FUN:REPT $CON:VO **cotton+ball**.

Coding explanations
$TOP = Conversational topic construction
  T00:   *No topic*: no sustained topic attempted; stray comment, attention request, off-topic comment
  NT0:   *New topic*: initiated successfully, at least one follow-up utterance occurs
  SPC: *Speaker continues*: same speaker on existing topic, directly relevant; not a new turn; must be on a topic, not continuing about "no topic"
  TN2, TN3, TN4, etc.: *Topic continuation*: new speaker on same topic, directly relevant; no more than 5 turns of asides occur since last utterance on this topic
FUN = Social Function
  GIVE: *Give information*: statement that describes a situation, communicates an idea, experience, or opinion
  ATTN: *Attention-getting*: question or statement which calls/directs attention to the speaker, *or* gives/acknowledges attention to another speaker
  AKSA: *Ask for an action*: question or command which requests that child or children do something, gives instructions or directions

Table 17.1 (cont'd)

QUKN: *Known-answer question*: question or request for information where the speaker knows the answer, is looking for a specific response

RESP: *Responding*: statement that responds to a question, inquiry, or fill-in-the-blank

EXPD: *Expanding*: rephrase with slight correction or expansion

CORR: *Correcting*: question, statement, or response contingent on previous utterance, which corrects it in terms of factual information

REPT: *Repeating*: direct echo or repetition of part or all of previous utterance

CON = Semantic Content

BO: *Books*: interaction about books and their content, such as discussion of book titles, authors, or characters

SW: *Scientific and world knowledge*: interaction relating to facts or concepts about the world

OA: *Ongoing activity*: interaction related to the immediate, shared physical context

VO: *Vocabulary*: interaction about the meanings of words, defining and discussing word meanings

[a]Jill B. Freiberg played a major role in the development and refinement of this coding system.

Acknowledgments

Work on this manuscript and some of the data reported was supported by grant #R324E060088A from the United States Department of Education.

Key Terms

CHAT   The name for the system of transcription used by the Child Language Data Exchange Information System (CHILDES) (MacWhinney, 1991). CHILDES includes a collection of language data as well as tools that enable computer-based transcript analysis.

Emergent literacy   Activity that reflects early understanding of print, its use, and the language typically employed when reading and writing prior to formal instruction.

Ethnographer   An anthropologist who studies settings (cultures, classrooms, communities) for an extended time by spending considerable time with the group being studied in an effort to understand the details of the community's beliefs and practices.

Lexical density   The balance between the use of words not previously used in a given text and the total number of words in the text. Different computer-based methods are used to analyze it.

Parametric statistics   Statistics used to analyze numerical data in an effort to provide generalizable knowledge.

Phonemic awareness   Ability to consciously reflect on or manipulate individual phonemes.

Rare words   Sometimes called "sophisticated words," these are words deemed as being somewhat uncommon for 4–year-olds. Computer-based methods have been devised to analyze for their prevalence.

Sociolinguist   A researcher who studies the social life of settings by carefully examining patterns in language use, attending to social factors such as power, interpersonal relationship, and context.

Time sampling   An approach to coding in which observers watch interactions for a predetermined interval and then code selected aspects of the interaction.

References

Brown, R. (1973) *A first language*. Cambridge, MA: Harvard University Press.

Burchinal, M., Vandergrift, N., Pianta, R., and Mashburn, A. (2010) Threshold analysis of association between child care quality and child outcomes for low-income children in pre-kindergarten programs. *Early Childhood Research Quarterly*, 25 (2), 166–176.

Cazden, C., John, V.P., and Hymes, D. (1972) *Functions of language in the classroom*. New York: Teachers College Press.

Dickinson, D.K. (1996) *Adult Roles*. Newton, MA.

Dickinson, D.K., and Caswell, L. (2007) Building support for language and early literacy in preschool classrooms through in-service professional development: effects of the Literacy Environment Enrichment Program (LEEP). *Early Childhood Research Quarterly*, 22, 243–260.

Dickinson, D.K., and Darrow, C.L. (in press) Methodological and practical challenges of broad-gauged language interventions. In T. Shanahan and C.J. Lonigan (eds), *Literacy in preschool and kindergarten children: the National Early Literacy Panel and beyond*. Baltimore: Brookes.

Dickinson, D.K., Darrow, C.L., Ngo, S.M., and D'Souza, L.A. (2009) Changing classroom conversations: narrowing the gap between potential and reality. In O.A. Barbarin and B.H. Wasik (eds), *The handbook of developmental science and early schooling: translating basic research into practice*. New York: Guilford.

Dickinson, D.K., Freiberg, J.B., Darrow, C.L., *et al.* (2009) Toward identifying an "active ingredient" responsible for improving receptive vocabulary in preschool children. Presented at the Annual Conference of the Institute for Educational Sciences, Washington, DC.

Dickinson, D.K., Howard, C., and Haine, R. (1998) *Teacher–Child Verbal Interaction Profile*. Newton, MA.

Dickinson, D.K., McCabe, A., and Clark-Chiarelli, N. (2004) Preschool-based prevention of reading disability: realities vs possibilities. In C.A. Stone, E.R. Silliman, B.J. Ehren, and K. Apel (eds), *Handbook of language and literacy: development and disorders* (pp. 209–227). New York: Guilford.

Dickinson, D.K., and Porche, M.V. (in press) The relationship between teacher–child conversations with low-income four-year-olds and grade four language and literacy development. *Child Development*.

Dickinson, D.K., and Smith, M.W. (1994) Long-term effects of preschool teachers' book readings on low-income children's vocabulary and story comprehension. *Reading Research Quarterly*, 29 (2), 105–122.

Dickinson, D.K., and Tabors, P.O. (eds) (2001) *Beginning literacy with language: young children learning at home and school*. Baltimore: Brookes.

Harms, T., Clifford, R., and Crye, D. (1998) *Early Childhood Environment Rating Scale, Revised Edition*. New York: Teachers College Press.

Harste, J.C., Woodward, V.A., and Burke, C.L. (1984) *Language stories and literacy lessons*. Portsmouth, NH: Heinemann.

Heath, S.B. (1983) *Way with words: language, life and work in communities and classrooms*. Cambridge: Cambridge University Press.

Labov, W. (1972) *Language in the inner city: studies in the black English vernacular*. Philadelphia: University of Pennsylvania Press.

MacWhinney, B. (1991) *The CHILDES project*. Mahwah, NJ: Erlbaum.

Mandler, J.M., and Johnson, N.S. (1977) Remembrance of things parsed: story structure and recall. *Cognitive Psychology*, 9, 111–151.

McCabe, A., and Bliss, L.S. (2003) *Patterns of narrative discourse: a multicultural lifespan approach*. Boston: Allyn and Bacon.

McDermott, R.P., and Hood, L. (1982) Institutionalized psychology and the ethnography of schooling. In P. Gilmore and A.A. Glatthorn (eds), *Children in and out of school: ethnography and education* (pp. 232–249). Washington, DC: Center for Applied Linguistics.

Meador, D., Vorhaus, E., and Wilson, S. (2009) *Tablet based Tools of the Mind fidelity system with Filemaker as the platform*. Nashville, TN: Peabody Research Institute, Vanderbilt University.

Mehan, H. (1975) *Learning lessons: the social organization of classroom behavior*. Cambridge, MA: Harvard University Press.

Ninio, A. (1980) Picture-book reading in mother–infant dyads belonging to two subgroups in Israel. *Child Development*, 51 (2), 587–590.

Phillips, S.U. (1972) Participant structure and communicative competence: Warm Springs children in community and classroom. In C.B. Cazden (ed.), *Functions of language in the classroom* (pp. 370–394). New York: Teachers College Press.

Purcell-Gates, V. (1988) Lexical and syntactic knowledge of written narrative held by well-read-to kindergartners and second graders. *Research in the Teaching of English*, 22, 128–160.

Reynolds, A.J., Ou, S.R., and Topitzes, J.W. (2004) Paths of effects of early childhood intervention on educational attainment and delinquency: a confirmatory analysis of the Chicago child–parent centers. *Child Development*, 75 (5), 1299–1328.

Schickedanz, J., and Dickinson, D.K. (2005) *Opening the world of learning: a comprehensive literacy program*. Parsippany, NJ: Pearson Early Learning.

Scribner, S., and Cole, M. (1981) *The psychology of literacy*. Cambridge, MA: Harvard University Press.

Smith, M.W., Dickinson, D.K., Sangeorge, A., and Anastasopoulos, L. (2002) *The Early Language and Literacy Classroom Observation toolkit (ELLCO)*. Baltimore: Brookes.

Snow, C.E. (1983) Literacy and language: relationships during the preschool years. *Harvard Educational Review*, 53 (2), 165–189.

Snow, C.E. (1991) The theoretical basis for relationships between language and literacy in development. *Journal of Research in Childhood Education*, 6 (1), 5–10.

Stanovich, K.E. (1986) Matthew effects in reading: some consequences of individual differences in the acquisition of literacy. *Reading Research Quarterly*, 21, 360–407.

Washington, J.A., and Craig, H.K. (1994) Dialectal forms during discourse of poor, urban, African-American preschoolers. *Journal of Speech and Hearing Research*, 37 (4), 816–823.

Wells, G. (1985) *Learning, language and education*. Philadelphia: NFER-Nelson.

Whitehurst, G.J., Falco, F.L., Lonigan, C.J., *et al.* (1988) Accelerating language development through picture book reading. *Developmental Psychology*, 24 (4), 552–559.

Further Reading and Resources

Dickinson, D.K., and Darrow, C.L. (in press) Methodological and practical challenges of broad-gauged language interventions. In T. Shanahan and C.J. Lonigan (eds), *Literacy in preschool and kindergarten children: the National Early Literacy Panel and beyond.* Baltimore: Brookes.

Dickinson, D.K., Flushman, T.R., and Freiberg, J.B. (2009) Language, reading and classroom supports: where we are and where we need to be going. In B. Richards, M.H. Daller, D. Malvern, *et al.* (eds), *Vocabulary studies in first and second language acquisition: the interface between theory and application* (pp. 396–429). Basingstoke: Palgrave-Macmillan.

Massey, S.L., Pence, K.L., Justice, L.M., and Bowles, R.P. (2008) Educators' use of cognitively challenging questions in economically disadvantaged preschool classroom contexts. *Early Education and Development*, 19 (2), 340–360.

Wasik, B.A., Bond, M.A., and Hindman, A. (2006) The effects of a language and literacy intervention on Head Start children and teachers. *Journal of Educational Psychology*, 98 (1), 63–74.

Weizman, Z.O., and Snow, C.E. (2001) Lexical output as related to children's vocabulary acquisition: effects of sophisticated exposure and support for meaning. *Developmental Psychology*, 37 (2), 265–279.

Zucker, T.A., Justice, L.M., Piasta, S.B., and Kaderavek, J.N. (2010) Preschool teachers' literal and inferential questions and children's responses during whole-class shared reading. *Early Childhood Research Quarterly*, 25 (1), 65–83.

See also http://peabody.vanderbilt.edu/Dickinson_David.xml.

18 Using the CHILDES Database

Roberta Corrigan

Summary

This chapter describes the Child Language Data Exchange System (CHILDES) and some examples of its use. CHILDES contains a set of transcriptions of language production, in standardized format, most of it as conversations between adults and children interacting in naturalistic settings, but some as elicited narratives. It also contains computer tools to analyze the transcripts. The database contains transcripts from monolingual speakers, bilingual speakers, and clinical populations. CHILDES can be used to address any research question in child language that requires spoken language data such as those contained in the database. The chapter describes a few issues involved in using CHILDES including sparse data, sources of variation in the database, and coding of categories.

The Child Language Data Exchange System (CHILDES) is a set of tools available on the internet for the study of first and second language acquisition. This chapter begins with a general picture of the CHILDES system, followed by a discussion of the wide range of questions that can be addressed using CHILDES and some questions that may be difficult to answer using it. The procedures section of the chapter describes issues in sampling CHILDES data, some CHILDES computer programs available for data analysis, and coding and reliability issues. The data analysis section includes a brief description of a few of the statistical matters that may arise in using corpus data. In the last part of the chapter I report in detail some of the decision processes I went through in using CHILDES for one of my own research projects (Corrigan, 2004).

Research Methods in Child Language: A Practical Guide, First Edition.
Edited by Erika Hoff.
© 2012 Blackwell Publishing Ltd. Published 2012 by Blackwell Publishing Ltd.

Aims of CHILDES Research

What is CHILDES?

CHILDES consists of a hierarchically arranged database of transcriptions of spoken language contributed by researchers who originally collected the data to conduct their own research. Most of the database consists of conversations between adults and children, done in a standardized format (Codes for the Human Analysis of Transcripts, CHAT). Each transcript is stored as a separate file, located in a folder labeled by the name of the researcher that contributed it. In addition to the database, CHILDES provides a set of computer programs for analyzing language and tools for linking transcripts to digitized audio or visual recordings (Computerized Language ANalysis, CLAN). Currently, CHILDES contains data from a wide range of monolingual speakers of different language groups including East Asian, Celtic, English (both US and UK), Germanic, Romance, and Slavic. In addition, there are corpora from bilingual speakers, clinical populations, and those containing narrative data. A separate database and programs called PhonBank are available for analyzing phonological properties of speech. The CHILDES collection continues to expand as new researchers donate their transcripts.

Full details of the CHILDES system are available in MacWhinney (2000); updated manuals for the database (including guidelines for its use and documentation for the corpora), for CLAN, and for CHAT are available online at http://childes.psy.cmu. edu/. The database and CLAN tools can be used online or can be downloaded to individual computers. CHILDES is part of the TalkBank system, which also includes databases on aphasia, adult bilingualism and second language acquisition, and corpora transcribed in conversational analysis format.

The CHILDES website provides detailed tutorials on the CHAT transcription format and the CLAN analysis tools. The current chapter is not intended to be a tutorial, but will discuss more general issues that arise when doing corpus research with CHILDES. I will focus on the database itself and on data manipulation with the CLAN programs rather than on data transcription using the CHAT system. However, anyone using CHILDES transcriptions must be familiar with basic CHAT notation in order to understand what they are viewing when they open a CHILDES file. Because particular methodological issues that might arise are dependent upon the research questions that are being addressed in a given study, this chapter will necessarily select only a small subset of issues to use as examples.

What Kinds of Questions Can Be Addressed Using CHILDES?

The databases are primarily used to address research questions that rely on how language is used by children and adults as they interact in naturalistic settings. As of November 2008, the CHILDES website (http://talkbank.org/usage/childesbib.pdf) listed more than 3,100 published articles that made use of CHILDES. One of the advantages of CHILDES is that researchers can use existing data to answer new research questions without collecting and transcribing their own data.

Thus, CHILDES serves as a basic source of both parent and child language data. In addition, Behrens (2008) suggests that large-scale corpora can be particularly useful in addressing three types of questions that previously would have been difficult to investigate, either because samples collected by individual researchers were too small to make trustworthy generalizations or because necessary computer tools were not available (see also Lieven and Behrens, Chapter 15 this volume).

First, are there differences in the frequency and distribution of adult language to other adults compared to their language addressed to children? For example, in Corrigan (2008) I took advantage of the fact that some of the English corpora in CHILDES take place in settings with multiple adults who talk to each other as well as to the child. I examined whether the semantic information in the discourse surrounding adjectives is different when adults address children compared to other adults. I found that even though adults rarely provide explicit definitions to the children, the linguistic contexts of their utterances contain more information about adjective meanings in adult–child conversations than in adult–adult conversations.

Second, are children's linguistic representations item-specific or more abstract? For example, Borensztajn, Zuidema, and Bod (2009) used an automatic procedure to identify the most probable multiword child utterances using distributional data from CHILDES files of three American English speaking children. They showed that the relative number of variable slots in productive units of grammar increased with age, supporting the notion that development proceeds from item-specific to abstract constructions.

Third, what are the effects of frequency on language learning, both across individuals and across groups? Two examples of statistical regularities available in the input language to young children that have been identified using CHILDES data include distributional information about transitivity-alternating verbs (Scott and Fisher, 2009) and co-occurrences between pronouns and verbs in child-directed speech (Laakso and Smith, 2007).

Questions That May Be Difficult To Answer with CHILDES

While the size of the CHILDES database may allow researchers to address questions that could not be answered with smaller samples, size can still be a limitation for researchers attempting to answer questions about infrequently produced words, constructions, or errors. Even though the 44-million-word database (including words across both adults and children speaking multiple languages) is the largest existing corpus of spoken language (MacWhinney, 2008), researchers may find that it is still too small.

In any corpus, a small set of frequent words makes up the majority of tokens, with most words occurring with very low frequency. The distribution of units larger than one word is even more skewed (Baroni, 2008). As a result, even large corpora do not sample all possible vocabulary or construction types. Pomikalek, Rychly, and Kilgarriff (2009) propose that to study rare items may require a corpus containing as many as a billion words. Tomasello and Stahl (2004) suggest that age of onset, order of acquisition, and error rate data are not reliable in language samples of 1 hour or less collected every week or every other week (typical of most CHILDES corpora). Discovering children's errors in small samples is difficult because errors are most likely to occur in low frequency structures (Rowland, Fletcher, and Freudenthal, 2008). Investigators wanting to study rare words or constructions (those that are produced only one or two times a day) or wanting to examine the relative frequency of linguistic structures or errors in child language may need to collect their own dense samples (Lieven and Behrens, Chapter 15 this volume; Tomasello and Stahl, 2004) or choose other elicitation or experimental techniques such as those described in other chapters in this volume in order to gather a sample large enough for study.

Procedural Issues

Which Parts of CHILDES Will Be Used?

Investigators must decide early in the research process, based on their individual research questions, whether to manipulate CHILDES data with CLAN, to use CHILDES data without CLAN, or to use other corpus data with CLAN tools and/or CHAT transcription format.

For example, many studies have attempted to simulate development of child language phenomena using CHILDES data, but have manipulated the data using non-CHILDES computational models. In an introduction to a special issue of the *Journal of Child Language*, MacWhinney (2010) describes eight studies where researchers input child-directed speech from CHILDES to various computational models that output aspects of child language ranging from word segmentation to aspects of syntax such as dative constructions.

Alternatively, language data that are not part of the CHILDES can be analyzed using CLAN tools. For example, in Corrigan (in press) I found that there was a correlation between pre-service teachers' vocabulary scores and the diversity and sophistication of the vocabulary in the books they chose to read aloud to their elementary school pupils. To determine vocabulary diversity, I typed the texts of the chosen children's books into CLAN and used the VOCD program in CHILDES to compute a measure of lexical diversity that is an alternative to the traditional type–token ratio (McKee, Malvern, and Richards, 2000).

Sampling and Grouping of Files

One of the most important methodological issues facing any researcher using the CHILDES databases is which sample of participants or language to examine. Because the files were donated by many different child language researchers, CHILDES is not intended to be a balanced corpus. This contrasts with some other existing corpora that were designed be representative of the types of language to be included within them (see Biber and Jones, 2008, for a discussion of some issues involved in corpus design). For example, the 10 million words of spoken language transcribed in the British National Corpus (BNC: http://www.natcorp.ox.ac.uk/) were collected in different contexts and selected from different ages, regions, and social classes in a demographically balanced way. CHILDES has similar sources of variation, but they are not systematically sampled. Researchers using CHILDES must think about what characteristics are relevant to their own research questions and select portions of the database that meet their criteria (essentially designing their own corpus). While published studies using CHILDES do report on which corpora they use, many of them do not give any insight as to why they made the sampling decisions that they made.

Longitudinal versus cross-sectional data

Some corpora in CHILDES are longitudinal while others contain cross-sectional data. The researcher may examine the language of one or two children in detail or may sum data across children. In either event, researchers must make decisions about sampling and/or grouping files. Should longitudinal data files be examined separately, maintaining the sampling scheme of the original researcher, or should files be grouped on some other basis? If multiple children are to be included, how many files will be chosen and how will they be categorized?

Grouping on the basis of language level

Mean length of utterance (MLU) is the most commonly used measure of language proficiency in child language research. The rationale for classifying children by MLU rather than by age is that children of the same chronological age will vary greatly in their language level (see Brown, 1973). MLUs are provided for some CHILDES files in their documentation. Otherwise, the CLAN program MLU can be used to do the computations. The default calculation is in morphemes, but this may be problematic for crosslinguistic comparisons because languages differ widely in morphological complexity (Brown, 1973). This has led some researchers to suggest that MLUs be calculated in words (Parker and Brorson, 2005), which can also be accomplished using CLAN programs.

For researchers who want to group children based on some other measure of syntactic complexity, CLAN programs could be used to compute type–token ratios (using the program FREQ), alternative measures of lexical diversity (VOCD), or scores on the developmental sentence score (Lee, 1984), which can now be computed automatically using the DSS program in CLAN. Norris and Ortega (2009) review a number of other measures of syntactic complexity, some of which could be computed with CLAN programs, noting that measures of subordination are frequently used in second language acquisition (SLA) research.

Other sources of extralinguistic variation

There are many other sources of variation in the CHILDES corpora including: type of language, family socioeconomic status, whether the child belongs to a clinical population or is typically developing, gender, type of discourse partner, general setting (e.g., laboratory or home), task within setting (e.g., interactive book reading, free play, meal time), and length of data files (either time or amount of language). In some cases, this variability could be beneficial to researchers who are interested in studying whether some of these factors affect language performance (e.g., see Domack, 2009, for a study that examines variation in gender, age, and SES). However, not all sources of variation in CHILDES may be present with enough frequency to study them systematically. Pomikalek, Rychly, and Kilgarriff (2009) suggest that variation studies require subcorpora where the expected frequency for the item being studied is between 30 and 40.

Researchers who do not want to directly examine sources of extralinguistic variation in their research should at least think about their potential effects on their research questions. The representativeness of a corpus depends not only on its total size in words, but also on the number of files from different categories and the number of words in each file (Biber and Jones, 2008). If a given source of variation, one that makes a difference in the language outcome variable, is over-represented in the chosen sample, then this may affect the generalizability of results. For example, suppose that a researcher is interested in the syntactic complexity of maternal speech to children. We know that parents' speech to their preschoolers is more complex during book reading than in other settings (Hoff, 2006). Suppose that a researcher has sampled many more files containing book reading to younger children than to older children. In this invented example, the researcher could erroneously conclude that parental speech is more syntactically complex to younger than to older children! In another example, suppose that a researcher wants to include both longitudinal and cross-sectional data in the same study. Hypothetically, this could result in the over-representation of a few children whose language is idiosyncratic in some way. Similarly, individual files within CHILDES vary greatly in length, again producing potential problems with over-representing certain children or time periods. In sum, the variability of the corpora within CHILDES is both a strength and a weakness that should be taken into account when designing studies.

Sampling language items

Another decision that must be made by researchers is what types of language items to examine in the participant samples they have chosen. As noted previously in this chapter, rare items are particularly problematic to locate in small samples. But even with language items that occur frequently enough, problems may arise if a researcher is interested in generalizing results beyond the particular language items that have been studied. An example from the literature may be illustrative. Reali and Christensen (2005) demonstrated that there is enough indirect evidence in child-directed speech to allow a simple statistical learning mechanism to discriminate correct from incorrect items for one type of auxiliary question, even when the input corpus is lacking the construction. They were careful to point out in their conclusions that their results were based on only one construction, but suggest that "we anticipate that there are likely to be other cases in which indirect statistical information (and/ or other cues) can lead to correct generalization of the structure" (2005, p. 1024). They argue that their results challenge poverty of stimulus arguments for language acquisition (the idea that there is not enough information available in the input to support the acquisition of some language structures, thereby necessitating innate grammatical knowledge). Kam *et al.* (2008) replicated the findings, but then extended the work to show that the statistical model did not perform well on related constructions in English and Dutch. They conclude that Reali and Christensen's (2005) findings on the subclass of auxiliary questions they studied "provides only the weakest encouragement for the belief that every other construction, when studied, will prove to have a comparably reliable statistical hallmark" (2008, p. 783). The important point in this example is that sampling only one example of language does not allow generalizations to all other language.

Choosing among CLAN Programs

In addition to sampling decisions, researchers wanting to analyze data using CLAN must decide which of the various programs can help them answer their research questions. This chapter has already mentioned MLU, VOCD, DSS, and type–token ratios calculated in FREQ as possible means for measuring syntactic complexity. FREQ also counts the frequency of words or codes (including parts of speech) in selected files or speakers within files, and outputs an alphabetical list of each word in the designated speakers/files. It can be used to calculate lemmas or root words as well as inflected forms. A few of the other commonly used CLAN programs and their functions are as follows: (1) STATFREQ summarizes word or code frequencies across files to be used as input to statistics programs; (2) FREQMERGE combines outputs from several frequency runs; (3) COMBO searches for specified combinations of utterances or character strings; (4) KWAL searches for specified key words and outputs the key words as well as the specified number of utterances preceding or following the words; (5) COOCCUR counts co-occurrences of words in clusters specified by the user (with a default cluster of two words); and (6) MAXWD finds the longest word or utterances in a file, and can also locate all the utterances that have a particular length or greater. The reader should consult the CLAN manuals on the CHILDES website for more details about these programs and for information on other available CLAN programs.

Coding and Interrater Reliability

Part of the rationale for standardizing transcripts in CHAT format is to increase the reliability of the transcriptions. All CHILDES corpora code the speakers on the main tiers of the transcript. All English language corpora (and those of many other languages, with work in progress to complete the entire database) are coded for part of speech and grammatical relations information on the dependent tiers following an utterance (for details see MacWhinney, 2008, and Sagae *et al.*, 2010). Any automatic tagging program generates a certain percentage of errors (about 6% in the current case). If that percentage of errors is unacceptable for addressing a particular research question, investigators using these coding categories may need to hand-correct the errors. Some CHILDES transcripts also contain other standard coding categories, described in detail in the CHAT manual on the CHILDES website, for example, speech acts, gestures, and speaker's errors. Some transcripts also contain other project-specific codes. If explanations of these codes and information about reliability of coding are not supplied in the documentation files for a particular corpus, researchers can go back to the original publication sources cited in CHILDES to locate the information.

Researchers who are using CHILDES transcripts will most often need to code categories that were not of interest to the original researcher. They will then need to measure reliability between coders. The CLAN program RELY allows multiple coders to score files. The program will then flag mismatches among coders which will facilitate calculation of interrater reliability.

Virtually all published materials using CHILDES present some type of rater reliability information on their categories.

Analysis of Corpus Data

Obviously, decisions made at earlier stages of the research, such as the research questions to be examined, how they are operationalized, and how sampling is to be accomplished, ultimately will determine the types of data analysis that will be used in a particular study. For example, if a decision was made to examine data from individual children without matching them on some measure of syntactic complexity, then grammatical development can only be examined within, not between children (e.g., Borensztajn, Zuidema, and Bod, 2009).

According to Gries (in press), data of two types can be extracted from corpora: (1) frequencies of words or constructions and their variability, and (2) frequencies and distributions of co-occurrences of linguistic elements. These data may be subjected to further statistical analyses, but sometimes they are simply presented descriptively. A number of studies that use the CHILDES databases report only frequencies (or percentages). Although observed absolute frequency is the most basic corpus statistic, it may lead to inaccurate conclusions if observed elements are unevenly distributed in a corpus (Gries, in press). Two major shortcomings of descriptive frequency counts are that they: (1) do not compare the counted unit in contexts where it is present versus those in which it is absent, and (2) do not determine whether the distributions could have occurred as a result of chance (Tummers, Keylen, and Geeraerts, 2005).

CHILDES studies that go beyond descriptive frequency counts use measures that run the full gamut of parametric and nonparametric tests available to researchers.

In contrast to experimental research, where a researcher can decide in advance which factors to vary and which to hold constant, in spontaneous data such as those contained in CHILDES, multiple factors vary simultaneously (Tummers, Keylen, and Geeraerts, 2005). Multifactorial methods including multiple regression, ANOVA, or cluster analysis are often useful in analyzing these data. Two previously cited studies serve as examples. Both ask whether surface regularities in the input provide the basis for induction of semantic categories. Laakso and Smith (2007) used hierarchical cluster analyses, principal components analyses, and log-likelihood ratios to analyze data from 22 CHILDES corpora in order to show that co-occurrences between pronouns and verbs in child-directed speech can help differentiate between physical (e.g., *push* or *pull)* and psychological verbs (e.g., *want* or *know*). Scott and Fisher (2009) evaluated data from 10 CHILDES corpora using cluster analyses to find that the distributional cues of verb transitivity, subject noun phrase animacy, and lexical overlap between subject and object positions could separate verbs into causal (e.g., *bounce* or *close*) versus unspecified object verbs (e.g., *eat* or *hit*).

An Example Study Using CHILDES

In the remainder of this chapter I will describe in some detail a study that I conducted (Corrigan, 2004) using the CHILDES database in order to illustrate some of the decisions that arise with its use.

Every Study Begins with a Research Question

The first step in doing research is to generate a question to be answered. An early decision to be made is whether the question can be answered using naturalistic data or whether an experimental methodology (such as those described in Part Two of this volume) would be more appropriate. For several years I had been examining connotative (evaluative) aspects of word meanings (e.g., Corrigan, 2002) and I was interested in how children learn them. I discovered that there was virtually no research in this area, partly because of difficulties in operationalizing what is meant by connotation. Could the notion of word connotation be operationalized in a way that took advantage of information available in corpora? The methods I had used with adults (semantic differential scales) were not appropriate for use with very young children. I had been reading corpus semantics literature investigating how word meanings can be established by examining their context in large segments of text. A basic idea in this literature is that words acquire meanings through their frequent co-occurrence with other words (Stubbs, 1995/2007). In particular, I was fascinated by the notion that word collocations can provide evidence for connotative (evaluative) meanings. For example, Stubbs notes that in 100 million words of text, *cause* most often occurs with negative collocates such as *death, damage, harm*; on the other hand, *provide* most often occurs with words that refer to desirable or necessary things such as *support, help, money*. I wondered whether the input to young children contained enough information to support the acquisition of connotative meaning. I chose to examine the word *happen*, which had been described in the corpus linguistics literature (Stubbs, 1995/2007) as having a negative connotation (common collocates are negative words such as *accidents*), because I knew it to be a word that is commonly used with young children. The specific research question then became whether or not *happen* is more likely to refer to negative rather than to positive events in adult–child conversations. I decided to look first at instances where adults used the word *happen* and then to examine children's uses of *happen* in their language.

Comparison Data

I chose to examine adult comparison data by looking at adults' uses of *happen* in another language corpus. In the Stubbs (1995/2007) data, I had noticed that the top 50 collocates of *happen* were grammatical words such as *what, something, nothing, whatever*. Stubbs did not attempt to systematically evaluate the referents of these words because he was looking only at a window of eight words on either side of *happen*. I wondered if I were to identify the referents of these words in more extended sequences of texts, whether they would also be negative in evaluation. I used the British National Corpus (BNC) Sampler, which is a 2 million word sample of the full BNC, split about equally between written and spoken texts. I found that the majority of uses of *happen* in this sample referred to negative referents.

Sampling from CHILDES

To find as many examples of *happen* as possible, I decided to use all the US English corpora that were available at the time that contained transcriptions of adults speaking to children. I split the children into four groups based on their MLUs rather than their ages. When MLUs were not provided in the database, I calculated them using CLAN. I first assigned children with cross-sectional data into the appropriate groups. To avoid over-representing data from children in longitudinal samples, I wanted each child represented in only one MLU group. I calculated the MLUs for each file in the database, then combined files that fell within the MLU ranges that I had decided upon. I then assigned the appropriate portion of each child's longitudinal data to one of the MLU groups (discarding data that did not fall into the chosen group). So, for example, if a child was assigned to the MLU 1.00–2.00 group, longitudinal data from only those sessions in which his or her MLU fell into this range were included. In the end, I was able to achieve my goal of keeping the percentage of *happen* utterances produced by adults approximately equal across groups. All group assignments were done before any coding of contexts to ensure that the outcomes of the scoring did not influence to which groups children were assigned. In the second part of the study, where I was looking at children's language rather than at child-directed language, I maintained the same groups, even though this produced unequal samples of child-produced *happen*.

Because this was a case study, I ignored issues of representativeness of sources of variation other than the MLU of the child and I also chose not to study constructions other than those containing *happen*. It could be that adults use *happen* more in some contexts (e.g., storybook reading) than in others. This might be problematic for interpreting the results if there were also differences in whether *happen* referred more to negative rather than to positive events only in some contexts. My subjective judgment is that this was not the case, but I did not test it directly.

Decisions about Procedures and Scoring

One of the many procedural decisions to be made included how to define the context of the *happen* utterances I scored. What was a reasonable window for the context surrounding an utterance? I arbitrarily decided upon three utterances on either side of *happen*. Another decision to be made was whether to include only the adult's context surrounding the utterance or to also include the child's utterances. Partly driven by a theoretical assumption that children and adults co-construct meaning, I decided to include both speakers' utterances in the context. I used the KWAL programs in CHILDES to gather these data. Having isolated *happen* and its surrounding context, I was ready to score whether each utterance occurred in a positive, negative, or neutral environment. I also had to decide how to score an episode if the context surrounding it contained a mixture of utterances judged to be positive, negative, and neutral.

Because I was producing new scoring categories that were not in the original data, I needed to check for the reliability of the coding. A sample of 47% of the adult-initiated episodes and 100% of the child-initiated episodes were scored by two coders. Disagreement as to whether the surrounding utterances were positive or negative occurred with only 1% and 2% of the adult-initiated and child-initiated episodes. The worst reliability occurred in trying to determine whether an utterance was positive or neutral.

Data Analysis Decisions

I chose to use chi-squares to analyze whether the observed frequency of negative compared to positive contexts surrounding *happen* was more frequent than expected for each age group. Chi-squares often involve decisions about whether to combine different categories in a contingency table if data are sparse. The adults produced enough instances of *happen* so that this was not an issue. With the child-initiated *happen* data, I collapsed children from the 1.00–2.00 and 2.00–3.00 MLU groups because of sparse data.

Results

I found that both adults and children were more likely to use *happen* to describe negative contexts as the children's language grew in complexity. I concluded that there was enough information available in the input for children to begin to acquire the evaluative meaning of the word.

Conclusions

Doing research with CHILDES involves many of the same decisions that a researcher must make in using any other method. Are spontaneous speech data the best source to answer the research question? If so, are there sufficient data available in CHILDES to address the question or should new, denser samples be collected? If CHILDES contains sufficient data, which corpora or subcorpora should be used? What will the comparison groups be, either within CHILDES or outside CHILDES? Which CLAN programs can best be used to assemble the necessary data to answer the research question, or should programs external to CHILDES be used? What language categories will be examined? Are the categories already coded in extant data files or will new coding be necessary? If so, how will reliability be assessed? How should the distributional frequency data on the categories be analyzed? In this chapter, I have given examples of a few of the studies using the CHILDES system and how they have addressed these methodological questions.

Key Terms

CHILDES   Child Language Data Exchange System.
Child Language Data Exchange System   An archive of transcripts of children's speech and computer tools to analyze them.
Corpus linguistics   A subset of applied linguistics that analyses large samples of spoken or written text stored in computerized databases.

References

Baroni, M. (2008) Distributions in text. In A. Ludeling and M. Kyoto (eds), *Corpus linguistics: an international handbook* (vol. 2, pp. 803–821). Berlin: de Gruyter.

Behrens, H. (2008) Corpora in language acquisition research: history, methods, perspectives. In H. Behrens (ed.), *Corpora in language acquisition research: history, methods, perspectives* (pp. xi–xxx). Amsterdam: Benjamins.

Biber, D., and Jones, J. (2008) Quantitative methods in corpus linguistics. In A. Ludeling and M. Kyoto (eds), *Corpus linguistics: an international handbook* (vol. 2, pp. 1286–1304). Berlin: de Gruyter.

Borensztajn, G., Zuidema, W., and Bod, R. (2009) Children's grammars grow more abstract with age: evidence from an automatic procedure for identifying the productive units of language. *Topics in Cognitive Science*, 1, 175–188.

Brown, R. (1973) *A first language: the early stages*. Cambridge, MA: Harvard University Press.

Corrigan, R. (2002) The influence of evaluation and potency on perceivers' causal attributions. *European Journal of Social Psychology*, 32, 363–382.

Corrigan, R. (2004) The acquisition of word connotations: asking "What happened?" *Journal of Child Language*, 31, 381–398.

Corrigan, R. (2008) Conveying information about adjective meanings in spoken discourse. *Journal of Child Language*, 35, 159–184.

Corrigan, R. (in press) Effects of pre-service teachers' receptive vocabulary knowledge on their interactive read-alouds with elementary school students. *Reading and Writing*.

Domack, A. (2009) "Let's read a book, Mommy": how gender, age, and socioeconomic status affect naturalistic conversations about literacy. Unpublished dissertation, University of Nebraska–Lincoln. *Dissertation Abstracts International Section A: Humanities and Social Sciences*, 70 (3-A), 796.

Gries, S.T. (in press) Useful statistics for corpus linguistics. In M. Almela (ed.), *New horizons in corpus linguistics*. Frankfurt: Lang.

Hoff, E. (2006) How social contexts support and shape language development. *Developmental Review*, 26, 55–88.

Kam, X.-N., Stoyenshka, I., Tornyova, L., *et al.* (2008) Bigrams and the richness of the stimulus. *Cognitive Science*, 32, 771–787.

Laakso, A., and Smith, L.B. (2007) Pronouns and verbs in adult speech to children: a corpus analysis. *Journal of Child Language*, 34, 725–763.

Lee, L. (1984) *Developmental sentence analysis*. Evanston, IL: Northwestern University Press.

MacWhinney, B. (2000) *The CHILDES Project: tools for analyzing talk* (3rd edn, vols 1 and 2). Mahwah, NJ: Erlbaum.

MacWhinney, B. (2008) Enriching CHILDES for morphosyntactic analysis. In H. Behrens (ed.), *Corpora in language acquisition research: history, methods, perspectives* (pp. 165–196). Amsterdam: Benjamins.

MacWhinney, B. (2010) Computational models of child language learning: an introduction. *Journal of Child Language*, 37, 477–485.

McKee, G., Malvern, D., and Richards, B. (2000) Measuring vocabulary diversity using dedicated software. *Literary and Linguistic Computing*, 15, 323–337.

Norris, J., and Ortega, L. (2009) Toward an organic approach to investigating CAF in instructed SLA: the case of complexity. *Applied Linguistics*, 30, 555–578.

Parker, M., and Brorson, K. (2005) A comparative study between mean length of utterance in morphemes (MLUm) and mean length of utterance in words (MLUw). *First Language*, 25, 356–376.

Pomikalek, J., Rychly, P., and Kilgarriff, A. (2009) Scaling to billion-plus word corpora. *Advances in Computational Linguistics*, 41, 3–14.

Reali, F., and Christensen, M. (2005) Uncovering the richness of the stimulus: structure dependence and indirect statistical evidence. *Cognitive Science*, 29, 1007–1028.

Rowland, C., Fletcher, S., and Freudenthal, D. (2008) How big is big enough? Assessing the reliability of data from naturalistic samples. In H. Behrens (ed.), *Corpora in language acquisiition research: history, methods, perspectives* (pp. 1–24). Amsterdam: Benjamins.

Sagae, K., Davis, E., Lavie, A., *et al.* (2010) Morphosyntactic annotation of CHILDES transcripts. *Journal of Child Language*, 37, 705–729.

Scott, R., and Fisher, C. (2009) Two-year-olds use distributional cues to interpret transitivity-alternating verbs. *Language and Cognitive Processes*, 24, 777–803.

Stubbs, M. (1995) Collocations and semantic profiles: on the cause of the trouble with quantitative studies. *Functions of Language*, 2, 23–55. Reprinted in W. Teubert and R. Krishnamurthy (eds), *Corpus linguistics: critical concepts in linguistics*. Routledge, 2007 (vol. 3, pp. 166–193).

Tomasello, M., and Stahl, D. (2004) Sampling children's spontaneous speech: how much is enough? *Journal of Child Language*, 31, 101–121.

Tummers, J., Keylen, K., and Geeraerts, D. (2005) Usage-based approaches in cognitive linguistics: a technical state of the art. *Corpus Linguistics and Linguistic Theory*, 1–2, 225–261.

Further Reading and Resources

Behrens, H. (2008) *Corpora in language acquisition resarch: history, methods, perspectives*. Amsterdam: Benjamins. A collection of papers particularly useful for detailing methodological issues involved in corpus research.

Gries, S.T. (2009) What is corpus linguistics? *Language and Linguistics Compass*, 3, 1–17. A very accessible introduction to using corpora in the study of language.

Ludeling, A., and Kyoto, M. (2009) *Corpus linguistics: an international handbook* (vols 1 and 2). Berlin: de Gruyter. A collection of 61 papers covering topics such as the history of corpus linguistics, how corpus linguistics relates to other disciplines such as sociolinguistics or lexicography, different types of corpora and how they are compiled, corpus annotation, statistical methods for corpus research, and uses for corpora.

Myles, F., and Mitchell, R. (2004) Using information technology to support empirical SLA research. *Journal of Applied Linguistics*, 1, 169–196. Describes the use of CLAN tools in second acquisition research with a corpus-based program of French L2 research.

Sokolov, J., and Snow, C. (1994) *Handbook of research in language development using CHILDES*. Mahwah, NJ: Erlbaum. Contains examples of original research that also provide tutorials on how to use the version of CLAN that was available at the time the book was published (there have been some changes, but much is still relevant).

http://childes.psy.cmu.edu/tools/email.html. A description of five Google group mailing lists devoted to child language learning, technical issues involving CHILDES, the Phon program, developmental pragmatics, and conversation analysis.

http://www.ling.lancs.ac.uk/staff/mark/lipps/lipps.htm. The Language Interaction in Plurilingual and Plurilectal Speakers (LIPPS) group is working on setting up a database called Language Interaction Data Exchange System (LIDES) of bilingual, mixed language that is modeled after CHILDES and uses CHAT transcription.

http://iascl.talkbank.org/clb.html. The *Bulletin of the International Association for the Study of Child Language* provides periodic descriptions of changes in the CHILDES system (new corpora, new CLAN programs, etc.).

Part IV Studying Multiple Languages and Special Populations

19 Crosslinguistic Research

Aylin C. Küntay

Summary

There is considerable variation among the languages of the world in terms of how the grammar is organized. Crosslinguistic research in child language compares developmental patterns in children acquiring differently organized languages. This comparative approach is crucial for testing universalist proposals about how children learn language in addition to demonstrating language-specific learning challenges and patterns. It is a flexible research framework: all the techniques covered in this book can be implemented crosslinguistically; children of any age and adults can be study participants; many domains of language development can be covered. Data from individual languages count as crosslinguistic research, especially if findings expand or challenge our knowledge about the acquisition of well-studied languages such as Indo-European. Recently, guided by linguistic typology, typologically comparative language development research has been especially prolific. In this chapter crosslinguistic research is exemplified in two domains of child language: (1) morphosyntactic development, and (2) pragmatic development.

Research Aims

Crosslinguistically framed language development research has had two overarching goals. The first goal tests claims of universalism, with the aim of uncovering the extent and limits of broad generalizations about children's language learning mechanisms.

Research Methods in Child Language: A Practical Guide, First Edition.
Edited by Erika Hoff.
© 2012 Blackwell Publishing Ltd. Published 2012 by Blackwell Publishing Ltd.

The second goal, focusing on language-specific particularism, studies how the linguistic organization of a certain language systematically influences the learner's language learning mechanisms (Slobin, 1997) or basic perceptual and cognitive mechanisms. These two goals are to be conceived as complementary. Followers of Slobin's pioneering enterprise in crosslinguistic research, for example, have variously demonstrated how children can learn language in general while also unraveling language-specific acquisition paths of learners.

Time and again, comparisons of linguistic systems have shown that most of the world's 6000 or so languages have radically different grammatical organizations than English. This variability naturally raises questions about what is universal and what is particular in language development. Taking heed of such diversity for the benefit of child language research, Slobin and his colleagues planted the seeds of crosslinguistic research by publishing *A field manual for cross-cultural study of the acquisition of communicative competence* in 1967. This manual was written to guide researchers in the methods of collecting comparable field data on the acquisition of communicative competence, which includes both linguistic knowledge and the socialization of such knowledge through child-rearing practices.

In principle, all the research techniques covered in this book could be administered within a crosslinguistic framework. The gist of the crosslinguistic approach is a comparative outlook on the linguistic and cognitive developmental trajectories of children exposed to different languages. On the surface, comparing paths of development across learners of multiple languages appears as simple replications of a technique in new linguistic communities and does not necessarily come across as a research innovation. However, especially when developmental data of different languages have been compared in a well-motivated way, crosslinguistic research has proven essential in addressing long-standing questions and opening new avenues in research about language development.

In crosslinguistic research, we see a prolific interface between child language studies and a field of linguistics called linguistic typology (Bowerman, 2011). Typologists operate with the goal of determining the limits of diversity that make it possible to group languages into types, determined by the status of languages on dimensions of variation (Slobin, 1997). Some of these variations stand out as properties that can potentially affect the trajectories of learning first languages. Child language researchers utilize these typological descriptions in generating comparative research questions across learners of languages with divergent properties and in determining the extent to which universalist accounts of language development provide an adequate account of how all languages are learned. In other words, in uniting methodological frameworks from the fields of linguistic typology and language acquisition, the crosslinguistic method stands out as a unique research approach that is simultaneously in search of universals and particulars.

One could adopt the crosslinguistic approach to assess any domain of language development from phonological to pragmatic development. The approach can be employed with populations of any age. Often, noncomparative work conducted with children exposed to any language other than English is considered crosslinguistic, owing to an implicit comparison to English (Stoll, 2009). Such studies often test the extent to which universalist theories of language development proposed on the grounds of research on Indo-European languages perform when tested with speakers of other languages. The second type of crosslinguistic work, termed "typological language acquisition" by Stoll (2009), operates with a well-motivated choice of comparisons across features of different languages. The prospects of the crosslinguistic approach in child language are staggering. Studies can be found for only about 2% of the world's languages (Stoll, 2009). Despite such sparseness, crosslinguistic studies have already supplied crucial contributions to the field of child language. Yet, of course, it is important to be aware of some the challenges of conducting crosslinguistic research.

In this chapter, the advantages and the challenges of employing a crosslinguistic approach will be demonstrated in two different research domains of child language development. The first area is morphosyntactic development, and the second is pragmatic development. The domains are: (1) argument structure comprehension, that is, determination of "who-did-what-to-whom" in simple sentences; and (2) exophoric usage of demonstrative pronouns, that is, reference to physically available entities with *this* or *that*.

Domain 1: Comprehension of Argument Structure

When exposed to a sentence such as *the bird is pushing the horse*, hearers need to figure out what exactly the roles of the bird and the horse are. Even if the meaning of the verb "push" is understood, a key task in sentence comprehension is to assign the status of the pusher and the pushee to the correct animals. The knowledge that allows us to achieve this comprehension is called argument structure knowledge. In English, we pay attention to the order of the nouns with respect to the verb to comprehend utterances; in other words, we use the word order of the sentence. In many other languages, who is pushing and who is being pushed are indicated by markers on the nouns referring to the animals, termed nominal case markers. Turkish, Serbian, and Croatian, for example, are nominal case marking languages; they indicate who is undergoing the action of pushing by a suffix on the noun standing for the pushee. Some other languages indicate roles of event participants with markers on verbs. Across languages, comprehension of the argument structure in sentences involves use of one or more of these cues. Studying the developmental status of this knowledge is a crucial component of assessing grammatical knowledge in children (see also Ambridge, Chapter 8 this volume; McKercher and Jaswal, Chapter 10 this volume).

Do children learning different languages develop the capacity to comprehend argument structure using similar or divergent cues? Based on research with English-speaking populations, researchers had originally proposed a "rigid word order" strategy, where children parse and produce sentences in the fixed order of subject, verb, and object (Bowerman, in press). This strategy received vindication in recent language comprehension studies (see Piotroski and Naigles, Chapter 2 this volume): English-speaking children use a canonical word order strategy as a mechanism to discover argument structure (i.e., who-did-what-to-whom) in the sentences they hear.

That is, upon hearing a transitive sentence such as *Z is VERBing C*, young children map Z onto an actor and C onto an undergoer of the activity implied by the verb.

For a while, the canonical word order strategy stood ground as a plausible candidate for being a universal discovery procedure about argument structure. But soon it encountered crosslinguistic testing with languages of variable word order and other typical ways of marking argument structure. Slobin and Bever (1982) asked preschool speakers of Turkish, English, Italian, and Serbo-Croatian to act out sentences using animal props. Crucially, the sentences were presented in various word orders and/or in the presence or absence of case markers on the nouns. The child speakers of the four languages were asked to use the animal toys in acting out sentences with normative vs variant word orders, either with or without case markers indicating the nonsubject grammatical role. The patterns of children's enactments revealed important language-specific strategies; for example, Turkish children employed nominal case markers in addition to normative word orders to derive sentence meaning. These results pointed towards a theoretical sharpening of the initial proposal, in that the canonical word order strategy had to be streamlined as the "canonical sentence schema." This crosslinguistic endeavor was responsible for showing in hindsight that it was the rigid word order characteristic of English, in essence a language-specific feature, that had been upheld as a promising universal mechanism. The crosslinguistic sentence act-out study served to discard a generalization, suggesting language-specific cues other than word order affect comprehension in morphologically complex languages.

It is still a debate today how early English children's use of normative word order develops to facilitate sentence comprehension productively. Using the intermodal preferential looking paradigm (see Piotroski and Naigles, Chapter 2 this volume; Golinkoff and Hirsh-Pasek, Chapter 5 this volume), where children are directed to look at the scene matching a sentential stimulus, Gertner, Fisher, and Eisengart (2006) have demonstrated that 21-month-old English learners will use SVO (subject–verb–object) order to distinguish reversible agent–patient nonsense actions paired with *novel* verbs (e.g., *the rabbit is gorping the fox*), showing that the SVO frame is already productive at this young age. Dittmar *et al.* (2008), on the other hand, show that such comprehension of novel reversible transitives depends on an initial training phase about familiar transitive constructions, arguing that early grasp of the transitive word order is tenuous for German and English learners. Slobin and Bever (1982) found that Turkish children's reliance on case markers emerged about a half-year earlier than English-speaking children's reliance on word order, demonstrating that Turkish children start using the salient case marking cue at the end of nonsubject nouns to comprehend argument structure during the early phases of language development.

As the debate for English learners continues, crosslinguistic studies are being conducted to determine whether children have an inclination to employ ordering patterns as a cue to comprehension if they are acquiring languages without a rigid word order. Gervain *et al.* (2008) turned to Italian and Japanese because these languages have opposing word orders, with more frequent function words coming before the less frequent content words in Italian (e.g., *sul tavolo*, on the table, "on the table") and vice versa for Japanese (e.g., *Kobe ni*, Kobe to, "to Kobe"). Building on this typological distinction, the methodology was to create "miniature artificial languages," where the order of frequent and infrequent nonsense words was manipulated. The babies' preferences for the two orders were tested via their head turns towards specific auditory stimuli (see Golinkoff and Hirsh-Pasek, Chapter 5 this volume). It was shown that Japanese and Italian 8-month-olds have already detected the ordering patterns of their respective languages; namely, that Italians babies tend to prefer ordering of more frequent nonsense words before less frequent nonsense words, whereas Japanese tend to show the opposite pattern. A recent inter-modal preferential looking study by Candan *et al.* (2010) also showed that Turkish 2-year-old children use word order as an indication of argument structure to match scenes to a noun–noun–verb sentence, although their relative uncertainty in making that match is higher than their English learning counterparts as revealed in their more frequent switches between the two alternative scenes (see Piotroski and Naigles, Chapter 2 this volume). Even in languages without a rigid word order, infants appear to learn to prefer more common ordering patterns of their native languages. Yet, how robustly the "basic word order" cue is used for derivation of sentential meaning across different languages and ages is a current target question of crosslinguistic methodology. For example, Chan, Lieven, and Tomasello (2009) find through an act-out study that Cantonese children learn to rely on word order for sentence comprehension after age 3, while English children show an earlier sensitivity, with German children being somewhere in between.

These studies which use sentences for children to act out with objects or to match to scenes have to make sure that both the linguistic stimuli and the visual stimuli such as props and pictures are comparable across languages. In the Candan *et al.* (2010) study comparing English, Turkish, and Mandarin learning children's sensitivity to word order, we filmed human actors costumed as animals so that we can use the same stimuli in all of the three settings. We avoided human faces as they would not look equally local to all the groups. In addition, we chose two animals the nouns for which end in consonants in Turkish, so that both nouns undergo the same vowel harmony rule when they are suffixed. We ensured that the audios of the sentences were spoken by the familiar dialect in all cultures, and included engaging child-directed attention getters in all the languages.

How should future crosslinguistic work proceed in addressing how children figure out argument structure in their language? Head turning, act-out, or classical inter-modal preferential looking procedures have been useful, but they do not zero in on how language comprehension builds up through real time. These methods character-istically merely reveal the statistically most prevalent preferences of children's language processing apparatus across entire trials of sentence comprehension (but see Piotroski and Naigles, Chapter 2 this volume, for descriptions of extensions of the classical intermodal preferential measure). There is now truly online child and adult psycholinguistic work examining moment-to-moment changes in cognitive processes during comprehension, tapped mostly through changes in direction and duration of eye gaze (see Swingley, Chapter 3 this volume; Trueswell, Chapter 12 this volume). This work demonstrates that comprehenders rapidly start predicting meanings about an entire construction's meaning from the first word on, revising interpretations when necessary upon encounter of subsequent words.

As a relevant example which was followed up by crosslinguistic research, in Snedeker and Trueswell (2004) participants were asked to move some objects around as they listened to instructions, and, importantly, their eye gazes were monitored throughout the trials, using the method of the visual world paradigm (see Trueswell, Chapter 12 this volume). In the critical conditions, the instructions were made ambiguous for guiding the choice of objects. The verb in the instructions was altered to lead to different semantic biases in sentences with similar prepositional phrases such as (1) **tickle** *the pig with the fan* (instrument biased), (2) **choose** *the cow with the fork* (modifier biased), (3) **feel** *the frog with the feather* (unbiased). For example, when the critical verb was one that typically appeared with an instrument as in (1), it was expected that hearing of the verb such as *tickle* would quickly divert the participants' attention to a potential instrument like a fan as a solitary object rather than a pig holding a fan, which was a distractor object. This hypothesis held true for both 5-year-olds and adults; both age groups were affected by the meaning of the sentence-initial verb in shaping their interpretations. Snedeker and Trueswell (2004) concluded that the verb meaning establishes a bias, affecting the participants' interpretation of the prepositional phrase well in advance of their encounter of the phrase. The participants' reliance on verb meaning over other cues in resolving structural ambiguities was used to support the idea that verbs are the primary linguistic units in predicting the remaining argument structure of a sentence.

Crosslinguistic research was essential to assess whether these findings and interpretations can be transferred to other languages. As seen in examples 1 to 3 above, verbs appear at the outset of sentences in English directives. Thus, their core role in predicting the rest of construction meaning could well be due to their initial position in the sentence. To test this hunch, Choi and Trueswell (2010) turned to Korean, a verb-final language, with an eyetracking study. Their experiments with 4- and 5-year-olds showed that, unlike adults, children had difficulty in remedying an initial destination-like interpretation of *naypkhin-ey* "napkin-on" when they encounter a verbal form such as *cipu-sey-yo* "pick up" instead of a verb congruent with their initial guess such as *nohu-sey-yo* "put." If verbs were the most informative elements of argument structure in all languages, a change in the trail of interpretation would have been less effortful and would have led to more error-free action patterns in children's enactments of the sentences. Thus, English children's failure to supersede the initially presented verb-biased information with disambiguating content appearing later in a sentence is then not indicative of a universal tendency to abide by verb meaning despite later incongruent information. Taken together, the English and the Korean studies point to the primacy of early-arriving cues over the late-arriving ones in online sentence meaning computation, as it is hard for preschool children to modify initial misinterpretations in light of later evidence.

This sequence of eye gaze studies is a good example of how crosslinguistic research can lead to streamlining of initial universalistic explanations. More studies should be conducted to determine whether other linguistic elements than the verb facilitate predictive processing of sentence meaning in variable word order languages. Kamide, Scheepers, and Altmann's (2003) study with a case marking language (German) showed that adults use case marking information on the initial noun to anticipate the rest of the argument structure of a sentence. Such experimental crosslinguistic studies should be carried out with child learners of morphologically complex languages, to determine whether anchors for parsing mechanisms differ across languages.

What these crosslinguistic and cross-sectional experimental studies set down are the components of argument structure knowledge, or how these components get differentially utilized during real-time language comprehension. Yet, the developmental processes driving such knowledge remain elusive. More crosslinguistic work should be directed towards search for these processes in child-directed discourse. The role of language that children hear in conversational sequences with caregivers is often proposed to be part of this developmental process, because unquestionably it is such child-directed language that displays the typological features of a language. Küntay and Slobin (1996) showed that Turkish mothers display many interesting features of the target language, such as word order alternations and range of morphology, via variation sets that are characterized by a sequence of utterances with a constant communicative intention but varying forms. Such studies complement what is lacking in purely experimental or typological studies by demonstrating the input characteristics, that is, how typological factors are manifested to the child in real interactions. Although recording, transcription, coding, and analysis of interactive discourse are effortful (see Rowe, Chapter 13 this volume), the outcome is well worth the effort. For example, Budwig, Narasimhan, and Srivastava (2006) demonstrated that rich morphosyntactic cues to the transitive–intransitive distinction in Hindi child-directed speech led to Hindi children's comprehension of such a distinction at an earlier age than English-speaking children. Stoll, Abbot-Smith, and Lieven (2009) examined child-directed speech in Russian, German, and English – languages with typologically varying flexibility in word ordering. Their question was whether the high degree of lexical repetitiveness found in the initial strings of English caregivers would carry over to typologically different languages; the analyses revealed that it did. Ural *et al.* (2009) found that the accusative morpheme is more effective than the number of nouns in child-directed utterances for a machine learner to determine the transitivity of a verb.

These recent studies notwithstanding, we still know very little about how actual child-directed discourse is structured in non-English languages (Stoll, 2009) and even less about how these patterns could be drawn out by the learner in acquisition of grammatical patterns such as argument structure. This situation of relative ignorance surely warrants effortful crosslinguistic research on caregiver–child discourse.

When researchers obtain discourse surrounding children across languages, it is important to make sure that the recorded contexts are relevant and have similar organizations in all the cultures considered. Tardif, Gelman, and Xu (1999), for example, showed that both English and Chinese children used more nouns in book-reading contexts and more verbs during toy-play contexts, and provided a qualification to an original proposal that Chinese learners have proportionally more verbs than nouns in their early vocabularies compared to English learners. Thus, it is important to choose or create comparable discourse contexts across cultures, especially if the samples of speech collected are small and do not allow for natural variation across a variety of activities. Other methodological considerations are who to include among the providers of speech to the target children and where to do the recording. In common practice, the children are recorded indoors in interaction with their mothers, i.e., primary caregivers. However, dyadic interactions between children and mothers, where children participate in interactions as legitimate communicative partners, might not be relevant in certain nonindustrialized or rural contexts. In a situation with Chintang learners in eastern Nepal, where toddlers play outside within groups of other children for most of the day, Stoll *et al.* (in press) placed a video camera and an external microphone close to the area where children played. Most recordings took place outside the house and included all the child-surrounding discourse. Thus, crosslinguistic researchers need to be watchful of the regular living arrangements of their participants so that they tap culturally relevant settings. In addition, it might not be appropriate to videotape in some cultures: some Turkish mothers did not allow us to record their faces during a block-construction task with their children, but permitted us to record their hands and voices.

Domain 2: Reference with Demonstrative Pronouns

Demonstrative pronouns such as *this*, *that*, *here*, and *there* provide a typical way to communicate about external objects and locations in conversations. Such forms are ubiquitous in interaction, but their meanings are not inherently but rather contextually specified. Because the usage of these so-called deictic forms speaks to the question of how communicative convergence takes place between interactive partners, their study lies at the heart of the field of linguistic pragmatics. Although demonstrative pronouns (and deictic systems in general) are pervasive in languages, linguistic typologists have just recently begun to explore how they work in diverse languages (Levinson, 2004).

The coverage of demonstrative pronouns is older in the field of child language, however. Child language researchers analyzing productions of language from transcripts could not escape noticing that demonstrative pronouns were frequent among the very early utterances. Clark and Sengul (1978) found that demonstratives used in conjunction with a pointing gesture are among the first few words that children produce. It is not surprising that the gestural-referential usage of demonstrative pronouns emerges before vocabulary development involving content words. With demonstratives, communicators can use pointing-like gestures to uniquely identify what exactly they are referring to among physical objects surrounding them. However, by their very nature of context dependency in naturalistic discourse, children's choice of certain demonstrative pronouns over others did not easily lend itself to an analysis of the dimensions that govern their usage.

Until recently, the literature of both linguistic typology and early child language work have made the assumption that demonstratives primarily encode spatial distinctions (Levinson, 2004; but see Diessel, 2006). In other words, the choice of a particular demonstrative form from a set (e.g., choice of *this* or *that*) was seen to be dependent on spatial factors such as degree of distance of the referent from a speaker or an addressee. Clark and Sengul (1978) found that young English speakers take several years to learn the "distance principle" as a semantic axis to govern their choice of a specific demonstrative from the paradigm, although demonstratives are very common in early child language. More recently, however, linguistic systems that encode nonspatial semantic dimensions came to the attention of linguistic typologists (Diessel, 2006; Levinson, 2004). What do these systems look like and what kind of developmental challenges do they pose to their learners in comparison to the spatial system exemplified in English?

Özyürek and Kita (2000) examined conversations among Japanese-speaking and Turkish-speaking adults and found that the three-way demonstrative systems in these languages were not entirely spatially oriented as proposed by the grammarians of the respective languages. In other words, a certain "third" pronoun, *şu* in Turkish and *so* in Japanese, was found to be used to direct an addressee's attention to a new referent, independently of the distance of this referent from the speaker or the addressee. In both languages, these attention-bidding pronouns could be used to refer to very near referents, such as spots on the speaker's body, or very far objects, such as buildings disappearing far in the horizon. The other two pronouns of the paradigm, i.e., *bu* and *o* in Turkish, were employed only when there was an already established shared attentional focus between the interlocutors. In those cases, *bu* was reserved for referents closer to the speaker and *o* for those that were near the addressee. The salient difference of this three-way system from the two-way system of demonstratives in English prompted a crosslinguistically framed study with Turkish children (Küntay and Özyürek, 2006).

Procedure

In order to study the acquisition of the three-way demonstrative system in Turkish, we conducted a cross-sectional, semi-experimental study with preschool children and adults working on a joint task in pairs. The task required from the participants was reconstructing a Lego® model based on a picture provided by the researcher, using several blocks of different sizes and colors. Such an activity, we thought, would confront an often-encountered challenge to effectively balance experimental control and ecological validity in studies with children learning any language, and could also easily be carried out by college-age adults. In addition, we wanted to maximize the occurrence of demonstrative pronouns with implicit task-based demands. In that regard, we expected that a task that calls for joint manipulation of physical objects with a visually accessible goal state (i.e., the pictured model) would elicit many demonstrative forms, leading to reference to objects in varying distances from both of the interactants. Further, to achieve the goal, speakers would often call for shifted attentional states from their recipients with regard to the referents, because there were many individual Lego pieces (both pictured and actual) that could be referred to at any point in the task. All these experimental manipulations would be created unobtrusively: that is, neither the adults nor the children could plausibly guess what exactly in their behaviors the researchers were interested in, being mostly preoccupied with perfecting their constructions. The task requires minimal training of experimenters and is appropriate for use in cultures where a request for playing with blocks is not totally unusual.

The Lego construction sessions of pairs of friends at the ages of 4 and 6, together with college-age adults, were video recorded for 12 minutes each. Video recording ensured that nonverbal behaviors accompanying demonstrative pronouns, such as gaze and gesture, would later be tracked. The transcripts of all the sessions were then obtained from the videotapes, and were first segmented into utterances. The task fulfilled its promise of providing a sizeable sample of demonstrative pronouns from all three of the age groups included. Over one-third (38%) of the utterances in adult conversations, and about 20% of the children's utterances, contained at least one demonstrative pronoun. All the utterances containing demonstrative pronouns were then tagged with respect to the type of the demonstrative pronoun, i.e., *bu*, *şu*, or *o*. We considered all the language-relevant morphological contexts where demonstratives were used (i.e., locative -*da*, accusative -*i*, dative -*a*) in addition to when they were used as adnominals (e.g., *bu parça* "this piece") as belonging to that certain type of the demonstrative. In tagging linguistic forms such as the three demonstrative pronouns in Turkish, researchers should take into consideration morphological and/or phonological variants of the target forms.

The obtained utterances with demonstratives were then coded by two trained coders as these coders watched the videotapes. These coders were not informed about the motivations and the expectations of the study. The codings included the relative distance of the referent from the speaker of the utterance and the presence of the addressee's eye gaze on the referent just before the use of the demonstrative by the speaker. To examine intercoder agreement, a third trained coder coded 25% of the utterances where demonstratives were used in respect to the referent's relative distance and the addressee's eye gaze on the referent. The interrater reliability was 86% for the distance measure, and 89% for the eye gaze measure. Some of the disagreements were actual errors, so these were corrected. For the cases of unresolvable ambiguity in the data in relation to the coding category, the original codings were retained.

If we were to obtain comparable data in another language, say in Japanese, it is important that the same stimuli are provided to the participants and the recording precision is equal in the two situations so that the same categories could be coded. Features such as relative distance and eye gaze status of the participants could be coded in any culture as long as the recording was done appropriately to allow such coding. The same extensive training should be given to coders so that they are familiar with the coding schema. In particular, when coders are coding for nonverbal features, video samples could be cross-coded by native speakers of languages other than that of the participants. Usually, being a native speaker is not a requirement for coding nonverbal behavior, and this procedure ensures that the two research groups have comparative fidelity.

Data

The procedure yielded a coded transcript as an output (see Rowe, Chapter 13 this volume; Corrigan, Chapter 18 this volume; Dickinson, Chapter 17 this volume). The coded data were first analyzed in terms of the distributional patterns of each type of demonstrative in the conversations of each group, using the chi-square test. In addition, we analyzed how each demonstrative usage co-occurred with the coded features of the conversational interaction, i.e., distance of referents and addressee's eye gaze patterns using repeated-measures ANOVA.

The distribution data indicated that in children's conversations the distribution of demonstrative pronouns differed from that in adults, i.e., children used more *bu* than *şu* instances while the adults used more *şu* than *bu* instances. Analysis of the demonstrative usage in relation to the nonverbal coding categories confirmed that one of the demonstrative pronouns in Turkish, *şu*, was used to invite the addressee's attention to focus on a referent, independent of this referent's spatial proximity to the interactants. As for the children's use of demonstratives, we showed that 4- and 6-year-old Turkish speakers are not yet at adult levels in using the contrast between *şu* and the other two demonstratives to manage their partner's attentional status. On the other hand, Turkish children took distance into account in their contrastive use of *bu* and *o*, reserving *bu* for close and *o* for farther away referents. The discrepancy of the child demonstrative pronoun system from the adult one in Turkish can be used to challenge a claim that demonstrative pronouns are basic and easy to acquire across languages (Diessel, 2006). When faced with the task of designing the most appropriate demonstrative form in fitting with the recipient's attentional status during fast-flowing conversations, Turkish 6-year-olds do not appear to perform at par with adults with regard to the pragmatic implications of the demonstratives.

The Küntay and Özyürek (2006) study is not strictly crosslinguistic in the sense that it does not involve any explicit comparison across different linguistic communities. However, it contains an implicit comparison because the divergence of the Turkish demonstrative pronoun system from the English one is conspicuous and the method used is as close to the naturalistic as possible. The methodological approach in this study is easily crosslinguistically transportable, and should clearly be replicated in languages with a similar system of demonstratives such as Japanese and more standard systems such as English.

Conclusion

In sum, the crosslinguistic approach can be fruitfully used to study morphosyntactic development or pragmatic development in addition to domains that are not demonstrated in this chapter. In combining the search for the "universal," the "particular," and the "typological" in language development (Slobin, 1997), the crosslinguistic framework could be adopted as complementary to any method covered in this book.

Acknowledgments

I would like to thank Reyhan Furman, Aslı Özyürek, and especially Letitia Naigles and Dan Slobin for reading earlier versions of this chapter, and providing tips and encouragement.

Key Terms

Argument structure   The number and type of noun phrases, and the relationship of these noun phrases with one another in a sentence, i.e., who-did-the-verb-to-what.

Demonstratives   Words that indicate which entities a speaker refers to and distinguish those entities from others, e.g., *this*, *that*, *these*, *those*.

Linguistic typology   A field of linguistics which systematically studies the similarities and differences in specific features across different languages.

Pragmatic development   Development that takes place to acquire knowledge about the communicative functions and conventions governing the use of language.

References

Bowerman, M. (2011) Linguistic typology and first language acquisition. In J.J. Song (ed.), *The Oxford handbook of linguistic typology* (pp. 591–617). Oxford: Oxford University Press.

Budwig, N., Narasimhan, B., and Srivastava, S. (2006) Interim solutions: the acquisition of early verb constructions in Hindi. In E.V. Clark and B.F. Kelly (eds), *Constructions in acquisition*. Stanford, CA: CSLI.

Candan, A., Küntay, A.C., Yeh, Y., *et al.* (2010) Crosslinguistic consistency and variation in children's sensitivity to word order. Unpublished manuscript, Koç University.

Chan, A., Lieven, E., and Tomasello, M. (2009) Children's understanding of the agent–patient relations in the transitive construction: cross-linguistic comparisons between Cantonese, German, and English. *Cognitive Linguistics*, 20, 267–300.

Choi, Y., and Trueswell, J.C. (2010) Children's (in)ability to recover from garden-paths in a verb-final language: evidence for developing control in sentence processing. *Journal of Experimental Child Psychology*, 106, 41–61.

Clark, E., and Sengul, C.J. (1978) Strategies in the acquisition of deixis. *Journal of Child Language*, 5, 457–475.

Diessel, H. (2006) Demonstratives, joint attention, and the emergence of grammar. *Cognitive Linguistics*, 17, 463–489.

Dittmar, M., Abbot-Smith, K., Lieven, E., and Tomasello, M. (2008) German children's comprehension of word order and case marking in causative sentences. *Child Development*, 79, 1152–1167.

Gertner, Y., Fisher, C., and Eisengart, J. (2006) Learning words and rules: abstract knowledge of word order in early sentence comprehension. *Psychological Science*, 17, 684–691.

Gervain, J., Nespor, M., Mazuka, R., *et al.* (2008) Bootstrapping word order in prelexical infants: a Japanese–Italian cross-linguistic study. *Cognitive Psychology*, 57, 56–74.

Kamide, Y., Scheepers, C., and Altmann, G.T.M. (2003) Integration of syntactic and semantic information in predictive processing: cross-linguistic evidence from German and English. *Journal of Psycholinguistic Research*, 32, 37–55.

Küntay, A.C., and Özyürek, A. (2006) Learning attentional contrasts in using demonstratives in conversation: what do language-specific strategies in Turkish reveal? *Journal of Child Language*, 33, 303–320.

Küntay, A., and Slobin, D.I. (1996) Listening to a Turkish mother: some puzzles for acquisition. In D.I. Slobin, J. Gerhardt, A. Kyratzis, and J. Guo (eds), *Social interaction, social context, and language: essays in honor of Susan Ervin-Tripp* (pp. 265–286). Mahwah, NJ: Erlbaum.

Levinson, S.C. (2004) Deixis and pragmatics. In L. Horn and G. Ward (eds), *The handbook of pragmatics* (pp. 97–121). Oxford: Blackwell.

Özyürek, A., and Kita, S. (2000) Attention manipulation in the situational use of Turkish and Japanese demonstratives. Paper presented at the Linguistic Society of America Conference, Chicago.

Slobin, D.I. (ed.) (1967) *A field manual for cross-cultural study of the acquisition of communicative competence*. Unpublished manuscript, University of California, Berkeley.

Slobin, D.I. (1997) The universal, the typological, and the particular in acquisition. In D.I. Slobin (ed.), *The crosslinguistic study of language acquisition. Vol. 5: Expanding the contexts* (pp. 1–39). Mahwah, NJ: Erlbaum.

Slobin, D., and Bever, T. (1982) Children use canonical sentence schemas: a crosslinguistic study of word order and inflections. *Cognition*, 12, 229–65.

Snedeker, J., and Trueswell, J.C. (2004) The developing constraints on parsing decisions: the role of lexical-biases and referential scenes in child and adult sentence processing. *Cognitive Psychology*, 49, 238–299.

Stoll, S. (2009) Crosslinguistic approaches to language acquisition. In E. Bavin (ed.), *The handbook of child language* (pp. 89–104). Cambridge: Cambridge University Press.

Stoll, S., Abbot-Smith, K., and Lieven, E. (2009) Lexically restricted utterances in Russian, German and English child directed speech. *Cognitive Science*, 33, 75–103.

Stoll, S., Bickel, B., Lieven, E., *et al.* (in press) Nouns and verbs in Chintang: children's usage and surrounding adult speech. *Journal of Child Language*.

Tardif, T., Gelman, S.A., and Xu, F. (1999) Putting the "noun bias" in context: a comparison of Mandarin and English. *Child Development*, 70, 620–635.

Ural, A.E., Yüret, D., Ketrez, N., *et al.* (2009) Morphological cues vs. number of nominals in learning verb types in Turkish: the syntactic bootstrapping mechanism revisited. *Language and Cognitive Processes*, 24, 1393–1405.

Further Reading and Resources

Berman, R.A., and Slobin, D.I. (1994) *Relating events in narrative: a crosslinguistic developmental study*. Hillsdale, NJ: Erlbaum.

Bowerman, M., and Brown, P. (eds) (2007) *Crosslinguistic perspectives on argument structure: implications for learnability*. Mahwah, NJ: Erlbaum.

Guo, J., Lieven, E., Budwig, N., *et al.* (2009) *Crosslinguistic approaches to the psychology of language: research in the tradition of Dan Isaac Slobin*. New York: Psychology Press.

Slobin, D.I. (1985–95) *The crosslinguistic study of language acquisition* (vols 1–5). Mahwah, NJ: Erlbaum.

Stoll, S. (2009) Crosslinguistic approaches to language acquisition. In E. Bavin (ed.), *The handbook of child language* (pp. 89–104). Cambridge: Cambridge University Press.

20 Studying Children in Bilingual Environments

Erika Hoff and Rosario Luz Rumiche

Summary

This chapter describes methods for assessing the language environments and language development of children exposed to two languages. The focus is on preschool children; the domains of language considered include receptive and productive language, covering phonology, the lexicon, and morphosyntax. Topics comprise (1) sample selection, including procedures for defining the samples to be studied, recruiting participants, and screening children for language impairment; (2) methods for measuring properties of bilingual environments, including caregiver interviews, the language diary, and recording and analysis of caregivers' child-directed speech; and (3) methods for measuring language knowledge in bilingually developing children, including the use of standardized tests, researcher-developed instruments, and the recording and analysis of spontaneous speech. Examples drawn from research are presented.

Research Aims

Reports of research on children who grow up in bilingual environments frequently begin with reference to one or both of the following facts:

1 Half the world's children grow up exposed to more than one language, yet most of the research on language development studies monolingual children (Grosjean, 1988; 2010).
2 The number of children in school who come from bilingual homes is large and growing, and – in the US and elsewhere – these children are statistically at risk

Research Methods in Child Language: A Practical Guide, First Edition.
Edited by Erika Hoff.
© 2012 Blackwell Publishing Ltd. Published 2012 by Blackwell Publishing Ltd.

for school failure (Federal Interagency Forum on Child and Family Statistics, 2002; Scheele, Leseman, and Mayo, 2010; Snow, Burns, and Griffin, 1998).

The lack of scientifically based information about the language development of children exposed to two languages and the concern about the low levels of academic achievement that characterize many groups of bilingual children worldwide underlie two central aims of research on bilingual development. One is the basic science aim of understanding the mental processes involved in bilingual development; the second is the applied aim of understanding the skills and needs of bilingual children in order to support their learning in school.

Within the basic science approach there are multiple questions one can ask. One can think of dual language exposure as a cognitive psychology experiment: what does the brain do given input that comes from two different linguistic systems? Can input from the two systems be distinguished? If so, how? Does the simultaneous acquisition of two languages challenge the language acquisition device, or is the human language acquisition capacity a bilingual (or even multilingual) capacity? When two languages are acquired, either simultaneously or in sequence, does the acquisition of one influence the rate or course of the acquisition of the other? Answers to these questions potentially reveal the nature of the language acquisition process and thus the nature of monolingual development as well. Children exposed to more than one language are also sometimes studied because they typically hear one of their languages more than the other and are more advanced in that language. Thus, bilingually developing children provide a within-subjects test of the effects of input on language development and of language knowledge on other aspects of language processing and growth (e.g., Conboy and Mills, 2006; Hoff *et al.*, in press; Marchman, Fernald, and Hurtado, 2010; Pearson *et al.*, 1997). Last, the ability to account for bilingual development is a test of the adequacy of theories of language acquisition because the correct theory of language acquisition must be able to account for monolingual and bilingual (and even multilingual) development.

Although research on bilingual development is in its infancy, it has already yielded insights regarding the process of language acquisition. For example, two findings from the study of bilingual children address the long-standing and yet continuing debate in the field regarding the degree to which language acquisition depends on language input or is the result of a more experience-independent maturational process. The first finding is that simultaneous bilinguals (or bilingual first language learners) acquire each language at a slower rate than do monolingual children. The second finding is that the rate at which bilingually developing children acquire each language is a function of how much they hear each language. Both these findings support the theoretical position that language acquisition is the result of children's analysis of the primary data provided to them through language exposure (e.g., Bialystok and Feng, 2011; Gathercole and Thomas, 2009; Hoff *et al.*, in press; Pearson *et al.*, 1997; Scheele, Leseman, and Mayo, 2010). Findings that children's ability to store and repeat sound sequences in each language are related to their exposure to each language also suggest that the basic process of phonological memory is itself a result of learning from input (Parra, Hoff, and Core, 2011). The finding that the speed with which bilingually developing children process words in their two languages differs as a function of their exposure to each language also attests to the effect of language exposure – in this case not only on children's acquisition of language knowledge, but also on children's ability to rapidly access what they know as they listen to speech (Conboy and Mills, 2006; Marchman, Fernald, and Hurtado, 2010).

Research with more applied motives has focused on questions such as how to assess bilingually developing children in order to identify those who are language impaired and on identifying factors in early skills that predict later literacy. The problem of assessment arises because there are not good descriptive data on the normative course of bilingual development, making it difficult to identify children who are not developing typically. Achieving a description of normative bilingual development is made difficult by the fact that bilingual children vary in the amount and nature of their language exposure (Genesee, 2006), but some progress has been made (see Gathercole, Thomas, and Hughes, 2008; Thordardottir, 2005; Thordardottir *et al.*, 2006). One topic within the research focused on literacy concerns early predictors of later reading. There is evidence, consistent with findings from monolingual children, that early oral language skills predict later reading (Hammer, Lawrence, and Miccio, 2007) and that reading skills in one language can benefit children's reading development in another language – more so if the languages and writing systems are similar (Oller and Jarmulowicz, 2007).

Other lines of research with bilingually developing children have investigated the effects of learning two languages on nonlinguistic cognitive processes. There is, for example, robust evidence that bilingual children show higher levels of inhibitory control than monolingual children, and research on this phenomenon promises to shed light on the basic processes underlying executive functions (Bialystok, 2009; Bialystok and Feng, 2011). There are also findings in the literature that bilingual children acquire theory of mind understandings at a slightly younger age than monolingual children (Goetz, 2003).

Procedures

Most, if not all, of the methods described in this book can be applied to the study of language development in children who live in bilingual environments. For example, researchers have studied the speech perception and language processing of what Werker has termed "bilingual-to-be" infants using habituation, looking-while-listening, and brain imaging techniques (e.g., Conboy and Mills, 2006; Marchman, Fernald, and Hurtado, 2010; Werker, Weikum, and Yoshida, 2006; Werker, Byers-Heinlein, and Fennell, 2009; and see Fennell, Chapter 1 this volume, Swingley, Chapter 3 this volume, and Kovelman, Chapter 4 this volume). Researchers have analyzed the spontaneous speech and standardized test performance of bilingually developing children (see Bialystok and Feng, 2011; Genesee and Nicoladis, 2007), obtained grammaticality judgments from bilingual children (e.g., Gathercole, 2002a; 2002b; 2002c), and used priming tasks to study language representation in bilinguals (see Vasilyeva, Waterfall, and Gómez, Chapter 11 this volume). The CHILDES database includes speech samples from bilingual children (see Corrigan, Chapter 18 this volume). There are, however, some methodical issues that are particular to the study of bilingually developing children, which we explore here, focusing on the methods we and others have used to study children from infancy to 4 years. Some of what we have learned from our efforts will apply to research with older children, but studying older bilingual children – typically in school settings – has its unique challenges. In particular, subject recruitment and selection are very different when one needs to secure the permission and cooperation of schools. In contrast, research with younger children requires only the permission and cooperation of caregivers – and, of course, the children. Descriptions of large-scale projects that have studied bilingual children in schools include Oller and Eilers (2002) and August and Shanahan (2006).

Defining Bilingual Environments and Bilingual Children

There is no agreed definition of either a bilingual environment or a bilingual child. In some of our research we have defined bilingual environments as those in which children experience two languages in one-to-one conversation and the less frequently heard language constitutes at least 10% of their language exposure. (We do have parents who volunteer their children in response to advertisements recruiting bilingual children because they believe that their children are becoming bilingual by watching bilingual television shows for children. We require that the language exposure be in conversation with the target child.) The logic behind the 10% criterion is that we want to study bilingual development and we suspect that there would not be much language development to measure in cases where children hear less than 10% of their input in that language. Whether children become bilingual when their less frequently heard language constitutes as little as 10% of their input is an empirical question. In our research with 22-month-olds, we have made the argument that they are "bilingually developing" because they produced some words in both languages. Although there is the belief that children need a language to be at least 20% of their input in order for the language to be acquired, there is no clear evidence for that view. The belief seems to have its origins in Pearson *et al.*'s (1997) observation that children who hear less than 20% of their input in one of their languages are reluctant to converse in that language, although these researchers were careful not to claim that the children did not know any of that language. These same children did, however, show that they had learned words in that less frequently heard language, as we have also found in our research (Hoff *et al.*, in press). (Whether that small amount of input is sufficient to sustain bilingual development in the longer run is a different question.) Some studies use a more restrictive criterion, including only children who hear their two languages in approximately equal proportions (see Fennell, Byers-Heinlin, and Werker, 2007; Sebastián-Gallés and Bosch, 2009).

The criterion one adopts in defining the sample needs to be guided by the aim of the research. If the aim is to ask the very interesting cognitive psychology question of what the mind does with input from two different language systems, then one could make an argument for including only children with balanced bilingual input. To take the logic a step further, if the question is what the mind does with dual language input over the course of first four years of life, then one might want to include only children with consistently balanced input over that period. Although adopting such stringent criteria may yield an elegant research design, implementation will quickly run afoul of reality. Very few children have balanced input, and the balance of language exposure changes as family circumstances and compositions change. We have taken the approach of trying to capture the variability in children's bilingual environments (and then studying its consequences) rather than trying to restrict the variability through selection criteria. Even with this inclusive approach, we have to reject some potential participants because they cannot clearly be categorized as bilingual or monolingual by our criteria. For example, the 2½-year-old child whose environment has been a monolingual English environment since the age of 2, but who had a Spanish-speaking nanny (or grandmother, or parent) in the home before then, would not be bilingual because she has no Spanish input, but we would not want to put her in a monolingual control group either because her infant exposure might still affect her language processing.

So far, we have been referring to research on children who have been exposed to two languages from birth – referred to as simultaneous bilinguals or bilingual first language learners (Genesee, 2006). Another variable in the environments of many bilingually developing children is the age at which their environment became bilingual. Children may be first exposed to a second language after infancy because of their own immigration or because they hear only their parents' heritage language until they enter school. These children who are first exposed to a second language at some later point are referred to as sequential bilinguals. There is virtually no research on the effects of the age of first exposure within the birth to 3-year period, and any cutoff point dividing simultaneous from sequential bilinguals is arbitrary. In our ongoing longitudinal research we have included children who hear only Spanish at home on the logic that eventually they are likely to be exposed to some English and we wish to study the effect of age of exposure within the preschool period. There is evidence from the study of internationally adopted children that first exposure to a language after the age of 2 may produce different outcomes than exposure before (Gauthier and Genesee, in press). Also, whether effects of differences in the age of first exposure are observable appears to depend on the measure employed (Abrahamsson and Hyltenstam, 2009) and on the age at which the children are assessed. On some measures, children catch up; on others, less so (Genesee, personal communication). In sum, there is no basis at this point for saying one definition of what constitutes a bilingual environment or a bilingually developing child is right and another wrong. It is important in designing research to realize that there is a decision to be made and that the decision may well have consequences for the findings obtained.

Recruiting Bilingual Participants

If the target population is bilingual, then the recruitment needs to be bilingual. The flyers and advertisements we place are in two languages; the website and the message on the lab telephone are in two languages. All the materials our participants see and our own interview protocol exist in two languages. All of the researchers who contact the participants are fully bilingual, and they follow the participant's lead in the choice of language to use. Because many parents of bilingual children may have limited skill in the community language, recruitment efforts might also appropriately be geared toward monolingual speakers of the minority or heritage language. When the target bilingual population is also a low-income population, extra efforts need to be made to recruit participants. Volunteer populations tend to be more educated and to have a higher income than the average in the population, and in many areas this may exclude most of the bilingual population. An extraordinary and very successful approach to attracting low-income bilingual participants is that taken by Anne Fernald's lab at Stanford University. They have created a satellite research lab in a rented house in a Latino neighborhood. The house also provides space for other services to Latino families, with the result that it is a close and familiar place to which families are much more comfortable going than to the Stanford University campus, high on the hill in Palo Alto.

Screening Bilingual Participants

In studies of basic processes in child language, it is standard to employ some means of excluding children who have a language learning impairment. It is not obvious how to do this with bilingually developing children. Because children exposed to and acquiring two languages have smaller single-language vocabularies than monolingually developing children of the same age and reach grammatical milestones slightly later than monolingually developing children (e.g., Hoff *et al.*, in press), any screening criterion applied equally to monolingual and bilingual children will be more restrictive when applied to bilingual children. That is, if the requirement for inclusion in the study is that the child be at the 10th percentile in at least one language, this requirement asks more of the bilingual child – who must reach the 10th percentile in one language in addition to knowing something in another – than of the monolingual children who need only reach the 10th percentile in one language. For some ages and some instruments, there may be a way around this dilemma (see below). Where a solution is not obvious, it is crucial for researchers to remember as they interpret their findings that their bilingual sample may be a more select group of children than their monolingual sample.

Assessing Bilingual Environments

Bilingual environments vary in more ways than do monolingual environments. In studying children in bilingual environments, merely describing the sample in terms of all the relevant parameters is a challenge. Most obviously, the balance of the two languages is different for different children, and very few have close to equal amounts of exposure to their two languages. Furthermore, even when amount of exposure is similar, other properties of exposure may differ among children and between languages within the same child. The two languages may be quite separated in experience or both languages may be used by the same people, in the same contexts, and even within the same conversation (De Houwer, 2009; Pearson, 2008). Children exposed to two languages may hear one or both of their languages from a restricted number of different people, and children in bilingual environments may hear their languages from both native and nonnative speakers to varying degrees (Fernald, 2006). The two languages may also differ in their functions. For instance, among Moroccan immigrants in The Netherlands, even when the heritage language (Tarifit-Berber) is the dominant language at home, Dutch is the language of home literacy activities. In contrast, among Turkish immigrants in The Netherlands, Turkish is used for home literacy activities (Scheele, Leseman, and Mayo, 2010). The larger social context is an additional parameter on which bilingual environments vary: a child's bilingual environment may reflect a bilingual community (e.g., Belgium or Quebec, Canada), an immigrant community within a larger monolingual community (e.g., the Turkish in the Netherlands; the Chinese in New York City), a community in which there is a widely used home language that differs from the language of commerce and government (e.g., many parts of Africa), or a more unique family circumstance (see De Houwer, 2009, and Pearson, 2008 for multiple examples).

We and others have used, or are using, three different methods to characterize children's bilingual environments: (1) interviews or questionnaires in which an adult family member answers questions about language use in the home; (2) the language diary method, in which the primary caregiver keeps a log of the target child's language experience; and (3) recordings of caregiver–child interactions.

Interviews/questionnaires

We have designed a questionnaire with more than 100 items which we administer in interview with the target child's primary caregiver. Our questionnaire was initially based on one developed and currently used by Virginia Marchman (e.g., Marchman and Martínez-Sussman, 2002), and it has evolved over the course of several studies as we think of more and more properties of children's environments that we wish to capture. We ask caregivers, for example, what languages are spoken in the home (in addition to the Spanish and English that are our focus, there is sometimes a third language spoken, for example, Quechua among natives of Peru). We ask who lives in the household, what their native languages are, who in the household is bilingual, and what percentage of the time they speak English and Spanish to the target child. We also ask for information about the child's language exposure with babysitters, in preschool, or in childcare. We ask what language is spoken in playgroups, church, sports activities, and more. We ask what language is used if there is book reading and how often, and in what language and how much the children watch television. Of course, other questions could also be asked (see, for example, Scheele, Leseman, and Mayo, 2010).

We have felt it necessary to ask these questions in a face-to-face interview in order to be sure the respondent is interpreting the question as we intended it. When we have given parents questionnaires to fill out on their own, some come back only partially completed and some come back with numbers that just do not add up.

When we take the time to ask these questions in interview, we have found that parents' estimates of their children's exposure to Spanish and English are strongly correlated with the amount of Spanish and English exposure later recorded in language diaries (see discussion of the language diary method below). The correlation between the estimated percentage of Spanish exposure and the percentage of diary time blocks with Spanish only was $r = 0.84$; the corresponding correlation for English was $r = 0.71$ ($n = 29$). In contrast, Vihman (personal communication, 2009) has reported that estimates of the balance of language exposure provided by parents in a phone intake interview do not produce reliable results. It takes approximately 20 minutes to conduct the home language environment interview, but we do it in the presence of the child and the time spent is also an investment in getting the child accustomed to the researcher's presence.

The language diary

It is valuable to have a more direct measure of children's language experience as well. The more direct measure provides a basis for validating the caregiver report measures obtained in interview, and it also provides a way to estimate parameters of language experience that participants cannot report on. The language diary is a procedure developed by De Houwer and Bornstein (2003) for their study of French–Dutch bilinguals in Belgium, which we have also used to study Spanish–English bilingual children in South Florida. This method depends on the cooperation and diligence of caregivers who keep a log of their children's language exposure for each day of the week, recorded on one day for each of seven weeks. We provide the caregivers with a spiral-bound book of diary pages with rows for each 30-minute period from 6:00 a.m. to 10:00 p.m. (with space for adding additional waking hours) and columns for indicating the language used during that period (English only, Spanish only, both languages), the people who interacted with the child (e.g., mother, mother and sibling), and the type of activity (e.g., breakfast, bath). We ask the caregivers not to use a testing day as one of the days they record. We call, email, or send a text message to the caregivers the evening before each scheduled recording day as a reminder. We try to schedule our visits so that we can look at the record of the first day shortly after it is recorded to make sure the caregivers understand and follow the instructions.

From the detailed records that caregivers provide in these language diaries, we have calculated measures of the children's relative exposure to English and Spanish (measured as the percentage of 30-minute periods in which the child heard only English or only Spanish), and the children's exposure to mixed input (measured as the number of 30-minute periods in which both English and Spanish were addressed to the child). We have also calculated the number of different speakers who addressed the child in each language and the number of different contexts experienced in each language over the course of seven days. By cross-referencing the diary record with information about household members in the language environment questionnaire we have also calculated the percentage of input in each language that was provided by native speakers of that language. We have found, using language diary data, that not only the amount but also certain properties of language exposure influence language development. In our sample, the number of different speakers who were sources of English and the percentage of English exposure that was provided by native speakers of English were both positive predictors of the children's English language development, over and above the effect of the amount of English exposure (Place and Hoff, in press).

We tried using this same diary method again when the children were 4 years old, and mothers reported that it was too difficult to keep records, largely because they were not with their 4-year-olds all day – as they were with their 25-month-olds. We have developed a brief telephone interview diary procedure as a substitute. This is clearly more subject to error, but we hope that by asking focused questions with well-practiced participants we can obtain reliable data. Following a prearranged schedule, we phone the primary caregiver in the evening of seven different days of the week – usually staggered across seven weeks, but we always make accommodations for individual schedules – and ask the caregiver to report for that day how much time the child spent in primarily English and primarily Spanish environments; how much time was spent reading books and watching television in each language; and who were the people who interacted with the child in each language.

Recording caregiver–child interaction

The interview and diary methods are means of measuring the amount and contexts of children's exposure to each language. In order to address questions of the quality of that exposure, it is necessary to obtain samples of speech in both languages the child hears. To do this we video record 30 minutes of adult–child interaction. We try to do this for both English and Spanish. We ask the families which person is the target child's primary source of each language, and we try to obtain recordings of interaction with each. In many cases, a bilingual mother is the primary source of both languages. Sometimes the only source of English is an older child, in which case we record interaction between the target child and that older sibling, and not all homes have a source of English. In order to obtain samples of both languages, we have recorded interaction on two different days and designated one the Spanish day and the other the English day. We have instructed the adults that today we will speak only in English (or Spanish). We nonetheless hear code switching in our language samples, because that is a property of language use in bilingual homes.

There is no perfect way to capture children's dual language experience. Recording everything the child hears using a system such as Language Environment Analysis (LENA: Lena Foundation, 2009) (see Naigles, Chapter 16 this volume) is obviously best in some ways. However, purchasing the LENA system is beyond the means of many research enterprises, and transcribing everything that LENA records is beyond the means of virtually all. We have decided to try to sample the English and Spanish the child hears for the purpose of measuring the quality of input and to rely on the other methods – self-report and language diary – for estimates of quantity.

Procedures for Assessing Bilingual Competency

Start with the obvious: if a child is learning two languages, then to accurately assess that child's language development requires assessment in both languages. One can move from there to the obvious problem that it may not be so easy to assess a child's competence in languages that the researcher does not speak and for which standardized tests, norms of development, and even proficient speakers who can serve as examiners are difficult to find. We have no solution to these problems (but see Paradis, Emmerzael, and Dunacan, 2010, for discussion and a suggestion). We will focus instead on the topic of how to assess the language competency of bilingual children who are acquiring two languages for which tests, norms, and native examiners are available, using our research on Spanish–English bilinguals to illustrate. We review two types of method: the use of standardized tests and the recording of spontaneous speech samples for later coding and analysis. One issue common to both sorts of procedures is ensuring that the methods are fully tapping the children's abilities in each language. We assess each language on a different day and use only that language to minimize the children's lapsing into their preferred language as we are testing their weaker one. Other researchers have gone even further in separating assessments by using different examiners who are either monolingual or pretend to be so (Páez, Tabors, and López, 2007).

Standardized tests

In our research with Spanish–English bilingually developing children, we have used the following standardized tests for which Spanish and English versions are available – or in one case, a Spanish–English bilingual version.

MacArthur inventories: MacArthur Communicative Development Inventory (Fenson et al., 1993); MacArthur–Bates Inventario del Desarrollo de Habilidades Comunicativas (Jackson-Maldonado et al., 2003). These well-known caregiver report inventories are available not only in English and Spanish but in multiple languages. They have been used with bilingual samples, and validated against spontaneous speech measures for bilingual samples (Marchman and Martínez-Sussman, 2002). We have found them to be excellent measures, with the following caveats: the norms are based on monolingual populations and the reference groups for the Spanish and English norms differ in socioeconomic status, making percentile scores noncomparable across languages. To illustrate, a 30-month-old child who knows 616 words on the English version is at the 65th percentile according to the English monolingual norms; a 30-month-old who knows 616 words on the Spanish versions is at the 80th percentile according to the Spanish monolingual norms. As a result, a bilingual child who knows the same number of words in English and in Spanish will look Spanish dominant if norm-referenced scores are used. Is such a child more advanced in Spanish? Perhaps this question is not a sensible question because we do not know that the normative rates of English and Spanish vocabulary acquisition are the same, but the available norms do not tell us that because the norming samples were not equated for socioeconomic status. With respect to grammar, it is clear that measures are not comparable across languages, but again the noncomparability of the reference groups precludes evaluating whether a child is at the same level relative to monolingual norms in both languages.

Expressive One-Word Picture Vocabulary Test (Brownell, 2000). This test consists of a series of pictures that the child is given to label. It was first developed for English, and subsequently modified and normed for use with Spanish–English bilingual children in the US. The problem with this test, for our research purposes, is that it is not two parallel tests of English and Spanish vocabulary – at least as it was designed. The way it is supposed to be administered to bilingual children is by first establishing which language is the bilingual child's dominant language and then administering the test in that language. If the child does know the word for a picture in her dominant language, she is then asked if she knows the word in the other language. Once the child provides one label in one language she is not asked for it in the other. Thus, this is a test of how many of these items the child has a word for in either language. This testing procedure in which a bilingual child answers in whichever language the child chooses is sometimes referred to as conceptual scoring, and it may be appropriate and very useful for purposes of assessing the child's total knowledge or conceptual understandings. This procedure does not, however, provide assessments of the child's knowledge of English and of Spanish. We use the EOWPVT differently in our research. We administer it entirely in English to assess the child's English, and then we use it entirely in Spanish (on a different day) to assess the child's Spanish. We also had to modify the procedure for establishing a basal because one of the first eight pictures is of a pair of scissors. At least among the bilingual children in our sample, *tijeras* is a later acquired word than its English equivalent *scissors*. Many children who cannot provide the label *tijeras* – and, if the standard procedure were followed, would not be tested for failing to establish a basal – go on to establish much higher basal scores when that item is skipped. We believe we obtain measures of the children's expressive vocabularies in both languages that, while not directly comparable, allow us to examine individual differences within a language.

Peabody Picture Vocabulary Test (PPVT); Test de Vocabulario en Imágenes Peabody (TVIP). These widely used tests of receptive vocabulary have separately normed versions in English and Spanish (see Pan, Chapter 7 this volume). Perhaps because the English version has been recently revised and the Spanish version has not, the stimulus materials for each version are not comparable. The stimuli for the English version are larger and in color, and many of the plates have more detail in the pictures than in the TVIP; the stimuli for the Spanish version are smaller and in black and white, and often contain less detail. We are currently studying the effect of these differences on the vocabulary scores children achieve; we have observed that children who have seen the color pictures of the English version are not particularly interested in the black and white version when it is presented.

Preschool Language Scale–4. This test is designed to provide assessments of children's English and Spanish language development. There are two versions, each normed against a monolingual sample. As with all tests in two languages, there is noncomparability. At many age levels there are items that have no equivalent in the other language. For example, one of the categories at the 2:6 to 2:11 level in the Spanish version is "understands several pronouns (me, mi, tú, tu)." There is no clear counterpart to this in English. Another, related problem is that when the same categories are in the Spanish and English versions, they may appear at different age levels across the two versions. For example, items that are designed to tap children's understanding of part/whole relationships (e.g., *the door of the car*) are in the 2:6 to 2:11 group on the English version, but their equivalents (e.g., *la puerta del carro*) are a 3:0 to 3:11 category on the Spanish version. Thus, a child might be administered the test of understanding part/whole relationships in English but not in Spanish, if that child did not know the pronoun system in Spanish and therefore did not advance to the next age level in testing. In terms of procedure, also, the test was designed for monolingual English- and Spanish-speaking populations. We found that we cannot use the productive part of the test because we cannot control what language a child will use to answer questions. We do not want to assume that a child is incapable of answering in Spanish just because she chooses to answer a question posed in Spanish in English. We use only the auditory comprehension portions of the test, and we administer them in each language (on separate days, in counterbalanced order).

Spontaneous speech samples

The samples of caregiver–child interaction that we record in order to assess properties of children's input also provide a language sample that can be used to assess the many aspects of children's language skills that are not tapped by standardized tests (see Rowe, Chapter 13 this volume). But as with standardized tests, there are unique difficulties in using speech samples either to compare bilingual children's skills in their two languages or to compare children within a language. Ideally, the child is recorded interacting with equivalent speakers of each language, but these do not always exist in a child's family. For some children, the only way to obtain a sample of spontaneous speech in English is in interaction with the examiner. For other children, family members are the child's source of both English and Spanish input, but they may differ in their proficiency of each language. For some children, an older sibling is the source of English input. There is good reason to believe that these differences among conversational partners – in language proficiency, in age, and in their relationship with the child – might affect the children's language use (Hoff, 2010). Other problems with drawing conclusions from spontaneous speech samples of bilingual children have been discussed elsewhere (e.g., Gutiérrez-Clellen *et al.*, 2000).

Data Analyses

As is true for the field of child language more generally, the first studies of young bilinguals frequently used very small samples. The limitations of small samples are particularly problematic when studying heterogeneous populations – which bilingual children certainly are. The heterogeneity of the environments and language skills of bilingual children, combined with the high variability in language skills that is characteristic of typically developing monolingual children, means that multivariate methods and large sample sizes are necessary to have adequately controlled and adequately powered tests of hypotheses. The heterogeneity of bilingual samples also argues for person-centered statistical techniques to identify types of bilingual environments and types of bilingual proficiency, and these too require larger samples than has been typical in the study of bilingual development (Laursen and Hoff, 2006). It is also important to have a control group of monolingual children, if comparisons are to be made, and that control group must match the bilingual sample with respect to SES. Comparison of bilingual children to monolingual norms is an extremely weak way to ask whether bilingually developing children differ from monolingual children.

Reactive Effects of Measurement

In our high-SES sample of Spanish–English bilingual households, virtually all the parents are bilingual themselves. (Note: they were not bilingual first language learners, as their children are, but as adults they are proficient in two languages.) These parents have chosen to expose their children to Spanish even though they could have done otherwise because they would like their children to develop competence in both English and Spanish. They ask us if they are doing the right thing. In our IRB forms we claim that one of the benefits of participating in this research for parents is the appreciation of their children's accomplishments that they will gain, and we clearly see that this is true as parents observe their children being tested. Parents ask us about bilingual development, how to promote it, and whether they are doing the right thing in exposing their children to Spanish. They often hear conflicting advice about the wisdom of their choice, and sometimes their concerns are part of their motivation for participating. We answer to the best of our abilities with appropriate disclaimers about the limits of our knowledge. For example, we say that children can learn two languages but that they need conversational input in both languages to do so. We encourage book reading as a type of interaction and suggest that TV is not the best source of language-advancing input. We tell parents that it is perfectly normal for their child to be behind monolingual children in English, because all our data show that it takes longer to acquire two languages than to acquire one. However, we do not dismiss the difficulty that this lag may pose for the child in school.

Summary

Studying language development in children who are exposed to and acquiring two languages potentially provides unique insights into the processes underlying all language acquisition. Moreover, description of the normative course of language development in bilingual children provides educators, clinicians, and policy makers with the information they need to serve the large and growing population of bilingual children entering school. Bilingual development can be studied using all the methods that are also applied to the study of monolingual development, but there are some challenges unique to the study of bilingual children. Because bilingual language experience can vary on more dimensions than monolingual experience, it is more complicated to characterize the language experience of bilingual children. Because the linguistic knowledge possessed by bilingual children can also vary on multiple dimensions, characterizing their language development is also more complex. This chapter has described the approach we have taken in our research with young Spanish–English bilingual children in trying to meet these challenges. The reader may be frustrated that we have raised issues more than we have provided solutions. Our answer to that anticipated frustration is that the field of childhood bilingualism is relatively new, and there is a great deal of work to be done. That work holds the promise of shedding new light on the mental processes that underlie language acquisition and of contributing to programs and policies that will support successful bilingual development and successful academic outcomes in bilingual children.

Acknowledgments

Preparation of this chapter was supported by grants HD054427 and HD060718 to the first author and HD060718-S1 to the second author from the National Institute of Child Health and Human Development. We thank Cynthia Core, Melissa Señor, and the many members of the Language Development Lab at Florida Atlantic University for their contributions to the work described. We thank Ivelisse Martínez-Beck for her comments on an earlier version of this chapter.

Key Terms

Bilingual first language learners   Another term for children who are simultaneous bilinguals.
Bilingually developing children   Children who are in the process of learning two languages. The point of this term is not to claim that the children will successfully achieve bilingualism.
Sequential bilingualism   Bilingualism in which first exposure to the second language begins sometime after exposure to the first language.
Simultaneous bilingualism   Bilingualism in which the child is exposed to both languages from birth and learns both languages at the same time.

References

Abrahamsson, N., and Hyltenstam, K. (2009) Age of onset and nativelikeness in a second language: listener perception versus linguistic scrutiny. *Language Learning*, 59, 249–305.
August, D., and Shanahan, T. (eds) (2006) *Developing literacy in second-language learners*. Report of the National Literacy Panel on Language-Minority Children and Youth. Mahwah, NJ: Erlbaum.
Bialystok, E. (2009) Bilingualism: the good, the bad, and the indifferent. *Bilingualism: Language and Cognition*, 12, 3–11.

Bialystok, E., and Feng, X. (2011) Language proficiency and its implications for monolingual and bilingual children. In A.Y. Durgunoglu and C. Goldenberg (eds), *Language and literacy development in bilingual settings* (pp. 121–138). New York: Guilford.

Brownell, R. (ed.) (2000) *Expressive One-Word Vocabulary Test* (3rd edn). Novato, CA: Academic Therapy.

Conboy, B.T., and Mills, D.L. (2006) Two languages, one developing brain: event-related potentials to words in bilingual toddlers. *Developmental Science*, 9, F1–F12.

De Houwer, A. (2009) *Bilingual first language acquisition*. Bristol: Multilingual Matters.

De Houwer, A., and Bornstein, M. (2003) Balancing on the tightrope: language use patterns in bilingual families with young children. Presented at the Fourth International Symposium on Bilingualism, Tempe, Arizona, April 30 to May 3.

Federal Interagency Forum on Child and Family Statistics (2002) *American's children: key national indicators of well-being*. Washington, DC: US Government Printing Office.

Fennell, C.T., Byers-Heinlein, K., and Werker, J.F. (2007) Using speech sounds to guide word learning: the case of bilingual infants. *Child Development*, 78, 1510–1525.

Fenson, L., Dale, P.S., Reznick, J.S., *et al.* (1993) *The MacArthur Communicative Development Inventories: user's guide and technical manual*. San Diego: Singular.

Fernald, A. (2006) When infants hear two languages: interpreting research on early speech perception by bilingual children. In P. McCardle and E. Hoff (eds), *Childhood bilingualism: research on infancy through school age* (pp. 30–44). Clevedon, UK: Multilingual Matters.

Gathercole, V.C.M. (2002a) Command of the mass/count distinction in bilingual and monolingual children: an English morphosyntactic distinction. In D.K. Oller and R.E. Eilers (eds), *Language and literacy in bilingual children* (pp. 175–206). Clevedon, UK: Multilingual Matters.

Gathercole, V.C.M. (2002b) Grammatical gender in bilingual and monolingual children: a Spanish morphosyntactic distinction. In D.K. Oller and R.E. Eilers (eds), *Language and literacy in bilingual children* (pp. 207–219). Clevedon, UK: Multilingual Matters.

Gathercole, V.C.M. (2002c) Monolingual and bilingual acquisition: learning different treatments of *that*-trace phenomena in English and Spanish. In D.K. Oller and R.E. Eilers (eds), *Language and literacy in bilingual children* (pp. 220–254). Clevedon, UK: Multilingual Matters.

Gathercole, V.C.M., and Thomas, E.M. (2009) Bilingual first-language development: dominant language takeover, threatened minority language take-up. *Bilingualism: Language and Cognition*, 12 (2), 213–237.

Gathercole, V.C.M., Thomas, E.M., and Hughes, E. (2008) Designing a normed receptive vocabulary test for bilingual population: a model from Welsh. *International Journal of Bilingual Education and Bilingualism*, 11 (6), 678–720.

Gauthier, K., and Genesee, F. (in press) Sequential dual language learning in adopted children from China: a longitudinal study. *Child Development*.

Genesee, F. (2006) Bilingual first language acquisition in perspective. In P. McCardle and E. Hoff (eds), *Childhood bilingualism: research on infancy through school age* (pp. 45–67). Clevedon, UK: Multilingual Matters.

Genesee, F., and Nicoladis, E. (2007) Bilingual first language acquisition. In E. Hoff and M. Shatz (eds), *Blackwell handbook of language development* (pp. 324–342). Chichester, UK: Wiley-Blackwell.

Goetz, P.J. (2003) The effects of bilingualism on theory of mind development. *Bilingualism: Language and Cognition*, 6 (1), 1–15.

Grosjean, F. (1988) Studying bilinguals: methodological and conceptual issues. *Bilingualism: Language and Cognition*, 1, 131–149. Reprinted in F. Grosjean (2008), *Studying bilinguals*. Oxford: Oxford University Press.

Grosjean, F. (2010) *Bilingual: life and reality*. Oxford: Oxford University Press.

Gutiérrez-Clellen, V.F., Restrepo, M.A., Bedore, L., *et al.* (2000) Language sample analysis in Spanish-speaking children: methodological considerations. *Language, Speech, and Hearing Services in Schools*, 31, 88–98.

Hammer, C.S., Lawrence, F.R., and Miccio, A.W. (2007) Bilingual children's language abilities and early reading outcomes in Head Start and kindergarten. *Language, Speech, and Hearing Services in Schools*, 38, 237–248.

Hoff, E. (2010) Context effects on young children's language use: effects of conversational setting and partner. *First Language*, 30, 461–472.

Hoff, E., Core, C., Place, S., *et al.* (in press) Dual language exposure and early bilingual development. *Journal of Child Language*.

Jackson-Maldonado, D., Thal, D.J., Fenson, L., *et al.* (2003) *El inventario del desarrollo de habilidades comunicativas: user's guide and technical manual*. Baltimore: Brookes.

Laursen, B., and Hoff, E. (2006) Person-centered and variable-centered approaches to longitudinal data. *Merrill-Palmer Quarterly*, 52, 377–389.

Lena Foundation (2009) www.lenafoundation.org.

Marchman, V.A., Fernald, A., and Hurtado, N. (2010) How vocabulary size in two languages relates to efficiency in spoken word recognition by young Spanish–English bilinguals. *Journal of Child Language*, 37, 817–840.

Marchman, V.A., and Martínez-Sussmann, C. (2002) Concurrent validity of caregiver/parent report measure of language for children who are learning both English and Spanish. *Journal of Speech, Language, and Hearing Research*, 45, 983–997.

Oller, D.K., and Eilers, R. (eds) (2002) *Language and literacy in bilingual children*. Clevedon, UK: Multilingual Matters.

Oller, D.K., and Jarmulowicz, L. (2007) Language and literacy in bilingual children in the early school years. In E. Hoff and M. Shatz (eds), *Blackwell handbook of language development* (pp. 368–386). Oxford: Blackwell.

Páez, M.M., Tabors, P.O., and López, L.M. (2007) Dual language and literacy development of Spanish-speaking preschool children. *Journal of Applied Developmental Psychology*, 28, 85–102.

Paradis, J., Emmerzael, K., and Sorenson Duncan, T. (2010) Assessment of English language learners: using parent report on first language development. *Journal of Communication Disorders*.

Parra, M., Hoff, E., and Core, C. (2011) Relations among language exposure, phonological memory, and language development in Spanish–English bilingually-developing two-year-olds. *Journal of Experimental Child Psychology*, 108, 113–125.

Pearson, B.Z. (2008) *Raising a bilingual child*. Random House.

Pearson, B.Z., Fernández, S.C., Lewedeg, V., and Oller, D.K. (1997) The relation of input factors to lexical learning by bilingual infants. *Applied Psycholinguistics*, 18, 41–58.

Place, S., and Hoff, E. (in press) Properties of dual language exposure that influence two-year-olds' bilingual proficiency. *Child Development*.

Scheele, A.F., Leseman, P.P.M., and Mayo, A.Y. (2010) The home language environment of monolingual and bilingual children and their language proficiency. *Applied Psycholinguistics*, 31, 117–140.

Sebastián-Gallés, N., and Bosch, L. (2009) Developmental shift in the discrimination of vowel contrasts in bilingual infants: is the distributional account all there is to it? *Developmental Science*, 12, 874–887.

Snow, C.E., Burns, M.S., and Griffin, P. (1998) *Preventing reading difficulties in young children*. Washington, DC: National Academy Press.

Thordardottir, E.T. (2005) Early lexical and syntactic development in Quebec French and English: implications for cross-linguistic and bilingual assessment. *International Journal of Language and Communication Disorders*, 40, 243–278.

Thordardottir, E. (in press). The relationship between bilingual exposure and vocabulary development. *International Journal of Bilingualism*.

Thordardottir, E., Rothenberg, A., Rivard, M.-E., and Naves, R. (2006) Bilingual assessment: can overall proficiency be estimated from separate measurement of two languages? *Journal of Multilingual Communication Disorders*, 4, 1–21.

Werker, J.F., Byers-Heinlein, K., and Fennell, C.T. (2009) Bilingual beginnings to learning words. *Philosophical Transactions B*, 364, 3649–3663.

Werker, J.F., Weikum, W.M., and Yoshida, K.A. (2006) Bilingual speech processing in infants and adults. In P. McCardle and E. Hoff (eds), *Childhood bilingualism: research on infancy through school age* (pp. 1–18). Clevedon, UK: Multilingual Matters.

Further Reading and Resources

Center for Early Care and Education Research – Dual Language Learners. A national research center housed at the Frank Porter Graham Child Development Institute, charged with advancing the capacity of the research field to improve assessment and measurement and examine and improve early care and education practices for children who are dual language learners. http://cecerdll.fpg.unc.edu/.

De Houwer, A. (2009) *Bilingual first language acquisition*. Bristol, UK: Multilingual Matters.

Genesee, F., and Nicoladis, E. (2007) Bilingual first language acquisition. In E. Hoff and M. Shatz (eds), *Blackwell handbook of language development* (pp. 324–342). Chichester, UK: Wiley-Blackwell.

Journal of Applied Psycholinguistics (2007) Special issue devoted to childhood bilingualism.

McCardle, P., and Hoff, E. (2006) *Childhood bilingualism: research on infancy through school age*. Clevedon, UK: Multilingual Matters.

Shatz, M., and Wilkinson, L.C. (eds) (2010) *The education of English language learners*. New York: Guilford.

21 Studying Children with Language Impairment

Karla K. McGregor

Summary

This chapter presents a summary of methods specific to the study of children with language impairment. The first section concerns research meant to describe the nature of childhood language impairment. The importance of selection criteria for recruiting participants with the diagnosis of interest and measures for describing heterogeneity within this participant group are stressed. Appropriate procedures for selecting and matching normally developing comparison groups are reviewed. In the second section, the summary turns to research meant to establish high level, high quality translational data that can serve as a basis for evidence-based practice. The evidence ladder and the guidelines for publishing research at given levels of the ladder are reviewed. In the final section, the summary stresses the importance of including children with language impairments in studies meant to address broad, fundamental questions about human language development. Their inclusion helps to ensure an accurate description of language development, forces completeness in causal accounts, and enables useful tests of these accounts.

The questions posed by those of us who study childhood language impairment overlap extensively with the questions posed by investigators who study normal language development; thus, our methods overlap as well. All of the methods discussed in other chapters of this book have been used in the study of children affected by language impairment. That said, there are some unique reasons to study childhood language impairment and thus, some unique methods as well. As methods are interesting only in so far as they allow us to answer questions, I have organized

Research Methods in Child Language: A Practical Guide, First Edition.
Edited by Erika Hoff.
© 2012 Blackwell Publishing Ltd. Published 2012 by Blackwell Publishing Ltd.

this chapter according to three general questions that we in the subfield ask about language impairment: what is the nature of the problem; what are the best clinical practices for addressing the problem; and what does the problem of language impairment tell us about normal language development?

What Is the Nature of the Problem?

Selection Criteria

Children with language impairments are a heterogeneous population; therefore, in studies of childhood language impairment broadly defined, aggregate results can be misleading and generalizable conclusions can be elusive. The most common way to reduce heterogeneity within the participant sample is to limit enrollment to participants with a given diagnosis. Frequently diagnoses are based in part or full on behavioral profiles of strengths and weaknesses. Therefore, as a first step, tests, samples, and probes are used to establish the behavioral profile and thereby ensure that potential participants present with the diagnosis of interest. Consider two examples. In a 2009 paper, Evans, Saffran, and Robe-Torres identified 6–14-year-olds with specific language impairment on the basis of composite expressive language scores from the Clinical Evaluation of Language Fundamentals–3 (Semel, Wiig, and Secord, 1995) that fell at or below 1.5 standard deviations below the mean for the standardization sample. In their 2007 paper, Eigsti, Bennetto, and Dadlani identified 3–6-year-olds as having autism spectrum disorders on the basis of scores at or higher than 5 and 6, respectively, on the communication and social reciprocity subscales of the Autism Diagnostic Interview–Revised (Lord, Rutter, and Le Couteur, 1994) and the Autism Diagnostic Observation Schedule (Lord *et al.*, 1999) along with parent reports of early delays in development. These are fairly representative examples of selection criteria used to identify specific language impairment and autism spectrum disorders. However, difficult decisions are reflected in these (and any) examples, namely, which standardized tests to administer – ideally ones with excellent psychometric properties that tap the defining features of the impairment of interest (Plante and Vance, 1994) – and which cutoffs to use – ideally those that maximize both sensitivity and specificity (Lahey, 1990).

Whereas these measures assist the investigator in including children with the diagnosis of interest, others are used to exclude children who present with other diagnoses. To return to Evans, Saffran, and Robe-Torres (2009), excluded from participation were children who failed to meet the following: nonverbal IQs of 85 or greater, as measured by the Leiter International Performance Scale (LIPS: Roid and Miller, 1997); normal hearing acuity based on ASHA (1997) guidelines for hearing screening; normal or corrected-to-normal vision; and normal oral and speech motor abilities. The first of these exclusions ruled out low intelligence and the remainder ruled out frank deficits in sensory or motor domains, any of which could also yield deficits in language. In Eigsti, Bennetto, and Dadlani (2007), children were excluded if they fit criteria for other types of spectrum disorders, namely, Asperger syndrome or pervasive developmental disorder not otherwise specified.

Investigators further reduce heterogeneity within their participant groups by limiting enrollment according to a number of other variables. In Evans, Saffran, and Robe-Torres (2009), all children were monolingual English speakers. In Eigsti, Bennetto, and Dadlani (2007), all children in the autism group were verbal, speaking in at least two-word phrases, and fairly high functioning, with mean nonverbal IQ scores in the low average range.

Individual Differences

Despite our best efforts to recruit a homogeneous group of participants, each of whom clearly presented with a given diagnosis of interest, the nature of development in general and developmental impairments in particular is such that participants may still vary greatly one from the other. Investigators often administer additional tests to describe these differences and to subgroup participants. Grouping according to whether expressive language or receptive language or both are affected is one common strategy; grouping according to severity level is another.

Once the experiment itself is completed, investigators often explore individual differences within the results. Some procedures that lend themselves to analysis of individual differences (along with an example article in which that procedure has been applied to the study of individual differences in children's language) include descriptive statistics (Nation *et al.*, 2004); correlation (Gathercole, Adams, and Hitch, 1994); signal detection theory (Mervis and Klein-Tasman, 2004); modified *t*-tests (McGregor, Sheng, and Smith, 2005); maximum likelihood estimation (Evans, Kass, and Viele, 1997); and growth-curve analysis (Hadley and Holt, 2006).

Group Comparisons

The measures discussed heretofore serve to identify a clinical group of interest and to explore variations among individuals within that group. To understand the nature of language impairment, comparison to other groups who, in principle, are just like the affected children but do not present with language impairment, is also necessary. Because developmental impairments, by definition, affect people as they develop, understanding of the impairment is limited without comparison to unaffected people who are in similar stages of development. Via such comparisons, we can begin to tease apart the pieces of the language profile that are attributable to the impairment from those attributable to the immature state. Two comparison groups are most typical: age-mates and IQ-mates.

Age-mates are children with no history or current signs of language impairment (or any other developmental impairment) who are highly similar in chronological age to the children of interest. IQ-mates are children who have no history or current signs of the impairment of interest (e.g., Down syndrome) but who are similar to the affected children of interest in intellectual ability (e.g., nonsyndromic mental retardation). To ensure the similarity of the groups in terms of IQ, they are matched on the basis of their performance on a standardized IQ test. Matching is done on the basis of raw scores if the two groups vary in chronological age or standard scores if they do not. Because of problematic psychometric properties, matching IQ-mates to the affected group of interest on the basis of age-equivalency scores is not recommended (Lahey, 1990; Mervis and Klein-Tasman, 2004).

Age-mates are an appropriate comparison group if the population of interest is unaffected by intellectual deficits (e.g., children with specific language impairment). IQ-mates are an appropriate comparison group otherwise. The logic of the latter is as follows. Consider that children with Down syndrome, for example, have IQs that fall within the mild-to-moderate range of mental retardation; therefore, they are likely to perform significantly lower than age-mates with normal IQs on any measure of language we might administer. If, instead, we compare their language performance to children who have similar levels of mental retardation but who do not have Down syndrome, we can begin to isolate the features of language impairment that are common to Down syndrome from those that are associated with intellectual disabilities more globally defined (see also Abbeduto, Kover, and McDuffie, Chapter 22 this volume).

Whereas age-mates and IQ-mates help us to judge the extent and nature of the language impairment relative to expected developmental attainments, a third sort of comparison group, language-mates, helps us to judge attainments in one aspect of language relative to another. Language-mates, like age-mates, have no history or current signs of impairments but, unlike age-mates, they are very similar to the affected children of interest in some aspect of language development because they are chronologically younger. Some common indices of matching include number of words in the expressive vocabulary, mean length of utterance (MLU), or raw scores on a given standardized test of language. Raw scores are, again, preferable to language-age-equivalency scores. To illustrate the utility of language-mates, consider children with specific language impairment matched to language-mates on the basis of MLU. Given that MLU gives some indication of general morphosyntactic development during the preschool years, one might be surprised to learn that children with specific language impairment typically omit grammatical morphemes at a significantly higher rate than their language-mates matched on the basis of MLU. This frequently replicated finding indicates that, in specific language impairment, the development of grammatical morphology lags behind the development of the morphosyntactic system more generally defined which, in turn, leads to the characterization of specific language impairment as involving "extraordinary limitations in grammatical morphology" (Leonard, 1998, p. 59).

Matching can be pairwise or groupwise. For pairwise matching, an individual is selected for the comparison group because he or she is highly similar to one individual in the affected group. Some decision must be made about the closeness of the match. Take age matching: the tightness of the match required depends on the age range of interest. A 6 month difference in age is an unacceptable match if we are interested in 2-year-olds, as language development is extremely rapid at that age (plus 6 months is equivalent to one-quarter of the total life experience of a 2-year-old!). On the other hand, matching to within 6 months of age if we are interested in 16-year-olds may be acceptable given slower rates of change in language at that age.

For groupwise matching, the goal is that, on the matching variables, the groups are characterized by highly similar means and distributions. Most investigators go on to demonstrate via statistical tests that their groups are very similar. To do so, we typically use a t-test. In the more conventional use of t-tests, we are careful to set a low alpha level, typically $p = 0.05$ or lower, to minimize the risk of a type I error (i.e., concluding that there is a difference when there is none). In this less conventional use our goal is the reverse, i.e., we seek to demonstrate similarity; therefore, the greater risk here is a type II error (i.e., concluding that there is no difference when there is one). To minimize type II error, we must set a high alpha level. Mervis and Robinson (2003) suggest a minimal alpha of 0.50 to conclude that groups are well matched on a given variable. A p-value less than 0.20 is unacceptable and those between 0.20 and 0.50 are ambiguous (Frick, 1995). Mervis and John (2008) provide a convincing demonstration of the importance of setting alpha at 0.50 or higher. When children with Williams syndrome were poorly matched to unaffected peers on the basis of relational vocabulary size, it appeared that they had particular deficits in spatial vocabulary; when groups were adequately matched, $p > 0.50$, this was obviously not the case.

Of course comparisons to age-mates, IQ-mates, or language-mates would be meaningless if potential confounds were not taken into account. Comparison groups must be highly similar to the group of interest in other demographic characteristics known to influence language development and usage. These include, but are not limited to, socioeconomic status, geographic region, gender, and the particular languages and number of languages being learned.

Despite their utility, there are some disadvantages to the use of matched control groups. In the case of language- and IQ-mates, investigators must make a theory-dependent decision as to which measure is relevant for the particular experimental question of interest. This can be difficult. Moreover, investigators typically rely on a single measure collected at a single point in time for matching. The validity of using a single measure, say MLU, as a proxy for assessing development in a complex domain, say syntax, has obvious limits. The validity of measuring at a single point in time is also questionable. This is especially true if the study includes affected children of widely different skills matched to unaffected children of widely different ages; the faulty assumption underlying such practice is that performance is not influenced by development (Tager-Flusberg, 2004). If no significant difference is obtained between the younger unaffected controls and the older affected children, we are often tempted to conclude that the affected children are functioning on a given task at a level commensurate with their language level. However, this conclusion ignores the additional years of experience and development that characterize the affected group, and it ignores the possibility that the null finding reflects independent effects for the presence of the language impairment and for age that are similarly large (Plante *et al.*, 1993).

In response to these limitations, Thomas and colleagues (2009) recommend instead that investigators compare the clinical population of interest to normal controls on the basis of developmental trajectories for the particular experimental task of interest. By collecting either longitudinal or cross-sectional data from controls who range from the youngest level of functioning to the oldest chronological age represented in the affected group, investigators can determine whether the performance of each affected individual fits anywhere on the normal trajectory and whether dissociation between any two measures that is observed for an affected individual is observed for any unaffected individuals. There are a number of advantages to this approach, but paramount among them is that development is appropriately considered. More traditional age-matched comparisons do not allow conclusions about change over time in either the affected or the unaffected groups. This is especially critical given that children with language impairment will follow alternative developmental pathways and these, in large part, shape the profiles of strengths and weaknesses that characterize the impairment (Karmiloff-Smith, 1998).

What Are the Best Clinical Practices for Addressing the Problem?

Whereas nuanced and accurate descriptions of the nature of language impairment across childhood are crucial to our basic understanding, they do not allow any direct conclusions about clinical management of the problem. For this, translational research methods are required. Via such methods we develop an evidence base that will support effective clinical practice, be it prevention, diagnosis, or intervention. Evidence-based practice is a movement that began in medicine but spread to allied health professions and education. The clinician who conducts evidence-based practice makes decisions in light of his or her own clinical expertise and experience, the client's needs and goals, and, importantly, the highest quality scientific evidence available. The investigator, then, is held to the task of producing this quality evidence.

Familiar standards of scientific quality apply; for example, we strive to minimize threats to internal and external validity. However, evidence is also ranked by type of design: designs that yield evidence that is transferable and directly applicable to clinical or educational settings comprise the highest rungs of the evidence ladder. Basic or "bench" research is a very low level of evidence because it is not transferable.

Case studies ($n = 1$) or case series ($n > 1$) with little or no experimental control also constitute a low level of evidence. Single-subject designs invoke excellent experimental controls via alternating or multiple baselines across behaviors and/or participants but, like case studies and case series, they allow for limited generalization because of the small n involved. Case-control studies are comparisons of two groups (e.g., two groups affected by spoken language impairment), one with an outcome of interest (e.g., age-appropriate reading ability) and one without (e.g., poor reading ability). The goal is to determine retrospectively whether the groups varied in the intervention of interest (e.g., reading taught via a phonics approach). In a cohort study, two groups of affected individuals are identified; one receives the intervention and the other does not. The groups are followed and their outcomes compared. These children are not randomly assigned to groups; thus groups can be identified retrospectively (lower) or prospectively (higher). The gold standard of intervention research is the randomized controlled clinical trial. As the name conveys, prospective participants are randomly assigned to an experimental or a control group. These groups are followed and their outcomes are compared to draw conclusions about the effectiveness of the intervention. Ideally these experiments are double blinded, that is the intervention is hidden from the child and parent receiving the intervention, the clinician administering the intervention, and the investigator interpreting the results, but this is an unachievable ideal in some studies of intervention for children with language impairment. When higher levels of evidence are not feasible or not appropriate for the question at hand, replications involving lower level designs are an effective alternative.

Investigators must not only design studies to reflect a given level of evidence but also report their studies in a standardized manner to facilitate the clinician's evaluation and consumption of the results. Journal editors typically require that authors follow the Consolidated Standards for Reporting Trials (CONSORT: Moher, Schulz, and Altman, 2001) when publishing the results of randomized controlled trials. CONSORT includes a 22-item checklist of requirements for the title, abstract, introduction, methods, results, and discussion of the paper. The intention is to help the reader judge the validity, reliability, and relevance of the findings. The guidelines also are of great help to other investigators who wish to include the work in a meta-analysis. Comparable guidelines exist for reporting nonrandomized designs (TREND: des Jarlias *et al.*, 2004) and systematic reviews or meta-analyses (QUOROM: Moher *et al.*, 1999).

It is important to emphasize that a high level of evidence does not necessarily equate to a high quality study. There are examples of poorly executed and well-executed studies at any level of the evidence ladder. Moreover, right-thinking people may disagree with the organization of the evidence ladder. Given the huge amount of variability within a given diagnostic group, one could argue that single-subject designs, wherein the participant is his or her own control, are the only reasonable approach. Single-subject designs are immune to ecological fallacy, that is, to the mistaken assumption that effects at the aggregate level are necessarily representative of effects at the individual level. Such designs also render moot the problems associated with control group comparisons as discussed above.

Single-subject designs sample response to an intervention repeatedly over time within a few participants (Gliner, Morgan, and Harmon, 2000). In the reversal or ABAB version, the participant is observed for the behavior of interest until stability is evident (A), then intervention is introduced (B) and the participant is observed for consequent change in the behavior. Once change asymptotes, the intervention is withdrawn (A) to see whether the behavior diminishes. Once stable, the second course of intervention is introduced (B). The wax and wane of the behavior in response to administration and withdrawal of the intervention is good evidence that the intervention is causing change. In the multiple baselines version, a number of baseline observations are made simultaneously across different participants or across different behaviors within a given participant. Once stable, the intervention is introduced to only one participant, or for the purpose of modifying only one behavior. The other participants/behaviors are continually monitored. If the participant/behavior that is the subject of the intervention changes but the participants/behaviors that remain in baseline do not, there is good evidence that the intervention itself is the cause of the change.

What Does the Problem of Language Impairment Tell Us about Normal Language Development?

Although most would agree that advances in our understanding of childhood language impairments and their clinical management are worthy research goals, fewer may have considered research on childhood language impairment as a means of advancing description and explanation of language development more broadly defined. In this final section, I turn away from childhood language impairment and its clinical management as a focus of study *per se* and toward methods that make use of these impairments as natural experiments for addressing fundamental questions about human language.

"The Average Child is a fiction ..." wrote Bates, Dale, and Thal (1995, p. 26) in a compelling argument for the study of individual differences in language development. As they point out, even if we limit our view to children who are normally developing, growth rates are characterized by enormous variation from child to child, reflecting the interaction of genetic and environmental factors that are at play. Take, for example, the normative data from the MacArthur–Bates Communicative Development Inventories (MCDI: Fenson *et al.*, 2007). At 24 months, the 10th to 99th percentiles equate to a range of 77 to 658 words in the expressive vocabulary. Once we consider children below the 10th percentile, an often-used clinically significant cutoff, we might find children who are producing no words at this age. This variation remains stable across developmental time. Even after controlling for age, gender, birth order, socioeconomic status, and mother's and father's education and occupation, the infant versions of the MCDI scales account for significant variance in the toddler versions (Bates, Dale, and Thal, 1995). Across the school years as well, relative differences between children with and without language impairment are stable (Law, Tomblin, and Zhang, 2008). To be accurate, any description of language development must encompass this variety; to be complete, any causal model must account for individual differences (see also Golinkoff and Hirsh-Pasek, Chapter 5 this volume, for a discussion of individual differences).

Not only does the study of children across the full range of the distribution yield descriptive validity, it enables tests of theoretical accounts of language development. In the preface to her 1994 book on the study of atypical language, Tager-Flusberg emphasizes the value in using developmental language impairment as a natural experiment for investigating factors that influence language development and she traces this approach to Lenneberg (1967). As she notes, normal development involves rapid changes in all domains. Impaired development is more uneven, slower in some domains than others, and therefore it is easier to unravel the developmental relationships (or lack thereof) between domains.

Take as an example one fundamental question: to what extent is the child's syntactic system modular? This question stems from an enduring debate about the possible dimensions of the language system and the extent to which these dimensions involve different mechanisms of acquisition, neural representation, and use. Essential to answering this question is an examination of associations and dissociations between syntax and other language systems.

One approach is to take advantage of extreme cases – children who cluster in the tails of the normal distribution – because in these cases dissociations are more readily apparent than in cases that cluster around the mean. In McGregor, Sheng, and Smith (2005), my colleagues and I recruited toddlers who had precocious lexical development, defined as scores at the 90th percentile or above on the expressive vocabulary portion of the MCDI. The question was whether they would have precocious syntax as well or whether, instead, scores tapping the lexical and syntactic domains would dissociate. In McGregor *et al.* (2010), we recruited older children on the basis of clinically low scores on measures of expressive syntax and asked the converse question: would they have deficits in expressive vocabulary as well or would scores tapping the lexical and syntactic domains dissociate? By selecting children on the basis of extreme scores (extremely high lexical scores in the former case, extremely low syntactic scores in the latter), it should be easier to identify dissociations. However, in both studies we found tight associations between the expressive lexicon and the grammar, whether in younger children or older, and whether in precocious children or impaired. These data complement those based on children within the average range and lend validity to the conclusion that lexical production and syntax are closely linked.

Tomblin and Zhang (2006) addressed the same general question by examining subgroups within a large longitudinal sample of children that included the entire distribution, both children with and without language impairment, and across four points in development: kindergarten, second, fourth, and eighth grades. These children took standardized tests that tapped receptive and expressive vocabulary and syntax (sentences). The investigators asked whether receptive and expressive abilities and lexical and syntactic abilities are distinct dimensions of the language system and, importantly, whether any dimensions change over developmental time. To test for dimensionality, they first applied a modified parallel analysis. This is an exploratory factor analysis (exploratory in that it did not involve any *a priori* assumptions about the model of best fit) performed on individual items from the standardized tests. Essentially it tells whether items tap one or a number of dimensions of language. The result was that the items predominantly tapped a single dimension; however, for the eighth grade sample only, there was some evidence of a difference between vocabulary and syntax. This was followed by a confirmatory factor analysis (confirmatory in that it tested the assumption of a unidimensional vs two-dimensional model) performed on composite scores classified as receptive–expressive or vocabulary–syntax. The result was confirmation that a two-factor model involving vocabulary and syntax was a somewhat better fit than a unidimensional model. Both were good fits for the data in the lower grades; by the eighth grade, however, the two-dimensional model was clearly better. This study is exemplary in that it involved (1) a longitudinal sample that (2) ranged widely in ability from impaired to advanced and that (3) was analyzed with sophisticated statistical methods. The results reveal something very important about language development writ large: neither vocabulary and syntax nor receptive and expressive abilities are independent dimensions of language during the early school years but, by eighth grade, vocabulary and syntax begin to function more independently. This evidence provides crucial support for long-standing hypotheses about the emergence of language modules over the course of development (Karmiloff-Smith, 1998).

Final Thoughts

Although we share many methods with those who study normal language development, those of us who study childhood language impairments make use of special methods for identifying and describing affected children and for determining the best clinical management practices. As our questions become more sophisticated and nuanced, so must our methods. The limitations in describing language impairment at a single point late in development are obvious and the solution – longitudinal studies that follow children from *in utero* – is costly. However, we have the foundational evidence to support requests for such funds. Likewise, if we are to build a sufficient evidence base, we must rise to the challenge of large-scale randomized controlled trials, again a costly endeavor. I think we may be further behind here but, thanks to the evidence-based practice movement, we do have a better understanding of the design of clinical trials and a stronger motivation for conducting them than ever before. Finally, decades of research on childhood language impairment reveal the value of this subfield in informing and testing theories of language development, but only to the extent that investigators use valid methods and make savvy interpretations that recognize the complexities of teasing apart the effects of impairment from the effects of development. I think, given the current state of the art, that we are in an excellent position to do so.

Key Terms

Age-equivalency score   The chronological age in a population of test takers (the norming sample collected by the test developers) for which a given score is the median score. For example, a 4-year-old whose raw score corresponds to an age-equivalent score of 5 years obtained the same score as the median score earned by 5-year-olds in the norming sample. Because age equivalencies do not convey variation within the norming sample, we do not know whether this performance is exceptionally good; in fact, the difference between the median scores for the 4- and 5-year-olds in the norming sample could be quite small.

Asperger syndrome   An autism spectrum disorder characterized by significant difficulties in social interaction as well as restricted and repetitive patterns of behavior and interests. Language and cognition are spared; however, the social use of language is problematic.

Autism spectrum disorder   A range of disorders characterized by social deficits, restricted and repetitive patterns of behavior and interests, and impaired verbal and nonverbal communication. Severity varies from mild to severe across individuals; mental retardation may or may not be present.

Down syndrome   A genetic disorder caused by an extra copy of chromosome 21. People with Down syndrome most typically present with moderate mental retardation but severity will vary from individual to individual. Speech production and expressive language are typically more impaired than receptive language; morphosyntax is often weaker than vocabulary.

External validity The extent to which findings can be generalized from the laboratory to other settings and from the participants in the study to other populations.

Internal validity The extent to which a causal relation between two variables in an experiment is properly demonstrated and the extent to which alternative explanations for the outcome can be dismissed.

Meta-analysis A method wherein the investigator gathers current research published on a given topic and then reanalyzes the data using a common measure of effect size.

Pervasive developmental disorder not otherwise specified A condition in which a person presents with some but not all of the diagnostic features of autism spectrum disorders.

Sensitivity The proportion of affected cases correctly identified by a given test; how well a test avoids false negatives.

Specificity The proportion of unaffected cases correctly identified by a given test; how well a test avoids false positives.

Specific language impairment Primary developmental language impairment. Morphosyntax, text-level grammar, and verbal working memory are areas of relative weakness; pragmatics and phonology are areas of relative strength. These children present with no gross abnormalities in sensory acuity or nonverbal cognition, although subtle problems in these domains are often characteristic.

Standard scores How far above or below a test performance falls relative to the mean earned by the test takers in the norming sample collected by the test developers. The mean is set at 100; a standard deviation is set at 15. Scores that fall from 1 standard deviation below the mean to 1 standard deviation above (i.e., 85–115 points) represent 66% of the norm group; a range ± 2 standard deviations represents 95% of the norm group. For example, if a 4-year-old's raw score converts to a standard score of 115, she performed 1 standard deviation better than the average 4-year-olds in the norming sample.

Systematic review A literature review written by an author who has used explicit methods to perform a thorough search and critical evaluation of individual research studies to identify valid evidence pertaining to a single question of interest.

Translational research The scientific process of translating basic research findings into practical applications for the population or question under study.

Williams syndrome A neurodevelopmental disorder caused by deletions of genes from the long arm of chromosome 7. People with Williams syndrome present with mild to moderate mental retardation. Although initially delayed, language ability is a strength relative to visual-spatial processing.

References

ASHA (1997) Guidelines for audiologic screening. American Speech–Language–Hearing Association. Available from www. asha.org/policy.

Bates, E., Dale, P., and Thal, D. (1995) Individual differences and their implications for theories of language development. In P. Fletcher and B. MacWhinney (eds), *Handbook of child language* (pp. 96–151). Oxford: Blackwell.

Des Jarlais, D.C., Lyles, C., Crepaz, N., and the TREND Group (2004) Improving the reporting quality of nonrandomized evaluations of behavioral and public health interventions: the TREND statement. *American Journal of Public Health*, 94, 361–366.

Eigsti, I.M., Bennetto, L., and Dadlani, M.B. (2007) Beyond pragmatics: morphosyntactic development in autism. *Journal of Autism and Developmental Disorders*, 37, 1007–1023.

Evans, J., Kass, R., and Viele, K. (1997) Response time and verbal complexity: stochastic models of individual differences in children with SLI. *Journal of Speech and Hearing Research*, 40, 754–764.

Evans, J.L., Saffran, J.R., and Robe-Torres, K. (2009) Statistical learning in children with specific language impairment. *Journal of Speech, Language, and Hearing Research*, 52, 321–335.

Fenson, L., Marchman, V.A., Thal, D.J., *et al.* (2007) *MacArthur–Bates Communicative Development Inventories: user's guide and technical* manual (2nd edn). Baltimore: Brookes.

Gathercole, S.E., Adams, A.M., and Hitch, G.J. (1994) Do young children rehearse? An individual-differences analysis. *Memory and Cognition*, 22, 201–207.

Gliner, J.A., Morgan, G.A., and Harmon, R.J. (2000) Single subject designs. *American Academy of Child and Adolescent Psychiatry*, 39, 1327–1329.

Hadley, P.A., and Holt, J.K. (2006) Individual differences in the onset of tense marking: a growth-curve analysis. *Journal of Speech, Language, and Hearing Research*, 49, 984–1000.

Karmiloff-Smith, A. (1998) Development itself is the key to understanding developmental disorders. *Trends in Cognitive Sciences*, 2, 289–298.

Lahey, M. (1990) Who shall be called language disordered? Some reflections and one perspective. *Journal of Speech and Hearing Disorders*, 55, 612–20.

Law, J., Tomblin, J.B., and Zhang, X. (2008) Characterizing the growth trajectories of language impaired children between 7 and 11 years of age. *Journal of Speech, Language, and Hearing Research*, 51, 739–749.

Lenneberg, E. (1967) *Biological foundations of language*. New York: Wiley.

Leonard, L. (1998) *Children with specific language impairment*. Cambridge, MA: MIT Press.

Lord, C., Rutter, M., and Le Couteur, A. (1994) Autism Diagnostic Interview–Revised: a revised version of a diagnostic interview for caregivers of individuals with possible pervasive developmental disorders. *Journal of Autism and Developmental Disorders*, 24, 659–685.

Lord, C., Rutter, M., DiLavore, P.C., and Risi, S. (1999) *Autism Diagnostic Observation Schedule–WPS (ADOS–WPS)*. Los Angeles: Western Psychological Services.

McGregor, K.K., Berns, A.J., Owen, A.J., *et al.* (2011) Associations between syntax and the lexicon among children with or without ASD and language impairment. *Journal of Autism and Developmental Disorders*. DOI 10.1007/s10803-011-1210-4.

McGregor, K., Sheng, L., and Smith, B. (2005) The precocious two-year-old: status of the lexicon and links to the grammar. *Journal of Child Language*, 32, 563–585.

Mervis, C.B., and John, A.E. (2008) Vocabulary abilities of children with Williams syndrome: strengths, weaknesses, and relation to visuospatial construction ability. *Journal of Speech, Language, and Hearing Research*, 51, 967–982.

Mervis, C.B., and Klein-Tasman, B.P. (2004) Methodological issues in group-matching designs: α levels for control variable comparisons and measurement characteristics of control and target variables. *Journal of Autism and Developmental Disorders*, 34, 7–17.

Mervis, C.B., and Robinson, B.F. (2003) Methodological issues in cross-group comparisons of language and/or cognitive development. In Y. Levy and J. Schaeffer (eds), *Language competence across populations: toward a definition of specific language impairment* (pp. 233–258). Mahwah, NJ: Erlbaum.

Moher, D., Cook, D.J., Eastwood, S., *et al.* (1999) Improving the quality of reports of meta-analyses of randomized controlled trials: the QUOROM statement. *Lancet*, 354, 1896–1900.

Moher, D., Schulz, K.F., and Altman, D.G. (2001) The CONSORT statement: revised recommendations for improving the quality of reports of parallel group randomized trials. *BMC Medical Research Methodology*, 1. http://www.biomedcentral.com/1471-2288/1/2.

Nation, K., Clarke, P., Marshall, C.M., and Durand, M. (2004) Hidden language impairments in children: parallels between poor reading comprehension and specific language impairment? *Journal of Speech, Language, and Hearing Research*, 47, 199–211.

Plante, E., Swisher, L., Kiernan, B., and Restrepo, M.A. (1993) Language matches: illuminating or confounding? *Journal of Speech and Hearing Research*, 36, 772–776.

Plante, E., and Vance, R. (1994) Selection of preschool language tests: a data-based approach. *Language, Speech, and Hearing Services in Schools*, 25, 15–24.Frick, R.W. (1995) Accepting the null hypothesis. *Memory and Cognition*, 23, 132–138.

Roid, G., and Miller, L. (1997) *Leiter International Performance Scale–Revised*. Wood Dale, IL: Stoelting.

Semel, E., Wiig, E., and Secord, W. (1995) *Clinical Evaluation of Language Fundamentals–3*. San Antonio, TX: Psychological Corporation.

Tager-Flusberg, H. (ed.) (1994) *Constraints on language acquisition: studies of atypical children*. Hillsdale, NJ: Erlbaum.

Tager-Flusberg, H. (2004) Strategies for conducting research on language in autism. *Journal of Autism and Developmental Disorders*, 34, 75–80.

Thomas, M.S.C., Annaz, D., Ansari, D., *et al.* (2009) Using developmental trajectories to understand developmental disorders. *Journal of Speech, Language, and Hearing Research*, 52, 336–358.

Tomblin, J.B., and Zhang, X. (2006) The dimensionality of language ability in school-age children. *Journal of Speech, Language, and Hearing Research*, 49, 1193–1208.

Further Reading and Resources

Guidelines for selecting and administering standardized tests, collecting language samples, and developing nonstandard probes to elicit language appear in:
Paul, R., and Norbury, C. (2007) *Language disorders from infancy through adolescence: assessment and intervention* (3rd edn). Philadelphia: Elsevier Health Sciences.

For more discussion on the value of assessing individual and group differences see:
Lubinski, D. (2000) Scientific and social significance of assessing individual differences: "Sinking shafts at a few critical points." *Annual Review of Psychology*, 51, 405–444.

Detailed steps for construction and analysis of developmental trajectories appear in:
Thomas, M.S.C., Annaz, D., Ansari, D., *et al.* (2009) Using developmental trajectories to understand developmental disorders. *Journal of Speech, Language, and Hearing Research*, 52, 336–358.

Guidance on the design of single-subject experiments appears in:
McReynolds, L.V., and Thompson, C.K. (1986) Flexibility of single-subject experimental designs. Part I: Review of the basics of single-subject designs. *Journal of Speech and Hearing Disorders*, 51, 194–203.

Kearns, K.P. (1986) Flexibility of single-subject experimental designs. Part II: Design selection and arrangement of experimental phases. *Journal of Speech and Hearing Disorders*, 51, 204–213.

Excellent resources for teaching and learning about evidence-based practice can be accessed from the Dartmouth Biomedical Libraries at:
http://www.dartmouth.edu/~library/biomed/guides/research/ebm-teach.html.

22 Studying the Language Development of Children with Intellectual Disabilities

Leonard Abbeduto, Sara T. Kover, and Andrea McDuffie

Summary

In this chapter, we focus on methods for assessing language in individuals with intellectual disabilities. The Centers for Disease Control estimates that 1 in 83 school-age children in the United States meet criteria for an intellectual disability, and virtually all of these children have significant problems with acquiring and using language. Research on language and intellectual disabilities is focused largely on questions about variations in language development relative to other domains of the individual's functioning (e.g., nonverbal cognition), across different components of language, as a function of differences in etiology of the intellectual disability, and relative to differences in experience. We outline the special challenges in measuring language in individuals with intellectual disabilities and describe some of the methods we have developed to deal with these challenges. These methods include standardized protocols for collecting expressive language samples, laboratory-based analogs of various dimensions of social interaction, and procedures for measuring the dynamic processes of language learning and use. These methods are motivated by the goal of stripping away the types of social scaffolding and nonlinguistic factors that shape language in naturalistic contexts and make it difficult to unambiguously characterize the language strengths and weaknesses of individuals with intellectual disabilities.

Research Methods in Child Language: A Practical Guide, First Edition.
Edited by Erika Hoff.
© 2012 Blackwell Publishing Ltd. Published 2012 by Blackwell Publishing Ltd.

Intellectual disability is defined by (1) impairments in cognitive functioning (typically defined as an IQ two or more standard deviations below the mean for the population), (2) limitations in the ability to function independently and meet the demands of daily life, and (3) an onset before the age of 18 years (AAID, 2010). The Centers for Disease Control (CDC) estimates that 1 in 83 school-age children in the United States meet criteria for an intellectual disability (http://www.cdc.gov/ncbddd/dd/mr3.htm). Until quite recently, the causes of most cases of intellectual disability were unknown. Recent advances in genetics, particularly molecular genetics, however, have led to the identification of close to 1000 genetic conditions producing intellectual disability (Dykens, Hodapp, and Finucane, 2000). In light of the connections between language and cognition that characterize development, it is not surprising that intellectual disabilities are almost invariably associated with significant language impairments (Abbeduto *et al.*, 2006a). Nevertheless, interesting questions remain about the nature, extent, correlates, and causes of language impairments in this population, as well as about variations in those impairments, especially in relation to differences in etiology.

Questions Motivating Research on Language Development and Intellectual Disabilities

Although the relationship between language and cognition has been hotly debated for decades, the bulk of the empirical evidence to date supports the claim that the learning mechanisms that drive language development cannot be entirely specific to the processing of linguistic information (e.g., Saffran, 2002). Moreover, there is considerable evidence that social interactions with caregivers motivate and provide a context for many facets of language development, from sounds to syntax (e.g., Tomasello, 1999). Children with intellectual disabilities have impairments that, by definition, extend to numerous aspects of the human cognitive system. In addition, this group of children experiences nonnormative linguistic and social environments (Abbeduto *et al.*, 2006a). Thus, there is little doubt that, on average, their language development will be impaired and, perhaps, different in important respects relative to same-age typical peers.

At the same time, however, the interrelationships between language and cognitive development and experience are quite complex, nuanced, and dynamic across the life course (Abbeduto *et al.*, 2006a). Moreover, there is substantial variation among children with intellectual disabilities in the degree of their cognitive impairments and in the quality of the environments in which they hear and practice language (Abbeduto *et al.*, 2006a). In addition, etiological differences are associated with different profiles of cognitive impairments (and comorbid challenging behaviors and conditions), as well as with differences in the affected children's experiences of the world. For example, children with Down syndrome have impairments in auditory working memory that are more pronounced than are those in spatial working memory (at least early in development), whereas children with fragile X syndrome, a single-gene disorder and the leading inherited cause of intellectual disabilities, display relatively more synchrony between their auditory and spatial memory delays (Dykens, Hodapp, and Finucane, 2000). Such etiology-related differences might lead to differences in the extent and nature of language impairments.

In summary, there is seldom reason to ask whether language is impaired in children with intellectual disabilities; it almost certainly will be. However, the following are all fruitful questions to be addressed through empirical research:

1   Are language impairments or delays more or less serious than those in other domains of psychological or behavioral functioning? Perhaps the most high profile line of research addressing this question has been focused on Williams syndrome. This syndrome was originally put forth as providing evidence of modularity because affected individuals were thought to have largely age-appropriate language despite severe intellectual disability, although more recent findings have refuted these early claims (Mervis, 2009).

2   Are impairments or delays variable across different components or dimensions of language? There is evidence, for example, that lexical development either keeps pace with, or is in advance of, nonverbal cognitive development in individuals with Down syndrome, whereas syntax, especially expressive syntax, is delayed relative to lexical development and nonverbal cognition in these individuals (Martin *et al.*, 2009).

3   Are there etiology-related differences in the profile of language impairments or patterns of language development? In our research, for example, we have found that limitations in many areas of syntax are more pronounced in individuals with Down syndrome than in age- and cognitive-ability-matched individuals with fragile X syndrome (e.g., Finestack and Abbeduto, 2010). Answers to this question are useful in generating hypotheses about causal factors, including at the genetic level, in language development and disorders.

4   What are the concurrent and predictive relationships between linguistic and nonlinguistic development for individuals with intellectual disabilities? In the case of Down syndrome, for example, receptive syntax levels have been found to be related to hearing status and auditory memory, but not visual-spatial memory (Miolo, Chapman, and Sindberg, 2005). Although largely correlational in nature, research addressing this question can lead to the identification of the specific psychological and behavioral causes of language impairments in individuals with intellectual disabilities.

5   What aspects of the environment promote or hinder language development in individuals with intellectual disabilities? Although we think of the cognitive impairments that define intellectual disabilities and other attributes of the affected child as primary in producing language impairments, there is considerable evidence that environmental factors, such as parental responsiveness, can have profound effects on the language outcomes of children with intellectual disabilities. Maternal responsivity, for example, predicts later language outcomes for children with fragile X syndrome (Warren *et al.*, 2010).

Challenges in Studying Language Development and Intellectual Disabilities: Implications for Methods

Answering any of the questions outlined in the preceding section presupposes that one has a method for measuring the linguistic construct of interest and that group differences or age- or developmental-level-related changes in the measure reflect variations in that construct. In this section, we consider a number of challenges in developing such methods.

One challenge is that an individual's performance on any measure is likely to reflect not only his or her linguistic ability, but also the influence of his or her capabilities and tendencies in other domains that are of little or no interest to the researcher (or clinician). Suppose, for example, that the goal is to determine whether a child can understand the syntax of a passive sentence (e.g., *The bird is chased by the frog*). One approach would be to ask the child to point to the drawing that matches the sentence in the case in which there are two drawings, one depicting a frog chasing a bird and the other a bird chasing a frog. If the child points to the incorrect drawing, is it because he or she has not yet mastered the passive construction? Or is it because the child has a hearing loss, was inattentive when the examiner spoke the sentence, was unable to inhibit responding before "being sure," has a visual impairment that makes discrimination of the relevant details of the drawings difficult, or was unable to remember the sentence for the length of time needed to scan the drawings?

Of course, the problem of measurement error is also faced by researchers studying language development in typical children. The problem might be more complicated in the case of intellectual disability, however, because addressing the research question of interest often involves comparisons to typical children matched on one or more measures of cognitive ability (e.g., mental age) or comparisons among matched groups of individuals with different types of intellectual disability (e.g., Down syndrome vs Williams syndrome). Despite matching, these groups often differ on many other aspects of their functioning and these differences might affect their performance on the language measure of interest. So, for example, matching individuals with Down syndrome and Williams syndrome on a measure of auditory memory will lead to a mismatch on visual-spatial memory (with the latter being more impaired on average for individuals with Williams syndrome). If the language measure taps visual-spatial ability in any way, then group differences on the language measure might reflect "true" language differences, "irrelevant" differences in visual spatial ability, or both (see also McGregor, Chapter 21 this volume, for a discussion of matching).

A second challenge to studying language in children with intellectual disabilities arises from the social nature of virtually any task or test used to measure language. Consequently, the performance of the child with an intellectual disability can be influenced by the characteristics or behavior of the other person(s) involved in the interaction. If expressive syntax is being assessed via language samples collected during free play with an examiner, for example, the extent to which the examiner asks yes–no rather than open-ended questions can affect conclusions about the child's skill: a high rate of yes–no questions leads, not surprisingly, to a high rate of yes and no answers and thus a lower mean length of utterance (MLU) and a lower frequency of complex sentences than would be obtained if the examiner asked open-ended questions. As another example, suppose turn-taking or topic-continuation ability is assessed in free play with a parent. Because many parents are likely to adjust their behavior to their child's, it might appear that the child is quite skilled at turn taking (e.g., few overlapping turns) or topic continuation (e.g., a large number of consecutive speaking turns maintaining the same topic); however, these numbers might reflect more about the parent's ability to read the child's signals and to scaffold the child's communication. Put differently, the child might look considerably less skilled if interacting with a peer or unfamiliar adult, who is less inclined or skilled at "masking" the child's limited turn-taking and topic-continuation skills.

A third challenge to developing methods for studying language in individuals with intellectual disabilities involves moving beyond a single measure of language ability to measures that focus on the specific dimensions or aspects of language of interest to the researcher (or clinician). Indeed, research to date has made clear that language is not a unitary ability and that language can "come apart" in different ways so that some parts may be more impaired or delayed than other parts. Syntax, for example, is more impaired than vocabulary, on average, in individuals with Down syndrome (Martin *et al.*, 2009). But even discriminating between the broad components of language may not be sufficient; for example, there are syndrome-related differences as to which aspects of pragmatics are most challenging (Abbeduto *et al.*, 2006b).

Moving beyond a single measure of ability, however, is difficult for two reasons. First, although there are many standardized tests of language ability that have the advantage of allowing comparisons to a normative sample, having well-documented test–retest properties, etc., they often yield only relatively gross summary scores (e.g., a receptive language standard score) that aggregate over multiple dimensions of language that can mask interesting variations. Second, and more importantly, research on language challenges in individuals with intellectual disabilities is often highly inductive rather than hypothesis driven. Consequently, there is a tendency to rely on measures that embody rather "traditional" distinctions between different aspects of language (e.g., between vocabulary and syntax or between receptive and expressive language) rather than those that are informed by hypotheses about the nature of the underlying learning or processing deficits that characterize the individuals in question.

Our laboratory has employed a variety of methods for dealing with these challenges to measuring language delays and impairments in individuals with intellectual disabilities. In the following sections, we briefly present a few of these methods.

Methods for Measuring Language

Language Sampling

The analysis of spontaneous language samples, particularly in comparison to standardized assessments, is especially useful for studying language development in children with intellectual disability. First, whereas a standardized test might yield a single omnibus score for expressive language ability, samples of spontaneous language provide rich data with the opportunity to extract an array of variables that reflect specific domains of ability. Aspects of language production such as MLU, intelligibility, lexical diversity, use of grammatical morphemes, and syntactic complexity are easily accessible from transcribed language samples, as are pragmatic aspects of language use, such as repetitive language and contingent turn taking. Second, a language sampling protocol can be readily adapted to any age or developmental level, thereby avoiding the floor effects so often associated with standardized tests, which make it difficult to identify potentially important differences among individuals with intellectual disabilities at lower ability levels. Third, language sample analysis is a contextualized and culturally sensitive method of language assessment that might provide a more accurate estimate of communicative language ability, in particular for children who are challenged by the demands of social interaction. Thus, comparisons of spontaneous spoken language performance across individuals or groups can address a range of research questions about relative patterns of strength and weakness, over a wide range of ages and ability levels, and with good generalizability to everyday communicative contexts.

Contexts for language sampling

As described above, the characteristics and behavior of the conversational partner interacting with the individual with intellectual disability and the variability in the resulting interactions can pose a challenge to research. In spontaneous language sampling, however, important dimensions of the social interaction can be controlled or manipulated in such a way as to answer theoretically and practically relevant questions. For example, language sampling contexts vary in the extent to which they elicit maximum performance in different aspects of language ability (Southwood and Russell, 2004). Interview-style conversations draw more utterances and utterances with higher MLU relative to free play (Southwood and Russell, 2004). In our research, we have demonstrated that children and adolescents with intellectual disability of mixed etiology produce more communication attempts per minute in a conversational context than in narration, whereas the language produced in the narrative context is likely to have a higher MLU than in conversation (Abbeduto *et al.*, 1995). Thus, the language sampling protocol can be constructed to isolate the aspects of language ability of interest or to examine the impacts of the characteristics of the sampling context on language ability.

We have also found that arriving at a more comprehensive picture of language abilities can be accomplished through the use of both interview-style conversation and narration from a wordless picture book. In particular, adolescent and young adult males with fragile X syndrome only, those with comorbid fragile X syndrome and autism, and those with Down syndrome display higher MLU in narration than conversation, but higher lexical diversity, dysfluency, and rate of talk in conversation than in narration (Kover and Abbeduto, 2010). Although the presence and content of the storybook provides helpful visual scaffolding, these same features also constrain lexical diversity in narration. Increased dysfluency and rate of talk in conversation are likely attributable to the reduced structure relative to narration. Thus, utilizing multiple language sampling contexts is vital for understanding profiles of abilities in individuals with intellectual disabilities.

Standardizing language sample elicitation

Although language sampling is a flexible methodology, procedures for language sample elicitation must be standardized to the extent possible to make valid comparisons between language sampling contexts or etiological groups. Characteristics of the sampling context (e.g., the conversational partner, the extent of prompting or structure, the book in narration or toys in free play) can affect the language produced by children, and thus variations in materials and experimenter behavior can hinder interpretation of findings (Southwood and Russell, 2004). Even the amount of talk and rate of questioning by a conversational partner can influence the amount of child talk and MLU (Johnston *et al.*, 1993). Thus, a failure to standardize the sampling context makes it difficult to interpret differences across individuals, disorders, and studies because participant ability and sampling conditions are confounded.

Using standardized sampling contexts, several researchers have documented differential effects of context across groups and group differences in the face of the same task demands. For example, Miles, Chapman, and Sindberg (2006) found that adolescents with Down syndrome achieved a higher MLU in a narrative task compared to an interview-style conversation, whereas typically developing children matched on receptive language ability did not differ between contexts, which suggests that nonlinguistic task demands might be especially important for individuals with Down syndrome. In our research, we found that adolescents with fragile X syndrome used fewer types of narrative evaluation, but were more grammatically correct, than adolescents with Down syndrome matched on nonverbal cognitive ability; however, group differences were not present for number of utterances, MLU, or number of different word roots (Keller-Bell and Abbeduto, 2007). By standardizing the collection of language samples, linguistic phenotypes can be further refined and etiology-specific intervention targets identified.

Summary

Language sampling can be quite useful when conducted in a constrained manner, with a constant set of materials, and in a scripted, yet naturalistic, manner by trained examiners or clinicians. A limitation of language sample analysis is the resource-intensive nature of the work, in terms of the time required both to administer spontaneous language sampling protocols and to transcribe the resultant sample. Although assessment time cannot be circumvented, transcription is facilitated by software programs such as Systematic Analysis of Language Transcripts (SALT: Miller and Iglesias, 2006), which generate analyses automatically and can accommodate coding systems beyond the standard output (see also Rowe, Chapter 13 this volume).

Laboratory-Based Analogs of Social Interaction

As discussed in the previous section, standardized language sampling offers a solution to several of the challenges faced by researchers interested in assessing language in individuals with intellectual disabilities. By requiring that the participant's communicative partner is an adult "confederate" who behaves in standardized or scripted ways and focuses on predetermined and standardized topics and materials, many aspects of language performance can be measured and attributed to the child's language skills rather than, for example, the scaffolding provided by a highly skilled partner. Often, however, language sampling is not sufficient to address the question of interest. The researcher may be interested in an aspect of language expression that occurs too infrequently to be assessed in a brief language sample, or it may be difficult to create the conditions that allow the full depth of the child's mastery (or lack of mastery) of the skill of interest to be assessed in a standardized, yet relatively naturalistic, language sampling context.

These limitations of language sampling procedures have led us to also use lab-based analog tasks. Although different from naturalistic linguistic interactions in many respects, these tasks nonetheless mimic the relevant aspects of those interactions and "pull" for the language behaviors and skills of interest. We have used such analog tasks to study several important pragmatic skills across a number of populations and age ranges. Here we describe two such tasks.

Producing referential descriptions

In a recent study, we used an analog task to examine the skills required to make clear the referents of one's talk when in the role of speaker (Abbeduto *et al.*, 2006b). There is considerable evidence that this is a domain of substantial impairment in individuals with intellectual disability (e.g., Brownell and Whiteley, 1992); however, our interest was in the possibility of syndrome-related variations in the extent and profile of impairments. In our task, the participant assumed the role of speaker, and a researcher, whose behavior was highly scripted, played the role of listener. The two partners were separated by an opaque partition, which required that the participants use only verbal means of communication. The participant and listener each had an identical set of four novel shapes. The participant's task on each trial was to describe a shape (i.e., target) so that the listener could select that shape from his or her set. The shapes were abstract geometric forms that had no universally agreed upon label. On some trials, the listener feigned noncomprehension, thereby highlighting the need for the participant to create descriptions that disambiguated the target for the listener. Each shape recurred several times across trials, although not necessarily on consecutive trials. Thus, this task was analogous to a conversation in which the participant would be providing information about several related topics that he or she had experienced, but that the listener had not.

We conducted several analyses of the talk that the participants generated during the task and found different pragmatic profiles for adolescents and young adults with fragile X syndrome and those with Down syndrome. Both groups were less likely than were younger, nonverbal mental-age-matched typically developing children to create unique (i.e., one-to-one) mappings between their descriptions and the shapes (e.g., referring to a specific shape as "house" every time it appeared). Instead, the syndrome groups were more likely to extend the same description to multiple shapes (e.g., referring to two different shapes as "house"), thereby failing to conform to a fundamental tenet of conversation (i.e., distinguish the referents for your listener).

Although there were no differences between the two syndrome groups in the use of unique mappings, they differed in other aspects of their performance in the task. The participants with fragile X syndrome were less likely than either those with Down syndrome or those with typical development to use consistent descriptions across recurrences of a given shape. Instead, the participants with fragile X syndrome were more likely to use a new description each time the shape was talked about (e.g., referring to a shape as "house" on one trial and then calling it "piano" on a subsequent trial). Such inconsistency violates expectations established previously in the interaction, thereby increasing the listener's processing burden. In contrast, the participants with Down syndrome were less likely than either the youth with fragile X syndrome or the typically developing children to use referential frames (e.g., "it's like house" or "it's kind of an ice cream cone"). Instead, the youth with Down syndrome tended to provide a description without the scaffolding of a referential frame (e.g., "it's a house" or "it's an ice cream cone") to assist their listener's processing. In short, the youth with fragile X syndrome and the youth with Down syndrome each created problems for their listeners, but because of different pragmatic deficits.

Identifying and correcting comprehension problems

We also used an analog task to study noncomprehension signaling by adolescents and young adults with fragile X or Down syndrome and nonverbal mental-age-matched typically developing children (Abbeduto *et al.*, 2008). Again, previous research had shown noncomprehension signaling to be an area of substantial impairment for individuals with intellectual disabilities (e.g., Fujiki and Brinton, 1993), but our interest was in the possibility of syndrome-related differences in the impairment. Such signaling requires monitoring one's understanding of incoming messages, identifying messages that are not understood, determining the reason for the comprehension problem, and formulating a linguistic signal that will elicit the information needed for clarification (e.g., *which toy?*). Failure to signal noncomprehension can seriously disrupt an interaction, especially because early misunderstandings will have a "snowball" effect as the interaction progresses.

We used a task in which the participant was the listener and responded to simple directions from an examiner by moving one of several potential referents into a scene in a book. Many of the directions were clear and unambiguous; however, about 60% were designed to create noncomprehension. Three types of problematic directions were created. In incompatible directions, the examiner requested an action on an absent referent (e.g., "Put the red lamp on the desk" when the available referents were a yellow lamp and a green lamp). In novel directions, the examiner used an unfamiliar word for the referent (e.g., "Put the azure balloon in the sky" when the referents were a blue balloon and a red balloon). In ambiguous directions, there were multiple exemplars of the referent's category (e.g., "Put the hat on the man" when the referents were a brown hat and a gray hat). Thus, this laboratory task is analogous to a range of social interactions involving direction following, but while providing a more concentrated "dose" of comprehension problems to ensure that there was a sufficient number of opportunities for assessing noncomprehension signaling.

All three groups did quite well on the unambiguous messages, responding with an action on the correct referent and without signaling noncomprehension; however, the two syndrome groups were less likely to signal noncomprehension of problematic messages than were typically developing comparison children. The relative difficulty of the different problem types, however, was similar across the three participant groups: noncomprehension signals were more likely, and diagnostic group differences were less pronounced, for incompatible directions than for ambiguous or novel directions. These results suggest that the development of one or more of the behaviors entailed in noncomprehension signaling is severely delayed in individuals with fragile X syndrome or Down syndrome. Nevertheless, development in this domain is not qualitatively different from that seen in typically developing individuals.

Summary

As illustrated by these two studies, aspects of language development that would be difficult, if not impossible, to assess in naturally occurring interactions or even with standardized language sampling tasks can be assessed by creating analogs of the components of language use of interest. Such tasks strip away those aspects of real social interaction that interfere with the measurement of the aspects of language development of interest and create concentrated opportunities for the participant to demonstrate the language behaviors of interest. Nevertheless, the generalizability of the findings from such tasks to naturally occurring interactions remains an open question.

Real-Time Measures of Language Learning and Processes

In the previous sections, we have described several methods for measuring language development in individuals with intellectual disabilities. These methods provide valuable information about an individual's level of language skill or, put differently, the progress he or she has made in accumulating the elements and behaviors that make up language competence. These measures do not, however, provide information about the dynamic processes that characterize the ways in which that individual has acquired those elements and behaviors. Information about the ways in which individuals with intellectual disabilities learn language would be particularly useful for planning interventions, allowing us not simply to target what information or behaviors the individual needs to learn but to facilitate more effective ways of learning language. We now turn briefly to two types of methods we have begun to employ to gain insights into the learning processes of individuals with intellectual disabilities.

Fast mapping

The term "fast mapping" was first introduced by Carey and Bartlett (1978) in a classic study of word learning in preschool-aged children. Broadly speaking, fast mapping describes an associative learning process by which children are able to rapidly infer a correspondence between a novel label and a speaker's intended referent. According to Rice, Buhr, and Nemeth (1990), the experimental fast-mapping paradigm provides a conservative metric of children's initial and incomplete comprehension of a novel word and, for a given child or group of children, can reveal the minimum input conditions that are necessary for the first stages of a novel word's acquisition and thereby the learning processes brought to bear by the child.

Although fast mapping was initially investigated in typically developing children with extensive prior vocabulary knowledge, researchers also have used the paradigm to examine vocabulary acquisition in typically developing infants and toddlers at the earliest stages of language development. For very young children, behavioral fast-mapping paradigms generally have focused upon identifying the types of social, affective, and attentional cues required to support referential understanding when the correspondence between label and object is not made explicit.

These types of studies have revealed a steady age progression in the ability of typically developing children to use a variety of contextual cues to infer the speaker's referential intent. By 18 months of age, for example, typically developing toddlers are able to follow and respond to adult eye gaze direction and learn a new word even when the adult's referential focus is discrepant from their own (Baldwin, 1993). Children of this age can also learn a new word in contexts in which the target object is not visible to the child when the novel label is provided (Tomasello, Strasberg, and Akhtar, 1995). By 24 months of age, typically developing children can learn a new word by interpreting an adult's emotional reaction (Tomasello and Barton, 1994) or by identifying what is novel in the discourse context from the speaker's perspective (Akhtar, Carpenter, and Tomasello, 1996).

Fast-mapping paradigms have also been extended to examine the process of word learning in children with intellectual and related developmental disabilities. Baron-Cohen, Baldwin, and Crowson (1997), for example, demonstrated that, when the speaker's direction of gaze coincided with the child's, children with autism (mean age 9 years) were able to make word–object associations as often as language-matched controls. When there was a discrepancy between the child's focus of attention and the speaker's (i.e., discrepant labeling), however, children with autism made mapping errors because they did not attend to the speaker's gaze. These authors suggest that the fast-mapping process is intact for school-aged children with autism, but that the ability to make appropriate mappings is impaired, presumably due to a deficit in attention following.

In our own lab, we are currently using three different fast-mapping paradigms to investigate how 4–10-year-old children with fragile X syndrome only, comorbid fragile X syndrome and autism, and idiopathic autism, as well as nonverbal mental-age-matched typically developing 2–5-year-olds, use social and affective cues to learn new words. The tasks being administered measure novel word learning based upon the participant's use of speaker's eye gaze direction, emotional reaction, and understanding of the speaker's knowledge state. Importantly, all of the tasks include multiple trials to assess word learning, as well as familiar object probes to assess task compliance and generalization probes to assess whether the participant has extended their initial word learning to other exemplars in the same category as the target object. A baseline measure of fast-mapping performance that directly pairs novel labels and objects in an ostensive manner is also being administered. The primary goal of this research is to uncover potential differences in the use of social cues in fast mapping according to diagnostic condition, with the expectation being that autism is associated with particularly serious impairments in this regard.

Although standardized tests, language sampling, and analog tasks can provide information about the extent to which an individual or group of individuals has acquired language knowledge, the use of a behavioral fast-mapping paradigm is one approach to providing insights into the process by which language is learned. Importantly, analyzing fast-mapping task performance not only can inform our theories of language acquisition but can have direct treatment implications as we come to understand the kinds of environmental scaffolding necessary to support lexical learning in different syndrome groups.

Eyetracking and preferential looking

Measures of looking time have been used extensively to assess comprehension in typically developing infants and toddlers. In a looking-while-listening paradigm, for example, the child typically views two pictures, a target and distractor, side-by-side on a screen while listening to an auditory stimulus (Fernald *et al.*, 2008). Both accuracy in comprehension (i.e., the proportion of time spent looking to the target during a window of time relative to the auditory stimulus) and speed of processing (i.e., the time between the auditory stimulus of interest and the child's gaze shift from the distractor to the target) can be assessed, allowing researchers to address questions about how a child recognizes or interprets a word or grammatical construction. Looking time tasks actually comprise a single family of paradigms based on eye gaze and eye movements, which can involve either high-tech infrared eyetrackers or lower-tech methods, and can accommodate studies of visual search and anticipatory looking.

Processes of language acquisition can also be assessed with looking time paradigms. Gertner, Fisher, and Eisengart (2006), for example, found that typically developing toddlers extend syntactic knowledge about word order to interpret novel verbs, evidenced by looking longer to a video in which the agent was the subject of the sentence (e.g., a duck acting on a bunny) than to a video of the reverse relationship (e.g., a bunny acting on a duck) while listening to transitive sentences (e.g., *The duck is gorping the bunny!*). Studies of this type can be extended to children with intellectual disabilities and other populations about which little is known with respect to language learning mechanisms.

In addition to permitting precise measurement of comprehension or learning, eye gaze paradigms provide several advantages over traditional assessments used with children with intellectual disability. First, these paradigms were developed to assess early language processing and thus are developmentally appropriate for a wide age range of children with intellectual disabilities. Second, the incidental nature of the tasks places negligible response demands on the child, which is significant for those stressed by face-to-face assessments. Third, the minimal demands allow for maximal compliance from children who might otherwise be challenging to test. Lastly, the effects of impulsivity and poor fine-motor control seen in some children with intellectual disability may be diminished in these assessments.

The utility of looking time measures has been demonstrated in studies of children and adolescents with a range of developmental disorders, including Williams syndrome and autism (e.g., Nazzi, Paterson, and Karmiloff-Smith, 2003; Swensen *et al.*, 2007). In our own lab, we are currently exploring the use of preferential looking tasks to assess the interpretation of specific syntactic constructions with familiar and novel verbs (e.g., active and passive reversible sentences in the form of *The bird is chased by the frog*) in boys with fragile X syndrome or autism and typically developing boys with similar levels of nonverbal cognitive ability. The goal of these studies is to identify the aspects of syntactic comprehension that are most challenging to boys with fragile X syndrome and autism.

Summary

Fast-mapping and looking time measures can complement research on profiles of ability, etiological differences, and environmental influences by allowing researchers to assess the dynamic learning processes underlying language development. Looking time measures are especially useful for children who might be difficult to reliably assess using other techniques.

Conclusion

Assessing language in individuals with intellectual disabilities poses many challenges because of the complex interrelationships among linguistic and nonlinguistic impairments in the performance of any task. We have tried to illustrate some of the ways we have addressed these challenges in our research. It is important to recognize, however, that no task is perfect in the sense of being a pure measure of only the construct of interest. Minimally, this caution needs to be kept in mind when interpreting the results of any single measure. Perhaps more importantly, the lesson should be that a multi-pronged assessment using different measures designed to tap the same construct should be used whenever possible.

Acknowledgments

Preparation of this chapter was supported by NIH grants R01HD024356, R01HD054764, and P30HD003352.

Key Terms

Autism A developmental disability defined by behavioral criteria, although there is evidence of a substantial genetic contribution to risk. Defined by impairments in three domains – social reciprocity, communication, and restricted interests and stereotyped behaviors – along with an onset early in development. Individuals with autism display a wide range of language and cognitive impairments. Early language ability is one of the best predictors of adult outcomes in terms of independent living and adaptive functioning.

Down syndrome A genetic condition involving triplication of all or part of chromosome 21. The leading genetic cause of intellectual disability. The condition is associated with a characteristic profile of physical symptoms and health conditions, as well as a behavioral profile that includes especially serious delays in language, problems with articulation, severe impairments in auditory memory, and a high rate of ear infections and hearing loss.

Fragile X syndrome The leading inherited cause of intellectual disability, caused by a mutation in a single gene on the X chromosome. Because it is X linked, males are more likely to be affected and more severely affected, on average, than females. Affected individuals often also meet diagnostic criteria for autism or have many of the symptoms of autism.

Intellectual disability A condition defined by (1) impairments in cognitive functioning (typically defined as an IQ two or more standard deviations below the mean for the population), (2) limitations in the ability to function independently and meet the demands of daily life, and (3) an onset before the age of 18 years.

Mental age A score derived from a standardized test of cognitive ability that is designed to link an individual's level of performance to a point on the typical developmental curve. For example, a mental age of 4 years means that the individual's level of performance meets expectations for a typical 4-year-old on that test irrespective of the individual's chronological age. There are substantial statistical limitations associated with such scores.

Williams syndrome This condition is caused by the deletion of a small set of genes on chromosome 7. Many individuals with Williams syndrome meet criteria for intellectual disability, but many fall in the average range of intelligence. In addition to problems in the cognitive domain, heart problems are common. Language is a relative strength, but contrary to early claims, is not spared (i.e., age appropriate) in most affected individuals.

References

AAID (2010) *Intellectual disability: definition, classification and systems of supports* (11th edn of AAIDD definition manual). Washington, DC: American Association on Intellectual and Developmental Disabilities.

Abbeduto, L., Benson, G., Short, K., and Dolish, J. (1995) Effects of sampling context on the expressive language of children and adolescents with mental retardation. *Mental Retardation*, 33 (5), 279–288.

Abbeduto, L., Keller-Bell, Y., Richmond, E.K., and Murphy, M.M. (2006a) Research on language development and mental retardation: history, theories, findings, and future directions. In L.M. Glidden (ed.), *International review of research in mental retardation*. New York: Academic.

Abbeduto, L., Murphy, M.M., Kover, S.T., *et al.* (2008) Signaling noncomprehension of language: a comparison of fragile X syndrome and Down syndrome. *American Journal on Mental Retardation*, 113, 214–230.

Abbeduto, L., Murphy, M.M., Richmond, E.K., *et al.* (2006b) Collaboration in referential communication: comparison of youth with Down syndrome or fragile X syndrome. *American Journal on Mental Retardation*, 111, 170–183.

Akhtar, N., Carpenter, M., and Tomasello, M. (1996) The role of discourse novelty in children's early word learning. *Child Development*, 67, 635–645.

Baldwin, D. (1993) Infants' ability to consult the speaker for clues to word reference. *Journal of Child Language*, 20 (2), 395–418.

Baron-Cohen, S., Baldwin, D., and Crowson, M. (1997) Do children with autism use the speaker's direction of gaze strategy to crack the code of language? *Child Development*, 68 (1), 48–57.

Brownell, M.D., and Whiteley, J.H. (1992) Development and training of referential communication in children with mental retardation. *American Journal on Mental Retardation*, 97, 161–171.

Carey, S., and Bartlett, E. (1978) Acquiring a single new word. *Papers and Reports on Child Language Development (Stanford University)*, 15, 17–29.

Dykens, E.M., Hodapp, R.M., and Finucane, B.M. (2000) *Genetics and mental retardation syndromes: a new look at behavior and interventions*. Baltimore: Brookes.

Fernald, A., Zangl, R., Portillo, A., and Marchman, V.A. (2008) Looking while listening: using eye movements to monitor spoken language comprehension by infants and young children. In I.A. Sekerina, E.M. Fernandez, and H. Clahsen (eds), *Developmental psycholinguistics: on-line methods in children's language processing* (pp. 97–135). Philadelphia: Benjamins.

Finestack, L.H., and Abbeduto, L. (2010) Expressive language profiles of verbally expressive adolescents and young adults with Down syndrome or fragile X syndrome. *Journal of Speech, Language, and Hearing Research*, 53, 1334–1348.

Fujiki, M., and Brinton, B. (1993) Comprehension monitoring skills of adults with mental retardation. *Research in Developmental Disabilities*, 14, 409–421.

Gertner, Y., Fisher, C., and Eisengart, J. (2006) Learning words and rules: abstract knowledge of word order in early sentence comprehension. *Psychological Science*, 17 (8), 684–691.

Johnston, J.R., Miller, J.F., Curtiss, S., and Tallal, P. (1993) Conversations with children who are language impaired: asking questions. *Journal of Speech and Hearing Research*, 36 (5), 973–978.

Keller-Bell, Y.D., and Abbeduto, L. (2007) Narrative development in adolescents and young adults with fragile X syndrome. *American Journal on Mental Retardation*, 112 (4), 289–299.

Kover, S.T., and Abbeduto, L. (2010) Expressive language in male adolescents with fragile X syndrome with and without co-morbid autism. *Journal of Intellectual Disability Research*, 54 (3), 246–265.

Martin, G.E., Klusek, J., Estigarribia, B., and Roberts, J.E. (2009) Language characteristics of individuals with Down syndrome. *Topics in Language Disorders*, 29, 112–132.

Mervis, C.B. (2009) Language and literacy development of children with Down syndrome. *Topics in Language Disorders*, 29, 149–169.

Miles, S., Chapman, R., and Sindberg, H. (2006) Sampling context affects MLU in the language of adolescents with Down syndrome. *Journal of Speech, Language, and Hearing Research*, 49, 325–337.

Miller, J., and Iglesias, A. (2006) *Systematic Analysis of Language Transcripts (SALT)*, English and Spanish (version 9). Computer software. Language Analysis Lab, University of Wisconsin–Madison.

Miolo, G., Chapman, R.S., and Sindberg, H.A. (2005) Sentence comprehension in adolescents with Down syndrome and typically developing children: role of sentence voice, visual context, and auditory-verbal short-term memory. *Journal of Speech, Language, and Hearing Research*, 48, 172–188.

Nazzi, T., Paterson, S., and Karmiloff-Smith, A. (2003) Early word segmentation by infants and toddlers with Williams syndrome. *Infancy*, 4 (2), 251–271.

Rice, M.L., Buhr, J.C., and Nemeth, M. (1990) Fast mapping word learning abilities of language-delayed preschoolers. *Journal of Speech and Hearing Disorders*, 55, 33–42.

Saffran, J.R. (2002) Constraints on statistical language learning. *Journal of Memory and Language*, 47, 172–196.

Southwood, F., and Russell, A.F. (2004) Comparison of conversation, freeplay, and story generation as methods of language sample elicitation. *Journal of Speech, Language, and Hearing Research*, 47, 366–376.

Swensen, L.D., Kelley, E., Fein, D., and Naigles, L.R. (2007) Processes of language acquisition in children with autism: evidence from preferential looking. *Child Development*, 78 (2), 542–557.

Tomasello, M. (1999) *The cultural origins of human cognition*. Cambridge, MA: Harvard University Press.

Tomasello, M., and Barton, M. (1994) Learning words in nonostensive contexts. *Developmental Psychology*, 30, 639–650.

Tomasello, M., Strasberg, R., and Akhtar, N. (1995) Eighteen month old children learn words in nonostensive contexts. *Journal of Child Language*, 23, 157–176.

Warren, S.F., Brady, N., Sterling, A., et al. (2010) Maternal responsivity predicts language development in young children with fragile X syndrome. *American Journal on Intellectual and Developmental Disabilities*, 115, 54–75.

Recommended Reading and Resources

AAID (2010) *Intellectual disability: definition, classification and systems of supports* (11th edn of AAIDD definition manual). Washington, DC: American Association on Intellectual and Developmental Disabilities.

Abbeduto, L., Brady, N., and Kover, S. (2007) Language development and fragile X syndrome: profiles, syndrome specificity, and within-syndrome differences. *Mental Retardation and Developmental Disabilities Research Reviews*, 13, 36–46.

Abbeduto, L., and McDuffie, A. (2010) Genetic syndromes associated with intellectual disabilities. In C.L. Armstrong and L. Morrow (eds), *Handbook of medical neuropsychology: applications of cognitive neuroscience* (pp. 193–221). New York: Springer.

Canfield, M.A., Honein, M.A., Yuskiv, N., et al. (2006) National estimates and race/ethnic-specific variation of selected birth defects in the United States, 1999–2001. *Birth Defects Research and Clinical and Molecular Teratology*, 747–756.

Condouris, K., Meyer, E., and Tager-Flusberg, H. (2003) The relationship between standardized measures of language and measures of spontaneous speech in children with autism. *American Journal on Speech–Language Pathology*, 12, 349–358.

Cowan, P.A., Weber, J., Hoddinott, B.A., and Klein, J. (1967) Mean length of spoken response as a function of stimulus, experimenter, and subject. *Child Development*, 3, 191–203.

Dykens, E.M., Hodapp, R.M., and Finucane, B.M. (2000) *Genetics and mental retardation syndromes: a new look at behavior and interventions*. Baltimore: Brookes.

Finestack, L.H., Richmond, E.K., and Abbeduto, L. (2009) Language development in individuals with fragile X syndrome. *Topics in Language Disorders*, 29, 133–149.

Hodapp, R.M. (1998) *Development and disabilities: intellectual, sensory, and motor impairments*. New York: Cambridge University Press.

Johnston, J.R. (2001) An alternate MLU calculation: magnitude and variability of effects. *Journal of Speech, Language, and Hearing Research*, 44 (1), 156–164.

Mervis, C.B., and Robinson, B.F. (2005) Designing measures for profiling and genotype/phenotype studies of individuals with genetic syndromes or developmental language disorders. *Applied Psycholinguistics*, 26, 41–64.

Tager-Flusberg, H., Rogers, S., Cooper, J., *et al.* (2009) Defining spoken language benchmarks and selecting measures of expressive language development for young children with autism spectrum disorders. *Journal of Speech, Language, and Hearing Research*, 52, 643–652.

Walker-Andrews, A.S., Haviland, J.M., Huffman, L., and Toci, L. (1994) Brief report: preferential looking in intermodal perception by children with autism. *Journal of Autism and Developmental Disorders*, 24 (1), 99–107.

Index